THE
STRATEGY-
FOCUSED
ORGANIZATION

THE

STRATEGY-FOCUSED ORGANIZATION

HOW BALANCED SCORECARD COMPANIES THRIVE IN THE NEW BUSINESS ENVIRONMENT

ROBERT S. KAPLAN
DAVID P. NORTON

HARVARD BUSINESS SCHOOL PRESS
BOSTON, MASSACHUSETTS

Library of Congress Cataloging-in-Publication Data
Kaplan, Robert S.
   The strategy-focused organization : how balanced scorecard companies thrive in the new business environment / Robert S. Kaplan, David P. Norton.
      p. cm.
   Includes index.
   ISBN 1-57851-250-6 (alk. paper)
     1. Strategic planning. I. Norton, David P. II. Title.

HD30.28 .K3544 2000
658.4'012--dc21

                                                    00-033515

The paper used in this publication meets the requirements of the American National Standard for Permanence of Paper for Publications and Documents in Libraries and Archives Z39.48-1992.

Contents

Preface

IN THE PREFACE TO OUR FIRST BOOK, *The Balanced Scorecard*, we stated, "The book, while as comprehensive and complete as we could make it, is still a progress report. . . .We are confident . . . that innovating companies . . . will expand the structure and use of the scorecard even further. So perhaps in a few years readers can look forward to the sequel."

That forecast was highly accurate on all counts. Since 1996, we have seen the initial set of adopters thrive and prosper by using the Balanced Scorecard as the centerpiece of their management systems and processes. And many other organizations now have adopted the Balanced Scorecard and achieved remarkable results. Adopters throughout the world include large and small, manufacturing and service, mature and rapid-growth, public and private, and for-profit and not-for-profit organizations. As we go to press, *The Balanced Scorecard* has been translated into nineteen languages, attesting to its universal appeal and applicability.

We first developed the Balanced Scorecard in the early 1990s to solve a measurement problem. In knowledge-based competition, the ability of organizations to develop, nurture, and mobilize their intangible assets was critical for success. But financial measurements could not capture the value-creating activities from an organization's intangible assets: the skills, competencies, and motivation of employees; databases and information technologies; efficient and responsive operating processes; innovation in products and services; customer loyalty and relationships; and political, regulatory, and societal approval. We proposed the Balanced Scorecard as the solution to this performance measurement problem.

But we learned that adopting companies used the Balanced Scorecard to solve a much more important problem than how to measure performance in the information era. That problem, of which we were frankly unaware when first proposing the Balanced Scorecard, was how to implement new strategies. Statistics from various sources documented that organizations encountered major difficulties and often failed when implementing new strategies. In contrast to this general experience, we observed that a high proportion of the early Balanced Scorecard adopters effectively implemented new strategies and realized positive returns within twelve to twenty-four months. We realized that a new organizational form had emerged—the "Strategy-Focused Organization." Executives of adopting organizations were using the Balanced Scorecard to align their business units, shared service units, teams, and individuals around overall organizational goals. They were focusing key management processes—planning, resource allocation, budgeting, periodic reporting, and the management meeting—on the strategy. Vision, strategy, and resource allocation flowed down from the top; implementation, innovation, feedback, and learning flowed back up from the front lines and back offices. With their new focus, alignment, and learning, the organizations enjoyed nonlinear performance breakthroughs. The whole truly became much more than the sum of its parts.

We are indebted to many people for helping us understand how to make an organization strategy focused. We have learned from and been inspired by leaders of exemplary organizations:

Brian Baker and Bob McCool	Mobil North America Marketing and Refining Division
Gerry Isom and Tom Valerio	CIGNA Property & Casualty Division
Robert Gordon	Store 24
Norman Chambers	Halliburton Energy Development
Michael Hegarty and Lee Wilson	Chemical and Chase Banks, now at AXA
Bill Catucci	AT&T Canada, now at Equifax
Larry Brady	FMC Corporation, now at UNOVA
Pam Syfert	City of Charlotte, North Carolina

Governor Gary Locke and Joe Dear	State of Washington
Dr. Jon Meliones	Duke Children's Hospital
Vanessa Kirsch and Kelly Fitzsimmons	New Profit, Inc.
Tris Chapman	Southern Gardens Citrus
Kathleen Bradley Kapsalis	May Institute
Elaine Brennan	Montefiore Hospital

Many people created change from within their organizations to generate the rich experiences and successful implementations that we describe in the book:

Jay Forbes	Nova Scotia Power
Mike Brown and Doug Schultz	United Parcel Service
Ron Mambu	FMC Corporation
Richard Magnus	Subordinate Courts, Singapore
Guillermo Babatz	Grupo Bal, Mexico
Steve Kirn	Sears, Roebuck and Co.
Cheryl Thomas and William Ehrhorn	Fannie Mae
Steven Relyea	University of California, San Diego
Ted Francavilla	Chemical and Chase Banks
Ed Lewis	Mobil NAM&R
Todd D'Attoma	Mobil NAM&R, Lubricants
Stephen Mournighan	U.S. Department of Energy Procurement
Lori Byrd	U.S. Department of Transportation
Julie Chesley and M. Wenger	National Reconnaissance Office
Dennis Wymore	Shell Oil Company

Eileen Moser	United Way of Southeastern New England
Lisa Schumacher and Nancy Elliott	City of Charlotte, North Carolina
John Davis	Nationwide Financial Services
Marc de Quervain	ABB Switzerland
Al Derden	Texaco
Wolfgang Schmidt-Soelch	Winterthur International
James Noble and Martin Shotbolt	General Motors
Garrett Walker	GTE Service Corporation
Randy Numbers and Mary Gray	J. P. Morgan

In addition, we learned from the innovative implementations done by our colleagues at the Balanced Scorecard Collaborative: Michael Contrada, Geoffrey Fenwick, Laura Downing, Bill Hodges, Terry Brown, Ann Nevius, Rob Howie, Cynthia Baird, Mario Bognanno, Dave Foster, Randy Russell, and Gaelle Lamotte; and those formerly at Renaissance Worldwide—Francis Gouillart, Sean Hogan, Ryan English, and Timothy Henry.

Our collaborators at Harvard Business School Press—Carol Franco, President; Hollis Heimbouch, Senior Editor; Constance Devanthéry-Lewis, Managing Editor; Barbara Roth, Senior Manuscript Editor; and Laura Noorda, Production Manager—provided inspiration and outstanding support.

We appreciate the assistance of all these many people in helping us create this book.

Robert S. Kaplan and David P. Norton
Boston and Lincoln, Massachusetts, June 2000

Creating the Strategy-Focused Organization

THE ABILITY TO EXECUTE STRATEGY. A study of 275 portfolio managers reported that the ability to execute strategy was more important than the quality of the strategy itself.[1] These managers cited strategy implementation as the most important factor shaping management and corporate valuations. This finding seems surprising, as for the past two decades management theorists, consultants, and the business press have focused on how to devise strategies that will generate superior performance. Apparently, strategy formulation has never been more important.

Yet other observers concur with the portfolio managers' opinion that the ability to execute strategy can be more important than the strategy itself. In the early 1980s, a survey of management consultants reported that fewer than 10 percent of effectively formulated strategies were successfully implemented.[2] More recently, a 1999 *Fortune* cover story of prominent CEO failures concluded that the emphasis placed on strategy and vision created a mistaken belief that the right strategy was all that was needed to succeed. "In the majority of cases—we estimate 70 percent—the real problem isn't [bad strategy but] . . . bad execution," asserted the authors.[3] Thus, with failure rates reported in the 70 percent to 90 percent range, we can appreciate why sophisticated investors have come to realize that execution is more important than good vision.

Why do organizations have difficulty implementing well-formulated strategies? One problem is that strategies—the unique and sustainable ways by which organizations create value—are changing but the tools for measuring strategies have not kept pace. In the industrial economy, companies created value with their tangible assets, by transforming raw materials into finished products. A 1982 Brookings Institute study showed that tangible book values represented 62 percent of industrial organizations' market values. Ten years later, the ratio had dropped to 38 percent.[4] And recent studies estimated that by the end of the twentieth century, the book value of tangible assets accounted for only 10 percent to 15 percent of companies' market values.[5] Clearly, opportunities for creating value are shifting from managing tangible assets to managing knowledge-based strategies that deploy an organization's intangible assets: customer relationships, innovative products and services, high-quality and responsive operating processes, information technology and databases, and employee capabilities, skills, and motivation.

In an economy dominated by tangible assets, financial measurements were adequate to record investments in inventory, property, plant, and equipment on companies' balance sheets. Income statements could also capture the expenses associated with the use of these tangible assets to produce revenues and profits. But today's economy, where intangible assets have become the major sources of competitive advantage, calls for tools that describe knowledge-based assets and the value-creating strategies that these assets make possible. Lacking such tools, companies have encountered difficulties managing what they could not describe or measure.

Companies also have had problems attempting to implement knowledge-based strategies in organizations designed for industrial-age competition. Many organizations, even until the end of the 1970s, operated under central control, through large functional departments. Strategy could be developed at the top and implemented through a centralized command-and-control culture. Change was incremental, so managers could use slow-reacting and tactical management control systems such as the budget. Such systems, however, were designed for nineteenth- and early twentieth-century industrial companies and are inadequate for today's dynamic, rapidly changing environment. Yet many organizations continue to use them. Is it any surprise that they have difficulty implementing radical new strategies that were designed for knowledge-based competition in the twenty-first century? Organizations need a new kind of management system—one explicitly designed to manage strategy, not tactics.

Most of today's organizations operate through decentralized business units and teams that are much closer to the customer than large corporate staffs. These organizations recognize that competitive advantage comes more from the intangible knowledge, capabilities, and relationships created by employees than from investments in physical assets and access to capital. Strategy implementation therefore requires that all business units, support units, and employees be aligned and linked to the strategy. And with the rapid changes in technology, competition, and regulations, the formulation and implementation of strategy must become a continual and participative process. Organizations today need a language for communicating strategy as well as processes and systems that help them to implement strategy and gain feedback about their strategy. Success comes from having strategy become everyone's everyday job.

Several years ago, we introduced the Balanced Scorecard.[6] At the time, we thought the Balanced Scorecard was about measurement, not about strategy. We began with the premise that an exclusive reliance on financial measures in a management system was causing organizations to do the wrong things. Financial measures are lag indicators; they report on outcomes, the consequences of past actions. Exclusive reliance on financial indicators promoted short-term behavior that sacrificed long-term value creation for short-term performance. The Balanced Scorecard approach retained measures of financial performance, the lagging indicators, but supplemented them with measures on the drivers, the lead indicators, of future financial performance.

But what were the appropriate measures of future performance? If financial measures were causing organizations to do the wrong things, what measures would prompt them to do the right things? The answer turned out to be obvious: *Measure the strategy!* Thus all of the objectives and measures on a Balanced Scorecard—financial and nonfinancial—should be derived from the organization's vision and strategy. Although we may not have appreciated the implications at the time, the Balanced Scorecard soon became a tool for managing strategy—a tool for dealing with the 90 percent failure rates.

Several of the first companies that asked us to help them adopt the Balanced Scorecard—Mobil Oil Corporation's North America Marketing and Refining Division, CIGNA Corporation's Property & Casualty Division,

Chemical Retail Bank, and Brown & Root Energy Services' Rockwater Division—were underperforming; they were losing money and trailing the industry. Each organization had recently brought in a new management team to turn performance around. Each new management team introduced fundamentally new strategies in an effort to make their organizations more customer-driven. The strategies did not simply rely on cost reduction and downsizing; rather, they required repositioning the organization in its competitive market space. More important, the new strategies required that the entire organization adopt a new set of cultural values and priorities. In retrospect, we had been asked to introduce the Balanced Scorecard into four worst-case scenarios: failing, demoralized organizations that needed their workforces of up to 10,000 employees to learn and understand a new strategy and change behavior that had been imbedded for decades.

Mobil North America Marketing and Refining

In 1992, Mobil North America Marketing and Refining Division, a $15 billion per year division of Mobil Oil Corporation,[7] ranked last among its industry peers in profitability, producing an unacceptably low return on investment and requiring a cash infusion of about $500 million from the parent company just to maintain and upgrade facilities. A new management team developed a new customer-focused strategy. The team decentralized the organization into eighteen market-facing business units with P&L accountability and restructured central staff functions into fourteen shared service groups. The Balanced Scorecard was introduced in 1994 to communicate and manage the rollout of the new strategy.

Results came quickly. After years of below-average performance, including ranking at the bottom of its peer group in 1992 and 1993, Mobil moved to the number one position in 1995, with profits 56 percent above the industry average (see Figure 1-1). This turnaround was accomplished within two years of introducing a new strategy, a new organization, and the Balanced Scorecard performance management process. What is more impressive, Mobil maintained industry leadership for the next four consecutive years. Brian Baker, executive vice president of the division in early 1998, commented on the organization's success: "In 1997 we hit the number 1 ranking for our third consecutive year, which is unprecedented for a major oil company. . . . The Scorecard gets the lion's share of the credit. We created a performance mind-set with the Balanced Scorecard."

Figure 1-1   Mobil NAM&R's Relative Profitability, 1990–98

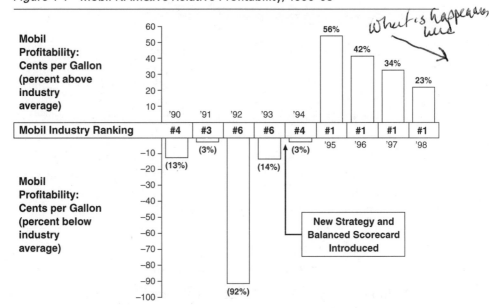

CIGNA Property & Casualty Insurance

In 1993, the Property & Casualty Division of CIGNA lost nearly $275 million, making its performance the worst in the industry. The division was near bankruptcy. Although its poor performance was due in part to a few major catastrophes, almost all of its lines of business were marginal. The new turnaround management team developed a new strategy—to become a "specialist"—by focusing on niches in which it had an informational comparative advantage. The management team deployed the new strategy to its twenty-one business units in 1994, using the Balanced Scorecard as the core management process.

The results were rapid and dramatic. Within two years, CIGNA Property & Casualty had returned to profitability and sustained and improved its performance during each of the next four years. By 1998, the company's profitability positioned it strongly within the industry with many of its businesses exhibiting top quartile performance. At the end of 1998, the parent company spun off the Property & Casualty Division for $3.45 billion. According to Gerald Isom, president of CIGNA Property & Casualty, the Balanced Scorecard played an important role in this success story:

"CIGNA used the Balanced Scorecard to manage its transformation from a generalist company to a top-quartile specialist."[8]

Brown & Root Energy Services' Rockwater Division

Rockwater, an undersea construction company of Brown & Root Energy Services (part of the Halliburton Corporation) headquartered in Aberdeen, Scotland, served major offshore oil and gas producers. Rockwater was losing money in 1992. Norm Chambers, the new division president, introduced the Balanced Scorecard to his management team in 1993 to help clarify and gain consensus for a new strategy based on developing customer value-added relationships rather than offering customers the lowest price. By 1996, Rockwater was first in its niche in both growth and profitability. Chambers noted: "The Balanced Scorecard helped us improve our communication and increase our profitability."[9]

Chemical (Chase) Retail Bank

Chemical Retail Bank's implementation started shortly after the merger of Manufacturers Hanover and Chemical Bank in 1992. Michael Hegarty, president of the Retail Bank, deployed the scorecard as part of a new strategy: to diversify the bank's business away from the increasingly commodity-oriented checking and savings accounts delivered through expensive branches in the New York metropolitan area. Chemical, as a newly merged bank, would have to close hundreds of now-redundant branches. By using the scorecard to communicate an intense focus on targeted customers, the retail bank was able to accomplish the cost savings expected from the merger while minimizing the losses of targeted customers, and, in fact, simultaneously expanding its revenue base with the targeted customer base. Chemical's retail profits evolved as shown:

Year	Profits
1993 (base year)	x
1994	8x
1995	13x
1996	19x

The improvement represented hundreds of millions of dollars annually during the bank's first three years of managing with the Balanced Scorecard. Hegarty noted: "The Balanced Scorecard has become an integral part of our change management process. The Scorecard has allowed us to look beyond financial measures and concentrate on factors that create economic value."[10]

In contrast with the difficulty most organizations experience in implementing strategy, these four early adopters all used the scorecard to support major strategic and organizational changes. And the "long run" came quite soon. The companies enjoyed substantial benefits from their new strategies early in their implementation activities.

The Balanced Scorecard made the difference. Each organization executed strategies using the same physical and human resources that had previously produced failing performance. The strategies were executed with the same products, the same facilities, the same employees, and the same customers. The difference was a new senior management team using the Balanced Scorecard to focus all organizational resources on a new strategy. The scorecard allowed these successful organizations to build a new kind of management system—one designed to manage strategy. This new management system had three distinct dimensions:

1. Strategy. Make strategy the central organizational agenda. The Balanced Scorecard allowed organizations, for the first time, to describe and communicate their strategy in a way that could be understood and acted on.

2. Focus. Create incredible focus. With the Balanced Scorecard as a "navigation" aide, every resource and activity in the organization was aligned to the strategy.

3. Organization. Mobilize all employees to act in fundamentally different ways. The Balanced Scorecard provided the logic and architecture to establish new organization linkages across business units, shared services, and individual employees.

These organizations used the Balanced Scorecard to create Strategy-Focused Organizations. They beat the long odds against successful strategy execution.

THE PRINCIPLES OF STRATEGY-FOCUSED ORGANIZATIONS

When talking about how they achieved these breakthrough results, the executives continually mention two words: *alignment* and *focus*. How does focus create breakthrough performance? Think of the diffuse light produced in a well-lit room by thousands of watts of incandescent and fluorescent lamps. Compare that warm, diffuse light with the brilliant beam of light that comes from the tiny battery in a handheld laser pointer. Despite its limited resources (two 1.5 volt batteries), the pointer produces a blinding light by emitting all the laser's photons and light waves in phase and coherent. The laser operates nonlinearly; it leverages its limited power source to produce an incredibly bright and focused beam of light. Similarly, a well-crafted and well-understood strategy can, through alignment and coherence of the organization's limited resources, produce a nonlinear performance breakthrough.

The Balanced Scorecard enabled the early-adopting companies to focus and align their executive teams, business units, human resources, information technology, and financial resources to their organization's strategy (see Figure 1-2).

Our research of successful Balanced Scorecard companies has revealed a consistent pattern of achieving such strategic focus and alignment. Although each organization approached the challenge in different ways, at different paces, and in different sequences, we observed five common prin-

Figure 1-2   Aligning and Focusing Resources on Strategy

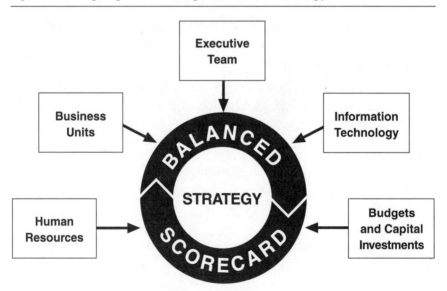

ciples at work. We refer to these as the principles of a Strategy-Focused Organization (see Figure 1-3).

Principle 1: Translate the Strategy to Operational Terms

The speed with which the new strategies delivered results indicates that the companies' successes were not due to a major new product or service launch, major new capital investments, or even the development of new intangible or "intellectual" assets. The companies were, of course, developing new products and services and investing in both hard, tangible assets

Figure 1-3 The Principles of a Strategy-Focused Organization

and softer, intangible assets. But they could not have benefited much in two years from such investments. To achieve the results we have just described, the companies capitalized on capabilities and assets—tangible and intangible—that existed already within their organizations. The companies' new strategies and the Balanced Scorecard had unleashed the capabilities and assets that were hidden (or frozen) within the old organization.

In effect, the scorecard provided the "recipe" that enabled ingredients already existing in the organization to be combined for long-term value creation. Think how making a meal requires a combination of raw materials (the ingredients), tangible capital and assets (cooking implements, an oven, and a stove), and intangible, human capital (the chef). But a great meal requires a recipe to take advantage of all these tangible and intangible assets. The recipe is the critical soft asset. It transforms the raw ingredients, physical assets, and intangible assets—each with little stand-alone value—into a great meal, with considerable value. The recipe corresponds to a company strategy that combines internal resources and capabilities to create unique value propositions for targeted customers and market segments. The companies in our sample were successful with the Balanced Scorecard because they engaged all employees, not just the lead chef, to implement and improve the recipe.[11]

The Balanced Scorecard provides a framework to describe and communicate strategy in a consistent and insightful way. We can't expect to implement strategy if we can't describe it. Unlike in the financial domain, where standard frameworks such as general ledgers, income statements, and balance sheets exist to document a financial plan, no generally accepted frameworks exist for describing strategy. There are as many ways of describing a strategy as there are strategy theorists and methodologies.

Since introducing the Balanced Scorecard in 1992, we have worked with more than two hundred executive teams in their design of scorecard programs. We always started the design by asking, "What is the strategy?" From this base of experience, we developed a general framework for describing and implementing strategy that we believe can be as useful as the framework—income statement, balance sheet, statement of cash flows—used by financial managers for financial planning and reporting. The new framework, which we call a "strategy map," is a logical and comprehensive architecture for describing strategy. It provides the foundation for designing a Balanced Scorecard that is the cornerstone of a new "strategic management system."

Strategy maps and Balanced Scorecards address the shortcomings of the industrial age's tangible asset measurement systems. The measurement linkages of cause-and-effect relationships in strategy maps show how the intangible assets are transformed into tangible (financial) outcomes. Financial measurement systems record the stand-alone book values of tangible assets—cash, accounts receivable, inventory, land, plant, and equipment. These types of assets have values largely independent of who owns them. Intangible assets, in contrast, usually have little stand-alone value; their value arises from being embedded in coherent, linked strategies. The scorecard's use of quantitative, but nonfinancial, measures—such as cycle time, market share, innovation, satisfaction, and competencies—allows the value-creating process to be described and measured, rather than inferred. The customer value proposition describes the context in which intangible assets such as skilled, motivated employees and customer information systems become transformed into tangible outcomes such as customer retention, revenues from new products and services, and, ultimately, profits. The strategy map and its corresponding Balanced Scorecard measurement program provide a tool to describe how shareholder value is created from intangible assets. Strategy maps and Balanced Scorecards constitute the measurement technology for managing in a knowledge-based economy.

By translating their strategy into the logical architecture of a strategy map and Balanced Scorecard, organizations create a common and understandable point of reference for all their units and employees.

Principle 2: Align the Organization to the Strategy

Synergy is the overarching goal of organization design. Organizations consist of numerous sectors, business units, and specialized departments, each with its own strategy. For organizational performance to become more than the sum of its parts, individual strategies must be linked and integrated. The corporation defines the linkages expected to create synergy and ensures that those linkages actually occur—a task, however, that is easier said than done.

Organizations are traditionally designed around functional specialties such as finance, manufacturing, marketing, sales, engineering, and purchasing. Each function has its own body of knowledge, language, and culture. Functional silos arise and become a major barrier to strategy implementation, as most organizations have great difficulty communicating and coordinating across these specialty functions.

Strategy-Focused Organizations, however, break through this barrier. Executives replace formal reporting structures with strategic themes and priorities that enable a consistent message and consistent set of priorities to be used across diverse and dispersed organizational units. New organization charts are not necessary. Business units and shared service units become linked to the strategy through the common themes and objectives that permeate their scorecards. Often, ad hoc organizations emerge to focus on scorecard strategic themes. In all cases, successful companies use the Balanced Scorecards in a coordinated manner across their organizations to ensure that the whole exceeds the sum of the parts.

Principle 3: Make Strategy Everyone's Everyday Job

The CEO and senior leadership team of the adopting organizations we studied could not implement the new strategy by themselves. They required the active contributions of everyone in the organization. We refer to this as the movement of strategy from the 10 (the senior executive team) to the 10,000 (everyone in the company). How do you move strategy from the boardroom to the backroom and thus to the front lines of daily operations and customer service?

Strategy-Focused Organizations require that all employees understand the strategy and conduct their day-to-day business in a way that contributes to the success of that strategy. This is not top-down direction. This is top-down communication. Individuals far from corporate and regional headquarters—at the oil refinery in Texas, at the gasoline station in New Hampshire, and at the claims desk in Des Moines—are the ones who will find improved ways of doing business that will contribute to achieving the organization's strategic objectives.

Executives use the Balanced Scorecard to help *communicate* and *educate* the organization about the new strategy. Some observers are skeptical about communicating strategy to the entire organization, fearing that valuable information could be leaked to competitors. To this criticism, Mobil's Brian Baker responds: "Knowing our strategy will do them little good unless they can execute it. On the other hand, we have no chance of executing our strategy unless our people know it. It's a chance we'll have to take."

Companies can educate their employees about surprisingly sophisticated business concepts. To understand the scorecard, employees had to learn about customer segmentation, variable costing, and database marketing. Instead of assuming that the workforce was incapable of understanding these ideas, the companies made concerted efforts to educate employees at all levels of the organization about these key strategic components.

The companies then cascaded the high-level corporate and business unit scorecards to lower levels of the organization; in many cases personal scorecards were used to set *personal objectives*. The strategy and scorecard were communicated *holistically*. Instead of cascading objectives through the chain of command, as is normally done, the complete strategy was communicated in a top-down fashion. Individuals and departments at lower levels could develop their own objectives in light of the broader priorities. Many pleasant surprises resulted from this process, as individuals identified areas outside their functional responsibility in which they could contribute.

Finally, each of the successful organizations linked *incentive compensation* to the Balanced Scorecard. Most executives opted for a team-based, rather than an individual based, system for rewarding performance. They used the business unit and division scorecards as the basis for rewards, an approach that stressed the importance of teamwork in executing strategy. Compensation could be based on up to twenty-five strategic measures. Instead of promoting confusion, as many feared, the scorecard compensation systems heightened the employees' interest in all components of the strategy and furthered their demand for knowledge and information about scorecard measures. Strategy indeed became everyone's everyday job, because everyone understood it and was motivated to execute it.

Principle 4: Make Strategy a Continual Process

For most organizations, the management process is built around the budget and operating plan. The monthly management meeting is devoted to a review of performance versus plan, an analysis of variances of past performance, and an action plan for dealing with those variances. There is nothing wrong with this approach per se. Tactical management is necessary. But for most organizations, that's all there is. There are no meetings at which managers discuss strategy. Our research indicates that 85 percent of management teams spend less than one hour per month discussing strategy. Is it any wonder that strategies fail to be implemented when strategy discussions don't even appear on the executive agenda and calendar? Strategy-Focused Organizations use a different approach.

The successful Balanced Scorecard companies introduced a process to manage strategy. We refer to this as a "double-loop process"—one that integrates the management of tactics (financial budgets and monthly reviews) and the management of strategy into a seamless and continual process. Because a process for managing strategy hadn't previously existed, each organization developed its own new approach. Three important themes emerged in the implementations.

First, organizations began to *link strategy to the budgeting process*. The Balanced Scorecard provided the yardstick for evaluating potential investments and initiatives. Chemical Retail Bank's initial motivation for using the scorecard was to provide a strategic rationale for screening investments. More than seventy different requests for funding had been submitted. The bank found that more than 50 percent of these requests had no impact on the scorecard. These were discarded as " nonstrategic." It also found that around 20 percent of the measures on the scorecard had no initiatives associated with them. So it developed a process for managing strategic initiatives. While this process took place within the annual budget process, the strategic initiatives were treated differently. Companies have discovered that they need two kinds of budgets: a *strategy budget* and an *operational budget*. This distinction is essential. Just as the Balanced Scorecard attempts to protect long-term initiatives from short-term suboptimization, the budgeting process must also protect the long-term initiatives from the pressures to deliver short-term financial performance.

The second and most significant step was the introduction of a *simple management meeting* to review strategy. As obvious as this policy sounds, such meetings didn't exist in the past. Now, management meetings were scheduled on a monthly or quarterly basis to discuss the Balanced Scorecard so that a broad spectrum of managers could have a say in the strategy. A new kind of energy stirred. People used terms such as *exciting* to describe the events. Information feedback systems had to be designed to support the process. Initially, these systems were designed for the needs of the executive team. But several of the organizations went a step further. They created *open reporting*, making the performance results available to everyone in the organization. Building on the principle that "strategy is everyone's job," they empowered "everyone" by giving each employee the knowledge needed to do his or her job. At CIGNA, a first-line underwriter could learn about performance reports before a direct-line executive if she happened to be monitoring the feedback system. This created a set of cultural issues that revolutionized traditional approaches to power and performance.

Finally, a *process for learning and adapting the strategy* evolved. The initial Balanced Scorecards represented hypotheses about the strategy; they were the best estimate, at time of formulation, of the actions that would engender long-term financial success. The scorecard design process helped to make the cause-and-effect linkages in the strategic hypotheses explicit. As the scorecard was put into action and feedback systems began reporting progress, the organizations could test the strategy's hypotheses. Some, such as Brown & Root, did the testing formally, using statistical correlations between measures on the scorecard to determine if, for example, employee empowerment programs were increasing customer satisfaction and improving processes. Others, such as Chemical Retail Bank, tested the hypotheses more qualitatively during meetings at which managers validated and refined the programs being used to drive service quality and customer retention. Still others used the meetings to determine if new strategic opportunities had emerged that weren't currently on their scorecard. In each case, ideas and learning emerged continually from within the organization. Rather than waiting for next year's budget cycle, the priorities and the scorecards could be updated immediately. Much like a navigator guiding a vessel on a long-term journey, always sensing the shifting winds and currents and adapting the course, the executives of the successful companies used the ideas and knowledge generated by their organization to constantly fine-tune their strategies. Instead of being an annual event, strategy became a continual process.

Principle 5: Mobilize Change through Executive Leadership

The first four principles focus on the Balanced Scorecard tool, framework, and supporting processes. It is important to stress that you need more than processes and tools to create a Strategy-Focused Organization. Experience has repeatedly shown that the single most important condition for success is the ownership and active involvement of the executive team. Strategy requires change from virtually every part of the organization. Strategy requires teamwork to coordinate these changes. And strategy implementation requires continual attention and focus on the change initiatives and performance against targeted outcomes. If those at the top are not energetic leaders of the process, change will not take place, strategy will not be implemented, and the opportunity for breakthrough performance will be missed.

A successful Balanced Scorecard program starts with the recognition that it is not a "metrics" project; it's a change project. Initially, the focus is on *mobilization* and creating momentum, to get the process launched. Once the organization is mobilized, the focus shifts to *governance*, with emphasis on fluid, team-based approaches to deal with the unstructured nature of the transition to a new performance model. Finally, and gradually over time, a new management system evolves—a *strategic management system* that institutionalizes the new cultural values and new structures into a new system for managing. The various phases can evolve over two to three years.

The first phase, *mobilization,* must make clear to the organization why change is needed; the organization must be unfrozen. John Kotter describes how transformational change begins at the top, with three discrete actions by the leaders: (1) establishing a sense of urgency, (2) creating the guiding coalition, and (3) developing a vision and a strategy.[12] The leaders of successful Balanced Scorecard organizations clearly followed this mode. Several of the adopting companies were experiencing difficult times. The obvious threat of failure and job loss was a motivating factor that created receptivity for change. But the role of the Balanced Scorecard in driving change and breakthrough performance should not be limited to distressed or failing companies. Often, executives at companies that are already doing well create stretch targets to ensure the organization does not become complacent. They use the scorecard to communicate a vision for future performance that is dramatically better than the present. The first job for executive leadership at a Strategy-Focused Organization is to make the need for change obvious to all.

Once the change process is launched, executives establish a *governance process* to guide the transition. This process defines, demonstrates, and reinforces the new cultural values to the organization. Breaking with traditional power-based structures is important. The creation of strategy teams, town hall meetings, and open communications are all components of this transition governance.

As the process evolves, executives modify their existing management system to consolidate progress and reinforce the changes. The patterns were different in each organization we studied. For example, CIGNA linked executive compensation to the scorecard in the first year, whereas Mobil waited until the second year. CIGNA and Mobil cascaded the scorecard to the very bottom of the organization, whereas Chemical Retail Bank went only halfway. Each organization linked the Balanced Scorecard to its formal planning/budgeting process at the first available cycle. Regardless of the sequence, though, each organization gradually built a new management system that ended up looking very similar to one another's. By linking traditional processes such as compensation and resource allocation to a Balanced Scorecard that described the strategy, they created a *strategic management system*. The scorecard described the strategy while the management system wired every part of the organization to the strategy scorecard.

For good executives, of course, there is no "steady state." By embedding the new strategy and new culture into a management system, however, companies can create a barrier to future progress. The competitive landscape is constantly changing, so strategies must constantly evolve to reflect shifts in opportunities and threats. Strategy must be a continual process. The art of leadership is to delicately balance the tension between stability and change.

OTHER EXAMPLES

While we have the most sustained experience with the four organizations described earlier in the chapter, the application and performance breakthroughs are by no means limited to these examples, these industries, or even the companies for which we served as consultants. Many companies in every industry worldwide have realized successes from use of the Balanced Scorecard to create Strategy-Focused Organization. We briefly describe several examples here and provide more details in chapters throughout the book.

AT&T Canada, Inc.

In 1995, AT&T Canada, Inc. (then known as Unitel Communications, Inc.) had more than C$300 million in operating losses and was close to defaulting on its debt. In a 1995 survey of employee satisfaction in 500 North American companies, AT&T Canada had placed far below the median. In December 1995, AT&T and the banks brought in Bill Catucci as CEO to rescue the company. Catucci turned the company around by focusing on process improvements and a new strategy, guided by a Balanced Scorecard strategic management system.

By the end of 1998, AT&T Canada had virtually eliminated its losses and was generating positive cash flow, a considerable accomplishment during a period when the price of a long-distance phone call from Toronto to Vancouver had dropped by a factor of 10. The customer base expanded from 350,000 to more than 700,000 when growth of the telecommunications market was only 4 percent. Revenue per employee increased from $273,000 in 1995 to more than $370,000 in 1998. The $250 million in new equity invested three years earlier now had an estimated market value of $1.2 to $1.5 billion—a substantial turnaround from the company's near-death experience of just three years earlier. The 1998 survey of 500 North American companies showed that AT&T Canada's employee satisfaction scores were 50 percent higher than the average performance of the top 10 percent of companies in the sample. The improved performance provided the basis for a merger in 1999 with MetroNet Communications Corporation, Canada's largest competitive local exchange carrier, in a transaction valued at approximately $7 billion.

Zeneca Ag Products North America

Zeneca Ag Products North America, a $1 billion business employing 1,800 people, developed, manufactured, and sold products for the agricultural industry. Zeneca was one of the world's top three suppliers of crop protection products and also at the leading edge in applying biotechnology to improve food quality.

The catalyst for the development of a Balanced Scorecard was poor financial performance in 1992, the worst in the company's history. Few new products were in the pipeline, inventory was out of control, and customers viewed the company as lacking in innovation. The product range was too broad for efficient management and included many unprofitable products. There was an urgent need to focus the company. The president and the executive team of Zeneca, aided by consultants, formed the guiding coalition for the change.

They used the Balanced Scorecard to make a new mission and strategy a reality, and to link incentive pay to strategic performance. Zeneca deployed the scorecard to the entire organization in early 1995. Since that time, the growth of sales has been double the industry average and the profit margin exceeded competitors' average each year. Customer survey results were positive, and all critical success factors continued to improve. The Balanced Scorecard also provided an excellent mechanism for securing the support of the parent company for agreement on performance goals at the beginning of each year.

Southern Gardens Citrus

Even small companies have benefited from using the Balanced Scorecard to implement strategy. Southern Gardens Citrus, a Florida-based citrus processor and subsidiary of U.S. Sugar Corp., with 175 employees, developed its Balanced Scorecard in 1995. The company wanted to create a high-performance, collaborative environment. Vice President/General Manager Tristan Chapman used his equipment supplier FMC Corporation (another early Balanced Scorecard adopter) to assist in delivering the new strategy of operational excellence.

Chapman's management team introduced the first Balanced Scorecard in the summer of 1995, with plantwide measures, accompanied with a pay-for-performance process. The results of the program were dramatic. At a time when many small agricultural processors were failing and leaving the business, Southern Gardens survived and enjoyed significant performance improvements:

Performance Area	94/95	97/98	% Improvement
Shipments out of spec.	30.0	1.2%	96
On-time delivery	89.0	98.0	82
Extractor utilization*	100.0	134.0	34
Yield*	100.0	106.4	6
Rework	6.2	1.9	69
Employee absenteeism	10.0	1.0	90
Employee turnover*	100.0	31.0	69
Cost per pound (¢)	28.8	19.7	32

* Indexed: 94/95 = 100

Southern Gardens was the most efficient citrus processor in the world for the 1996 through 1999 seasons. It received The Kroger Co. Supplier of the Year Award in 1996, 1998, and 1999.

University of California, San Diego

The Balanced Scorecard also has been successfully applied to government, nonprofit, and educational institutions, as we discuss in Chapters 5 and 7. As one leading example, the University of California, San Diego, was looking for ways to improve productivity and customer satisfaction among its administrative service units, such as the bookstore, housing office, police force, and travel office. Vice Chancellor Steven Relyea introduced the Balanced Scorecard approach to the 27 service units in 1994.[13] The results were far reaching. The payroll department reduced errors by 80 percent. The financial office reduced the time to process expense reimbursement checks from six weeks to as little as three days. The innovative program has received wide recognition, including winning the 1999 Rochester Institute of Technology/USA Today Quality Cup for Education.[14]

Duke Children's Hospital

Duke Children's Hospital (DCH), an academic children's hospital within the Duke University Health System in Durham, North Carolina, was experiencing increases in cost per case of 35 percent from 1994 to 1995. Its eight-day average length of stay was 15 percent over target. It was losing money, its staff was dissatisfied, and its recent process improvement initiatives were unsuccessful. Yet it was asking the medical center for an additional $40 million for expansion programs. Dr. Jon Meliones at DCH led a Balanced Scorecard program that eventually reached all of DCH's pediatric facilities, including two large hospitals in the region that DCH acquired as the program was rolling out. Dr. Meliones used the Balanced Scorecard method as a call to action to begin "practicing smarter" medicine.

The near-term results from the scorecard, initiatives, and process improvements were dramatic (see Figure 1-4). These efforts resulted in nearly a $30 million reduction in cost and a $50 million increase in net margin. All results were achieved while improving clinical outcomes and staff satisfaction. Through the use of the Balanced Scorecard to focus and align the clinical, academic, and administrative staffs to a new strategy, DCH im-

Figure 1-4   Duke Children's Hospital's Balanced Scorecard

	Measure	Before	After	% Improvement
Financial	▪ Operating Margin	−$50m	+$10m	
Perspective	▪ Cost per Case	$14,889	$11,146	−25%
	▪ Family Satisfaction	4.3	4.7	+11%
Customer	▪ Would Recommend	4.3	4.7	+11%
Perspective	▪ Discharge Timeliness	50%	60%	+20%
	▪ Medical Plan Awareness	47%	94%	+100%
	▪ Length of Stay	8 days	6 days	−25%
Internal	▪ Readmission Rate			
Perspective	- Intensive Care Unit	11%	4%	−63%
	- Intermediate Care	11%	7%	−36%

proved patient and physician satisfaction and loyalty while achieving dramatic 25 percent reductions in cost per case and length of stay. And the results came quickly, within two to three years.

United Parcel Service

What about an organization that was not in financial difficulty? Is the Balanced Scorecard only for companies experiencing declining performance? Consider the experience of UPS. In 1994, the company was enjoying record profits. But CEO Oz Nelson understood that the market was changing and the company would be in danger within five years unless it made dramatic changes. Many new opportunities were arising from e-commerce and global expansion, and UPS had to become a more customer-focused company, one that understood its customers better and could deliver what they wanted.

UPS had long had an operational-excellence focus. Ninety percent of its measurements were financial, usually reported with lags of forty-five days or more. Employees said that they had little understanding of how their day-to-day work affected company performance. Nelson wanted the company and its employees to refocus on quality measures of key processes. So the company defined four key point-of-arrival (POA) metrics—customer satisfaction, employee relations, competitive position, and time in transit—and created the corporate Balanced Scorecard with the four perspectives containing measures and goals aligned to these metrics.[15] The scorecard became the measurement vehicle to align all eleven UPS regions, sixty districts, and more than 300,000 employees worldwide. The goal was to have a clear line of sight from every employee's everyday job to the company's overall business objectives.

In 1999, within five years of launching the project, UPS executives believed they had succeeded in transforming the company into a more nimble, customer-focused, and solutions-oriented business that was at the leading edge of technology and e-commerce opportunities. UPS revenues were growing at nearly 10 percent annually, in an industry with 3 percent to 4 percent growth. Profitability had improved by 30 and 40 percent in 1998 and 1999. In 1999 *Forbes* named UPS "Company of the Year," and *Business Week* described UPS's delivery people as "the foot soldiers of the dot.com revolution." Along with initiatives in technology and marketing, the Balanced Scorecard helped drive this performance. In the words of one UPS executive, "The Balanced Scorecard provided a road map—the shared vision of our future goals–with action elements that let everyone contribute to our success."

We discuss the UPS Balanced Scorecard process more comprehensively in Chapter 9. We mention it here to indicate that becoming a Strategy-Focused Organization is best done before a division or company has encountered the financial difficulties experienced by Mobil, CIGNA, AT&T Canada, and Zeneca Ag. Ideally, the scorecard should be used by organizations that are about to embark on an aggressive growth strategy—to guide the journey, to develop the management system for rapid growth, and to align existing and soon-to-be-hired employees to the strategy for acquiring, retaining, and deepening relationships with targeted customers.

A NEW APPROACH TO MANAGING

The Balanced Scorecard has evolved since we first developed and introduced the concept as a new framework for measuring organization performance. It was originally proposed to overcome the limitations of managing only with financial measures. Financial measures reported on outcomes, lagging indicators, but did not communicate the drivers of future performance, the indicators of how to create new value through investments in customers, suppliers, employees, technology, and innovation. The Balanced Scorecard provided a framework to look at the strategy used for value creation from four different perspectives:

1. Financial. The strategy for growth, profitability, and risk viewed from the perspective of the shareholder.

2. Customer. The strategy for creating value and differentiation from the perspective of the customer.

3. Internal business processes. The strategic priorities for various business processes, which create customer and shareholder satisfaction.

4. Learning and growth. The priorities to create a climate that supports organizational change, innovation, and growth.

With the Balanced Scorecard, corporate executives could now measure how their business units created value for current and future customers. While retaining an interest in financial performance, the Balanced Scorecard clearly revealed the drivers of superior, long-term value and competitive performance.

We quickly learned that *measurement* has consequences beyond just reporting on the past. Measurement creates focus for the future because the measures chosen by managers communicate to the organization what is important. To take full advantage of this power, measurement should be integrated into a *management system*. Thus we refined the Balanced Scorecard concept and showed how it could move beyond a performance measurement system to become the organizing framework for a strategic management system (see Figure 1-5).[16] A strategy scorecard replaced the budget as the center for management processes. In effect, the Balanced Scorecard became the operating system for a new strategic management process.

As organizations managed with the scorecard, they made further discoveries. The speed and magnitude of the results achieved by the early adopters revealed the power of the Balanced Scorecard management system to focus the entire organization on strategy. To achieve such intense strategic focus the organizations had instituted comprehensive, transformational change. They redefined their relationships with the customer, reengineered fundamental business processes, taught their workforces new skills, and deployed a new technology infrastructure. Also, a new culture

Figure 1-5 Starting from a New Premise

From a Management Control System

***Designed around a Short-Term, Control-Oriented
Financial Framework***

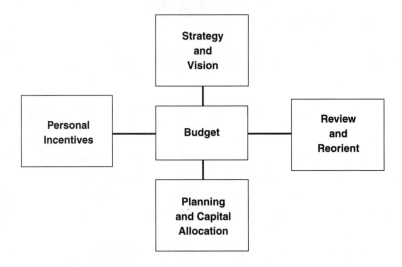

To a Strategic Management System

***Designed around a Longer-Term
Strategic View***

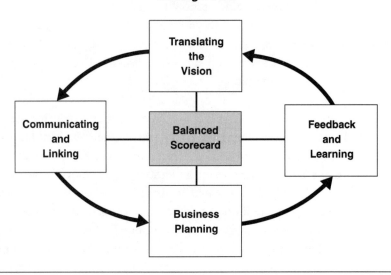

emerged, centered not on traditional functional silos but on the team effort required to support the strategy. The management system provided the mechanism to mobilize and guide the process of change. But this new culture involved even more than a management system. Companies created a new kind of organization based on the requirements of their strategy—hence the term *Strategy-Focused Organization.* For the companies we studied, creating a Strategy-Focused Organization was not a homogeneous approach similar to, for example, qualifying for ISO 9000 or submitting an application for the Baldrige Award, processes by which a standard set of requirements can be applied. Strategies differed so that the organizational changes differed from company to company. The common feature, however, was that every Strategy-Focused Organization put strategy at the center of its change and management processes. By clearly defining the strategy, communicating it consistently, and linking it to the drivers of change, a performance-based culture emerged that linked everyone and every unit to the unique features of the strategy.

Companies are moving away from performance management systems linked exclusively to financial frameworks. In the early decades of the twentieth century, Dupont Corporation and General Motors Corporation developed the return-on-investment metric as an integrating device for the multidivisional firm.[17] By the mid-twentieth century, multidivisional firms were using the budget as the centerpiece of their management systems. In the 1990s, companies had extended the financial framework to embrace financial metrics that correlated better with shareholder value, leading to economic value added (EVA) and value-based management metrics. But even today's best financial frameworks do not capture all the dynamics of performance in today's knowledge-based competition.

Recognizing the limitations of managing only with financial numbers, many companies adopted quality as their central rallying cry and organizing framework during the 1980s and 1990s. Companies strove to win national quality awards—Malcolm Baldrige in the United States, the Deming Prize in Japan, and EFQM in Europe—and to emulate Motorola, Inc., and General Electric by adopting six sigma programs. But quality alone was insufficient, as were the pure financial measures the quality programs hoped to replace. Several companies that won national quality awards soon found themselves in financial distress.

Beyond financial and quality measures, some companies have emphasized customer focus, implementing programs to build market-focused organization and establishing customer relationship management systems. Others have opted for core competencies or reengineering of fundamental business processes. Still others have emphasized strategic human resources management, showing how motivated, skilled employees can create economic value, or have deployed information technology for competitive advantage. Each of these perspectives—financial, quality, customers, capabilities, processes, people, and systems—is important and can play a role in creating value in organizations. But each represents only one component in the network of management activities and processes that must be performed to generate superior, sustainable performance. To focus on and manage only one of these perspectives encourages suboptimization at the expense of broader organizational goals. Companies have to replace any narrow or specific focus with a comprehensive view in which strategy is at the heart of the management systems.

Strategy-Focused Organizations use the Balanced Scorecard to place strategy at the center of their management processes. The Balanced Scorecard makes a unique contribution by describing strategy in a consistent and insightful way. Before the development of strategy scorecards, managers had no generally accepted framework for describing strategy: They could not implement something that they couldn't describe well. So the simple act of describing strategy via strategy maps and scorecards is an enormous breakthrough.

Having the scorecard, however, may be necessary but not sufficient to beat the odds against successful strategy implementation. From working with the world-class executives on whom this book is based, we have learned that they succeeded by using the Balanced Scorecard as the central framework for a new performance management process. This process produced significant performance improvements rapidly, reliably, and in a sustainable manner. The approach, while building on solid historical foundations, was tailored to the needs of the new economy. This book provides a roadmap for those who wish to create their own Strategy-Focused Organization.

NOTES

1. "Measures That Matter," Ernst & Young (Boston, 1998), 9.
2. Walter Kiechel, "Corporate Strategists under Fire," *Fortune,* 27 December 1982, 38.
3. R. Charan and G. Colvin, "Why CEO's Fail," *Fortune,* 21 June 1999.

4. M. B. Blair, *Ownership and Control: Rethinking Corporate Governance for the Twenty-First Century* (Washington, DC: Brookings Institute, 1995), Chapter 6.

5. Research conducted by Professor Baruch Lev of New York University, referenced in A. M. Webber, "New Math For a New Economy," *Fast Company,* January–February 2000, 217–24.

6. R. S. Kaplan and D. P. Norton, "The Balanced Scorecard: Measures That Drive Performance," *Harvard Business Review* (January–February 1992): 71–79.

7. The sales figure excludes excise taxes collected at gasoline pumps for the government.

8. "Letters to the Editor," *Harvard Business Review* (March–April 1996): 170.

9. "Letters to the Editor," *Harvard Business Review* (March–April 1996): 172.

10. "Letters to the Editor," *Harvard Business Review* (March–April 1996): 172.

11. We have adapted the recipe metaphor from Paul Romer, the contemporary pioneer in the economic growth literature.

12. John Kotter, *Leading Change* (Boston: Harvard Business School Press, 1996).

13. You can access the UCSD Balanced Scorecard project on the Internet: http://www-vcba.ucsd.edu/performance/.

14. *USA Today,* 7 May 1999, 7B.

15. The POA measures were long-range company goals to signal when UPS had "arrived" at achieving its targeted performance.

16. Robert S. Kaplan and David P. Norton, *The Balanced Scorecard: Translating Strategy into Action* (Boston: Harvard Business School Press, 1996).

17. H. Thomas Johnson and Robert S. Kaplan, *Relevance Lost: The Rise and Fall of Management Accounting* (Boston: Harvard Business School Press, 1986), 61–124.

How Mobil Became a Strategy-Focused Organization

MOBIL NORTH AMERICA MARKETING AND REFINING (NAM&R) is perhaps our best example of putting the five principles of a Strategy-Focused Organization into practice. Bob McCool became chief executive of NAM&R in 1992; his executive vice president, Brian Baker, succeeded him in 1996. Together they transformed an underperforming organization that was inwardly focused, bureaucratic, and inefficient into the leader in its industry—a turnaround that improved operating cash flow by more than $1 billion per year. Mobil NAM&R successfully implemented a strategy that required a significant marketplace repositioning concomitant with substantial cost reductions and operational improvements. Even more impressive, however, Mobil created an organization capable of sustaining competitive advantage in a mature, commodity, and fiercely competitive industry. Placing the Balanced Scorecard at the center of its management processes, Mobil achieved industrywide profit leadership from 1995 up through its merger into ExxonMobil Corporation in late 1999. Its experience illustrates well the power of the five principles of a Strategy-Focused Organization.

TRANSLATE THE STRATEGY TO OPERATIONAL TERMS

The process starts by building a Balanced Scorecard that describes and communicates the strategy. Therefore, management must have a clear understanding of its strategy.

Historically, Mobil attempted to differentiate its commodity product (gasoline) through a product leadership strategy that stressed brand image and unique product characteristics. Its major competitors, however, pursued a similar strategy, and largely neutralized Mobil's attempt at product differentiation. Most competition still took place around price and location. Because of the nature of the industry—capital intensive, a high cost of raw materials, a commodity product—Mobil and its competitors devoted much of their energies to cost reduction and productivity.

As McCool and Baker contemplated a new strategy, they wanted to do more than just lower costs and become more efficient across its value chain. Some of Mobil's competitors had access to low-cost crude, so that a pure cost leadership strategy would be difficult to sustain in the long run. Mobil wanted a strategy for growth and differentiation. It wanted to find ways to attract customers who purchased more gasoline than average, purchased more premium than regular-blend products, were willing to pay higher prices for a better buying experience, and would purchase products other than gasoline at a retail station. Mobil's strategy, therefore, was two-pronged: (1) reduce costs and improve productivity across its value chain, and (2) generate higher volume on premium-priced products and services. If successful, Mobil's margins would improve through both components.

Financial Perspective

Mobil started its scorecard by defining its high-level financial objective: to increase *return on capital employed* (ROCE) from its current level of 7 percent (below the cost of capital) to 12 percent within three years.[1] The executives believed that an increase of this magnitude—in a mature, slow-growth, commodity industry with at least a half-dozen major competitors and many smaller players—was indeed a stretch target.

Mobil planned to improve its high-level ROCE measure by using two financial themes: *productivity* and *growth*. The productivity theme consisted of two components: cost reduction and asset intensity. Cost reduction would be measured by operating cash expenses versus the industry (using cents per gallon to normalize for volume), with the goal of being the industry cost leader.[2] Asset productivity would enable Mobil to handle greater volumes from its growth strategy without expanding its asset base. For this objective, it selected a measure of cash flow, net of capital spending, to indicate the benefits from generating more cash (i.e., throughput) from existing assets plus any benefits from inventory reductions.

Mobil's financial growth theme also consisted of two components. The first, volume growth, was for sales from its basic gasoline products (and home heating oil and jet fuel) to grow faster than the industry average. In addition to pure volume growth, Mobil wanted a higher proportion of its sales in its premium product grades. So it set two measures for this growth component: volume growth rate versus industry growth rate, and percentage of volume in premium grades.

The second growth component represented the opportunity to sell products other than gasoline to retail customers. An important component of Mobil's growth theme was a customer-driven strategy built around sales of convenience store products. New revenue could also come from sales of automobile services and products such as car washes, lubricants, oil changes, minor repairs, and common replacement parts. Mobil set a financial growth objective to develop new sources of revenue, and it measured this objective by nongasoline revenues and margins. Thus the financial perspective (see Figure 2-1) incorporated objectives and measures for both productivity and growth strategies.

Figure 2-1 Mobil NAM&R's Strategy Map: *Financial Perspective*

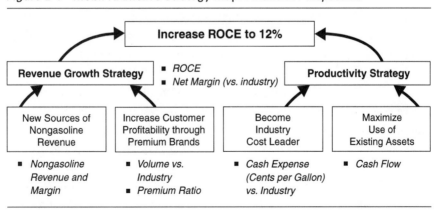

The juxtaposition of two contrasting strategies (productivity versus growth) is a frequent cause of strategic failure. Organizations become confused by apparent contradictions and fall back to one-dimensional behavior. This was clearly a risk and a challenge for Mobil. Their Balanced Scorecard, however, allowed it to define and to clarify these contradictions, to make the organization aware of the tradeoffs and to manage them—across their internal value chain—in a visible and effective way. The scorecard provided the communication vehicle for the new, more complex financial strategy.

Customer Perspective

Mobil struggled initially to understand how it could generate the desired growth in volume, margins, and nongasoline revenues. Like other companies, Mobil had historically attempted to market a full range of products and services to all consumers. It matched prices, however, of discount stations operating near a Mobil station so that it would not lose market share. Attempting to be a full-line producer while lowering price to avoid losing customers to low-priced discount stations explained a lot about Mobil's poor financial performance in the early 1990s.

When they met to discuss ways to develop a new profitable growth strategy, the executives expressed quite divergent views about why customers might be willing to pay a $0.06 to $0.10 per gallon premium to purchase Mobil gasoline. Eventually, they turned to the Gasoline Marketing Department, which had just completed a study that revealed five distinct consumer segments among the gasoline-buying public (see Figure 2-2).

The executives could now see that price-sensitive consumers constituted only 20 percent of all gasoline purchasers. Another segment, Homebodies, had little loyalty to any brand or station. But three segments wanted more than a commodity purchase.

Mobil now faced a critical strategic choice. It could compete for the price-sensitive consumers, by lowering costs throughout its value chain, including at the gasoline station, so that it could be profitable even at the lowest prices charged to consumers. Alternatively, Mobil could attempt to attract three segments—Road Warriors, True Blues, and Generation F3— by offering a superior buying experience. But it could not do both. Strategy is about choice. For Mobil to deliver a superior buying experience, it would have to invest in larger stations, more gasoline pumps at each sta-

Figure 2-2 Mobil's Growth Strategy: Understand the Customer

Road Warriors 16%	Generally higher-income, middle-aged men who drive 25,000 to 50,000 miles a year . . . buy premium gasoline with a credit card . . . purchase sandwiches and drinks from the convenience store . . . will sometimes wash their cars at the carwash.
True Blues 16%	Usually men and women with moderate to high incomes who are loyal to a brand and sometimes to a particular station . . . frequently buy premium gasoline and pay in cash.
Generation F3 27%	Fuel, Food, and Fast: Upwardly mobile men and women—half under 25 years of age—who are constantly on the go . . . drive a lot and snack heavily from the convenience store.
Homebodies 21%	Usually housewives who shuttle their children around during the day and use whatever gasoline station is based in town or along their route of travel.
Price Shoppers 20%	Generally aren't loyal to either a brand or a particular station, and rarely buy the premium line . . . frequently on tight budgets.

tion, technology at the gas pump, convenience stores, auxiliary car services (such as car washes and service bays for minor repairs and maintenance), and training for station personnel. Such a policy raises costs at the gasoline station that would make it impossible to be profitable if prices remained at the lowest level in the industry.

Ideally, with five different consumer segments, a company could contemplate having five different distribution systems to satisfy each segment. Such a policy, however, is often expensive and complex to implement and difficult to explain to consumers.[3] Mobil couldn't have different types of gasoline stations—Mobil for Road Warriors, Mobil for Generation F3, and Mobil for Price Shoppers. It had to choose. Mobil's strategic choice was to target consumers in the first three segments (Road Warriors, True Blues, and Generation F3) and offer a great buying experience that would sustain premium prices, even for its commoditylike products.

In its customer perspective, therefore, Mobil selected the outcome measure to be market share in the three targeted segments. Measuring total market share would represent an undifferentiated strategy, perhaps no strategy at all, attempting to be all things to all consumers. The differentiation strategy demanded a measure consistent with targeting specific consumer groups. Mobil wanted to be the number one choice for Road Warriors, True Blues, and Generation F3. Share of segments for these three groups was the logical outcome measure for the customer perspective.

But companies cannot stop with outcome measures alone. Mobil needed to define the value proposition that it must deliver to attract, retain, and deepen its relationship with customers in the three targeted segments. Again, market research was critical; the research had identified the attributes that constituted a great buying experience. These included the following:

- Immediate access to a gasoline pump (to avoid waiting for service)
- Self-payment mechanisms at the pump (to avoid waiting to pay)
- Covered area for gasoline pumps (to protect customers from rain and snow)
- One hundred percent availability of product, especially premium grades (to avoid stockouts)
- Clean restrooms
- Satisfactory exterior station appearance
- Safe, well-lit station
- Convenience store, stocked with fresh, high-quality merchandise
- Speedy purchase
- Ample parking spaces near convenience store
- Friendly employees
- Availability of minor car services

Mobil summarized these attributes as offering customers "a fast, friendly serve." But how could all the attributes of the fast, friendly serve buying experience be measured? Mobil decided that the consumer's buying experience was so central to its strategy that it invested in a new measurement system: the "mystery shopper." Mobil hired an independent third party to send a representative (the mystery shopper) to every Mobil station every month to purchase fuel and a snack and to evaluate the experience based on twenty-three specified attributes. A summary of the ratings would constitute the mystery shopper score for that station that month. Mobil had learned how difficult it was to *brand its product*. Now it would attempt to *brand the buying experience.*

The mystery shopper rating represented the value proposition that Mobil would offer its targeted customers. If Mobil's theory of the business were valid, increases in the mystery shopper score would translate into increases in market share in the three targeted segments. Note that Mobil did not expect that its market share in the nontargeted segments—Price Shoppers and Homebodies—would increase, as consumers in these segments did not necessarily value the improved buying experience enough to generate loyalty and pay the higher prices that Mobil would be charging at the gasoline pump.

At this point, Mobil had a fairly simple set of objectives and measures for the customer perspective: three outcome measures (share of three targeted segments) and a summary measure of the value proposition (mystery shopper score) expected to drive the outcomes.

The customer perspective, however, was not complete. Mobil did not sell directly to its end-use consumers. Like companies in many industries, Mobil's immediate customer was the independent owner of the gasoline station. These franchised retailers purchased gasoline and lubricant products from Mobil and sold to consumers in Mobil-branded stations. If end-use consumers were to receive a great buying experience, then the independent dealers had to deliver that experience. Dealers were clearly a critical part of Mobil's new strategy.

In the past, Mobil did not consider their retailers or distributors as components of its strategy. Relationships could even be adversarial. Every cent that Mobil reduced the price of gasoline to the dealer, to reduce the dealer's cost of goods sold, 1 cent would be subtracted from Mobil's top line (revenues). This old strategic view put Mobil and its dealers in a zero-sum-game situation. Mobil now realized that its strategy could not possibly succeed unless it stopped treating dealers as rivals. Dealers had to be brought into the strategy and deliver on the strategy every day in every transaction conducted with consumers.

In a sharp departure from the past, Mobil adopted an objective to increase its dealers' profitability. Mobil set a stretch target to have its dealers become the most profitable franchise operators in the country so that it could attract and retain the best talent. The new strategy emphasized creating a positive-sum game, increasing the size of the reward that could be shared between Mobil and its dealers so that the relationship would be win-win.

The higher reward came from several sources. First, the premium prices that Mobil hoped to sustain at its stations would generate higher revenues. Second, by increasing the market share in the three targeted segments, a higher quantity of gasoline would be sold, and a higher percentage of the purchases would be for premium grades (especially purchases by True Blues and Road Warriors). Third, the dealer would also have a revenue stream from the sale of nongasoline products and services—convenience store and auxiliary car services—a portion of which would also flow back to Mobil.

Mobil therefore set an objective to create the win-win relationship with dealers and measured this objective by the gross profits that could be split between the dealers and Mobil. The customer strategy could now be represented by linked measures in the customer perspective (see Figure 2-3).

Mobil's customer strategy involved a virtuous cycle. Motivated, independent dealers would deliver a great buying experience that would attract an increasing share of targeted customers. These customers would buy premium products and services at premium prices, creating increased profits for both Mobil and its dealers, who would continue to be motivated to offer the great buying experience. The strategy would generate the quality revenue growth for Mobil's financial strategy. The objectives and measures in Mobil's customer perspective were not generic, undifferentiated measures such as customer satisfaction or customer loyalty. They were specific, fo-

Figure 2-3 Mobil NAM&R's Strategy Map: *Customer Perspective*

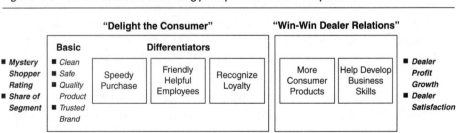

cused measures, derived from the strategy, and that clearly communicated the new strategy.

Internal Business Process Perspective

With a clear picture about the outcomes desired in the financial and customer perspectives, Mobil now turned to the objectives and measures in the internal business process perspective. For direct linkages to the customer objectives, Mobil identified two important internal processes:

1. Develop new products and services
2. Generate dealer profits from nongasoline revenues

The first objective signaled the desire to enhance the buying experience of consumers by developing new offerings at the gasoline station. The second objective supported both the new win-win relationship with dealers and Mobil's financial objectives. If dealers could generate increased revenues and profits from products other than gasoline, then dealers would rely less on profits from gasoline sales to meet their profit targets. This would leave more of a profit share for Mobil, while still allowing its dealers to be the most profitable in the industry. Mobil also recognized that an important internal process was to train its dealers to be better managers of the gasoline station, service bays, and convenience store—another contributor to dealer profitability.

In addition to processes aimed at improving customer objectives, Mobil included several objectives and measures in its internal business process perspective for its basic refining and distribution operations. Measures for these operations stressed low cost, consistent quality, reductions of asset downtime, and the elimination of environmental, safety, and health-threatening incidents. Most of these measures related to the cost reduction and productivity themes in the financial perspective.

One could question why a company following a differentiation strategy used so many internal measures relating to cost reduction and productivity. The answer is quite simple. Because Mobil produced mostly commodity products (gasoline, heating oil, jet fuel), it could not use higher prices to recover any higher costs or inefficiencies incurred in its basic manufacturing and distribution operations. The differentiation, for Mobil's new strategy, occurred at the gasoline station, not in its refineries, pipelines, distribution terminals, or trucking operations. Little that happened prior to the final point of purchase created a differentiated product from the consumer's perspective. If the basic operations of refining and distribution did not create a differentiated product or service, then any higher costs incurred in these processes could not be recovered in the final selling price. Therefore, Mobil had to follow an operational excellence strategy in its basic operating processes. Having several measures in the internal process perspective for cost reduction, fixed asset productivity, and yield improvements signaled this strategy.

The measures of quality (being on time and on specification) and retail product availability supported some part of the consumer's value proposition. But most of the benefit supported the operational excellence strategy in its production and distribution operations. The major objective in regard to environmental, health, and safety (EHS) factors used measures such as safety incidents, days away from work, and environmental incidents. Again, some of the benefits from improved EHS performance contributed to cost reduction and increased productivity. The head of the division felt that safety incidents were an important leading indicator, believing that if employees' carelessness led to personal harm, it is likely that they were not paying much attention to the physical assets of the company either. The EHS measures, however, also contributed to Mobil being a good citizen in its communities, and for the well-being of its employees. Mobil executives valued these community and employees objectives and wanted them to be featured on the Balanced Scorecard.

Thus Mobil's internal business process objectives and measures supported both its differentiated strategy with consumers and dealers and its financial objectives for cost reduction and improved productivity. Figure 2-4 shows a simplified representation of this perspective.

Learning and Growth Perspective

The final set of objectives provided the foundation for Mobil's strategy: skills and motivation of its employees and the role for information technology. The project team identified three strategic objectives for the learning and growth perspective:

1. Core Competencies and Skills
   - Encourage and facilitate our people to gain a broader understanding of the marketing and refining business from end to end

Figure 2-4 Mobil NAM&R's Strategy Map: *Internal Process Perspective*

- Build the level of skills and competencies necessary to execute our vision
- Develop the leadership skills required to articulate the vision, promote integrated business thinking, and develop our people

2. Access to Strategic Information
   - Develop the strategic information required to execute our strategies

3. Organizational Involvement
   - Enable the achievement of our vision by promoting an understanding of our organizational strategy and by creating a climate in which our employees are motivated and empowered to strive toward that vision

The measures to support these three objectives, however, proved to be among the most difficult to specify. Ideally, Mobil wanted to identify the specific skills and information each individual should have to enhance internal process performance and deliver the value proposition to its customers; these might include, for example, measures such as strategic competency availability percentage and strategic systems availability. The company had to defer actual measurement, however, until it could develop the measurement instruments. For the third objective, Mobil implemented an employee survey designed to measure people's awareness about the new strategy and their motivation to help the company achieve its targets.

With the learning and growth perspective specified, Mobil now had a complete representation of its new strategy. It had finished the first process in creating a Strategy-Focused Organization by translating its vision and strategy into a set of objectives and measures in the four perspectives (see Figure 2-5). These could be represented in a strategy map (see Figure 2-6) that graphically portrayed the cause-and-effect linkages of the objectives and measures across the four perspectives. The objectives and measures, and their representation in a map, could now be linked and communicated clearly to the rest of the organization.

Building a Balanced Scorecard should be neither a search for the best measures nor a benchmarking exercise to find out what other companies are measuring in their scorecards. Rather, the scorecard-building process should follow Mobil NAM&R's steps:

- Assess the competitive environment
- Learn about customer preferences and segments
- Develop a strategy to generate breakthrough financial performance
- Articulate the balance between growth and productivity
- Select the targeted customer segments
- Determine the value proposition for the targeted customers
- Identify the critical internal business processes to deliver the value proposition to customers and for the financial cost and productivity objectives
- Develop the skills, competencies, motivation, databases, and technology required to excel at internal processes and customer value delivery

At the end of this process, the organization will have a scorecard of objectives and measures that truly reflects the strategy. An outside observer should be able to infer the organization's strategy from its scorecard measures and the linkages among them. When this test has been passed, the organization is ready to deploy the scorecard through the next four processes to create the Strategy-Focused Organization.

ALIGN THE ORGANIZATION TO THE STRATEGY

Most organizations consist of multiple divisions, multiple business units, and a collection of shared service units. Such organizations must link their

Figure 2-5 Mobil NAM&R's Balanced Scorecard

	Strategic Themes	Strategic Objectives	Strategic Measures
Financial	Financial Growth	F1 Return on Capital Employed F2 Existing Asset Utilization F3 Profitability F4 Industry Cost Leader F5 Profitable Growth	■ ROCE ■ Cash Flow ■ Net Margin Rank (vs. Competition) ■ Full Cost per Gallon Delivered (vs. Competition) ■ Volume Growth Rate vs. Industry ■ Premium Ratio ■ Nongasoline Revenue and Margin
Customer	Delight the Consumer	C1 Continually Delight the Targeted Consumer	■ Share of Segment in Selected Key Markets ■ Mystery Shopper Rating
	Win-Win Dealer Relations	C2 Build Win-Win Relations with Dealer	■ Dealer Gross Profit Growth ■ Dealer Survey
Internal	Build the Franchise	I1 Innovative Products and Services	■ New Product ROI ■ New Product Acceptance Rate
		I2 Best-in-Class Franchise Teams	■ Dealer Quality Score
	Safe and Reliable	I3 Refinery Performance	■ Yield Gap ■ Unplanned Downtime
	Competitive Supplier	I4 Inventory Management	■ Inventory Levels ■ Run-out Rate
		I5 Industry Cost Leader	■ Activity Cost vs. Competition
	Quality	I6 On Spec, on Time	■ Perfect Orders
	Good Neighbor	I7 Improve EHS	■ Number of Environmental Incidents ■ Days Away from Work Rate
Learning and Growth	Motivated and Prepared Workforce	L1 Climate for Action L2 Core Competencies and Skills L3 Access to Strategic Information	■ Employee Survey ■ Personal Balanced Scorecard (%) ■ Strategic Competency Availability ■ Strategic Information Availability

Figure 2-6 Mobil NAM&R's Strategy Map

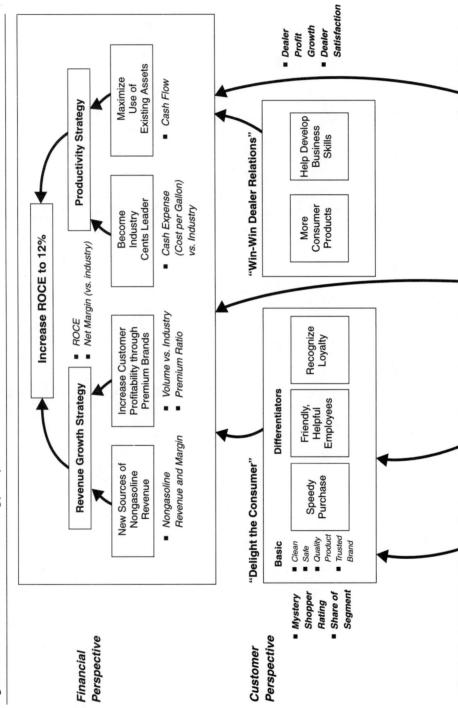

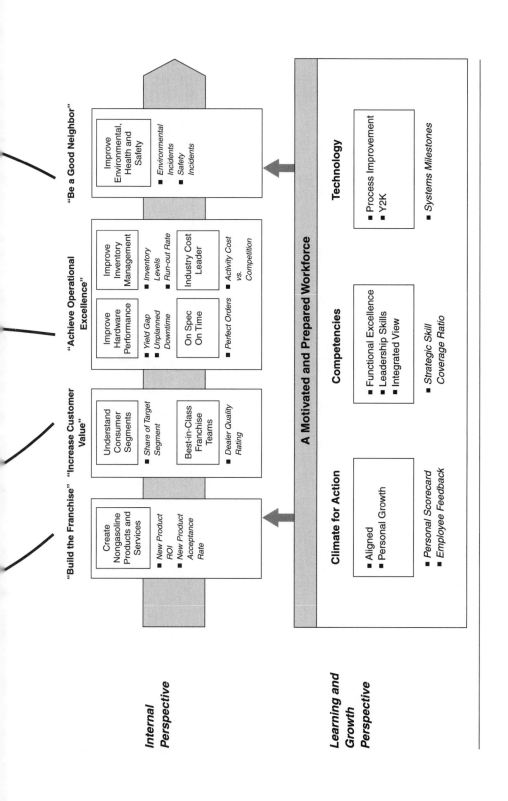

high-level scorecard, developed at the corporate or division level, down to their decentralized organizational units. This creates alignment and synergy across the organization, which is the second principle of a Strategy-Focused Organization.

As part of its new strategy of customer focus, Mobil had dissolved its centralized, functional organization and created eighteen geographic business units that could each react to the company's local market conditions in different ways. In addition, the previously centralized staff functions had been transformed into fourteen shared service units (e.g., information services, finance, planning and analysis, human resources, and environment and safety) that had to sell services to the local business units and get agreement from them on prices and levels of service provided. The new organization created two challenges for senior management. The first was figuring out how to keep these thirty-two entities focused on the same high-level strategy. The second was upgrading the skills of the newly appointed business unit and shared service heads. The business unit heads had all grown up within a structured, top-down, functional organization. Only the top two senior executives had accountability for a P&L statement. Everyone else either managed costs (as a manager of a refinery, pipeline, or distribution facility) or revenues (as a district sales manager). Bob McCool saw a problem with the transition to the new organization:

> We were taking people who had spent their whole professional life as managers in a big functional organization, and we were asking them to become the leaders of more entrepreneurial profit-making businesses, some with up to $1 billion in assets. How were we going to get them out of their historic area of functional expertise to think strategically, as general managers of profit-oriented businesses?[4]

The Balanced Scorecard became the mechanism both to create strategic awareness and skills among the new unit managers and to align the strategies of the decentralized units with each other and with the division. The scorecard developed by the NAM&R Leadership Team became the template for the creation of strategies elsewhere in the organization. The scorecard developed at the division established the major objectives that were common for the entire organization:

- Achieve financial returns (as measured by ROCE)
- Delight targeted consumers with a great buying experience of food and fuel

- Develop win-win relationships with dealers and retailers
- Improve critical internal processes—low cost, zero defects, on-time deliveries
- Reduce environmental, safety, and other health-threatening incidents
- Improve employee morale

These high-level objectives were then transmitted throughout the organization by incorporating them in scorecards developed by individual business units. Each unit formulated a strategy appropriate for its target market, but each strategy had to be consistent with the themes and priorities of the NAM&R template. Each of the eighteen geographical business units translated its strategy into a Balanced Scorecard. The eighteen scorecards were customized to local circumstances—competitors, market opportunities, and critical processes—but were still based on the high-level divisional scorecard. As McCool noted,

Mobil in the Midwest is not the same as Mobil in New England, or on the West Coast. In each market, the consumer looks at us differently, our competition in each region is different, and the economics of operating in each market are different. I don't want to dictate a solution from Fairfax [headquarters]. We have a basic strategy and set of support programs that we can roll out to each NBU [Natural Business Unit]. We do have a few constraints: we want our dealers to operate under a sign that says "Mobil," there's a basic design for the station and for the C-store that we want to share across regions, and we think we have a winning segmentation strategy with fast and friendly service. But if an NBU thinks it has a better driver for success, I'm willing to hear it. I want the NBU head to tell me, here's my business, this is my vision and strategy, and this is how I am going get there from here.[5]

With these guidelines, each business unit developed its own scorecard in light of its local situation.[6] Measures at the individual business levels did not have to add up to a divisional measure. The business unit managers chose local measures that would *influence* the measures on the divisional scorecard, but the measures were not necessarily a simple decomposition of the higher-level scorecard. Many of the measures on the New England Sales and Distribution (NES&D) unit scorecard resembled those on the high-level scorecard. But several measures on the national scorecard did not appear, as NES&D did not have any refineries in its district. And NES&D introduced several new measures. One of them, called Dealer Commitment, sought to align local dealers with Mobil's desired "fast, friendly serve" buying experience. The New England scorecard reflected the percentages of dealers who had bought into the Dealer Commitment initiative. This was the district's way of measuring a win-win relationship with its dealers. Other regions, however, could adopt quite different approaches. So the measures for this objective were different across the eighteen regions and therefore could not be aggregated into a division-level measure. But each region had developed initiatives and measures that reflected its local circumstances and culture of how it would implement a strategic alliance with the dealers in its region. In this process, the strategies of all organizational units became aligned so that the cumulative impact of each unit performing well would be reinforced by the actions of all other units.

The next level of linkage occurred when Mobil deployed Balanced Scorecards for all of its shared service units. These units now had to sell services to the natural business units and get agreement from them on prices and levels of service provided.

To get the staff functions (or shared service organizations) responsive to business unit needs, Mobil formed buyers' committees. Each committee had three to five representatives from business units who worked out an annual agreement with a shared service unit. Rigorous negotiations occurred annually between the buyers' committee and the shared service unit's executive team on the menu of services that the service unit proposed to supply and the cost of supplying each service type. Marty Di Mezza, head of the Gasoline Marketing shared service unit, recalled the change in culture that this new organizational arrangement required:

> *We had to go through a major mental change: from a direction-giving organization to a service provider. Our people would have to learn how to partner with the NBUs to assist them in accomplishing their strategies. . . .*
>
> *For the first time in Mobil's history, we had to put together a bundle of services that someone else had to agree to buy. We had never before asked people whether they were willing buyers.*[7]

The discussions eventually culminated in a service agreement describing the set of services that the business units wanted the service unit to supply and an authorized budget for the supply of these services. Often services that the shared service group wanted to offer were not perceived as valuable by the business units' buyers' committee, so the services were discontinued. In other cases, the buyers' committee wanted the service but not at the prices being quoted. The shared service unit would then reduce some of the functionality, or bells and whistles as they called them, to deliver a lower-cost basic service. The converse also occurred. The buyers' committee often identified services that were high priority for them, which the shared service unit had not proposed to offer. Di Mezza commented on the negotiating process: "It was an iterative process, revising our menu of services and reallocating our manpower and expense resources to the objectives that the field organization wanted to accomplish. But it was a learning and bonding process as we went through each iteration of the scorecard and service agreement."[8]

Once the service agreements had been obtained, all fourteen shared service units constructed their balanced scorecards. Each shared service unit developed its own strategy for functional excellence, but the strategies had to be directed at helping the business units and the division achieve their strategies. The customer perspective of the shared services' Balanced Scorecards reflected the business units' satisfaction with the delivered services. In this way, the shared service unit success measures were linked to the measures on business unit scorecards and the NAM&R scorecard.

At the end of this process, each of Mobil NAM&R's thirty-two decentralized units had developed its unique strategy. But each strategy was linked to the others and, ultimately, to common organizational themes and objectives (see Figure 2-7).

Traditional organizations use a hierarchical chain of command to direct high-level objectives downward so as to become subobjectives for each business unit. When, as typically occurs, such objectives are expressed in financial terms only—such as the business unit's target for ROCE or contribution to EVA—little opportunity for integration or synergy occurs across business and shared service units. When, however, business and shared service units develop Balanced Scorecards, linked to the corporate/divisional level scorecard, all organizational units become aligned to common and reinforcing strategic themes. Integration is achieved through these common strategic themes.

MAKE STRATEGY EVERYONE'S EVERYDAY JOB

The third principle of a Strategy-Focused Organization is to link every employee to the business unit and corporate strategy. Everyone should under-

Figure 2-7 Linking Shared Services Scorecards to Business Unit and Corporate Strategies

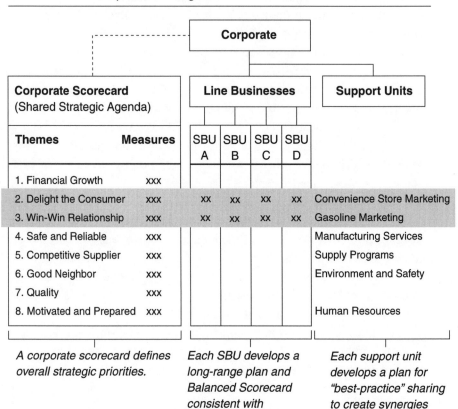

A corporate scorecard defines overall strategic priorities.

Each SBU develops a long-range plan and Balanced Scorecard consistent with corporate strategic agenda.

Each support unit develops a plan for "best-practice" sharing to create synergies across SBUs.

stand the organization's strategy and be motivated to help the organization achieve its strategic objectives. The Balanced Scorecard is used to *communicate* strategic objectives to employees, not to *command* them about what to do. Strategy-Focused Organizations want employees to align their day-to-day activities to accomplish strategic objectives and to find new, innovative, and often cross-functional and cross-unit opportunities for contributing to organizational objectives.

Mobil's executive team faced the challenge of realigning an organization that had traditionally looked inward to one that would have an external customer focus. The realignment could not be done just at the top. It had to take place at the grassroots level. For its strategy to succeed, Mobil would have to make *everyone* aware of the strategy and accountable for its success. The scorecard provided the bridge to translate the strategy at the top into operational actions at the bottom—on the front lines and in the back offices—where strategy must be effectively implemented. Brian Baker of Mobil expressed the importance of employee awareness and commitment to the strategy:

I am accountable for a large organization, spread over a large geographic area. At the end of the day, success comes from individuals at the front line of operations. You've got an operator at a refinery, sitting in front of a computer screen controlling a process unit at 3 A.M. on Sunday. Frankly, management is not around. My fate, in a very real sense, is determined by that person's attitude, whether that person is paying attention. Thirty seconds of inattention at the wrong time can shut down that refinery, stopping production. If you're going to drive the business you have to drive it down to that individual who is at the front line, making the decision.

Mobil used a comprehensive and continuing communication process, based on the Balanced Scorecard, to make sure that everyone understood the strategy. Mobil's deployment of the Balanced Scorecard started with a member of the executive leadership team visiting every site in North America. At the site meeting, the employees received a one-page brochure (see Figure 2-8) that summarized the new initiatives being launched. Note that the words *balanced scorecard* never appeared on this brochure. The brochure summarized the scorecard with eight new strategic themes drawn from each of the following four scorecard perspectives:

1. Financial (return on capital)
2. Customer (delight the customer, win-win relationships with dealers)
3. Internal Business Process (low cost, safe and reliable, on-time and on-spec, good neighbor)
4. Learning and Growth (motivated and prepared)

The brochure reinforced the message by explaining how the organization intended to *measure* Mobil's progress along these eight strategic themes. The brochure communicated the new direction for Mobil in a

Figure 2-8 Mobil NAM&R's Educational Brochure

NAM&R Strategic Themes

Will guide us to our vision and are defined above each graph.

NAM&R Strategic Measures

Will keep us focused on achieving NAM&R's strategic themes. They are explained in the graphs and the bulleted text accompanying them.

Financially Strong

Reward our shareholders by providing a superior long-term return which exceeds that of our peers.

ROCE

Income divided by capital employed including all allocations

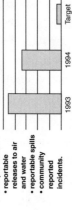

1993 1994 Target

7% 8% 12%

Delight the Consumer

Understand our consumers' needs better than anyone and offer them products and services which exceed their expectations.

Mystery Shopper

The Mystery Shopper program rates how well each of our stations is delivering the "best buying experience."

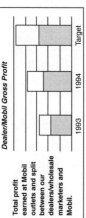

1993 1994 Target

Win/Win Relationship

Improve Dealer/Wholesale Marketer profitability through customer-driven products and services and by developing their business competencies.

Dealer/Mobil Gross Profit

Total profit earned at Mobil outlets and split between our dealers/wholesale marketers and Mobil.

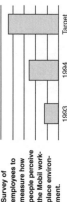

1993 1994 Target

Safe & Reliable

Maintain a leadership position in safety while keeping our refineries fully utilized.

Days Away from Work *Manufacturing Reliability*

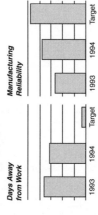

1993 1994 Target 1993 1994 Target

Competitive Supplier

Provide product to our terminals at a cost equal to or better than the competitive market maker.

Activity Cost vs. Competition

Our cost to deliver product to the terminal vs. lowest cost provider.

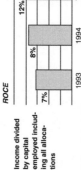

1993 1994 Target

Good Neighbor

Protect the health and safety of our people, the communities in which we work, and the environment we all share.

Environmental Index

Composite of:
- reportable releases to air and water
- reportable spills
- community reported incidents.

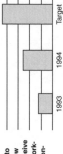

1993 1994 Target

On Spec On Time

Provide quality products supported by quality business processes that are on time and done right the first time.

Quality Index

Composite of:
- product off spec
- order shipped late
- business process errors
- customer complaints
- cost of rework.

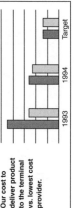

1993 1994 Target

Motivated & Prepared

Develop and value teamwork and the ability to think Mobil, act locally.

Climate Survey

Survey of employees to measure how people perceive the Mobil workplace environment.

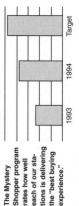

1993 1994 Target

simple, credible way. Mobil wanted to avoid the natural skepticism and cynicism among jaded employees that yet another new corporate initiative (i.e., the Balanced Scorecard) had been launched.

The executives visiting each site explained the new strategic directions and answered questions from employees about either the strategic themes or their measurement. For example, truck drivers were initially skeptical about how they could affect any of the strategic themes; they knew their job—to deliver product to customers. How would this new direction affect them?

The executive could explain relatively easily how the truck drivers could affect internal process measures. By driving safely and avoiding accidents, the drivers would improve performance on all four internal measures: contributing to lower costs, being reliable, being on time, and being a good neighbor. By driving the prescribed routes and not getting lost, they could maintain low costs and schedules. The drivers understood these impacts easily but then went on to question the two customer measures. The executive explained the win-win relationship with dealers, and asked the drivers to treat the dealers as valued customers when delivering the product to them. The executives also explained the new market segmentation strategy and the mystery shopper program that would evaluate buying experiences at every North American Mobil station. They pointed out how drivers could contribute to one aspect of the "perfect buying experience" by arriving on time with the appropriate grades of gasoline and lubrication products so that no dealer would be out of stock. At the same time, however, the drivers were also learning about all the other attributes of the "perfect buying experience," even though they couldn't control these.

Soon, however, some truck drivers started calling in from the field after having delivered gasoline to a station:

You had better get someone from region up to this station fast. If a mystery shopper showed up there, the station would flunk and our "delight the consumer" score would be destroyed. The Mobil sign is broken, half the lights are out, the restrooms are filthy, the convenience store is serving stale doughnuts and running out of stock, and the employees are yelling at the customers. This is not the new Mobil strategy of "fast, friendly service."

On their own, and without central direction, the truck drivers had become a critical part of the organization's frontline market research organization. Even though they couldn't control the buying experience, they could influence it—once they knew about it and understood it—in ways that the senior executive team could not have anticipated. Nor could the senior executive teams, had they thought about it, commanded the truck drivers to perform such a local intelligence function. But by communicating the high-level strategy to the frontline personnel, and explaining it to them so that they understood fully the message, the people closest to the customer buying experience started to innovate and help in the strategy implementation in unexpected ways.

Another early win from the communications program occurred when Mobil's technology group developed and quickly launched the Speedpass, a small device carried on a key chain. The device, when passed in front of a photocell on the gasoline pump, identified the consumer and the credit or debit card to which the purchase should be charged. The Speedpass made the gasoline purchase even faster and friendlier. Consumers did not have to hunt through their wallets or purses to find a credit card; the payment mechanism was already on the same chain as the keys being used to drive their car. The Speedpass soon became a strong differentiator for Mobil, and its popularity spread rapidly. In 1997 and subsequent scorecards, managers modified their scorecards to include new objectives for Speedpass penetration with both consumers and dealers.

The powerful and compelling aspect of this story was how the Speedpass came to be developed. Joe Giordano, a planning manager in the Marketing Technology group, learned from the Balanced Scorecard about the importance of speed in the purchasing transaction. He conceptualized how a simple device might enable a consumer to handle the entire purchasing transaction without having to use credit cards or to punch numbers onto a keypad. Giordano worked with a gasoline pump manufacturer and a semiconductor company to develop the Speedpass, not a particularly advanced technology, but one that enhanced the buying experience for millions of Mobil's retail customers. Senior executives knew the strategy but didn't know enough about technology to propose innovative solutions for the strategy. The breakthrough idea, just like the feedback from the truck drivers, came from a manager deep within the organization seeing how he could make a major contribution to the organization's strategy.

Mobil reinforced its communication strategy by deploying its human resource systems to create personal linkages. Individuals had their annual objectives tied to the scorecard. The human resources department developed integrated and comprehensive training and development mechanisms to provide all employees with the tools they needed to accomplish their personal and organizational objectives.

After the communication and linkage to personal objectives, Mobil reinforced the strategy by linking incentive compensation to the Balanced Scorecard. In 1996, Mobil NAM&R instituted a new, three-tiered approach for all its salaried employees. The bonus plan was part of a new variable pay compensation program. Because of salary freezes during Mobil's difficult times in the early 1990s, employees' base pay was now, on average, only 90 percent of competitive market wages. Rather than restoring pay parity through a one-time salary increase, the executive leadership team instituted a program that would pay up to a 30 percent annual cash bonus.

The bonus program used three tiers of performance:

1. A corporate component (10 percent) based on the two corporate financial performance competitive rankings
2. A division component (6 percent) based on the NAM&R Balanced Scorecard metrics
3. A business unit component (14 percent) based on key performance indicators, from the business unit or shared services Balanced Scorecard metrics

The corporate component was based on performance relative to Mobil's top seven competitors on two financial measures: ROCE and earnings-per-share (EPS) growth. This component awarded a bonus of between zero and 10 percent, depending on Mobil's relative ranking on ROCE and EPS growth among its industry peer group. The second component (between zero and 6 percent) was awarded based on the performance of the NAM&R divisional scorecard. And the third component (between zero and 14 percent) was based on business unit Balanced Scorecard performance.

Targets for the measures were established so that the full 30 percent bonus would only be received if Mobil ranked at the top of the industry in every measure.[9] If Mobil performed at the bottom of the industry, then no cash bonus would be earned. And if Mobil performed in the middle of the industry, then only about a 10 percent cash bonus would be awarded (see Figure 2-9). With this plan, poor performance led to poor pay (compensation of up to 10 percent below industry norms). Average performance led to average compensation, and outstanding performance led to top-in-class pay.

Figure 2-9 Mobil NAM&R's Incentive Plan

	Poor	Average	Best in Industry
Base Pay	90%	90%	90%
Corporate Award (return on capital, earnings growth)	0–1	3–6	10
NAM&R/SBU M&R (30%) SBU (70%)	0	5–8	20
Total Pay (% of market)	91%	98%–104%	120%

Mobil had no explicit compensation link to individual performance. The rewards were based on business, division, and corporate performance. The plan did allow for individual awards, to be administered within a narrow range, to adjust for performance not captured by the metrics. Business unit managers were awarded a fixed "pot of money" for such individual awards, and this allowance could not be overspent.

McCool commented on the receptivity of managers and employees to the new variable pay plan based on Balanced Scorecard performance:

We were also fortunate that when Mobil asked us to go to a pay-for-performance plan we could use our scorecard measures. Variable pay plans only work if you have a good set of metrics. Managers accepted the compensation plan based on the scorecard since they believed the measures represented well what they were trying to achieve.[10]

Baker felt that basing variable pay on a balanced set of indicators was superior to relying only on financial measures. In the short run, financial measures could be influenced by short-term factors beyond managers' control, including economywide and industry effects, interest rates, weather, commodity prices, and exchange rates. Well-performing managers could get penalized when the market was weak, and poor managers rewarded when markets were strong. The scorecard gave more visibility into variables that were both more under the direct control of managers and more sustainable for creating future economic value.

In March 1997, after the first year (1996) with the new variable pay plan, Brian Baker conducted the first of what would become an annual meeting to review the prior year's performance. As all the employees walked into the large cafeteria where the meeting was held, they could see a large replica of a paycheck on the front wall. The "balanced paycheck" was made out to Mobil NAM&R employees for $60 million.

Baker told the employees he had some good news and some bad news. Which did they want to hear first? Several employees asked to hear the bad news first and get it out of the way. At that point Baker reached up to the large balanced paycheck, pulled it down and ripped it up in front of everyone: "That is what you would have earned if you had hit the stretch targets for all of our measures. But we didn't hit those targets, so you did not earn the $60 million."

A palpable gloom settled over the audience, until one brave soul finally asked, "What's the good news?" Baker responded by reaching under the podium, unfolding another balanced paycheck and, with assistance, mounted it on the front wall. This one was made out for $35 million. "We actually had a very good year to which you all contributed a great deal. Your share of the $35 million incentive award will be in your next paycheck. Everyone is getting a cash bonus of 17 percent of annual pay. Thank you very much for your efforts. Let's make it happen again next year."

The process followed by Mobil NAM&R—new organizational structure, new measurement system, communication, and personal goals and compensation linked to strategic outcomes—aligned individuals to the organization's new strategy. Mobil was able to develop a shared vision of its strategy. When employees clearly understood the strategic objectives and the value proposition for consumers and dealers, a stream of innovative suggestions and ideas began to flow from frontline employees (truck drivers) and technologists to help the organization succeed. The organization had accomplished strategic linkages from the top down to its business units, shared services, and employees.

This third principle of becoming a Strategy-Focused Organization requires communication, personal goal setting, and linkages to incentive compensation. When successfully accomplished, all individuals make strategy their everyday job. Baker concluded, "Until you tie compensation to the scorecard, you don't have credibility. When you tie it to compensation, they know you mean it."

MAKE STRATEGY A CONTINUAL PROCESS

Once the divisional scorecard was launched, Mobil's executive leadership team reviewed it each year and updated it to reflect new opportunities and competitive conditions. With the updated strategic information at the division level, the business units formulated their plans and targets for the upcoming year, including decisions about initiatives and capital spending. These plans provided the basis for targeted performance during the next year. In effect the business units and the division now had a "budget" for performance on both the financial and nonfinancial strategic measures on the scorecard. Building the performance targets into the compensation system closed the loop from strategy to operations.

The management meetings, centered on the Balanced Scorecard, were distinctly different from those in the past, which had focused solely on financial measures. Bob McCool commented on the difference: "In the past, we were a bunch of controllers sitting around talking about variances. Now we discuss what's gone right, what's gone wrong. What should we keep doing, what should we stop doing? What resources do we need to get back on track, not explaining a negative variance due to some volume mix."[11]

Brian Baker described how he used face-to-face meetings to review the strategies of his business units and shared service organizations:

I went into these reviews thinking they would be long and arduous. I was pleasantly surprised how simple they were. Managers came in prepared. They were paying attention to their scorecards and using them in a very productive way—to drive their organization hard to achieve the targets. . . .

Basically, there's no way I can understand and supervise all the activities that report to me. I need a device like the scorecard where the business unit managers are measuring their own performance. My job is to keep adjusting the light I shine on their strategy and implementation, to monitor and guide their journeys, and see whether there are any potential storms on the horizon that we should address.[12]

McCool echoed the role for these meetings to coach managers and learn about strategy, not to assign blame. "The process enables me to see how the NBU managers think, plan, and execute. I can see the gaps, and by understanding the manager's culture and mentality, I can develop customized programs to make him or her a better manager."[13]

The new governance process emphasized learning, team problem solving, and coaching. Review meetings looked to the future, exploring how to implement strategy more effectively and what changes should be made to the strategy, based on what had been learned from the past. This made strategy implementation a continual, not an episodic, process.

Management teams need to have stimulating, challenging discussions about whether the organization remains on its trajectory for long-term, breakthrough performance, or whether new ideas, new knowledge, and new threats and opportunities have occurred that require a strategic course shift. The Balanced Scorecard provides the agenda for management meetings designed for such strategic feedback and learning. In Strategy-Focused Organizations, strategy is a continual process, not an annual event.

MOBILIZE LEADERSHIP FOR CHANGE

Perhaps the most puzzling and problematic aspect of creating Strategy-Focused Organizations is how to sustain the effort. Many companies have managers who have read the articles and the books, attended the conferences and the seminars, and returned to their organizations to lead inspiring projects that developed wonderful, strategic Balanced Scorecards. But not all of these companies were able to sustain the energy to deliver the results we reported in Chapter 1. What helps to distinguish organizations that sustain their projects to breakthrough performance from those that tried it but never delivered the results?

When Bob McCool became head of Mobil NAM&R in 1992, he made it clear that the performance of the past was not acceptable; things had to change. Working with his leadership team, he developed a vision and a strategy for how these changes would be achieved. The Balanced Scorecard played an instrumental role in this process. While the pieces of the strategy existed, they were fragmented; some observers referred to it as "strategy du jour." The Balanced Scorecard helped to make this a single, integrated strategy. Heads of shared service units—marketing, human resources, and information technology, among others—were included in the membership of the leadership team to ensure that information about customers, people, and technology were incorporated in the strategic thinking and planning. Several of these key ingredients had been lacking in past discussions. Accountability for pieces of the strategy was now clearly established within the team.

McCool and Brian Baker played central roles in communicating the new strategy and the Balanced Scorecard throughout the organization, devising new compensation systems linked to the scorecard and revising the planning and budgeting processes to support the strategy. They also reinforced the strategy and the scorecard at every opportunity, especially in their face-to-face meetings with employees and managers.

First Quarter, 1995

A critical incident occurred early in 1995 that revealed the commitment of the executive leadership team both to the new strategy and to the Balanced Scorecard. The winter (first quarter) of 1995 was unusually warm in North America. Sales of home heating oil and natural gas were below normal, and Mobil's revenues fell far short of the budget. In April 1995, McCool led a meeting at headquarters to review the first quarter's results. People entered the room trembling, as they knew that financial performance would be below expectations and that, in the past, poor financial results had led to people being fired. McCool opened his remarks by confirming people's fears that the first quarter results had fallen far below plan. But he continued in an unexpected way:

> From what I can see, we had a good quarter even though financial results were disappointing. The poor results were caused by unusually warm winter weather that depressed sales of natural gas and home heating oil. As you know, this is also the first quarter we are operating with the Balanced Scorecard, so I can see performance across a broader set of indicators. Market shares in our key customer segments were up. Refinery operating expenses were down. And the results from our employee-satisfaction survey were high. In all the areas we could control, we moved the needle in the right direction. We actually had a pretty good quarter. Keep up the good work.

The audience was stunned. Never before had a senior executive of the company congratulated and encouraged them after disappointing financial performance. But what had McCool seen? The poor financial performance was due to unusual external conditions that the employees could not control. The nonfinancial measures on the scorecard, which employees could influence and control, were all moving in favorable directions. McCool confirmed his belief in the strategy when he confidently told the employees to stay the course, to keep improving the performance driver measures on the scorecard. And his faith was soon confirmed: By the end of the year, Mobil had become the most profitable company in the industry.

We often describe the nonfinancial measures on the Balanced Scorecard as leading indicators. But the measures may be not only *leading*; they are also *sustainable*. In the short run, financial results can be affected by temporary factors—the weather, interest rates, exchange rate movements, energy prices, and economic cycles. But what determines how the organization does in the long run is how well it is positioned relative to its competitors. If organizations can continue to invest, even during economic downturns, in customer relationships, process improvements, new product development, and employee capabilities, they can improve their position relative to competitors, so that when the external environment improves, they will enjoy profits much higher than the industry average. How senior executives react during short-term downturns speaks volumes about the commitment of the organization to creating long-term, sustainable value.

Sustaining the Scorecard

Once the Balanced Scorecard had been installed at Mobil, it became the agenda for an annual meeting of the top 125 managers in January to discuss scorecard objectives, measures, and targets for the new year and to share best practices across the business units and shared service units. The meeting was called the "Balanced Scorecard Conference," but, of course, the meeting was about the division's strategy and its execution. When the major meeting of the Executive Leadership Team and senior managers is labeled the "Balanced Scorecard Conference," managers throughout the organization don't have any trouble interpreting the commitment of senior executives to using the scorecard to create the Strategy-Focused Organization.

The responsiveness of the new system to the evolution of the strategy can be powerful. Brian Baker described it this way: "I firmly believe that if I change one measure on my scorecard, change will happen." Baker is saying that by changing a measure on the scorecard, 7,000 people become aware of it, their compensation will be affected by it, and millions of dollars of initiatives will be shifted by it. When the changes are integrated into the management system in this way, the change has been institutionalized.

The role of the Executive Leadership Team evolved over time. Bob McCool retired in 1996. Brian Baker was promoted from executive vice president to the head of NAM&R, and Baker further emphasized the use of the scorecard, ensuring continuity of direction. He maintained the use of the scorecard in discussions with business unit managers for compensation, for planning and budgeting, and for monthly management reviews, thereby reinforcing the central role of the scorecard in Mobil's management system.

Inspired and dedicated middle managers can sustain quality improvements, local process improvements, and many other change programs. Middle managers can also implement programs that have been ordered from centralized corporate staff groups. But creating an entire organization that is aligned to and focused on the strategy requires the active and ongoing leadership of the senior executive team as occurred at Mobil. We are skeptical that significant results can be delivered with the Balanced Scorecard without such active leadership and ongoing reinforcement.

RESULTS

Mobil launched its Balanced Scorecard project in 1994. The following year, 1995, was the first in which Mobil operated with a scorecard. To expand on the results reported in Chapter 1, we collected data from the company for the five years from 1994 to 1998 (in late 1999, Mobil merged with Exxon to become ExxonMobil). Figure 2-10 shows the elements of Mobil's dramatic turnaround to industry-leading profitability.

The *productivity strategy* created a 20 percent reduction in the cost of refining, marketing, and delivering a gallon of gasoline. Mobil produced the equivalent of about 12 billion gallons of gasoline per year, so that even small changes in operating costs per gallon had an enormous impact on the bottom line. Better utilization of existing assets created additional improvements in cash flow. The productivity strategy was accomplished using several key drivers:

- Product quality improved each year for four consecutive years
- Annual yield losses were reduced by 70 percent
- Safety incidents resulting in lost work were reduced by 80 percent
- Environmental incidents were reduced by 63 percent

Figure 2-10 The Mobil Story (NAM&R)

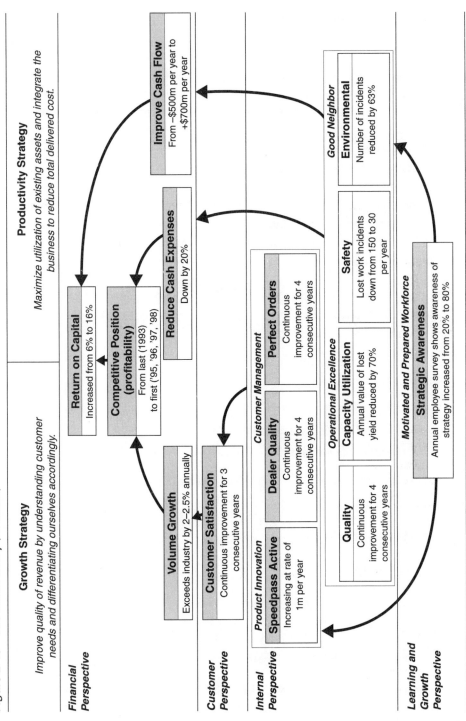

The *growth strategy*, with its new value proposition for targeted customer segments, produced increased customer satisfaction, which led to increased revenue from nongasoline merchandise and gasoline volume growth that exceeded industry averages by more than 2 percent per year. The innovative Mobil Speedpass was one of the drivers of rapid service. Improved dealer training and quality ensured professional and friendly service. The Perfect Order program, which improved quality for four consecutive years, strengthened Mobil's relationships with commercial and industrial customers.

None of this success would have occurred without a complete cultural shift at the grassroots of the organization. Annual human resource surveys showed that only 20 percent of the workforce understood Mobil's strategy in 1994. By 1998, awareness and understanding exceeded 80 percent.

SUMMARY

Mobil NAM&R applied the five principles of a Strategy-Focused Organization to achieve breakthrough performance:

1. Translate the strategy to operational terms
2. Align the organization to the strategy
3. Make strategy everyone's everyday job
4. Make strategy a continual process
5. Mobilize leadership for change

By applying these principles, Mobil integrated and aligned the entire organization to the new strategy. With such focus and alignment, it was gratifying but not surprising that Mobil could implement its new strategy rapidly and effectively.

NOTES

1. Many companies are now using value-based financial metrics, such as economic value added, as alternatives to ROCE. Mobil was a company that emphasized ROCE, but its story would have been unaffected had an alternative shareholder value metric been chosen.
2. Note that operating expenses exclude the cost of purchased raw materials, such as crude oil. Thus while Mobil could be the industry leader for its operating expenses, a competitor that had access to lower-cost crude oil could have a lower total cost per gallon produced.

3. See M. Porter, "What Is Strategy?" *Harvard Business Review* (November–December 1996): 61–78, for an example of a failed Continental Airlines strategy that attempted to offer two different levels of service for business travelers and price-sensitive leisure travelers.

4. R. S. Kaplan, "Mobil USM&R (A): Linking the Balanced Scorecard," 9-197-025 (Boston: Harvard Business School, 1996), 3.

5. Ibid., 6.

6. The details of this process for two of the local business units (New England Sales District, and Lubricants) are described in R. S. Kaplan, "Mobil USM&R (B): New England Sales & Distribution," 9-197-026 (Boston: Harvard Business School, 1996), and "Mobil USM&R (C): Lubricants Division," 9-197-027 (Boston: Harvard Business School, 1996).

7. R. S. Kaplan, "Mobil USM&R (D): Gasoline Marketing," 9-197-028 (Boston: Harvard Business School, 1996), 1.

8. Ibid., 2.

9. In Chapter 10, we describe in detail the interesting target-setting process used by Mobil.

10. Kaplan, "USM&R (A)," 9.

11. Ibid.

12. Ibid., 9–10.

13. Ibid., 9.

TRANSLATING THE STRATEGY TO OPERATIONAL TERMS

DO YOU NEED A FINANCIAL PLAN? Call any of the major accounting firms and ask for their assistance. The results they deliver will be strikingly similar. Each plan will have a pro forma income statement, balance sheet, cash-flow forecast, and capital plan. The actual contents of the plans may differ, based on the knowledge and experience of the accountant, but the structure will be the same.

Look at how the situation changes when you need a strategic plan. You can go to any of the major strategy consulting firms for help, but the results they deliver will not be similar in any way. One firm will look at your port-folio of businesses. Another will focus on processes. A third may analyze customer segments and value propositions. Others will stress shareholder value, core competencies, e-strategy, or change management. Unlike fi-nancial management, strategy has no generally accepted definitions or framework. There are as many definitions of strategy as there are strategy gurus.

Why is this a problem? In this era of knowledge workers, strategy must be executed at all levels of the organization. People must change their be-haviors and adopt new values. The key to this transformation is putting strategy at the center of the management process. Strategy cannot be exe-cuted if it cannot be understood, however, and it cannot be understood if it cannot be described. If we are going to create a management process to implement strategy, we must first construct a reliable and consistent framework for describing strategy. No generally accepted framework existed, however, for describing information age strategies. The financial framework worked well when competitive strategies were based on acquiring and managing tangible assets. In today's knowledge economy, sustainable value is created from developing intangible assets, such as the skills and knowledge of the workforce, the information technology that supports the workforce and links the firm to its customers and suppliers, and the organizational climate that encourages innovation, problem-solving, and improvement. Each of these intangible assets can contribute to value creation. But several factors prevent the financial measurements—used in traditional, industrial age, management control systems—from measuring these assets and linking them to value creation.

1. Value Is Indirect. Intangible assets such as knowledge and technology seldom have a direct impact on the financial outcomes of revenue and profit. Improvements in intangible assets affect financial outcomes through chains of cause-and-effect relationships involving two or three intermediate stages. For example:

   - Investments in employee training lead to improvements in service quality

   - Better service quality leads to higher customer satisfaction

   - Higher customer satisfaction leads to increased customer loyalty

   - Increased customer loyalty generates increased revenues and margins

   The financial outcomes are separated causally and temporally from improving the intangible assets. The complex linkages make it difficult if not impossible to place a financial value on an asset such as "workforce capabilities."

2. Value Is Contextual. The values of intangible assets depend on organizational context and strategy. They cannot be valued separately from the organizational processes that transform them into customer and financial outcomes. For example, a senior investment banker in a firm such as Goldman Sachs has immensely valuable capabilities for developing and managing customer relationships. That same person, with the same skills and experience,

would be worth little to a company, such as E*TRADE.com, that emphasizes operational efficiency, low cost, and technology-based trading. The value of most intangible assets depends critically on the context—the organization, the strategy, the complementary assets—in which the intangible assets are deployed.

3. Value Is Potential. Tangible assets, such as raw material, land, and equipment, can be valued separately based on their historic cost—the traditional financial accounting method—or on various definitions of market value, such as replacement cost and realizable value. Industrial age companies succeeded by combining and transforming their tangible resources into products whose value exceeded their acquisition cost. Profit margins measured how much value was created beyond the costs required to acquire and transform tangible assets into finished products and services.

    Companies today can measure the cost of developing their intangible assets—the training of employees, the spending on databases, the advertising to create brand awareness. But such costs are poor approximations of any realizable value created by investing in these intangible assets. Intangible assets have potential value but not market value. Organizational processes, such as design, delivery, and service, are required to transform the potential value of intangible assets into products and services that have tangible value.

4. Assets Are Bundled. Intangible assets seldom have value by themselves (brand names, which can be sold, are an exception). Generally, intangible assets must be bundled with other assets—intangible and tangible—to create value. For example, a new growth-oriented sales strategy could require new knowledge about customers, new training for sales employees, new databases, new information systems, a new organization structure, and a new incentive compensation program. Investing in just one of these capabilities, or in all of them but one, would cause the new sales strat-egy to fail. The value does not reside in any individual intangible asset. It arises from creating the entire set of assets along with a strategy that links them together.

The Balanced Scorecard provides a new framework to describe a strategy by linking intangible and tangible assets in value-creating activities. The scorecard does not attempt to "value" an organization's intangible assets. It does measure these assets, but in units other than currency (dollars, yen, and euros). In this way, the Balanced Scorecard can use strategy maps of cause-and-effect linkages to describe how intangible assets get mobilized and combined with other assets, both intangible and tangible, to create value-creating customer value propositions and desired financial outcomes.

In Chapter 3, we develop the concept of a strategy map, a logical architecture that defines a strategy by specifying the relationships among shareholders, customers, business processes, and competencies. Strategy maps provide the foundation for building Balanced Scorecards linked to an organization's strategy. Chapter 4 presents strategy maps and scorecards for several private sector organizations. These illustrate how a range of strategies can be represented in strategy maps. Chapter 5 provides analogous strategy scorecards for nonprofit, public sector, and health care organizations.

Building Strategy Maps

WHEN WE FIRST FORMULATED THE BALANCED SCORECARD in the early 1990s, we built strategy scorecards from a clean sheet of paper. We let the story of the strategy emerge onto the four perspectives through executive interviews and interactive workshops. We have now analyzed the hundreds of strategy scorecards built since that time and have mapped the patterns into a framework that we call a strategy map. A strategy map for a Balanced Scorecard makes explicit the strategy's hypotheses. Each measure of a Balanced Scorecard becomes embedded in a chain of cause-and-effect logic that connects the desired outcomes from the strategy with the drivers that will lead to the strategic outcomes. The strategy map describes the process for transforming intangible assets into tangible customer and financial outcomes. It provides executives with a framework for describing and managing strategy in a knowledge economy.

A Balanced Scorecard strategy map is a generic architecture for describing a strategy. As an example, the left-hand diagram in Figure 3-1 illustrates the architecture of a strategy map for a retail firm specializing in women's clothing. The cause-and-effect logic of this design constitutes the *hypotheses of the strategy*. The *financial* perspective contains two themes—growth and productivity—for improving shareholder value. The value proposition in the customer perspective clearly emphasizes the im-

Figure 3-1   A Fashion Retailer's Strategy Map

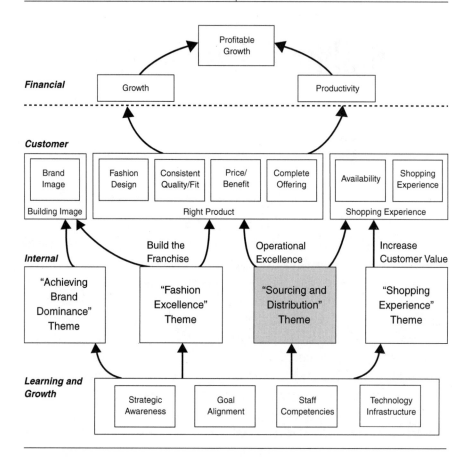

The Revenue Growth Strategy

"Achieve aggressive, profitable growth by increasing our share of the customer's closet"

The Productivity Strategy

"Improve operating efficiency through real estate productivity and improved inventory management"

portance of fashion, fit, and a complementary product line for the growth strategy. Four strategic themes in the internal perspective—brand dominance, fashion excellence, sourcing and distribution, and the shopping experience—deliver the value proposition to customers and drive the financial productivity theme. The right-hand diagram in the figure shows the detailed strategy map and Balanced Scorecard for one of the four strategic themes: sourcing and distribution. The diagram shows how this theme

Sourcing and Distribution Theme	Measurement	Target	Initiative
Financial — Profitability	■ Operating income	■ 20% increase	
Revenue Growth	■ Same store growth	■ 12% increase	■ Likes Program
Customer — Product Quality → Shopping Experience	■ Return rate 　—Quality 　—Other ■ Customer loyalty 　—Ever active 　—# units	■ Reduce by 50% each year ■ 60% ■ 2.4 Units	■ Quality Management ■ Customer Loyalty
Internal — "A" Class Factories ↔ Line Plan Management	■ Merchandise from "A" factories ■ Items in stock	■ 70% by year 3 ■ 85%	■ Corporate Factory Development Program
Learning — Factory Relationship Skills / Merchandise Buying/Planning Systems	■ % of strategic skills available ■ Strategic systems vs. plan	■ Year 1 (50%) 　Year 3 (75%) 　Year 5 (90%)	■ Strategic Skills Plan ■ Merchants' Desktop

affects the customer objectives of product quality and product availability that, in turn, drive customer retention and revenue growth. Two internal processes—the factory management program and the line planning process—also contribute to these objectives. The former determines the quality of the factories used for manufacturing the product, and the latter determines the quantities, mix, and location. New skills and information systems support both of these processes. The strategy map and scorecard for the sourcing and distribution theme define the logic of the approach to improving product, quality, and availability. The cause-and-effect relationships on the strategy map—and the measures, targets, and initiatives on the scorecard—comprise the strategy for this theme.

Strategy maps help organizations see their strategies in a cohesive, integrated, and systematic way. Executives often describe the outcome from constructing this framework as "the best understanding of strategy we have ever had." And beyond just understanding, strategy maps provide the foundation for the management system for implementing strategy effectively and rapidly.

The Balanced Scorecard overcomes the limitations of purely financial measurement systems by clearly portraying the value-creating processes and critical roles for intangible assets. The scorecard describes the multiple *indirect* linkages required to connect improvements in an organization's intangible assets—the ultimate drivers of knowledge-based strategies—to the tangible customer and financial outcomes from the strategy. The customer value proposition defines the *context* for how the intangible assets create value. For example, if "fashion and design" are part of the customer value proposition, then an intangible asset, such as merchandising skill, is necessary for the strategy to succeed. The strategic themes describe the "recipe" for combining the intangible ingredients of skills, technologies, and organizational climate with internal processes, such as sourcing and distribution, to create tangible outcomes—customer loyalty, revenue growth, and profitability. In this way, the Balanced Scorecard provides the measurement and management framework for knowledge-based strategies.

STRATEGY IS A STEP IN A CONTINUUM

Strategy does not (or should not) stand alone as a management process. A continuum exists that begins in the broadest sense, with the mission of the organization. The mission must be translated so that the actions of individuals are aligned and supportive of the mission. A management system should ensure that this translation is effectively made. Strategy is one step in a logical continuum that moves an organization from a high-level mission statement to the work performed by frontline and back-office employees.

If we are to build a consistent architecture for describing strategy, we must have a consistent way of positioning it relative to other management processes. Figure 3-2 presents a view of strategy that we have found effective in practice. The overarching *mission* of the organization provides the starting point; it defines why the organization exists or how a business unit fits within a broader corporate architecture.

Figure 3-2 Translating a Mission into Desired Outcomes

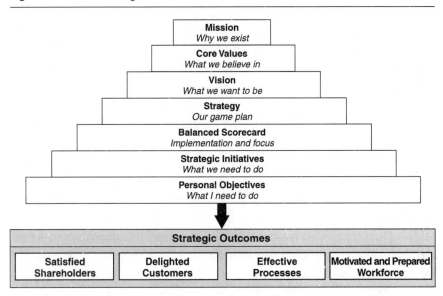

The mission and the *core values* that accompany it remain fairly stable over time. The organization's *vision* paints a picture of the future that clarifies the direction of the organization and helps individuals to understand why and how they should support the organization. In addition, it launches the movement from the stability of the mission and core values to the dynamism of strategy, the next step in the continuum. *Strategy* is developed and evolves over time to meet the changing conditions posed by the real world.

Creating the Vision and Linking It to Strategy at CIGNA's Property & Casualty Division

Gerry Isom accepted the presidency of CIGNA's Property & Casualty Division in 1993, inheriting an organization on the brink of failure. Business losses had been mounting. By 1998, the company's profitability positioned it strongly within the industry, with many of its businesses exhibiting top-quartile performance. Isom had to create a clear picture of what this organization could become over the next five years. He used the term *specialist* to define the basic change in strategy that could create a success. "Top quartile" defined a level of success that, while difficult to comprehend when the organization was on the brink of bankruptcy, implied an organization that people could be proud to be working for. The "five-year" goal gave a sense of perspective to the statement.

The vision creates the picture of the destination. The *strategy* defines the logic of how this vision will be achieved. Vision and strategy are essential complements. At CIGNA, the vision was appealing but lacked credibility until a strategy was developed to show how this vision would be accomplished. Isom used a very simple but clever technique to accomplish this; he "quantified" his vision. The insurance industry uses a measure called *combined ratio* as a surrogate for profitability. The ratio divides the expenses of the organization—claims paid plus operating expenses—by its revenues from premium income. In an ideal world, this ratio should be less than one (operating revenues exceed expenses). But because the cash from premiums received is invested until it is required for claims, top-quartile performers can have combined ratios of around 103, with the investment process providing an additional source of income to generate profitability.

In 1993, the Property & Casualty Division's combined ratio was nearly 140. The high-level strategy to achieve a top-quartile combined ratio is shown in Figure 3-3. The strategy had four themes:

Figure 3-3   CIGNA P&C's Strategy for Becoming a Top-Quartile Performer

Year	1993	1994	1995	1996	1997	1998
Combined Ratio	140		117	108–109		103–105

A (11 pts)
B (~ 6 pts)
C (~ 6 pts)
D

(~ 9 pts)   (~ 5 pts)

A Manage Producers	B Focus Geographically	C Upgrade the Underwriting Process	D Align Underwriting, Claims, Loss Control, and Premium Audit
■ Purge bad producers ■ Build good producers	■ SBU A: 20–25 states ■ SBU B: 10 states	■ Stress selection with adequate price ■ Train underwriters	■ Integrate learning

A. Manage producers (agents)

B. Focus geographically

C. Upgrade the underwriting process

D. Align the organization

A timeline was established, and rough goals for the reduction in the combined ratio were identified for each component of the strategy. In this way, the seemingly impossible goal of a 35-point reduction in the ratio was broken into pieces and then spread over time. Instead of one giant, impossible leap to the top quartile, the vision was decomposed into a strategy that comprised a series of smaller steps. The organization could now see how Isom's vision could, in fact, be accomplished. As Isom reported, "The structure of the scorecard helped us clarify our strategy and kept the organization *focused* on making our vision a reality."

The strategy specifies general directions and priorities. Translating the strategy into action is the next step in the continuum. For this to occur—for the strategy to drive the actions of thousands of people and the investment of millions of dollars—the language of the strategy must be made more specific. Strategy maps and the Balanced Scorecard provide the tools to translate general strategic statements into specific hypotheses, objectives, measures, and targets.

STRATEGY IS A HYPOTHESIS

Michael Porter describes the foundation of strategy as the activities in which an organization elects to excel: "Ultimately, all differences between companies in cost or price derive from the hundreds of activities required to create, produce, sell, and deliver their products or services. . . . [D]ifferentiation arises from both the choice of activities and how they are performed."[1]

The essence of strategy is choosing to perform activities differently from competitors so as to provide a unique value proposition. A *sustainable* strategic position, in Porter's view, comes from a *system* of activities, each of which reinforces the others.

The Balanced Scorecard—a descriptive and not a prescriptive framework—builds a view of strategy that, while developed independently of Porter's framework, is remarkably similar. The Balanced Scorecard design process builds upon the premise of *strategy as hypotheses*. Strategy implies the movement of an organization from its present position to a desirable but uncertain future position. Because the organization has never been to this future position, its intended pathway involves a series of linked hypotheses. The scorecard enables the strategic hypotheses to be described as a set of cause-and-effect relationships that are explicit and testable. Further, the strategic hypotheses require identifying the activities that are the drivers (or lead indicators) of the desired outcomes (lag indicators). The key for implementing strategy is to have everyone in the organization clearly understand the underlying hypotheses, to align resources with the hypotheses, to test the hypotheses continually, and to adapt as required in real time.

Figure 3-4 illustrates the architecture of a Balanced Scorecard. The scorecard defines the set of near-term objectives and activities, the drivers, that will differentiate a company from its competitors and create long-term customer and shareholder value, the outcomes. The process begins in a top-down fashion, clearly defining strategy from the perspective of the shareholder and customer. It asks, "What are the *financial* objectives for growth and productivity? What are the major sources of growth?" Once the financial objectives have been specified, the process continues by asking, "Who are the target *customers* that will generate revenue growth and a more profitable mix of products and services? What are their objectives, and how do we measure success with them?" The customer perspective also should include the value proposition, which defines how the company differentiates itself to attract, retain, and deepen relationships with targeted customers. Financial and customer objectives are desired outcomes, but they don't explicate how to achieve them. The *internal* business processes—such as product design, brand and market development, sales, service, and operations and logistics—define the activities needed to create the desired customer value proposition and differentiation, and the desired financial outcomes.

The fourth perspective recognizes that the ability to execute internal business processes in new and differentiated ways will be based on the organization infrastructure; the skills, capabilities, and knowledge of employees; the technology that they use; and the climate in which they work. We refer to these as the *learning and growth* factors.

Thus the architecture of the Balanced Scorecard has a top-down logic, starting with the desired financial and customer outcomes and then mov-

Figure 3-4   Defining the Cause-and-Effect Relationships of the Strategy

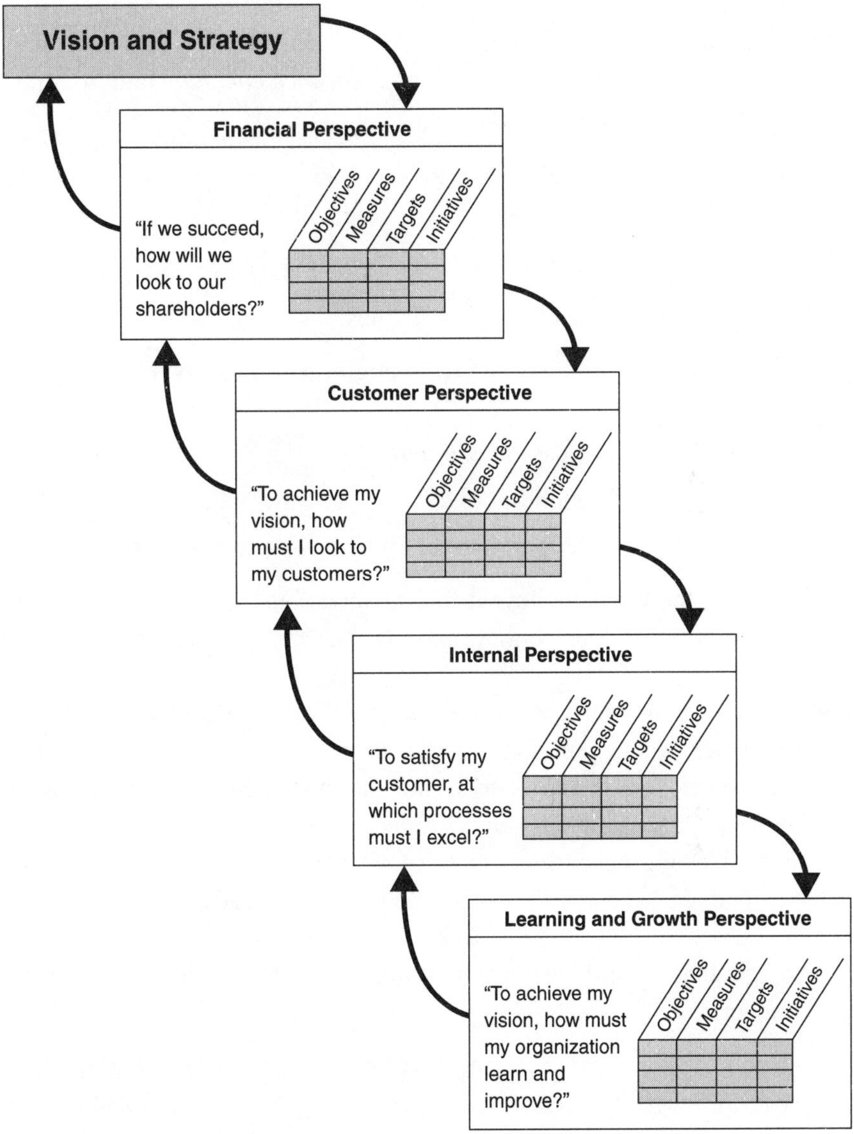

Vision and Strategy

Financial Perspective

"If we succeed, how will we look to our shareholders?"

Objectives | Measures | Targets | Initiatives

Customer Perspective

"To achieve my vision, how must I look to my customers?"

Objectives | Measures | Targets | Initiatives

Internal Perspective

"To satisfy my customer, at which processes must I excel?"

Objectives | Measures | Targets | Initiatives

Learning and Growth Perspective

"To achieve my vision, how must my organization learn and improve?"

Objectives | Measures | Targets | Initiatives

ing to the value proposition, business processes, and infrastructure that are the drivers of change. The relationships between the drivers and the desired outcomes constitute the hypotheses that define the strategy.

STRATEGY CONSISTS OF COMPLEMENTARY
STRATEGIC THEMES

In our experience, executives almost always separate their strategies into several focused themes. For example, an *insurance company* built its strategy around three strategic themes:

1. Improve operating efficiency
2. Grow profitable premiums in core segments
3. Develop a new fee-based solutions business

An *agribusiness firm* defined four themes:

1. Improve operating margin by reengineering supply chain processes
2. Reduce the cost of capital employed
3. Increase sales through improved retail channel alliances
4. Improve sales by helping farmers with new agronomic practices

These focused themes allowed the organizations to deal with the conflicting priorities of long-term versus short-term or growth versus profitability.

In general, strategic themes reflect what the management team believes must be done to succeed. The themes do not reflect financial outcomes such as "improved shareholder value" or customer outcomes such as "higher customer retention" and "higher market share." The strategic themes reflect the executives' view of what must be done internally to achieve strategic outcomes. As such, the themes typically relate to internal business processes.

Strategic themes provide a way to segment the strategy into several general categories.

1. Build the franchise: the long wave of value creation; developing new products and services and penetrating new markets and customer segments

2. Increase customer value: expand, deepen, or redefine relationships with existing customers (for instance, cross sell services, become trusted advisor and consultant, transform unprofitable customers) through multiple sales cycles

3. Achieve operational excellence: the short wave of value creation through internal productivity management and supply chain management that enables organizations to provide efficient, zero-defect, and timely production and delivery of existing products and services to customers. Also, the management of asset utilization and resource capacity

4. Be a good corporate citizen: manage relationships with external, legitimizing stakeholders, especially in industries subject to regulation (e.g., utilities, health care, broadcasting, telecommunications) or safety and environmental risk (e.g., petro-chemicals)

Each of the four strategic themes provides a "pillar" for the strategy (see Figure 3-5) and contains its own strategic hypothesis, its own set of cause-and-effect relationships, and, occasionally even, its own scorecard. The architecture based on strategic themes is so transparent that many executive teams, as we later discuss, use the themes to assign accountability for managing the execution of the strategy.

As further examples of strategic themes, consider a chemical company that was attempting to reposition itself by building full-service relation-

Figure 3-5 Architecture of a Strategy Map

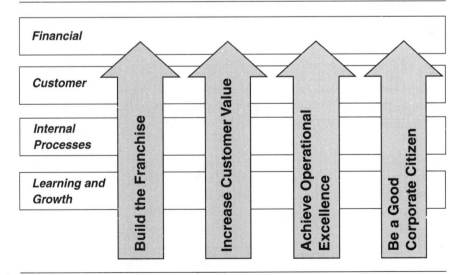

ships with its customers. It defined one simple objective for each of its four strategic themes (see Figure 3-6). A utility company defined four strategic themes as it prepared for deregulation, consolidating its core businesses while simultaneously moving into more customer-focused businesses (see Figure 3-7).

Figure 3-6   A Chemical Company's Strategic Themes

Build the Franchise	Increase Customer Value	Achieve Operational Excellence	Be a Good Corporate Citizen
■ Identify and capture new opportunities	■ Integrate seamlessly with our customer's value chain to deliver solutions	■ Maximize operational efficiencies to deliver products	■ Be a good corporate citizen and neighbor

Figure 3-7   A Utility Company's Strategic Themes

Build the Franchise	Increase Customer Value	Achieve Operational Excellence	Be a Good Corporate Citizen
"Grow the Business"	*"Increased Customer Focus"*	*"Secure the Base"*	*"Public Trust"*
■ Margins in emerging markets ■ Profitable growth in new markets	■ Service excellence ■ Value-added solutions	■ Manage assets and investments to improve cash flow ■ Effective governance	■ Maintain public support

The strategic themes define long-term ("build the franchise"), mid-term ("increase customer value"), and short-term ("operational excellence") value propositions for targeted customers. Balanced Scorecard strategy maps portray the cause-and-effect relationships of how the strategic themes drive improved customer and financial outcomes.

A CASE STUDY: STORE 24

We can illustrate the construction of strategy maps with Store 24, a New England–based convenience-store company. Store 24 has approximately 100 stores located in urban neighborhood settings—a "mature market" environment. Store 24 wants to create higher growth rates by increasing the amount of business from the young adult population, which is growing at higher than average rates.

The typical convenience store attempts to compete through "operational excellence" strategies, offering fast, friendly service, clean surroundings, good quality, and product selection tailored to its target customers. Store 24 seeks to differentiate itself by creating an interesting and enjoyable shopping experience, such as by offering innovative in-store promotions. In effect, Store 24 is attempting to shift the value proposition from operational excellence to customer intimacy.

The *financial* perspective of the strategy map (see Figure 3-8) shows how the high-level objectives (return on investment and earnings) are based on simultaneously managing growth and productivity. Growth arises from successful promotions that increase customer loyalty and sales in core categories. Productivity will be achieved by using standard industry approaches to improve labor productivity and increase inventory turnover.

Store 24 plans to differentiate itself in *customers'* eyes by providing "entertaining and unexpected fun" during the shopping experience. The company motto, posted in all stores, is "Store 24 Bans Boredom." A typical in-store promotion during the Halloween season finds toy spiders hanging from the ceiling, spooky background music, and employees wearing costumes.

Store 24's strategic themes are linked to key *internal processes*. To support its customer intimacy strategy, Store 24 must pay close attention to the in-store shopping experience. Accordingly, the company has made significant investments in staff training programs to ensure that this strategy is executed at the point of customer contact (the customer-management

Figure 3-8   Store 24's Strategy Map

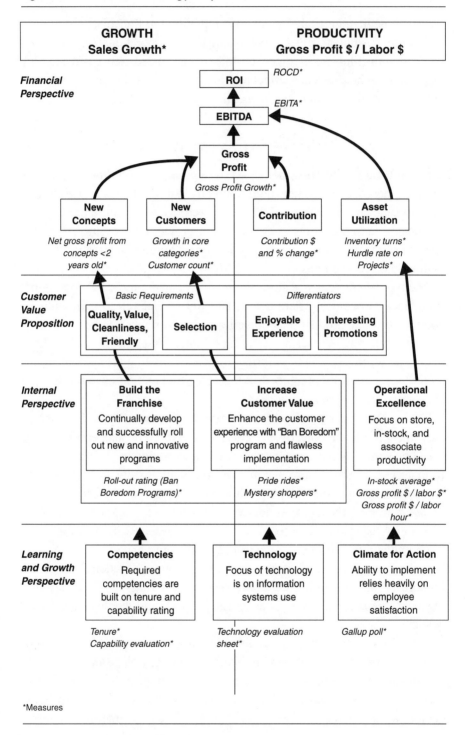

process). The innovation process focuses on the development of new promotions and layouts that will deliver on the promise to ban boredom. And the operations process is linked to a focus on cost and inventory management needed to meet productivity objectives.

The *learning and growth* strategy is aligned with the requirements for strategic business processes and customer differentiation. Because Store 24's strategy is totally dependent on the behavior of store personnel at the point of sale, the learning and growth strategy calls for retention of experienced store personnel who can sustain customer relationships. It also requires significant training for the staff, complemented by ongoing evaluation programs. The employee satisfaction measure on the scorecard shows that Store 24 recognizes that the employee is a true partner in the overall strategy.

The Store 24 strategy as described above is unique in the industry. We will elaborate on it and on Store 24's scorecard later in this chapter. In Chapter 12, we will describe how the strategy evolved and how the scorecard changed over time.

STRATEGY BALANCES CONTRADICTORY FORCES: THE FINANCIAL PERSPECTIVE

The development of a strategy map proceeds in a top-down fashion (as shown in Figure 3-4). It begins with the high-level *financial* strategy for growth, profitability, and shareholder value.[2] Creating shareholder value is the outcome that every strategy seeks to accomplish. A company will typically choose a single overarching or "dominant" objective as its long-term indicator of success. Historically, some version of the DuPont return on investment (ROI) or ROCE measure has been used as the overarching financial objective. More recently, companies have adopted various shareholder and value-based-management metrics such as EVA, cash-flow ROI, and variations of discounted cash flow.[3]

EVA's contribution as a financial metric is to go beyond accounting net income by recognizing an explicit capital charge for a business. The capital charge is calculated by applying a business-specific (and perhaps asset-specific) cost of capital to an organization's recorded assets. Thus EVA equals the (accounting) net income less the capital charge.[4] Businesses that are earning above their risk-adjusted cost of capital are said to be creating shareholder value, whereas businesses earning less than their cost of capital are destroying shareholder value. EVA addresses the defect in the ROI calculation of discouraging businesses from investing in projects that return above their cost of capital but below the (apparent) average cost of capital calculated by dividing net income by assets employed. EVA also addresses the defect in a pure accounting income calculation that ignores the cost of assets employed to generate accounting profits.

Whether companies use ROI, ROCE, EVA, or some other value-based metric as the high-level financial objective, they have two basic strategies for driving their financial performance: growth and productivity (see Figure 3-9). The revenue growth strategy focuses on developing new sources of revenue and profitability. It generally has two components:

1. Build the franchise. Develop new sources of revenue from new markets, new products, or new customers. This dimension of the strategy implies the greatest amount of change and requires the longest time to execute.

2. Increase customer value. Work with existing customers to expand their relationship with the company. This component tends to be intermediate term in duration and focuses on processes such as cross selling and solution development to deepen customer relationships.

Store 24, for example, focused on revenues generated from innovative promotions and the expansion of revenues from target segments as its growth strategy.

Figure 3-9   Building the Strategy Map: The Financial Perspective

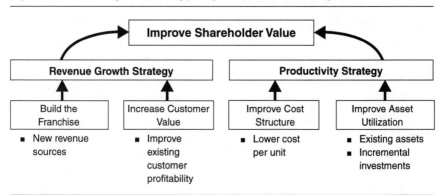

The productivity strategy features the efficient execution of operational activities in support of existing customers. Productivity strategies focus on cost reduction and efficiency. Like the revenue growth strategy, the productivity strategy generally has two components:

1. Improve cost structure. Lower the direct costs of products and services, reduce indirect costs, and share common resources with other business units.

2. Improve asset utilization. Reduce the working and fixed capital needed to support a given level of business by greater utilization, more careful acquisition, or disposal of parts of the current and fixed asset base.

Store 24 focused on inventory turnover and labor productivity as the key financial indicators for its productivity strategy.

The productivity strategy generally yields results sooner than the growth strategy. But one of the principal contributions of the Balanced Scorecard is to highlight the opportunities for enhancing financial performance through revenue growth, not just by cost reduction and asset utilization. Also, the balancing helps to ensure that cost and asset reductions do not compromise a company's growth opportunities. In fact, companies whose strategy features only the productivity element are likely to gain less benefit from the Balanced Scorecard. Financial metrics, such as process costs (available from a well-functioning, activity-based costing system), and productivity ratios provide an adequate language and reporting framework for a pure productivity strategy.

The link to strategy in the financial perspective arises as organizations choose a balance between the contradictory levers of growth and productivity. Companies that are in early-stage startup mode or see opportunity for extremely rapid growth will emphasize objectives and measures from the revenue growth strategy. Cost and productivity will be subservient, as these organizations spend heavily to develop and introduce new products and services and to extend into new markets and applications. Companies in the mature end of their lifecycle will emphasize the cost reduction and asset utilization components, as limited opportunities remain to find new customers or expand into new markets. Most companies are in the middle of their life cycle and therefore employ a "profitable growth" strategy that requires a balance of the contributions from revenue growth and from cost reduction and productivity. These companies will have a balance of measures across the two generic financial strategies.

Note also how the strategic themes, introduced earlier in the chapter, relate to the two financial strategies. Typically, the "building the franchise" and "increasing customer value" themes will drive the financial growth strategy, and "achieving operational excellence" will drive the productivity strategy. But the relationship is not one-to-one. Expanding the customer base can contribute to lower unit costs, and operational excellence can contribute to a better customer buying experience.

We now turn to the customer perspective that drives the revenue growth (financial) objective. We also discuss how to link customer outcomes to value propositions and the organization's strategic themes.

STRATEGY DESCRIBES A DIFFERENTIATED VALUE PROPOSITION

The core of any business strategy—connecting a company's internal processes to improved outcomes with customers—is the "value proposition" delivered to the customer. The value proposition describes the unique mix of product, price, service, relationship, and image that the provider offers its customers. The value proposition determines the market segments to which the strategy is targeted and how the organization will differentiate itself, in the targeted segments, relative to competition. A clearly stated value proposition provides the ultimate target on which the strategic themes of critical internal business processes and infrastructures are focused. We have found that approximately 75 percent of executive teams do not have a clear consensus around the customer value proposition. The development of this layer of the strategy map forces the team to clarify its understanding of the customer and is one of the most valuable parts of a Balanced Scorecard design process.

As we reviewed the value propositions of successful Balanced Scorecard users, we found that they matched well with the three different strategies, described by Treacy and Wiersema, that an organization uses to differentiate itself in the marketplace.[5]

1. Product leadership. "A product leadership company pushes its products into the realm of the unknown, the untried, or the highly desirable."[6] Sony Corporation and Intel Corporation epitomize this strategy.

2. Customer intimacy. "A customer-intimate company builds bonds with its customers; it knows the *people* it sells to and the products and services it needs."[7] The Home Depot, Inc. and Mobil have successfully executed this strategy.

3. Operational excellence. "Operationally excellent companies deliver a combination of quality, price and ease of purchase that no one else can match."[8] Companies such as Costco Wholesale Corporation, McDonald's Corporation, and Dell Computer Corporation are models of this strategy.

The claim (and good supporting evidence) is that successful companies excel at one of these three dimensions of value while maintaining "threshold standards" on the other two. For example, The Home Depot differentiates itself through the superior knowledge and helpfulness of its sales staff, a customer intimacy strategy. The company must still have excellent product selection, high-quality inventory management, and reasonable prices, but these are not the primary reasons for its targeted customers to shop there. Costco, on the other hand, provides the lowest cost to the consumer by selling items in bulk, at low prices, in a warehouse environment, which is an operational excellence strategy. The sales staff must be well trained, and the products offered must be recognized as high quality, but customers shop at Costco for convenience and low price, not the uniqueness of the product selection or sales support. Intel, Sony, and many pharmaceutical companies succeed by offering the best product for their customers' needs. Prices of product leadership companies are generally high and service is adequate but not necessarily exceptional. Customers purchase the products from these companies because of their unique capabilities and functionality.

Figure 3-10 shows the template that translates these generic strategy concepts into the strategy maps used for Balanced Scorecard design. Notice that different aspects of the value proposition become more crucial depending on the strategy. Companies following an operational excellence strategy need to excel at measures of competitive price, customer-perceived quality, and lead time and on-time delivery for purchasing. Companies following a product leadership strategy must excel at the functionality, features, and performance of their product or service. And companies following a customer intimacy strategy will stress the quality of their relationships with customers and the completeness of the solution offered to customers. For example, Store 24's *customer intimacy* strategy (recall

Figure 3-8) used a value proposition based on three differentiators: an exciting shopping experience, friendly employees, and interesting promotions. Product quality, price, and selection were basic requirements but not differentiators.

Figure 3-10 also provides a diagnostic check on whether an organization's Balanced Scorecard measures matches its strategy. We often encounter companies that espouse a strategy of product innovation or

Figure 3-10 Building the Strategy Map: The Customer-Value Proposition

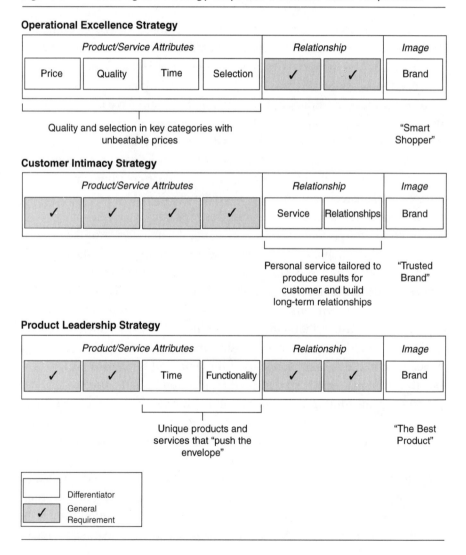

"value-added customer relationships." Yet their customer measures relate to customer satisfaction on operational dimensions such as defects, lead times, and price. No objectives or measures relate to the espoused strategy of product leadership or customer intimacy. By using the template of Figure 3-10, companies can detect when their measures are misaligned with their strategy.[9]

Targeted Customers and Customer Outcome Measures

The value proposition enables companies to define their targeted customers. Most markets consist of heterogeneous customers. Some customers value innovation the most, others value the close partnering relationships with their suppliers, and still others prefer low price, consistent quality, and ease of purchase. Strategy is about choice. As it selects the value proposition at which it will excel, a company also selects the customer segment or segments for whom that value proposition will be the differentiator, causing them to do business with the company. Targeted customers are those who place the highest importance, in their buying decision, on the attributes of the value proposition offered by the company.

It is important to identify clearly the company's targeted customers. They become the focus of the customer outcome measures in the company's Balanced Scorecard. The generic customer measures—satisfaction, acquisition, retention, account share, market share, and profitability—should be measured for targeted customers. Companies that choose a product leadership or customer relationship strategy will disappoint price-sensitive customers. Conversely, companies that offer standard products and services, at the lowest prices, will disappoint customers who value innovation or personalized service. For the scorecard to faithfully represent the strategy, the customer outcomes should be measured for the targeted customers who, the strategic hypothesis claims, most appreciate the value proposition selected by the company.

The idea of selecting some customers as more important than others may be unfamiliar and uncomfortable for many companies. But selection is about choice. Michael Porter expresses this position eloquently: "Strategy renders choices about what not to do as important as choices about what to do. Indeed, setting limits is another function of leadership. Deciding which target group of customers, varieties, and needs the company should serve is fundamental to developing a strategy. But so is deciding *not to serve* other customers or needs and *not to offer* certain features or services."[10]

Strategy is reflected in the customer perspective of the Balanced Scorecard through the emphasis of a particular value proposition and the measurement of outcomes for targeted customers.

The value proposition connects upward in the strategy map to the measurement of customer outcomes and then to the financial objectives. It also connects downward to the critical internal processes that enable the company to deliver its value proposition to targeted customers.

STRATEGY ALIGNS INTERNAL ACTIVITIES TO THE VALUE PROPOSITION

The customer value proposition and how it translates into growth and profitability for the shareholder is the foundation of strategy. But the customer value proposition and financial outcomes are the outcomes that organizations want to achieve. Strategy must not only specify the desired outcomes; it must also describe how they will be achieved. Again referring back to Porter, "The essence of strategy is in the activities—choosing to perform activities differently or to perform different activities than rivals."[11] Porter claims that *"activities are the basic units of competitive advantage."* The art of developing a successful and sustainable strategy is ensuring alignment between an organization's internal activities and its customer value proposition.

The activities of an organization are embodied in the internal business processes that comprise its value chain. We have found it useful to segment the value chain into four sets of business processes, corresponding to the four strategic themes introduced earlier in the chapter, as shown in Figure 3-11.

All of these processes are important and must be performed well by every organization. But companies must excel at the one process that has the maximum impact on its customer value proposition. The other two or three processes are supportive, not primary (see Figure 3-12).

A *product leadership* strategy would require a leading-edge innovation process that created new products with best-in-class functionality and brought them to market rapidly. Customer management processes might focus on rapid acquisition of new customers to consolidate the early mover advantage that a product leader creates.

A *customer intimacy* strategy, on the other hand, requires excellent customer management processes such as relationship management and solution development. The innovation process would be motivated by the

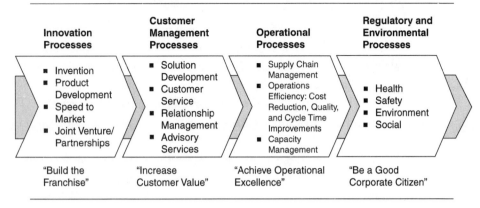

Figure 3-11 A Generic Organization's Value Chain

Innovation Processes	Customer Management Processes	Operational Processes	Regulatory and Environmental Processes
■ Invention ■ Product Development ■ Speed to Market ■ Joint Venture/ Partnerships	■ Solution Development ■ Customer Service ■ Relationship Management ■ Advisory Services	■ Supply Chain Management ■ Operations Efficiency: Cost Reduction, Quality, and Cycle Time Improvements ■ Capacity Management	■ Health ■ Safety ■ Environment ■ Social
"Build the Franchise"	"Increase Customer Value"	"Achieve Operational Excellence"	"Be a Good Corporate Citizen"

Figure 3-12 Identifying Strategic Internal Business Processes

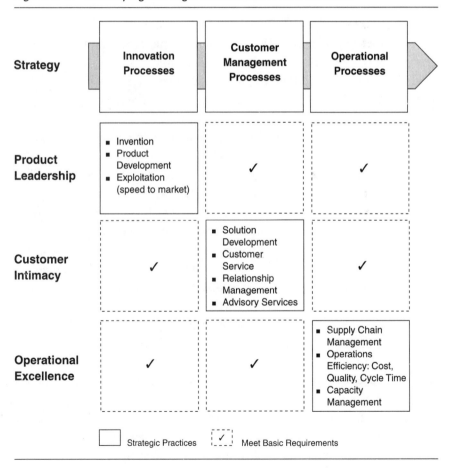

Strategy	Innovation Processes	Customer Management Processes	Operational Processes
Product Leadership	■ Invention ■ Product Development ■ Exploitation (speed to market)	✓	✓
Customer Intimacy	✓	■ Solution Development ■ Customer Service ■ Relationship Management ■ Advisory Services	✓
Operational Excellence	✓	✓	■ Supply Chain Management ■ Operations Efficiency: Cost, Quality, Cycle Time ■ Capacity Management

☐ Strategic Practices   ⌐✓⌐ Meet Basic Requirements

91

needs of targeted customers, focusing on those new product developments and service enhancements that contribute to better customer solutions.

A strategy for *operational excellence* emphasizes measures of the cost, quality, and cycle time of operating processes, excellent supplier relationships, and speed and efficiency of supply and distribution processes.

Many companies, unfortunately, espouse a strategy of innovation or developing value-adding customer relationships but choose internal business processes measurements that focus on cost and quality of manufacturing processes. These companies have a complete disconnect between their measurements and their strategy. It is not surprising that so many companies have difficulty implementing new growth strategies when their primary measurements emphasize cost reduction, standardization, and efficiency. Figure 3-12, like Figure 3-10, provides a diagnostic for companies to validate that the objectives and measures they select for their internal business process perspective match the priorities of their strategy.

Companies also can identify two new constituents in the internal business process perspective—suppliers and the public—that may be important for their strategy. The success of many companies—retailers such as Sears, Roebuck and Co., The Limited, Inc., and Wal-Mart Stores, Inc.; electronics manufacturers such as Hewlett-Packard Company and Sun Microsystems, Inc.; and automotive firms—depends on having great suppliers and great relationships with their suppliers. When outstanding supplier relationships are critical for a strategy, this objective should be incorporated in the operations process of the internal perspective.

Businesses such as telecommunications and utilities companies, whose prices and operations are regulated to some extent by the government, must have excellent relationships with these authorities and legislatures. Companies whose operations entail EHS risks need to comply with regulations in the communities where they operate. Beyond compliance, they may seek to achieve a reputation as a leader in EHS performance to enhance their ability to recruit and retain valuable employees, and to maintain and expand their physical presence in communities. When such regulatory and EHS considerations are vital for a successful strategy, companies include several objectives in a "good corporate citizen" strategic theme in the internal perspective.

Returning to our example of Store 24 (Figure 3-8), the critical internal process was providing a unique and attractive in-store shopping experience to support its customer intimacy strategy. The company made significant investments in staff training programs to ensure that this strategy was executed at the point of customer contact (the *customer management* process). The *innovation* process focused on the development of new promotions and layouts that enabled Store 24 to deliver on its promise to ban boredom.

STRATEGY TRANSFORMS INTANGIBLE ASSETS

We have explicated and illustrated how a strategy map organizes financial, customer, and internal process objectives by strategic themes, financial strategies, value propositions, and critical internal processes. We now address the foundation for all strategy: the learning and growth perspective.

The learning and growth strategy defines the intangible assets needed to enable organizational activities and customer relationships to be performed at ever-higher levels of performance. There are three principal categories for this perspective (see Figure 3-13):

1. Strategic competencies: The strategic skills and knowledge required by the workforce to support the strategy

2. Strategic technologies: The information systems, databases, tools, and network required to support the strategy

3. Climate for action: The cultural shifts needed to motivate, empower, and align the workforce behind the strategy

The learning and growth strategies are the true starting point for any long-term, sustainable change. Executive teams readily acknowledge the

Figure 3-13 The Learning and Growth Perspective

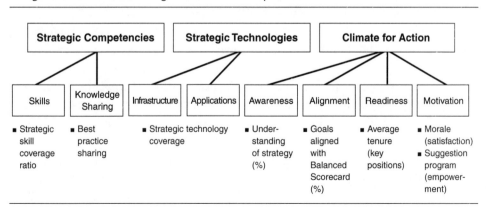

importance of this perspective but generally have low levels of awareness and consensus about how to define or achieve objectives in it. The thoughtful design of learning and growth strategies presents a major opportunity to improve the odds of successful strategy implementation.

By treating the learning and growth strategy after the three other perspectives have been defined, executives can align their human resources, information technology, and corporate climate objectives with the requirements from the strategic business processes and customer differentiation strategy. For example, Store 24's strategy (Figure 3-8) depended totally on the behavior of store personnel at the point of sale. Its learning and growth strategy called for the retention of experienced store personnel who could sustain customer relationships and provide the "fun" buying experience. The human resources strategy also required significant training for the staff, complemented by ongoing evaluation programs. The employee satisfaction measure on the scorecard recognized that the employee had to be a true partner with the strategy.

The work of Carla O'Dell and C. J. Grayson on knowledge management has built a complementary framework for thinking about learning and growth strategies. They describe the goal of knowledge management as "a systematic approach to find, understand, share and use knowledge to create value."[12] The greatest value comes when knowledge management is linked to the strategy and value proposition of the organization. As summarized in Figure 3-14, different value propositions require different knowledge management strategies. *Customer intimacy* requires employees to understand their customers so that they can build long-term relations with them. Lexus, for example, requires every employee to survey ten customers per month by phone. *Product innovators* must accelerate the time to develop and commercialize new products. Companies such as Eli Lilly and Company and The Dow Chemical Company use knowledge management approaches to manage patents, development cycles, and customer requirements. *Operational excellence* companies, in their quests to lower cost and improve quality, use best-practice sharing approaches to move winning approaches "from the best to the rest." Companies like Chevron Corporation or BP Amoco have used knowledge management to improve safety, reduce energy costs, and shorten construction cycles.

In knowledge-based organizations, the ability to improve business processes, consistent with a customer value proposition, depends on the ability and willingness of individuals to change behavior and focus their

Figure 3-14 Knowledge Management Strategies

Customer Intimacy	Product Innovation	Operational Excellence
■ Capture knowledge about customers ■ Understand customer needs ■ Empower front-line employees with information they need ■ Ensure that everyone knows the customer ■ Make company knowledge available to customers	■ Reduce time to market ■ Commercialize new products faster ■ Ensure that ideas flow (e.g., from customer service to R&D) ■ Reuse what other parts of the company have already learned	■ Reduce cost ■ Improve quality ■ Move know-how from top-performing units to others

Source: Based on material from Carla O'Dell, C. Jackson Grayson, "Knowledge Transfer: Discover Your Value Proposition," *Strategy and Leadership* (March–April 1999).

knowledge on the strategy. Some people have objected to placing the learning and growth perspective at the bottom of Balanced Scorecard diagrams. They feel this minimizes the importance of this perspective. Quite the contrary; we placed this perspective at the bottom because it is the foundation for everything else above it. Or, to use another metaphor, learning and growth objectives are like the roots of a tree. They are the source of support, nourishment, and growth for the beautiful foliage and blossoms (financial breakthroughs) that appear at higher elevations of the scorecard. The learning and growth initiatives are the ultimate drivers of strategic outcomes.

A STRATEGY MAP TEMPLATE

Figure 3-15 integrates the preceding development into a generic template for creating a strategy map. The growth theme in the financial perspective is realized through growth from fundamentally new sources ("build the franchise") and growth from expanded relations with existing customers ("increase customer value"). The productivity theme is achieved through expense and asset management.

Figure 3-15 Describing the Strategy: The Balanced Scorecard Strategy Map

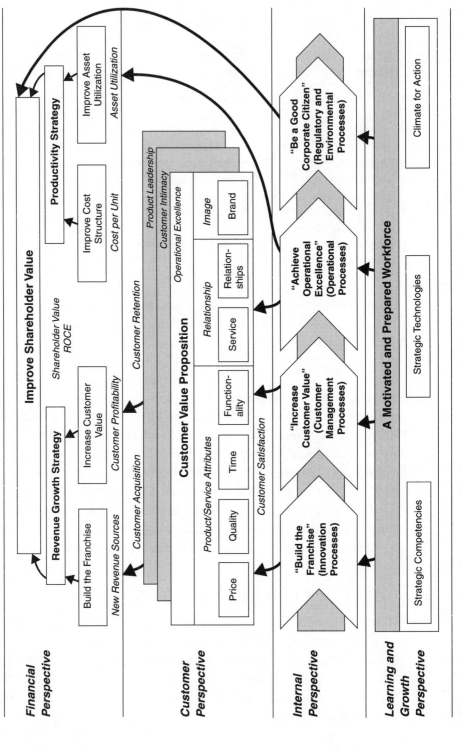

The *customer* perspective, the heart of the strategy, defines how growth will be achieved. The value proposition defines the specific strategy to compete for new customers or increased share of existing customer businesses. A clear definition of this value proposition is the most important single step in the development of a strategy map. The *internal* perspective defines the business processes and the specific activities that the organization must master to support this customer value proposition. The *learning and growth* perspective defines the competencies, know-how, technology, and climate needed to support these high-priority processes and activities. When properly constructed, the strategy map portrays an integrated and logical description of how the strategy will be accomplished.

In our consulting work, we have developed generic strategy maps for different industries and different classes of strategies; these include, for example, a company in the chemical industry following a product innovation strategy. The template is a starting point for the design process that then gets tailored for the particular organization. When we don't already have such an industry template, we start with the generic template in Figure 3-15 as the starting point. The templates help executive teams describe their strategies and improve exponentially the quality of their insights. They facilitate greater precision in defining the customer value proposition and increase awareness that internal processes, competencies, and technologies must be linked to that value proposition. Templates also foster a cause-and-effect mentality that encourages more innovative approaches to strategy implementation.

Templates are also useful to analyze or reverse-engineer an existing scorecard. A well-designed Balanced Scorecard should tell the story of the strategy. Thus if you were to begin with a scorecard, you should be able to reverse the logic and deduce the strategy. Mobil used this approach to evaluate the quality of the scorecards being used by its strategic business units (SBUs). The left-hand side of Figure 3-16 shows a partial view of the strategy map for the division's revenue growth theme. It shows, as described in Chapter 2, how customer and dealer satisfaction were to be created through nongasoline products, improved dealerships, and quality. Senior management then compared the scorecards being used by SBUs to this template. The scorecard of one unit, shown in the upper right, made no mention of a dealer. What was the message if this scorecard did, in fact, reflect its strategy? Were dealers not strategic? Had the SBU found a way to bypass the dealer? The unit shown in the lower right of Figure 3-16 made no mention

Figure 3-16 Reverse-Engineering a Scorecard to Describe the Strategy: The Mobil Experience

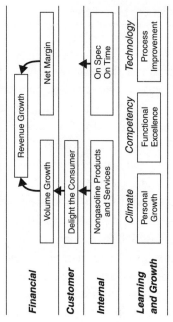

The Template
(Strategy Map: Partial)

Revenue Growth Strategy
Improve quality of our revenue by understanding customer needs and differentiating ourselves accordingly

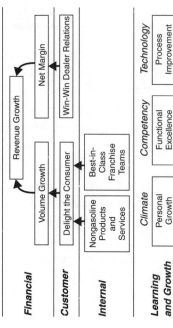

SBU A
"Did we eliminate the dealer?"

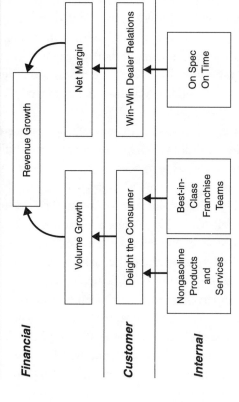

SBU B
"Have we achieved perfection?"

of quality on its scorecard. Again, what was the message? Was quality not strategic in this business? Applying the template to SBU scorecards, Mobil's executive team could identify gaps in the strategies being implemented at lower levels of the organization and ensure that the high-level strategies were truly reflected on local scorecards.

IMPLICATIONS FOR MEASUREMENT SYSTEMS

Performance measurement systems typically are aggregations of stand-alone measures, such as return on capital, customer satisfaction, and defect rates. Each measure can have an authoritative literature, practical experience, and even consulting firms that focus on the properties and measurement of the underlying phenomenon (financial performance, meeting customer expectations, and process quality). Conferences are convened on metrics to describe their subtleties and applications. But stand-alone measures are ultimately limited in their ability to describe and manage an organization's value-creating processes. Take a human resource measure, such as employee turnover. This measure can be refined by measuring turnover in various employee categories and degrees of criticality for the organization. A signal that employee turnover in a critical category last period was 10 percent will likely be useful to the organization. Benchmarking studies can improve the insight further by comparing the turnover rate to that of other companies in the same industry or geographical location. If the 10 percent turnover was lower than that experienced by 90 percent of comparable organizations, the recent performance can be considered quite good. But this benchmarked performance for retention of key employees still does not indicate anything about the *value* of decreasing key employee turnover. The value comes from noting a correlation between employee retention and customer satisfaction and loyalty, and a further correlation between customer loyalty and increased revenue. Organizational value comes not from increasing individual measures of an intangible asset or internal process but from linking changes in such measures to customer and financial outcomes.

The cause-and-effect linkages in Balanced Scorecard strategy maps describe the path by which improvements in the capabilities of intangible assets get translated into tangible customer and financial outcomes. Take, as an example, the experience of the undersea contractor, Rockwater, a division of Brown & Root Energy Services. Rockwater embarked on a strategy to improve its return-on-capital financial performance through two strategic themes: operational excellence—reducing costs and improving quality—and customer management—developing long-term partnerships with targeted (Tier I) customers. Both themes required new capabilities and attitudes on the part of the workforce (see Figure 3-17).

For the operational excellence theme, improved attitude and morale among employees led to a higher frequency of suggestions (linkage A1 in Figure 3-17). The suggestions in turn led to many improvements in work practices that significantly reduced the incidence of costly rework (linkage A2). The lower incidence of rework translated directly into lower project costs (A3), higher profitability, and a higher return on capital (A4). The project teams could also leverage their cost-reduction experiences into lower prices for future work for price-sensitive (Tier II) customers.

For the customer management strategic theme, the company could observe that its most satisfied value-seeking (Tier I) customers were serviced by employees who had scored highest on measures of attitude and alignment with Rockwater's strategy (linkages B1 and B2). These satisfied customers paid outstanding invoices with the shortest delays (linkage B3), thirty to ninety days faster than dissatisfied customers paid. The short collection period led to lower levels of working capital and higher cash flows leading directly (linkage B4) to an increased return on capital.

Measuring organizational performance requires such causal chains of value creation. Stand-alone measures cannot capture the means by which improvements in intangible assets and internal processes lead to increased performance in outcome measures. The linkages in strategy maps provide the recipes for such transformations and value creation. The three strategic themes described earlier in the chapter represent the linkages for value creation over three- to five-year planning horizons: near term, achieve operational excellence; medium term, increase customer value; and long term, build the franchise. Collectively, they enable executives to manage and balance the drivers of short- and long-term performance.

STAKEHOLDER AND KEY PERFORMANCE INDICATOR SCORECARDS

Many organizations say they have a Balanced Scorecard because they use a mixture of financial and nonfinancial measures. Certainly, such measurement systems are more "balanced" than ones that use financial mea-

Figure 3-17 Rockwater's Strategy Map

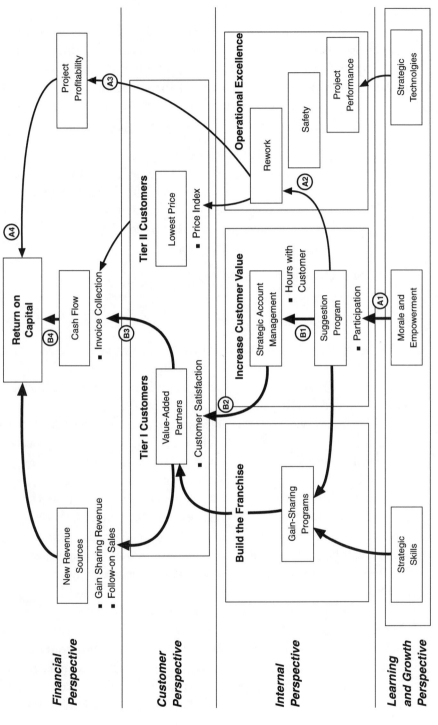

sures alone. Yet the underlying assumptions and philosophies that govern many of these scorecards are quite different from the strategy scorecards we have described in this chapter. We have observed two other scorecard types frequently used in practice: the stakeholder or constituent scorecard and the key performance indicator (KPI) scorecard.

Stakeholder (Constituent) Scorecards

The *stakeholder scorecard* identifies the major constituents of the organization—shareholders, customers, and employees—plus, often, other constituents such as suppliers and the community. The scorecard defines their goals for these different constituents, or stakeholders, and develops an appropriate scorecard of measures and targets for them.[13] For example, Sears built its initial scorecard around three themes:

1. "A compelling place to shop"
2. "A compelling place to work"
3. "A compelling place to invest"

Citicorp used a similar structure for its initial scorecard— "a good place to work, to bank, and to invest." AT&T Corporation developed an elaborate internal measurement system based on financial value added, customer value added, and people value added.

All these companies built their measurements around their three dominant constituents: customers, shareholders, and employees, especially using satisfaction measures for customers and employees, to ensure that each constituent felt well served by the company. In this sense, they were, apparently *balanced*. Missing from such scorecards, however, was any indication of *how* these balanced goals were to be achieved. A vision describes a desired outcome; a strategy, however, must describe *how* the outcome will be achieved and how employees, customers, and shareholders will be made satisfied. Thus a constituent scorecard is not adequate to describe the strategy of an organization and therefore is not an adequate foundation on which to build a management system.

The critical missing element of the constituent card is the identification of drivers that will achieve the goals—an explicit value proposition, innovation that will generate new products and services, customer management processes, a role for technology, and the specific skills and competencies of employees required to implement the strategy. In a well-constructed *strategy scorecard*, the value proposition in the customer perspective, all the processes in the internal perspective, and the learning and growth perspective components of the scorecard define the *how* that is as fundamental to the strategy as the outcomes that the strategy is expected to achieve.

Stakeholder scorecards have been used effectively in practice. They often are a first step on the road to a strategy scorecard. As organizations begin to work with stakeholder cards, they inevitably confront the question of *how*. This leads to the next level of strategic thinking and scorecard design. Both Sears and Citicorp quickly moved beyond their initial constituent scorecards, developing an insightful set of internal process objectives to complete the description of their strategy and, ultimately, achieving a strategy Balanced Scorecard. The stakeholder scorecard can also be useful as a corporate scorecard in which internal synergies across the SBUs are limited. Because each business has a different set of internal drivers, the corporate scorecard need only focus on the desired outcomes for the corporation's constituencies (including the community and suppliers). Each SBU then defines how it will achieve those goals and articulates these with its business unit strategy scorecards.

KPI Scorecards

KPI scorecards are found most frequently, but not exclusively, in manufacturing and health care organizations, especially those that have been implementing total quality management (TQM). The TQM approach and variants such as the Malcolm Baldrige Award criteria generate many measures to monitor their processes and progress. When migrating to a "Balanced Scorecard," they build on the base already established by classifying the many existing measurements into the four Balanced Scorecard categories. KPI scorecards can be found when the information technology group, which likes to put the company database at the heart of the program, triggers the scorecard design. KPI scorecards also arise from consulting organizations that like to sell and install large systems, especially so-called executive information systems.

KPI scorecards will be most helpful for departments and teams when a strategic program already exists at a higher level. In this way, the diverse indicators enable individuals and teams to define what they must do well to contribute to higher-level goals. Unless the link to strategy has been clearly thought through, however, the KPI scorecard can be a dangerous illusion.

Only a strategy scorecard, built using the principles articulated in this chapter and embedded in a strategy map, can create a Strategy-Focused Organization.

SUMMARY

Balanced Scorecards should not just be collections of financial and nonfinancial measures, organized into three to five perspectives. The best Balanced Scorecards reflect the strategy of the organization. A good test is whether you can understand the strategy by looking only at the scorecard. Many organizations, especially those that created constituent/stakeholder scorecards or KPI scorecards, fail this test.

Strategy scorecards, along with their graphical representation on strategy maps, provide a logical and comprehensive way to describe strategy. They communicate clearly the organization's desired outcomes and its hypotheses about how these outcomes can be achieved. They enable all organizational units and employees to understand the strategy and identify how they can contribute by becoming aligned to the strategy.

We do not claim to have made a science of strategy. The *formulation* of strategy is an art, and it will always remain so. The *description* of strategy, however, should not be an art. If we can describe strategy in a more disciplined way, we increase the likelihood of successful implementation. With a Balanced Scorecard that tells the story of the strategy, we now have a reliable foundation for the design of a management system to create Strategy-Focused Organizations.

NOTES

1. M. Porter, "What Is Strategy?" *Harvard Business Review* (November–December 1996): 62.

2. The primacy of the financial perspective applies to profit-seeking organizations. Nonprofit and government organizations typically require a modest rearrangement in the geography of the Balanced Scorecard, a topic we discuss in Chapter 5.

3. See R. Myers, "Metric Wars," *CFO Magazine* (October 1996); "Measure for Measure," *CFO Magazine* (November 1997); and "Valuing Companies: A Star to Sail By?" *The Economist,* 2 August 1997, 53–55, for a description and comparison of various value-based metrics being advocated.

4. In practice, the EVA calculation ends up being far more complex than this, involving consideration of the capitalization and amortization of R&D, acquisi-

tion, training, and marketing expenses. See G. B. Stewart III, *The Quest for Value: The EVA® Management Guide* (New York: HarperBusiness, 1991).

5. M. Treacy and F. Wiersema, *The Discipline of Market Leaders: Choose Your Customers, Narrow Your Focus, Dominate Your Market* (Reading, MA: Addison-Wesley, 1995).

6. Ibid., 35.

7. Ibid., 38.

8. Ibid., 31.

9. An alternative explanation for the mismatch between measures and strategy is that the company is espousing one strategy but implementing a quite different strategy.

10. Porter, "What Is Strategy?" 77.

11. Ibid., 64.

12. Carla O'Dell and C. Jackson Grayson, "Knowledge Transfer: Discover Your Value Proposition," *Strategy and Leadership* (March–April 1999): 10–15.

13. See A. A. Atkinson and J. H. Waterhouse, "A Stakeholder Approach to Strategic Performance Measurement," *Sloan Management Review* (Spring 1997), for an excellent exposition of stakeholder scorecards.

Building Strategy Maps in Private Sector Companies

IN CHAPTER 3, WE ILLUSTRATED THE ARCHITECTURE of Balanced Scorecard strategy maps with a company, Store 24, that was following a customer intimacy strategy. In this chapter, we illustrate the strategy maps developed for a product leadership company, National Bank Online Financial Services, and two other companies, Fannie Mae and Nova Scotia Power, Inc., that have followed operational excellence strategies. We also present the strategy maps for an agricultural chemicals company whose strategic themes tracked the evolution of strategy over time. Collectively, these examples reveal how organizations customize their Balanced Scorecards to specific strategies.

NATIONAL BANK ONLINE FINANCIAL SERVICES: PRODUCT LEADERSHIP

National Bank Online Financial Services (OFS), a division of National Bank, was among the first of the major U.S. banks to offer Internet access for online banking services.[1] In 1994, when the OFS division was established, only 20,000 customers used the bank's online service, and these customers used only a limited number of services. By early 1998, OFS had grown to have 350,000 customers. Douglas Newell, the executive vice president of the OFS division, set a goal to have 1 million online customers by the end of the decade. Achieving this growth, however, would require continued investments in technology (both hardware and software). Newell knew such investments could be difficult in the National Bank cost-focused culture, especially for a division that was treated as a cost center.[2] Newell felt that he needed a mechanism to communicate his strategy to both the bank's senior management and his employees. The CFO, Jane Darcy, reflected:

We're operating in an environment where new projects and opportunities come up continuously and our business environment and competitors are changing all the time. Alliances are constantly being forged and broken. Everyday, a newspaper story reports about a new technology, service offering or way of doing business that affects us. We needed a tool to help us synchronize our strategy with what we were doing on a daily basis and translate that into measurable results. Such a tool would enable us to communicate with senior management, with other departments in the bank and with our OFS employees.

Newell reinforced this need:

While we were very good at articulating the online vision. . . , we often had difficulty translating that vision into effective execution. We needed a mechanism that would help us ensure that our plans closely supported our vision, and then we needed a set of clearly articulated, objective measures of performance. In the Internet space everything is new. And we needed a better way to identify what was working and what wasn't working to further our goals.

OFS executives turned to the Balanced Scorecard as the mechanism to address the issues noted by Darcy and Newell. OFS, in its planning process, had already established three strategic themes:

1. Add and retain high-value and high-potential-value customers. Grow the customer base by differentiating offerings from the competition. In particular, focus on continued leadership in product and feature development and superior customer service. The team set a target to grow the customer base by 847,000 new customers: 450,000 migrated (existing National Bank) customers and 397,000 new customers.

2. Increase revenue per customer. Grow revenue per customer by continuing third-party alliance programs and cross selling both branded and nonbranded products. The target was to increase revenue per customer from $200 to $310.

3. Reduce costs per customer. Reduce cost per customer by increasing the customer base to spread fixed costs and develop cutting-edge, automated processes and support and self-help systems. The target was to reduce annual customer costs from $114 to $76.

By having these three strategic themes already established, the interdepartmental project team that had been created to build the initial Balanced Scorecard had a great starting point for its task. The team worked hard to define objectives and measures for each of the three strategic themes, eventually producing the strategy map shown in Figure 4-1. The process of drawing the linkage diagrams for the three strategic themes generated extensive debate. But the process of defining and drawing the strategic themes for the scorecard enabled people from across the division to reach a consensus about the strategy and how to implement it effectively. As one participant described it, "We spent weeks getting the linkage map right. We debated where every objective fit on the map. The discussions became heated at times. However, it was good for us to have a cross-functional discussion about each objective, because it helped everyone see how interrelated all objectives are."

We can analyze the OFS scorecard using the framework established in Chapter 3. Starting with the financial perspective, National Bank OFS identified a gap that existed between its ambitious profit targets and the profits that would be earned with the existing customer base and imbedded costs. The company used its three strategic themes to determine the specific amounts required to close the profit gap:

1. Increasing the number of customers

2. Increasing the revenue per customer

3. Decreasing cost per customer

OFS set stretch targets for each component that, taken together, yielded the desired profit improvement. This set the stage for moving to the customer perspective.

Figure 4-1 National Bank's Online Financial Service Strategy Map

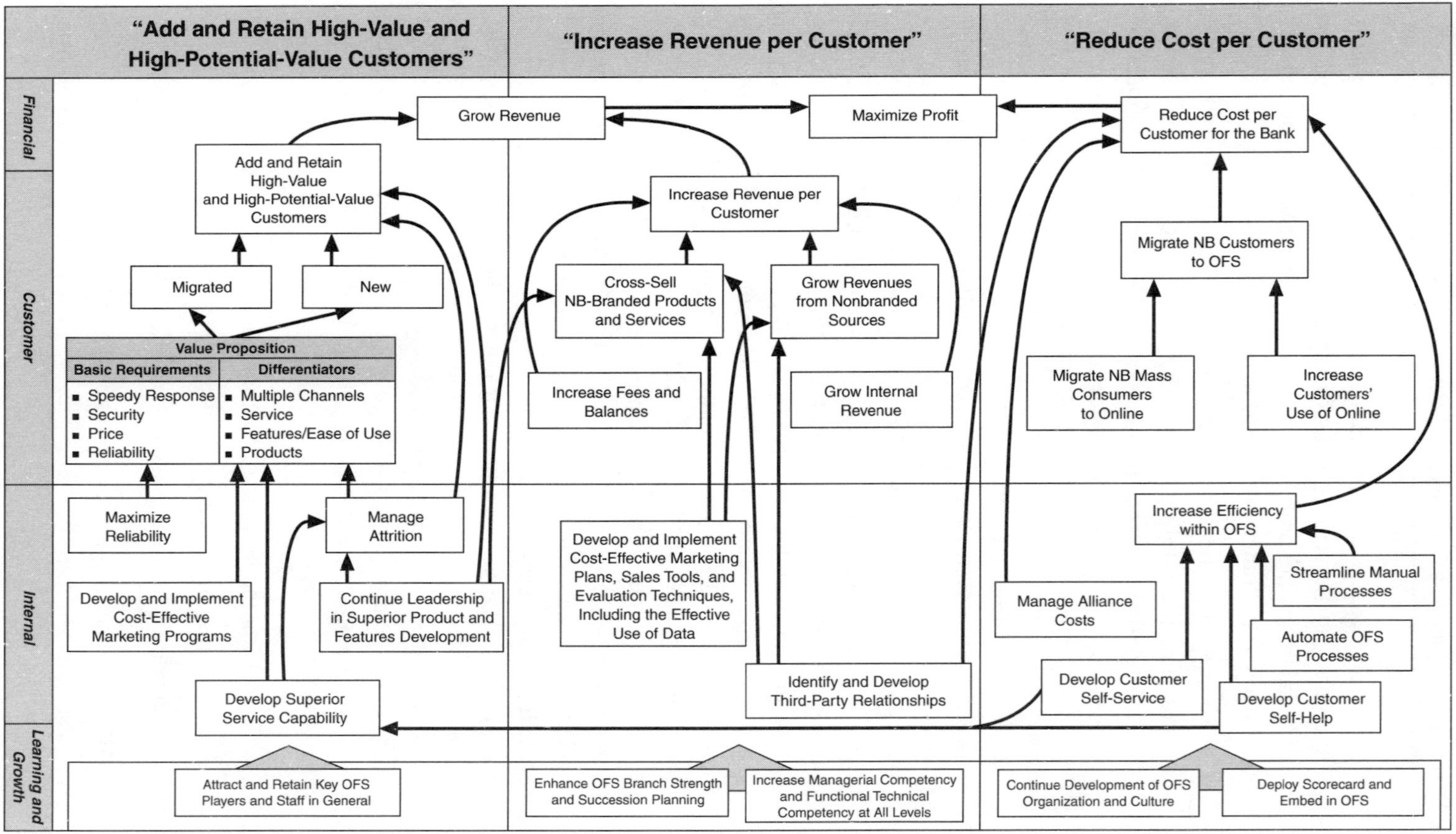

National Bank OFS was a *product leader*, the first in its market to leverage emerging Internet-based electronic technology to capture a mass market of banking customers. The strategy required OFS to introduce rapidly a broad portfolio of services that could be delivered through an electronic banking relationship. The OFS value proposition (Figure 4-1) focused on the product profiles that would accelerate the development of their customer base, thus consolidating their early mover advantage. The differentiators included multiple electronic channels to provide services, superior service, ease of use to expand the number of computer-literate customers, and a broad range of financial service products. The basic requirements included speed, response, security, fair price, and reliability.

The Balanced Scorecard project team identified the customer outcomes and drivers in each of the three strategic themes. The customer outcome measures for the first strategic theme—"add and retain high-value and high-potential-value customers"—were the number of incremental and total online customers and the total bank profit per online customer. The retention of customers was measured by customer satisfaction indicators and attrition rates. The measures for the value proposition proved controversial, particularly when the team was setting targets for the internal business process objectives to "maximize reliability" and offer "superior service capability." Newell wanted to set targets for these objectives that would be comparable to the availability and reliability that consumers experienced with their telephone service. Such targets were of a much greater magnitude than what Internet-based services were currently providing. But Newell eventually helped the entire group to understand that only by offering such dramatic improvements in reliability and access convenience would large numbers of customers shift to the Internet channel. So the process of arguing about the targets for critical Balanced Scorecard measures in the internal perspective eventually created a divisionwide consensus for breakthrough targets on availability and reliability.

The customer objectives for the second strategic theme, "increase revenue per customer," emphasized the importance of deepening relationships with existing customers. This could come from two sources: cross selling existing National Bank financial services to the OFS customer base, and selling entirely new products and services to customers through this channel. When these customer outcomes were translated to internal processes, the team identified two critical internal processes:

1. Improve partnerships with other National Bank business units. OFS personnel had to become familiar with National Bank products and develop skills in marketing them to OFS customers.

2. Establish alliances with third parties to develop and offer the new services.

As a specific example of third-party alliances, OFS customers could, with a couple of mouse clicks, send flowers to their moms on Mother's Day and gifts to dads on Father's Day. Such new services represented attractive revenue opportunities, as OFS retained the fees earned from these third-party transactions.

The third strategic theme—"reduce cost per customer"—was critical for success of the venture. Prices of financial services were plummeting. For example, competition from specialized discount brokerage firms had reduced online commissions from $90 to $270 per transaction down to around $10 to $25. OFS had to be able to offer this service at competitive prices and still be profitable. Also, the two other strategic themes had emphasized the premium customer, perhaps 20 percent of all banking customers, for whom OFS could become the personal banker for a range of banking, insurance, and investment products. But what about the other 80 percent of banking customers who use only a limited range of products? OFS could generate profits for National Bank if these customers would migrate from branch-based transactions that cost about $1.25 per transaction to online banking services in which transactions, under efficient operations, could be done at $0.01 per transaction. The theme to "reduce cost per customer" reflected the goal of moving customers who were marginally profitable in a bricks-and-mortar environment to profitable customers in a more efficient electronic channel. The key was to continually lower the cost of serving customers, and this included not only handling their transactions but minimizing the need for online personnel to problem-solve and troubleshoot when customers experienced difficulties. The cost reduction theme led to developing several important strategic objectives:

- Increase the customer base, as most of the operating costs were "fixed," independent of the number of customers using the online service[3]

- Increase the percentage of customers' transactions done online

- Reduce the cost of handling customer contacts, through streamlined processes

- Reduce the need for customer calls, through automated processes and extensive self-help capabilities

The last item—self-service capability—enabled customers to manage and monitor their banking transactions in much the same way that shippers can now track the progress of their package deliveries through Federal Express's online tracking service. Customers make fewer calls for information and help when they can access transactions online. By giving customers the ability to monitor their accounts and transactions online, OFS would lower its costs of service. But online transaction monitoring also contributed to another strategic theme—enhance customer service for high-value customers. With online tracking and self-help, customers felt more in control of their accounts and transactions, so they actually preferred to monitor their transactions online rather than via telephone. Thus the online tracking capability contributed to two strategic themes: cost reduction and enhanced customer service. The team reflected this linkage (see Figure 4-1) by connecting two objectives in the cost reduction strategic theme—"develop customer self-service" and "develop customer self-help"—to the "develop superior service capability" in the add and retain high-value customers strategic theme.

With objectives for the customer perspective completed for the three strategic themes, the OFS project team could now define objectives for its three general internal processes that would deliver on the value proposition and the strategic themes. The *innovation* process was fundamental to sustaining their product leadership strategy. OFS had to continually lead in the development of superior products and features. Third-party relationships were another source of new products. The *customer management* processes sought to exploit the benefits from the new products by migrating traditional branch banking customers to the new products now available on the technology-based channel. Within this new body of electronic customers, the team sought to cultivate a set of high-value customers who would use a broader range of services, thus increasing revenue per customer. The *operations* process, of course, focused on continual improvements in cost and service reliability.

The National Bank OFS strategy for learning and growth (Figure 4-1) was aimed at supporting rapid growth. A relatively small number of people had responsibility for developing the innovative new products required by the strategy. To take advantage of these new products, however, OFS had to expand the size of its workforce while maintaining high levels of quality and alignment to company objectives. The learning and growth objectives were defined as follows:

- Attract and retain key OFS players and staff
- Enhance OFS bench strength and succession planning
- Increase managerial competency and functional technical competency at all levels
- Continue development of the OFS organization and culture
- Deploy the scorecard and embed it in OFS

The project team grappled with the issue of how to align these five learning and growth objectives with strategic themes, as these objectives seemed necessary to achieve each of the three strategic themes. The team eventually decided to treat the learning and growth objectives as drivers behind all three themes, instead of aligning a subset of them under any one. They also decided that they would measure the learning and growth objectives annually.

Was the National Bank OFS strategy successful? In 1998, more than 450,000 National Bank customers were paying bills, checking account balances, conducting stock and bond trades, or applying for new accounts. In August 1999, the bank celebrated its millionth customer. National Bank had also received several awards as "Best Online Bank." On the internal measures, downtime on the OFS banking Web site decreased 71 percent from 1997 to 1998; this increased availability led to a significant decrease in customer calls for service. And the claim ratio on disputed payments also dropped by 50 percent in one year.

OFS soon began to use the scorecard to report to the National Bank chairman's office on the division's strategic objectives and measures. Financial measures alone could not summarize whether OFS's strategy was being implemented successfully either for itself or, more important, for the entire bank. The chief financial officer of OFS emphasized the importance of the scorecard in keeping the organization focused on vital operational issues, even while it exploited technology and managed customer relationships:

It helped us focus on process issues, making sure that we stayed proactive and avoided problems that would create bad customer experiences. Because of our focus on processes, we get really good early warning signs and avoid some of the operational problems that E-Trade, eBay, and other Internet-based services have experienced recently.

In addition to these applications, we discuss in Chapter 11 how OFS used the Balanced Scorecard to set priorities and select initiatives to enhance its strategy.

Long-term Internet Strategy: An Oxymoron?

The Balanced Scorecard has been applied successfully in virtually every industry, from long-cycle companies in pharmaceuticals to short-cycle ones in fashion retailing.[4] But technology-based companies like National Bank OFS are often said to be changing at Internet speed, seven to ten times faster than the normal pace of business. Does the Balanced Scorecard work in such environments? Some aspects of e-companies appear different. First, by using technology rather than real estate for infrastructure, e-companies can change their product portfolios and distribution channels seemingly overnight. Second, the industry is in a state of rapid flux and instability, so strategies are continually evolving and changing. At present, e-companies are staking out territory by attempting to compete simultaneously on price, service, customer intimacy, and innovation.

Yet e-companies that are continually evolving their strategies need a system for rapid strategy implementation even more than stable companies. These companies' strategies are still based on differentiated value propositions with underlying strategic hypotheses. The companies must communicate their strategies and value propositions to employees, test and learn about the strategies in real time, and quickly adapt the strategies. Rapid and effective strategy implementation is exactly the task that the Balanced Scorecard management system has been designed to do. Managers can use the scorecard to communicate the stable, long-run success measures as well as the new tactics—in the value proposition and in the internal business processes—that reposition the organization in its competitive environment. If, as we believe, success comes from aligning all employees, decentralized units, and initiatives to the strategy, fast-cycle companies should find the Balanced Scorecard an ideal management tool for quickly realigning the organization to a new strategy.

For example, consider the three strategic themes developed by National Bank OFS for its Balanced Scorecard:

1. Add and retain high-value and high-potential-value customers

2. Increase revenue per customer

3. Reduce cost per customer

These three themes are applicable to a broad range of rapidly-growing, Internet-based companies. Rather than becoming obsolete in two months, the themes are actually probably relevant and applicable for many years. The tactical details for implementing these objectives may change, but the strategic themes and most of the strategic objectives, particularly in the financial and customer perspectives, would stay the same—not just quarter to quarter but year to year. Thus we believe that the Balanced Scorecard can provide considerable value, not just to slow-cycle organizations such as Mobil and CIGNA, but also for organizations operating in continually evolving competitive marketplaces, such as online products and services.

The scorecard will help e-companies communicate enduring high-level strategic themes to all employees. Senior management can use the strategic themes and objectives to screen new initiatives, as we discuss in Chapter 11. Employees will continually examine their own priorities, opportunities, and day-to-day actions to determine whether they are contributing to the organization's strategic objectives. As employees learn about new threats, opportunities, capabilities, and technologies, they can assess what behaviors need to be modified and what new initiatives they can propose for the changed environment. At a high level, the senior management team will continually review and assess the value propositions they are offering to accomplish their high-level strategic objectives. Such reviews can lead to changes in the critical internal process objectives and measures, launching new initiatives or canceling existing initiatives. In this way, the scorecard continues to give the company a roadmap to the future, while facilitating the continual adaptation and change that must occur to cope with new opportunities and threats.

FANNIE MAE OPERATIONS: OPERATIONS EXCELLENCE

The Operations division of Fannie Mae provides an example of an operations excellence strategy. Fannie Mae, formerly a government agency but since 1968 a private shareholder-owned company listed on the New York

Stock Exchange, provides financial products and services that increase the availability and affordability of housing for low-, moderate-, and middle-income Americans. Fannie Mae's stated mission is to tear down barriers, lower costs, and increase the opportunities for home ownership and affordable rental housing for all Americans. Fannie Mae adds liquidity to the home mortgage market through two principal activities. First, it provides insurance by guaranteeing principal and interest payments on qualifying home mortgages. Second, Fannie Mae purchases home mortgages originated by local housing lenders and holds them for investments. At the end of 1999, Fannie Mae guarantees covered 23 percent of outstanding mortgage debt—a book value of $1 trillion. In portfolio, Fannie Mae held 11.7 million loans with a book value of $523 million.

The Fannie Mae Operations and Corporate Services division (OCS) handles what used to be called the "back office" for the insurance, purchase, and investment activities. It is the processing arm of the company, handling the massive quantity of principal and interest payments that flow into it each month. Traditionally, OCS had a simple mandate: *soundness and safety*. It had to ensure the integrity of processing operations and the security of the enormous quantity of funds that continually flowed through the company. OCS's secondary objective was cost-efficient operations. Historically, the company had been highly profitable. Unlike the situations at Mobil, CIGNA, or AT&T Canada, described in Chapter 1, no burning platform was raging at Fannie Mae to drive change. It was well run and doing fine. But Fannie Mae recognized that there was competitive advantage to be derived from leveraging operations capability, and the head of Operations wanted to expand by offering even more attractive, efficient, and responsive processing capabilities, including the flexibility to handle new types of financial instruments. The updated strategy for OCS was as follows:

1. Differentiate by becoming the most efficient, responsive processor in the industry

2. Support the company's revenue-enhancement strategy by developing a capability to process more complex products and services

The Balanced Scorecard would play two roles in this strategy. First, it would provide a mechanism to get the executive leadership together in one room to talk about the division's strategy rather than just how well their individual departments or functions were performing. Second, it would reposition OCS's role within Fannie Mae beyond being a large support division doing back-office work to becoming a value-adding contributor to the company's revenue growth strategy.

The financial perspective of OCS's Balanced Scorecard retained the historic emphasis on low-cost processing. The soundness and safety theme would be reinforced by continued focus on productivity and low-cost processing, enabling operations to "reliably and efficiently manage the current book of business." In addition, OCS now had a financial growth theme— to become more flexible and more customer-focused—thus enabling revenue growth to occur. This theme was based on leveraging relations with existing customers to identify new services and sources of revenue.

Defining the customer perspective generated extensive and interesting discussions that were primarily focused on identifying who the customer was for the operations division. Early on, it was recognized that the vast majority of external customer contact happens in Operations in the normal course of business, and Fannie Mae Operations wanted to leverage these contacts to add value in the operational channel. OCS historically thought more about functional excellence—low cost, efficient processing of a commodity product—than about customers. As an internal support organization, OCS clearly had internal customers, which it renamed "internal business partners." For them, OCS was to provide information about external customers, be responsive and collaborate on new opportunities, and partner with marketing and sales groups to provide value to end-use customers. In addition, OCS decided to recognize explicitly how it provided value to external customers. Operations wanted to work with lenders to develop a more integrated process from the point of underwriting and loan origination through ongoing loan servicing. Initially, the management team felt that as long as it offered its commodity products and services at the lowest price in the industry, it would be delivering the desired value to its external customers. The value proposition therefore had to emphasize "accurate, timely processing" and "lower processing cost" for the customer. OCS, however, wanted to move beyond a pure low-price strategy to more value-added customer relationships that leveraged the value of the information services it provided. For this strategy—to expand revenue growth through new products and services—OCS management had to also recognize its role in supporting noncommodity products. "Innovative new products" and "information" about markets were components of the new strategy based on product leadership. The complete customer perspective is shown in Figure 4-2.

Figure 4-2 Fannie Mae's Operational Excellence Strategy Map

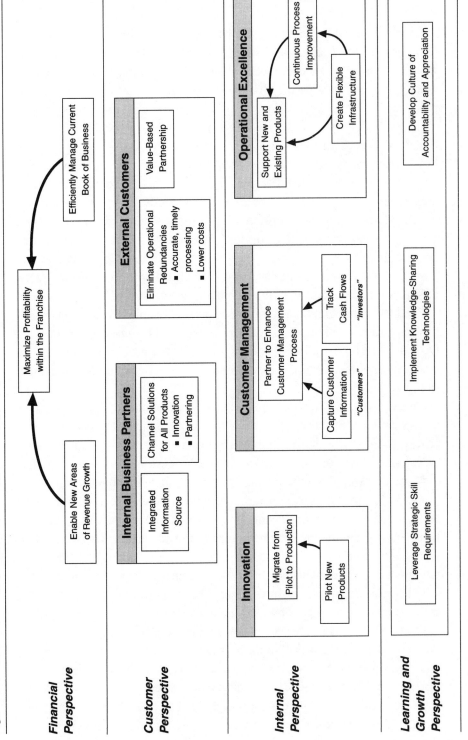

For the internal business process perspective, OCS had to start with its traditional base of safety and soundness for operational excellence. The focal point for the enhanced *operations* process strategy was to create a more flexible infrastructure that would support growth, both from new products and from acquisition. A continuous process-improvement program for both existing and new products would be critical to the operational excellence theme. For OCS's intent to move beyond operational excellence, the *customer management* process became highlighted. The knowledge gained by the OCS group about transaction volumes and complexity profiles enabled them to develop more cost-effective services for their customers. Similarly, information for investors about the timing of cash flows and their relationship to different investment vehicles created another asset to broaden the customer relationship. OCS personnel and Fannie Mae account managers would partner, using these information assets to enhance the customer management process. The management team defined two strategic themes for this process: "enable investor opportunities" and "leverage knowledge of our customer." The *innovation* process at OCS focused on the piloting and migrating of the new opportunities. The strategy maps for the four internal process strategic themes are illustrated in Figure 4-2.

The learning and growth strategy at OCS defined a set of strategic skills to support each of the four strategic themes. The people perspective was critical to complete the transition from Fannie Mae being a government-type bureaucratic organization to a flexible, customer-focused one. The new strategy would require people to change behavior and responsibilities. For example, the "improve operating capability" theme required improved skills in customer relations, teaming, and communications. These tasks had to be clearly communicated, recognized, and rewarded. The technology plan focused on capturing and sharing knowledge about customers, including knowledge management of the customer database and integration with the transaction processing system. The supporting culture focused on the creation of both accountability and achievement.

Once the OCS Balanced Scorecard had been developed, Larry Barnett, vice president of security trading operations, recalled, "The heavy lifting could really begin." It had to become imbedded in the OCS culture and management system. OCS selected "theme owners" for the four internal strategic themes. The theme owners organized discussions at which people from various departments and functions came together to talk about how they could contribute to the theme, not just report on their individual function and department. Discussions on new investments, initiatives, hiring, and skill development of existing personnel were tied back to how such actions contributed to accomplishing the strategic themes. The Balanced Scorecard became the agenda for monthly meetings and discussions. Managers helped frontline personnel to define local, departmental measures that would, in some cases, be reported daily to support the high-level divisional objectives and measures.

NOVA SCOTIA POWER, INC.: OPERATIONAL EXCELLENCE

Another operational excellence strategy was implemented at Nova Scotia Power, Inc. (NSPI), a regulated, investor-owned utility that supplies electricity to the Canadian province of Nova Scotia. In 1998, NSPI had 1,650 employees, revenues of C$750 million, and a net margin of 12.4 percent. David Mann, formerly corporate counsel at NSPI, became CEO in July 1996, and was faced with the challenge to position NSPI for a new world of deregulation in the electric utility industry. In late 1998, NSPI was separated from nonregulated energy enterprises and placed within a newly established holding company, NS Power Holding, Inc. NSPI could not increase its prices for electricity, despite internal and external cost pressures.

Working with a strategy consulting firm, Mann's senior management team had formulated a new strategic plan, but Mann wanted a measurement system to guide and gauge the success of the plan. In addition, NSPI had recently reorganized into SBUs, and Mann felt the need for a tool to unite the plans of the SBUs so that they would all be working toward the same overall goals. CFO Jay Forbes proposed that the Balanced Scorecard be used for these purposes. Forbes served as the executive sponsor for the development and implementation of the scorecard at NSPI.

The scorecard was based on the four strategies in the NSPI plan:

1. Cut costs (revised to "manage costs" in 1999)
2. Build customer loyalty
3. Build the business
4. Develop employee commitment

The corporate-level NSPI scorecard was simple (see Figure 4-3); each of the four strategic objectives could be aligned with a Balanced Scorecard perspective. The company emphasized building customer satisfaction and

Figure 4-3 Nova Scotia Power

Manage Costs		**Build Customer Loyalty**	
Objective	**Measure**	**Objective**	**Measure**
Environmental Performance	▪ Environmental performance index	Increase Customer Loyalty	▪ Customer loyalty rating
Operating Efficiency	▪ Total manageable costs/kWh sold ▪ Fuel cost/kWh generated	Customer Growth and Retention	▪ Sales volume (GWh sold)
Optimize Capital Utilization	▪ Percentage of actual capital spending economically justified ▪ Percentage of 2000 ACE plan approved on basis of economic justification	Reliability	▪ Outage performance index
Prepare for the Year 2000	▪ Percentage of all computerized systems compliant by 6/30/99 ▪ Percentage of effort complete on contingency planning by 9/30/99		

Build the Business		**Develop Employee Commitment**	
Objective	**Measure**	**Objective**	**Measure**
Maintain Confidence of Investment Community	▪ Net earnings	Safety	▪ All-injury frequency rate ▪ High potential incident ratio ▪ Reduction in public electrical contact incidents
		Competency Attainment	▪ Percentage of employees with development plans ▪ Percentage of employees with development plans achieving one or more development goals
		Employee Commitment	▪ Employee commitment survey results

loyalty and improving employee commitment while embarking on a vigorous cost-reduction program that would enable it to maintain profitability without raising rates.

The results were impressive. From 1996 to 1999, NSPI generated a sales volume increase of more than 13 percent and was able to deliver the higher revenues with 20 percent fewer employees. The combination contributed to a productivity improvement of nearly 36 percent, as measured by kilowatt-hours of sales per employee. The cost reductions were not achieved at a cost to the customer, the community, or employees. Customer satisfaction increased steadily; power interruptions and customer hours without power decreased to record low levels; environmental incidents decreased; and accidents dropped by 25 percent to a record low. Employee commitment surveys showed large year-to-year increases. Forbes commented on this performance for a regulated utility that had to absorb significant external price increases for fuel and for government-mandated pension charges:

> We have held price constant since 1996 despite cost increases in some areas. We have been able to absorb these increases and earn our allowed rate of return because we've been able to manage our costs more effectively through the use of the Balanced Scorecard. At the same time, we've been able to increase our safety, improve our reliability, improve customer service, and enhance our employee commitment.

AGRICHEM MANUFACTURING INDUSTRIES: MANAGING STRATEGIC THEMES OVER TIME

The strategy maps we have discussed so far give a snapshot of the organization's strategy. They represent the simultaneous strands that organizations manage to achieve their strategic objectives. Companies that are introducing new technologies and radically new products and relationships must also manage strategic themes over time. Initially the company may focus on productivity and process improvements to deliver short-term cost savings. Over time, the emphasis shifts to revenue growth, with new product introductions and new relationships with customers. The strategy culminates with the company occupying a new strategic niche, providing new and powerful value-added products and services to its customers.

AgriChem, a U.S. manufacturer of agricultural chemicals, provides a good illustration of the power of managing a time-sequenced set of strategic themes.[5] AgriChem blended active ingredients into packaged products. It sold the packaged chemicals to distributors, who sold and supplied farmers around the country. In 1993, AgriChem formulated an aggressive new three-year strategy to transform the value chain to its end-use customer, the farmer. The strategy consisted of five overlapping strategic themes:

1. Reengineer manufacturing
2. Redesign interface with distributors
3. Improve distributor operations
4. Invent new distributor-farmer interface
5. Pioneer precision agriculture

AgriChem developed separate strategy maps for each of the five themes so that it could focus on each one at the appropriate point in the three-year period. The goal was to double the company's high-level financial metric, return on net assets (RONA).

The first theme—reengineer manufacturing (see Figure 4-4)—was to deliver substantial financial benefits from cost reduction and enhanced productivity. This theme emphasized a new production planning software system (in the learning and growth perspective) that would produce efficiencies in supply and distribution (internal business process objectives). These improvements would enable AgriChem to reduce prices to its distributors (customer perspective) while still increasing its operating margins (financial perspective).

As AgriChem consolidated its gains from internal cost reduction and productivity improvements, it could start to improve the distribution system to its retailers (see Figure 4-5). Installing additional software modules that were focused on sales and marketing operations launched this second theme. The modules provided better information from retailer sales back to manufacturing operations. The close linkages enabled a breakthrough in operations. Orders from farmers came during a narrow time interval at the start of the growing season. Historically, AgriChem had to forecast how much and which products the farmers would order each year and stock retailers in advance. Even with good forecasting routines, the process still led to costly overstocks and understocks each year. If AgriChem could align its

Figure 4-4   Reengineer Manufacturing

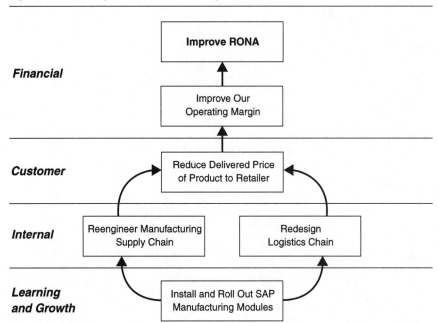

newly streamlined manufacturing processes (the first strategic theme) to orders received by its retailers from farmers, the company could manufacture much more product to order rather than to stock.

The third strategic theme (see Figure 4-6) emphasized improvements in the company's retailers' operations. By deploying some of AgriChem's new information technology for retailers, the company could reduce both its own cost and capital requirements and those of its retailers. As AgriChem became the retailers' most profitable supplier, the retailers would source more product from AgriChem, leading to higher profits for both.[6]

The first three strategic themes focused on improving AgriChem's operations, AgriChem's relationships with its retailers, and then retailers' operations. The next breakthrough in performance would come from using information technology to create efficiencies for farmers (see Figure 4-7). AgriChem wanted to develop a SmartCard for farmers that would link to

Figure 4-5   Redesign Interface with Distributors

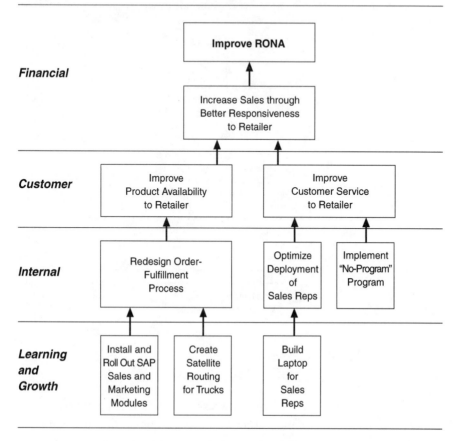

AgriChem's extensive database on individual farmers' operations. The farmer would interact with AgriChem's computers and databases to select the desired chemicals for the upcoming season. The farmer could then drive to the local retailer and identify himself with the SmartCard, and the appropriate chemicals would be automatically dispensed into the farmer's containers. This new process saved time, packaging, and inventory for the retailer and provided great convenience to the farmer.

The fifth and final strategic theme was the most ambitious and experimental of all (see Figure 4-8). This theme deployed advanced information technology directly to the end-use consumer by providing the farmer with desktop and tractor-top capabilities. AgriChem would develop a farmers' database enabling each farmer to forecast, at his desktop, the chemicals he

Figure 4-6   Improve Distributor Operations

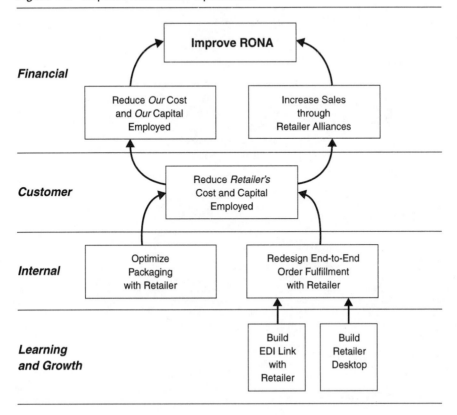

could best use based on his crops, land characteristics, terrain, planting patterns, and weather trends. The final program could be loaded on the tractor itself, which would automatically dispense seeds, fertilizer, and protection, using precise positioning information from global positioning satellite equipment. This precise planting program eliminated gaps and duplication of dispensing seed and fertilizer as the farmer traversed his fields. The revolutionary farming process in this fifth strategic theme had the largest potential for increasing AgriChem's revenue growth by forging an intense value-added relationship with end-use consumers.

AgriChem's full strategy map is shown in Figure 4-9. At its foundation were employee-focused programs to develop relationship-building skills and incentive programs and customer focus. While Figure 4-9 appears

Figure 4-7   Invent New Distributor-Farmer Interface

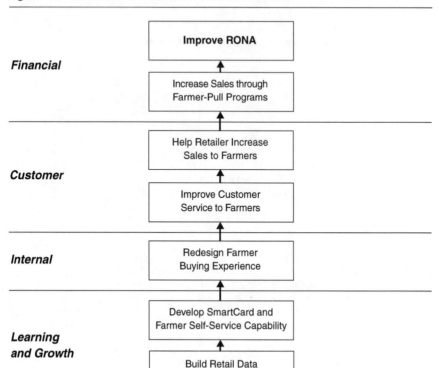

quite complex, it becomes simpler to both understand and manage when it is viewed as a sequential process moving from right to left on the diagram.[7] The later themes—which are more revenue-based and closer to the end-use consumer—build on and leverage the competitive advantages from the cost reductions and distribution efficiencies achieved in earlier stages. The vertical strategic themes of Figures 4-4 to 4-8 also provide a powerful accountability model. The company appointed a manager for each of the five strategic themes with the responsibility for delivering the performance targeted for each theme.

Company managers reported that the near-term operational improvements from the first two strategic themes yielded positive cash flow and gave employees confidence that helped to sustain investments for the more

Figure 4-8   Pioneer Precision Agriculture

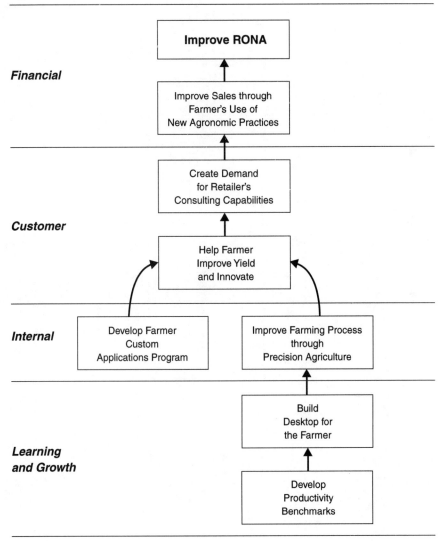

experimental revenue growth themes, especially numbers four and five. The company, in three years, doubled sales, increased RONA from 16 percent to 50 percent, and forged direct, long-term relationships with its end-use consumers.

Figure 4-9 AgriChem's Strategy Map

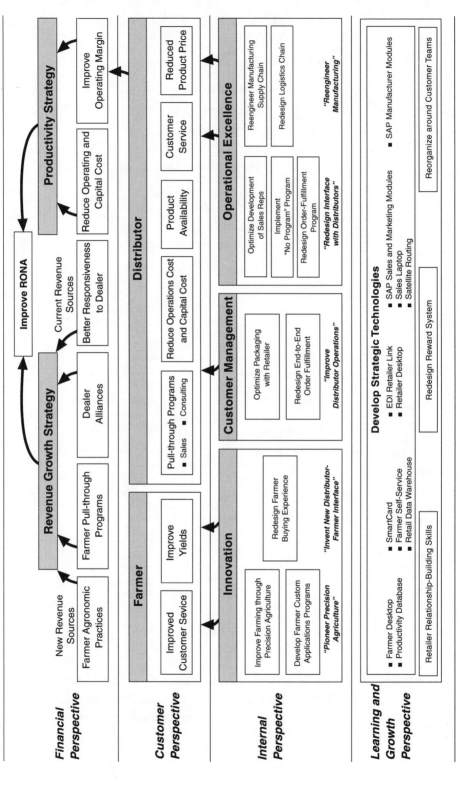

SUMMARY

In this chapter, we have illustrated how Balanced Scorecard strategy maps get constructed from the underlying strategy of the organization. The exemplar organizations developed and used the scorecard to translate their strategies into linked cause-and-effect relationships that could be easily understood and communicated to the entire organization. The process made the strategy transparent. Readers of the scorecard could infer the strategy from looking at the scorecard objectives and measures, and the linkages in the Balanced Scorecard strategy map.

NOTES

1. Disguised company name. Quotations from National Bank personnel may not be reprinted without permission of the Harvard Business School Press.
2. The fees and interest income earned from OFS's customers were attributed to the product divisions (checking accounts, savings accounts, credit cards, and so on). OFS covered its costs by charging nominal fees to the product groups based on customers' online transactions.
3. See the discussion of Internet economics in Carl Shapiro and Hal R. Varian, *Internet Rules: A Strategic Guide to the Network Economy* (Boston: Harvard Business School Press, 1998).
4. See Jeffrey R. Williams, *Renewable Advantage: Crafting Strategy through Economic Time* (New York: The Free Press, 1998), for discussion of how competitive strategy evolves at different rates in different industries.
5. We are grateful to Francis Gouillart, president of Emergence Consulting, for this example. Mr. Gouillart has been a leader in using the time-based themes approach of the Balanced Scorecard for describing strategy.
6. One can see here the role for activity-based cost systems so that retailers can understand the relative profitability of products sourced from their various suppliers; see Robert S. Kaplan and Robin Cooper, *Cost & Effect: Using Integrated Cost Systems to Drive Profitability and Performance* (Boston: Harvard Business School Press, 1998), 203–10.
7. Of course, the earlier themes would not be forgotten once their initial targets have been achieved. AgriChem would continue to improve its internal cost and productivity, its distribution to retailers, its dealers' processes, and its farmers' buying experiences.

Strategy Scorecards in Nonprofit, Government, and Health Care Organizations

IN 1996, THE MIGRATION OF THE BALANCED SCORECARD to the nonprofit and government sectors was in its embryonic stages. During the next four years, the concept became widely accepted and adopted in such organizations around the world. As we have reviewed the scorecards produced by these organizations, we have gained additional insights into effective use of the Balanced Scorecard in nonprofits and government agencies. In this chapter, we provide examples of how the Balanced Scorecard has been applied in government, nonprofit, and health care organizations.

ROLE FOR STRATEGY

In our experience, nonprofits and government agencies typically have considerable difficulty in defining clearly their strategy. We have seen "strategy" documents running upwards of fifty pages. And most of the document, once the mission and vision are articulated, consists of lists of programs and initiatives, not the outcomes the organization is trying to achieve. These organizations must understand Michael Porter's admonition (quoted in Chapter 3) that strategy is not only what the organization intends to do, but also what it decides not to do—a message that is particularly relevant for nonprofits and government departments.

Most of the initial scorecards in the nonprofit and government sector feature an operations excellence theme. These organizations take their current mission as a given and try to do their work more efficiently—reduce costs, incur fewer defects, and do it faster. Often the project builds off a recently introduced quality initiative that emphasizes local process improvement. It is unusual to find nonprofit organizations focusing on a strategy that can be thought of as product leadership or customer intimacy. As a consequence, their scorecards tend to be closer to the KPI scorecards described at the end of Chapter 3 than true strategy scorecards.

The City of Charlotte, North Carolina, however, followed a customer-based strategy by selecting an interrelated set of strategic themes to create distinct value for its citizens. The United Way of Southeastern New England, a nonprofit, also articulated a customer (donor) intimacy strategy. Other nonprofits—the May Institute, Inc. and New Profit, Inc.—selected a clear product leadership position. The May Institute uses partnerships with universities and researchers to deliver the best behavioral and rehabilitation care. New Profit introduces new selection, monitoring, and governing processes that are unique among nonprofit organizations. Montefiore University Hospital uses a combination of product leadership (in its centers of excellence) and excellent customer relationships—through its new patient-oriented care centers—to build market share in its local area. So government and nonprofit organizations can be strategic and build competitive advantage in ways other than pure operational excellence. But it takes vision and leadership to move beyond improving existing processes to a strategy that highlights which processes and activities are the most important to implement.

MODIFYING THE ARCHITECTURE OF THE BALANCED SCORECARD

Most nonprofits and government organizations had difficulty with the original architecture of the Balanced Scorecard, where the financial perspective was placed at the top of the hierarchy. Given that achieving financial success is not the primary objective for most of these organizations, the architecture can be rearranged to place customers or constituents at the top of the hierarchy.

In a private sector transaction, the customer both pays for the service and receives the service. The two roles are so complementary that most people don't even think about them separately. But in a nonprofit organization, donors provide the financial resources—they pay for the service—while another group, the constituents, receives the service. Who is the customer—the one paying or the one receiving? Rather than have to make such a Solomon-like decision, organizations can place both the donor perspective and the recipient perspective at the top of their Balanced Scorecards. They develop objectives for both donors and recipients and then identify the internal processes that will deliver desired value propositions for both groups of "customers."

In fact, nonprofit and government agencies should consider placing an overarching objective at the top of their scorecard that represents their long-term objective: for instance, a reduction in poverty or illiteracy or improvements in the environment. Then the objectives within the scorecard can be oriented toward improving such a high-level objective. For a private sector company, financial measures provide accountability to the owners, the shareholders. For a nonprofit or government agency, however, the financial measures are not the relevant indicators of whether the agency is delivering on its mission. The agency's mission should be featured and measured at the highest level of its scorecard. Placing an overarching objective on the Balanced Scorecard for a nonprofit or government agency clearly communicates the organization's long-term mission (see Figure 5-1).

Figure 5-1   Adapting the Balanced Scorecard Framework to Nonprofit Organizations

Even the financial and customer objectives, however, may need to be rethought for governmental organizations. Take the case of regulatory and enforcement agencies that monitor and punish violations of environmental, safety, and health regulations. As such an agency does its job—detecting transgressions and fining or arresting those who violate the laws and regulations—can it look to its "immediate customers" for satisfaction and loyalty measures? Clearly not; the true "customers" for such organizations are the citizens at large, who benefit from effective but not brutal or idiosyncratic enforcement of laws and regulations. Figure 5-2 shows a modified framework in which a government agency has three high-level perspectives:[1]

1. Cost incurred. This perspective emphasizes the importance of operational efficiency. The measured cost should include both the expenses of the agency and the social cost it imposes on citizens and other organizations through its operations. For example, an environmental agency may impose costs on private sector organizations. These are part of the costs of having the agency carry out its activities. The agency should be attempting to minimize the direct and social costs required to deliver the benefits in its mission.

2. Value created. This perspective identifies the benefits to citizens that are being created by the agency. This perspective will be the most problematic and difficult to measure. It will usually be hard

Figure 5-2   The Financial/Customer Perspectives for Public-Sector Agencies

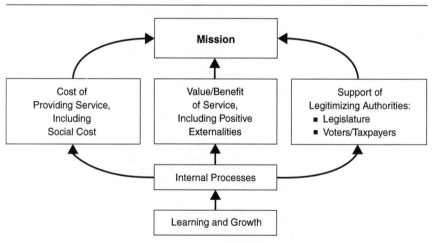

to quantify, financially, the benefits from improved education, reduced pollution, better health, less congestion, and safer neighborhoods. But the Balanced Scorecard still enables organizations to identify the outputs, if not the outcomes, from its activities and to measure these outputs. So surrogates for value created could include percentage of students acquiring specific skills and knowledge; density of pollutants in water, air, or land; improved morbidity and mortality in targeted populations; crime rates and perception of public safety; and transportation times. In general, public sector organizations may find they use more output than outcome measures. The citizens and their representatives—elected officials and legislators—will eventually make the judgments about the benefits from these outputs versus their costs.

3. Legitimizing support. An important "customer" for any government agency will be its "donor," the organization—typically the legislature—that provides the agency's funding. In order to ensure continued funding for its activities, the agency must strive to meet the objectives of its funding source—the legislature and ultimately citizens and taxpayers.

Thus a public sector organization may have three high-level objectives it needs to satisfy if it is to accomplish its mission: create value, at minimal cost, and develop ongoing support and commitment from its funding authority. From these three, the agency proceeds to identify its objectives for internal processes and learning and growth that will enable it to achieve the objectives in its three high-level perspectives.

With this background, we can now illustrate some of the principles with examples drawn from the public and nonprofit sectors.

GOVERNMENT ORGANIZATIONS:
STRATEGIC LOGIC IN THE PUBLIC SECTOR

The City of Charlotte

In 1990, the City of Charlotte already had a mission and a vision statement that communicated the city's desire to provide high-quality services to its citizens that would make it a "community of choice for living, working, and leisure activities."[2] But the City Council was unsure about how to implement the mission and vision; funding was incremental and spread across all operating departments. Pam Syfert, then deputy city manager, felt the need to establish a strategy and set priorities for city initiatives. Rather than continue with business as usual, Syfert wanted the city to focus its limited resources on those initiatives that would have the greatest impact on achieving its vision.

In the early 1990s, senior city staff, the mayor, and the City Council used their annual retreat to choose a few themes that would guide resource allocation and departmental programs for the next decade. The staff presented the mayor and City Council with fifteen possible focus areas.[3] The group debated the themes and eventually selected the following:

- Community safety
- Transportation
- City within a city (preserving and improving older urban neighborhoods)
- Restructuring government
- Economic development

To implement these five themes effectively, Syfert formed a core project team to translate the five themes into strategic objectives for a city Balanced Scorecard. The team decided to place the customer (citizen) perspective at the top of its scorecard. It established seven customer objectives (see Figure 5-3), two objectives each for community safety and restructuring government, and one each for the other three strategic themes.

As the team worked on the five strategic themes, it realized that many financial, internal, and learning and growth objectives were common across several themes. The team therefore built its initial scorecard for all five themes (as shown in Figure 5-3). The top-line—customer perspective—captured aspects of the five strategic focus areas, slightly renamed. Its objectives represented the key services the city was delivering for its citizens. The financial objectives became the enablers for helping the city achieve its customer objectives. It measured delivering the city's services at a good price, securing external partners for funding and services, and maintaining its solid tax base and credit ranking to fund high-priority projects. The internal and learning and growth objectives then supported both the financial and the customer objectives. The internal objectives encouraged the city to change and improve the way it delivered services, especially by forming partnerships within communities, and improving

Figure 5-3 City of Charlotte City Council's Strategy Map

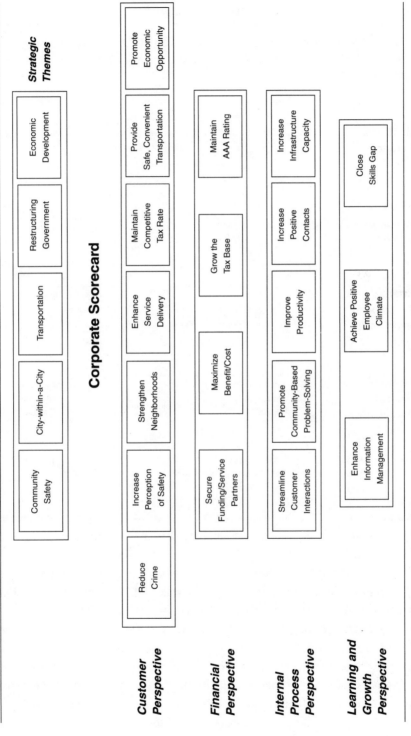

Source: Adapted from R. S. Kaplan, "City of Charlotte (A)," 9-199-036 (Boston: Harvard Business School, 1998), 12. Reprinted by permission of Harvard Business School.

Figure 5-4   Strategic Theme: City-within-a-City

Mission: *This focuses on comprehensively dealing with the economic develop-ment and quality of life issues in Charlotte's older, urban neighborhods, including residential and business areas.*

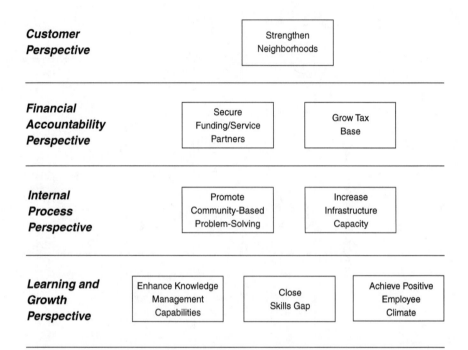

Source: Adapted from R. S. Kaplan, "City of Charlotte (A)," 9-199-036 (Boston: Harvard Business School, 1998), 115. Reprinted by permission of Harvard Business School.

productivity. And the learning and growth objectives identified whether the city was maintaining technology and its employee training and skills so that it could continually improve. The team developed descriptive state-ments for each of the nineteen objectives on the corporate scorecard.[4]

The strategic nature of the scorecard was highlighted when some de-partments—such as Fire, Wastewater Treatment, and Solid Waste Ser-vices—expressed disappointment that their activities did not appear on the corporate scorecard. Syfert told people in these departments that their work remained vitally important for the city and that their performance would be measured against departmental objectives. But she emphasized that each of these departments should also think how their operations could contribute to one or more of the city's top-level objectives:

"The ultimate goal is to make Charlotte a city where residents of all neighborhoods enjoy personal safety, decent and affordable housing, good jobs, adequate infrastructure, ready access to shopping, educational and recreational amenities, and effective representation through community-based organizations."

"Neighborhoods are this city's greatest asset."

Partnering with private and other funding sources extends and makes more effective the city's use of its resources.

Growing a neighborhood's tax base by attracting new businesses and encouraging the expansion and retention of existing ones is important to its economic vitality.

Promoting "community-based" problem-solving:
- Empowers neighborhood residents
- May reduce the level of city involvement to solve a problem
- Reduces duplication of effort
- Enhances delivery of city services

To succeed, we must support employees with the training and technical resources to facilitate solutions.

While focusing on the city's older urban neighborhoods, this problem-solving model will be shared as a best practice for managing similar issues in other city areas.

The corporate scorecard does not and cannot represent every important service delivered. For example, basic city services such as fire suppression, garbage collection or animal control are not represented individually on the corporate scorecard. These basic services are more appropriately addressed at a department or division level scorecard. The focus areas identify services the organization wants to improve or enhance to make Charlotte a community of choice for living and working.[5]

With the citywide scorecard now established as a template, the team then identified the relevant strategic objectives for each of the five themes and built separate scorecards for each theme (Figure 5-4 shows the scorecard for the "city-within-a-city" theme). The scorecards for the five strategic themes then became the basis for active discussions among city managers, from many different departments, about how these cross-departmental objectives could be achieved. We continue the Charlotte story later in the text, discussing in Chapter 6 how the city linked the corporate scorecard to individual departments and strategic themes and in Chapter 12 how the Charlotte scorecard was used interactively for reporting and learning.

FEDERAL GOVERNMENT AGENCIES

Scorecards are being developed by many U.S. government agencies, including units in the Department of Defense. The Balanced Scorecard concept has been endorsed by the National Partnership for Reinventing Government:

> *Why should you as a government leader try to achieve a balanced set of performance measures? . . . Because you need to know what your customer's expectations are and what your employee needs to have to meet those expectations. Because you cannot achieve your stated objectives without taking those expectations and needs into account. Most importantly, because it* works, *as can be seen from the success of our partners.*[6]

An early success occurred at the Veterans Benefit Administration (VBA) in the U.S. Department of Veterans Affairs. Initially the VBA formed a committee to determine how to comply with the Government Performance and Results Act (GPRA). The discussions soon evolved to the Balanced Scorecard and how this could help the agency both comply with the GPRA and become more effective. The VBA spent considerable time developing a consensus about its objectives, which was a challenge, as historically its five subbusinesses considered themselves to be quite different from one another. The committee learned that its existing measurement system ignored three important constituents: veterans (the beneficiaries), employees, and taxpayers. The committee developed a simple Balanced Scorecard. Even with only five measures, the scorecard provided a more balanced view of the VBA's mission and strategy:

1. Customer (veterans) satisfaction
2. Cost (taxpayer)
3. Speed
4. Accuracy
5. Employee development

Previously, VBA offices had been compared only on speed of processing. Now the scorecard enabled the comparison across the five scorecard measures, including customer satisfaction, which had not been measured before. A director concluded:

The scorecard is the basis for determining whether we meet our short-term and long-term strategic goals. It will ultimately be linked to our performance appraisal and rewards and recognition systems. All of our organizational design choices must be linked if we are to have a clear line of sight. The scorecard is the linchpin behind all of those choices.

In 1996, the Procurement Division in the U.S. Department of Transportation (DOT) was one of the first government agencies to adopt the Balanced Scorecard.[7] Lori Byrd, the project leader, reported that since then processing times have dropped dramatically and satisfaction measures have increased across the board:

The BSC has been recognized throughout the DOT as an important tool for facilitating culture change and promoting innovation within the Department. The procurement BSC served as an important pilot program that other major program areas have adopted and adapted. The procurement BSC has been a catalyst for the department at all levels and all programs.

Many other federal agencies, including the Federal Aviation Agency Logistics Center and the National Reconnaissance Office, have adopted the scorecard to align their organization to a strategy and become more accountable for performance.

International Applications

The city of Brisbane, Australia, followed a process essentially identical to that of Charlotte to produce a comprehensive citywide Balanced Scorecard program. In early 2000, the Australian cities of Cockburn and Melville won awards for their Balanced Scorecard performance measurement systems. Also in Australia, the government established in 1997 Centrelink, a new organization to provide a single source for information, assistance, and payments (such as social security) that previously were handled by a myriad of government departments and agencies. Centrelink immediately adopted the Balanced Scorecard as the mechanism for measuring progress in achieving its six high-level goals:

1. Establish partnerships with client departments to deliver results, provide value for money, and help customers toward financial independence

2. Increase customer and community involvement and satisfaction with services and results

3. Encourage people in Centrelink to be proud of their contribution and to feel that they are making a difference

4. Return an efficiency dividend to the Australian government

5. Develop innovative and personalized solutions, consistent with government policy

6. Be the first choice and benchmarked as the best practice in service delivery

Richard Magnus, the chief judge from the Singapore District and Magistrates' Courts, returned from attending a Harvard Business School executive program to lead the establishment of the Balanced Scorecard in the District and Magistrates' Courts system, one with 84 judges, 500 administrators, and 400,000 cases per year. The scorecard was piloted in the Small Claims Tribunal, probably the first application to the judicial sector in the world.[8]

After the scorecard was successfully piloted in the Small Claims Tribunal, the concept was rolled up to the Subordinate Courts, where it became the cornerstone of the management system there, and will be deployed to all the other subsidiary courts and administrative departments. The Subordinate Courts have started to link recognition and reward, but not actual monetary compensation, for excellent performers by presenting plaques and certificates, overseas study trips, and conference opportunities.

These experiences testify to the applicability and success of the scorecard across a wide range of governmental organizations.

THE NONPROFIT SECTOR

The Balanced Scorecard has become widely adopted in nonprofit organizations as well as government. We can provide a few examples.

The United Way of Southeastern New England

The United Way of Southeastern New England (UWSENE) was among the first to develop a Balanced Scorecard for a nonprofit organization.[9] United Way organizations enable individual donors to contribute, in an annual consolidated campaign at their workplace, to a wide range of human service programs in their communities.

Doug Ashby, chief professional officer (the CEO) of the UWSENE, felt that his current planning process was not sufficiently integrated with the organization's operations and looked to the Balanced Scorecard to provide the missing linkages. Much debate occurred about who were the customers of the UWSENE, what were the drivers of customer satisfaction, and which were the internal business processes that would deliver the products and services valued by customers.

Several different constituencies could have been represented in the customer perspective: donors, volunteers, employees, agencies, and the individuals who were the ultimate recipient or consumer of agency services. Ashby framed the strategic choice faced by the organization:

United Ways have three primary choices. They can be donor-focused, agency-focused, or community-focused.

Each of the three strategies is good, with the potential to yield positive end results. . . . Many United Ways switch strategies, say to meet specific community needs, for very good reasons but then are surprised when their agencies and donors get upset. UWSENE has definitely become a donor-focused organization, believing that if the donors are satisfied, then agencies will be provided for. That is why we chose the donor as the primary customer on the scorecard.[10]

Ashby's choice made the objectives for donors on the customer perspective relatively straightforward to articulate. The team then formulated initial internal business process objectives that would deliver the financial and customer objectives. Because the United Way functioned as a financial intermediary, collecting funds from a broad population of donors and disbursing the funds to community-based agencies, the team left the financial perspective at the top of the scorecard.

The UWSENE team discussed whether the four perspectives of a for-profit Balanced Scorecard were adequate and appropriate for its scorecard. Some suggested adding additional perspectives—say, for volunteers and for the agencies it funded to supply needed services to communities. Ashby, however, felt that the four basic perspectives had sufficient flexibility to include objectives that would address the organization's relationship with agencies and volunteers. This choice did bother some in the organization, who felt that the agencies were so critical to the mission of the UWSENE that they would have liked them to be featured with a separate perspective.

After several months, the team produced the scorecard shown in Figure 5-5. Reactions to the scorecard were favorable. One middle manager said, "You can relate to the BSC. It shows where you fit in the organization. You can see how you contribute to the customer or financial needs of the organization, and to staff advancement."[11] A member of the project team noted the enthusiasm among the staff for the Balanced Scorecard:

> We used to have strategic plans handed down from on high, and there wasn't the buy-in we now have from the BSC. It should start to change behavior.
> In the past, . . . those departments not involved with fundraising didn't get any recognition for the success of the organization. Now we will look to all the BSC measures to assess our success in reaching our goals.[12]

The May Institute

The May Institute, a Massachusetts nonprofit institution, is one of the country's largest providers of high-quality behavioral health care, education, and rehabilitation programs for children and adults. It has 2,000 employees and serves more than 8,000 individuals and family members each year through its nonprofit network of 160 programs in New England and the Southeast. The May Institute is also an active center of research and training, maintaining associations with more than forty universities and medical centers throughout the United States and several other countries.

The May Institute launched a Balanced Scorecard project to guide its expansion and to manage its increasing scope of operations. Chief Operating Officer Kathleen Bradley Kapsalis wanted to be able to evaluate where new projects fit within May's network of services and to evaluate new opportunities. Initially, the scorecard project struggled as it became imbedded with operational improvement projects and information technology initia-

Figure 5-5   United Way of Southestern New England's Balanced Scorecard

Perspective	Outcomes	Strategic Objectives
Financial	External Growth Internal Stability Community-Building	▪ Increase net amount of funds raised ▪ Balance internal income and expenses to maintain our 100% guarantee to others ▪ Increase amount of funds that go to services ▪ Increase amount of funds that go to proprietary products
Customer	Customer Satisfaction Market Growth Customer Retention	▪ Recognition ▪ Ease of giving ▪ Products that customers care about and that will improve the community ▪ Information on results ▪ Quality, timely service

Internal	Key Internal Business Processes Based on Quality
	
	Develop Innovative Products
	Maintain Viable Product Line
		▪ Improve key internal processes in the following areas:
		  - Fundraising
		  - Fund Distribution
		  - Community-Building
		  - Information Processing/Communications
		  - Pledge Processing
		  - Product Development
		  - Volunteer/Staff Development
		  - Customer Service
		  - Interdepartmental Communications
		▪ Develop a research and development process to come up with new, innovative products
		▪ Develop a consistent process for evaluating existing products and services

Learning and Growth	Employee Productivity Employee Satisfaction	▪ Training and development ▪ Technology ▪ Team ▪ Open and effective communication ▪ Agency assistance ▪ Employee ownership and involvement

Source: Adapted from R. S. Kaplan and Ellen L. Kaplan, "United Way of Southeastern New England (UWSENE)," 9-197-036 (Boston: Harvard Business School, 1996), 14. Repinted by permission of Harvard Business School.

tives. Existing project managers and technology consultants wanted to adapt the scorecard to support their local, continuous improvement initiatives, rather than to specify a strategic path for the future. Fortunately, the external Balanced Scorecard consultant kept the project team directed at the organization's higher-level strategic objectives. This project reinforced the difficulty that many nonprofit organizations have in distinguishing strategy from the myriad of initiatives they always have under way.

The May Institute did place its customer perspective at the top of its scorecard hierarchy. Reflecting the multiple constituencies of most non-profit organizations, the May Institute recognized several different types of customers in this perspective:

- Consumers (patients) and families
- Funders
- Academic community
- Media
- Legislators

Directly beneath the customer perspective, the May Institute placed the learning and growth perspective, feeling that the quality of its staff had the greatest impact on helping it to achieve its customer objectives.

The internal perspective featured several critical processes:

- To offer effective, comprehensive, and cost-effective care for consumers
- To safeguard rights, responsibilities, and ethics via the corporate compliance office
- To effectively collaborate and partner with other agencies and providers

A fourth process featured the important role of information systems for internal and external communication.

The financial perspective promoted the viability of the organization and developing performance-based compensation practices. The scorecard is portrayed in Figure 5-6.

Kapsalis emphasized how the Balanced Scorecard has been a wonderful teaching tool for her organization. Most of the May Institute's personnel give direct patient care and human services. The scorecard helped them to understand the importance of the business aspects of the organization, especially budgets and marketing activities. In contrast, May's board consisted mostly of businesspeople who understood finances well. For them, the scorecard communicated the role for human services and personnel development and allowed for more balanced discussions at board meetings. Beyond its communication role, the scorecard was used to highlight the

Figure 5-6   The May Institute's Balanced Scorecard

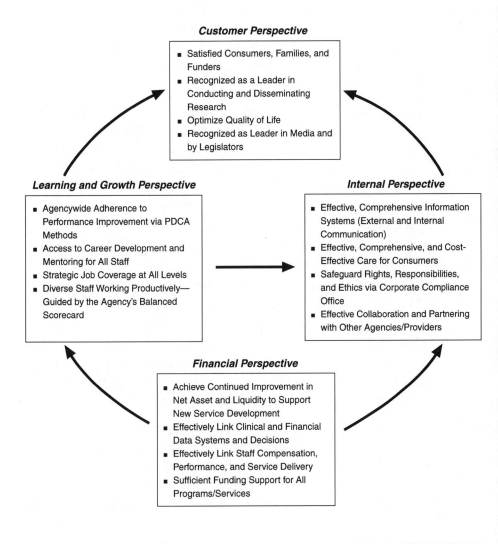

Our Mission: *Provide excellent Services, Research, and Training and meet the highest possible standards of behavioral health care and rehabilitation to our consumers, who face the challenges of autism, brain injury, mental retardation/developmental disabilities, and other physical and mental health issues.*

Working together we seek to contribute to every individual's independence and promote maximum community integration.

Customer Perspective

- Satisfied Consumers, Families, and Funders
- Recognized as a Leader in Conducting and Disseminating Research
- Optimize Quality of Life
- Recognized as Leader in Media and by Legislators

Learning and Growth Perspective

- Agencywide Adherence to Performance Improvement via PDCA Methods
- Access to Career Development and Mentoring for All Staff
- Strategic Job Coverage at All Levels
- Diverse Staff Working Productively— Guided by the Agency's Balanced Scorecard

Internal Perspective

- Effective, Comprehensive Information Systems (External and Internal Communication)
- Effective, Comprehensive, and Cost-Effective Care for Consumers
- Safeguard Rights, Responsibilities, and Ethics via Corporate Compliance Office
- Effective Collaboration and Partnering with Other Agencies/Providers

Financial Perspective

- Achieve Continued Improvement in Net Asset and Liquidity to Support New Service Development
- Effectively Link Clinical and Financial Data Systems and Decisions
- Effectively Link Staff Compensation, Performance, and Service Delivery
- Sufficient Funding Support for All Programs/Services

importance of human resources processes, particularly retention and re-cruitment, in a tight job market.

New Profit, Inc.

A novel Balanced Scorecard application was at the heart of a new nonprofit organization, New Profit, Inc. (NPI), a Boston-based venture capital phil-anthropic fund.[13] Vanessa Kirsch, founder of NPI, wanted to create a per-formance framework for the nonprofit sector. The new venture philanthropy fund was structured similar to that of a for-profit venture cap-ital firm. Kirsch and her general partners, funded by a small percentage of the fund's size, actively managed a portfolio of social enterprises.

NPI specified three principles to guide the fund's investment strategy:

1. Choose scalable organizations. The fund would seek out social en-trepreneurs who had proven track records and were seeking to grow their organizations. Grants would be directed at organiza-tions whose basic model could be expanded to increase their social impact and lead to self-sufficiency.

2. Establish a performance-based design. Both NPI and the organiza-tions it supported would be made accountable by reference to mu-tually agreed-on benchmarks based on measurable performance criteria. NPI committed to competitive capital allocation, with fund dispersal dependent on organizations reaching their goals.

3. Encourage active lifecycle investing and monitoring. The fund would commit to large investments in each portfolio organization over a three- to five-year span. In addition to funding, NPI would provide technical assistance to help the organization become more effective and grow. NPI expected to take board seats on its portfo-lio organizations.

Kirsch felt that the Balanced Scorecard would be critical for imple-menting her performance-based philanthropy fund: "The Balanced Score-card will become our agreement with the portfolio organizations as to what will be measured to evaluate performance. We will have a firm agreement and will be able to say that if you're not on this page, you are on the wrong page."[14]

Kelly Fitzsimmons, Kirsch's general partner, reinforced the centrality of the scorecard for NPI: "The scorecard will align all our stakeholders for creating social innovation and social returns. That means the boards, investors, fund managers, foundations, and social entrepreneurs can bring all their resources to bear in the right ways to strategic applications."[15]

The NPI project team, like the UWSENE, retained the financial perspective as its high-level objective: raise adequate capital and operating funds and use them in an efficient and sustainable manner. For the customer perspective, the team identified the investors in the fund as the primary customers. Thus the customer perspective would feature investor satisfaction as an important outcome measure.

Like the UWSENE debate about the role of agencies on their scorecard, the NPI team debated whether portfolio organizations were customers or part of the internal business processes that needed to be managed. After several iterations, the team finally decided that portfolio organizations warranted their own perspective because they were so critical to the success of NPI. The success of the portfolio organizations was central for investor satisfaction. Extending this principle, the team proposed that the scorecards from each portfolio organization should include a perspective to represent its contribution to NPI's strategic objectives. The scorecard approved for initial use at NPI is shown in Figure 5-7.

Kirsch also asked NPI's initial four portfolio organizations to develop their own Balanced Scorecards. These scorecards would have to demonstrate how the portfolio organizations contributed to NPI's mission for growth, scalability, and social impact.[16]

Beyond its role in managing internal operations and relationships with portfolio organizations, the Balanced Scorecard was used as the primary communication tool with NPI's board of directors and donors. One board member commented:

The BSC allows the board to be up-dated in a brisk way about what is happening across the organization, factoring in a breadth of issues ranging from those of the balance sheet to the softer aspects involving people and their knowledge. It gives us board members a framework so that discussions don't become monolithically focussed on how much money was raised.[17]

For potential investors, Kirsch used the Balanced Scorecard of NPI and its portfolio organizations to illustrate a highly attractive product-leadership value proposition. NPI would offer a unique (for the nonprofit sector) performance management system, along with active fund managers

Figure 5-7 New Profit's Balanced Scorecard

Mission: *New Profit, Inc., is a nonprofit venture philanthropy firm. Our goal is to affect large-scale social change by applying venture capital practices to philanthropy.*

Perspective	Strategic Objectives	Targets
Financial	**Fund Capitalization**—secure $5m in fund commitments **Operating Revenues**—secure $500k in operating funds from foundations and friends **Sustainability**—manage cash flow to maintain an operating surplus **Efficiency**—maintain ratio of 1:4 staff $/pro bono $	▪ Raise $4.5m ▪ Maintain operating cash flow with three-month surplus
Investor	**Build Investor Community**—engage them in key aspects of NPI network **Investor Satisfaction**—use satisfaction survey and interviews **Focused Investor Strategy**—develop investor segmentation	▪ Close three founding and three lead investors ▪ Achieve 80% satisfaction
Performance of Portfolio Organization	**Growth**—set specific growth targets with portfolio organizations **Social Impact**—increase the scope of portfolio organization's social impact **Balanced Scorecard Performance**—implement first scorecards for each portfolio organization **Satisfaction with Fund Services**—satisfaction from portfolio organizations regarding NPI and Monitor resources **Best Practices**—share best practices across portfolio organizations	▪ Create four scorecards with specific targets ▪ 80% performance for portfolio organizations ▪ Targeted number of shared learning and collaboration events
Internal Business Processes	**Portfolio Management**—implement performance management system **Define Leadership Position**—establish collaborative relationships with intellectual partners, establish best practices for performance, become policy spokesperson on philanthropic issues **Board and Governance**—expand and develop national board and develop academic board **Satisfaction with Fund Services**—satisfaction from portfolio organizations regarding NPI and Monitor resources **Plan NPI Institute**—plan for institute	▪ Finalize process with portfolio organizations ▪ Meet targets for press hits and invitations to speak ▪ Secure relationships with 100% of potential intellectual partners
Learning and Growth	**Fill Strategic Positions**—design strategy for attracting and retaining talented staff **Technology**—identify technology needs and plan for procurement **Knowledge Management**—develop system for improvement and learning related to key processes **Alignment**—open lines of communication exist between NPI investors and portfolio organizations	▪ Fill 100% of necessry strategic positions ▪ Finalize HR strategies for attracting and retaining staff

Source: Adapted from R. S. Kaplan, "New Profit Inc.: Governing the Nonprofit Enterprise," 100-052 (Boston: Harvard Business School, 1999), 15.

who would search out the best opportunities for investing and would work with the portfolio organizations to improve performance against stated objectives. An early investor enthusiastically endorsed the concept, made a significant financial commitment, and promised to give more based on performance: "Do well and you will get more."[18]

HEALTH CARE SECTOR

The complexities of developing and implementing strategy in health care institutions are quite obvious. To date, two of the scorecard's best strategic applications to health care have been instituted at Duke Children's Hospital in Durham, North Carolina, and Montefiore Hospital in the Bronx, New York.

Duke Children's Hospital

We reported in Chapter 1 on the successful results from the Duke Children's Hospital (DCH) program. Dr. Jon Meliones, head of Pediatrics Intensive Care Unit, launched that project after identifying several burning platform issues:[19]

- The organization was confused about which services were the most important to provide.
- There was no shared purpose among administration, staff, and physicians.
- The communication and coordination with referring pediatricians was poor.
- There were competitive threats to the organization's market position.
- The organization had great difficulty in balancing quality care, patient satisfaction, staff satisfaction, and education and research with its financial objectives.

First, DCH's leadership team developed mission and vision statements. This involved self-examination of institutional goals so as to ensure compatibility with the entire Duke Medical Center, benchmarking against national data, and defining centers of excellence based on existing strengths and projected needs. The vision became, "to provide patients, families, and primary care physicians with the best, most compassionate care possible, and excel at communication." The strategy hypothesized that with better communication and care, referrals and revenues would increase. In addition, the strategy wanted to reduce costs and length of stay to restore financial viability.

A multidisciplinary team at an executive workshop reviewed the mission, vision, and strategy and started to develop the scorecard for the strategy. After iterations, interactions, and active communication, the team reached consensus on the first scorecard (see Figure 5-8).

The team renamed the learning and growth perspective to research, education, and teaching, as this mission was so central for a health care unit in an academic medical center. The objective in this perspective was to involve the staff in the change process and to advance the field of children's care.

Once the scorecard had been communicated and accepted, the hard work began: how to make it happen. Employees generated many ideas to improve customer satisfaction. Meliones defined a two-dimensional grid to screen the initiatives: Effort involved (time and money) and potential impact on customer satisfaction. Only initiatives that could be of high impact were considered further; of these, DCH first assessed the low-cost ones and then the higher-cost ones. Soon people only generated ideas likely to be of high impact and, mostly, of low cost.

A whole range of new processes were implemented: care providers held a discussion each day about every patient to be discharged that day, the family was educated about treatments before a patient was released, and the primary care physician was informed about in-patient treatment and recommended treatment after discharge. Physicians received their monthly cost/case statistics and patient and referring physician satisfaction scores, benchmarked against the total physician population. They could now compare themselves against their colleagues and peers and search for ways to improve.

As described in Chapter 1, within three years and with an increase in case mix complexity, DCH's cost per case and average length of stay dropped by 25 percent, and satisfaction and loyalty increased among the hospital's customers—patients and physicians.

Montefiore Hospital

Montefiore Hospital, with an annual budget over $1 billion, is the university hospital for the Albert Einstein College of Medicine. It consists of two

Figure 5-8   Duke Children's Hospital's Balanced Scorecard

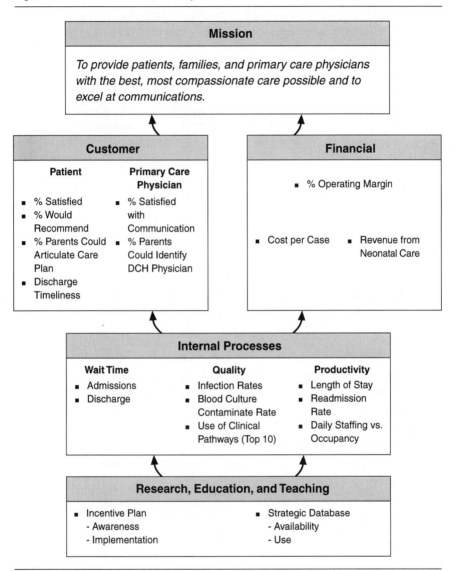

large Bronx, New York–based hospitals, a network of twenty-six primary care satellites, a large specialty-focused faculty practice, and 400,000 Home Care visits.

Montefiore's two hospitals, four miles apart, operated as separate divisions for over thirty years but were merged into a single operating division in 1996. The medical center faced the challenge of delivering health care to largely Hispanic, African American, and elderly people in the Bronx who had high rates of poverty and disease, while also striving to be a leader in education and research.

Appointed senior vice president responsible for the newly consolidated Acute Care Division in 1996, Elaine Brennan inherited an organization built around functional silos—hospital operations, clinical, and academic—and had no real authority. She participated in a planning process at the medical center to formulate a new strategy for Montefiore, GRIP:

Grow: volume and market share

Rebalance: academic and clinical staff

Infrastructure: information systems, state-of-the-art technology

Performance: setting targets and achieving them

The growth theme reflected two simple strategies:

1. Be "all things to some people," to develop a population-based approach focused on providing a full spectrum of health care services to specific populations (children, women, and seniors).

2. Be "some things to all people," to develop specialty centers to attract patients from outside the Bronx and maternal/child services to attract patients from lower Westchester County (adjacent to the Bronx).

The challenge was how to realign the bureaucratic, fragmented organization so that two formerly distinct and competitive hospital systems could pull together to implement the strategy.

Brennan decentralized the organization. She formed five clinical care centers, each of which would focus on the needs of a particular patient population, and three support centers. For example, the Heart Care Center would provide all cardiac-related services. Each care center was multidisciplinary, bringing together nursing, physician, and managerial personnel into a single organization. The care center would have control over a majority of services delivered to its inpatient and ambulatory customers and be jointly run by an executive-level manager, physician, and nurse. It would be responsible for outcomes along a variety of dimensions: revenue, cost, quality, service, work environment, employees. Brennan, of course, faced the problem of how to measure performance for the new care center organization. With Montefiore's existing system, 90 percent of the hospital's measurements were financial.

Brennan and her management team worked from October 1998 to June 1999 to define the architecture and content of a Balanced Scorecard management system using a nation-state-city metaphor. In this model, the nation would be the Montefiore's Acute Care Division; the states would be each of the eight care centers, and the cities would be individual services (cost centers). The group worked initially to build the Balanced Scorecard for the nation, and then moved into their care centers, based on the experience and the high-level strategic themes, to develop scorecards for their states and cities.

Figure 5-9 shows a simplified version of Montefiore's initial Balanced Scorecard. Like the one used at Duke Children's Hospital, it focused on patient satisfaction and clinical and administrative processes designed to produce benefits for patients. Most of the measures seem operational, designed to focus people's attention on improving processes for dealing with and treating patients and improving cost, quality, and timeliness. The strategic measures that were used to position Montefiore for the future are in the innovation and growth perspective. The volume and market share measures would reflect the "G" in the GRIP strategy to increase penetration in its immediate capture area, the Bronx, and to attract customers from neighboring areas—northern Manhattan and southern Westchester County—through its specialty centers and patient-oriented care centers. The measure on equipment's average life was a proxy that came from a market survey indicating that state-of-the-art equipment and innovation contributed to a referring physician's hospital choice. The percentage of revenue from new programs and the number of referring physicians reflected the success of the strategy to expand reach, penetration, and lines of service.

At the time of writing, while early signs are favorable, it is too soon to draw conclusions. Program growth has occurred in the Heart Care Center; the capacity to serve and the number of cases have increased; new alliances and joint ventures are being formed to implement the strategy; and recruitment efforts for physician and staff have been successful. Perhaps the most significant early success indicator has been the enthusiasm of the staff, both clinical and managerial, to the new organization, the clarity of the strategic objectives, and the new measurement and management system that fosters local decision-making and accountability. Brennan reflected on

Figure 5-9   Montefiore Hospital's Balanced Scorecard

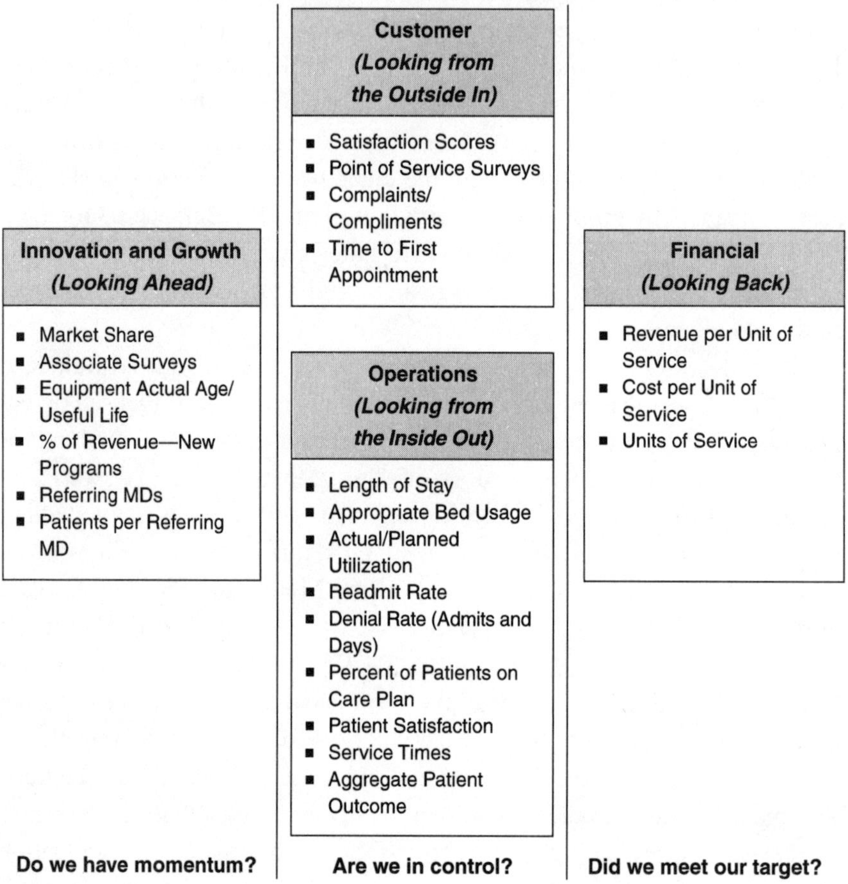

Customer
(Looking from the Outside In)

- Satisfaction Scores
- Point of Service Surveys
- Complaints/Compliments
- Time to First Appointment

Innovation and Growth
(Looking Ahead)

- Market Share
- Associate Surveys
- Equipment Actual Age/Useful Life
- % of Revenue—New Programs
- Referring MDs
- Patients per Referring MD

Financial
(Looking Back)

- Revenue per Unit of Service
- Cost per Unit of Service
- Units of Service

Operations
(Looking from the Inside Out)

- Length of Stay
- Appropriate Bed Usage
- Actual/Planned Utilization
- Readmit Rate
- Denial Rate (Admits and Days)
- Percent of Patients on Care Plan
- Patient Satisfaction
- Service Times
- Aggregate Patient Outcome

Do we have momentum?   **Are we in control?**   **Did we meet our target?**

the changes she helped to launch: "If you teach a bear to dance, be prepared to keep dancing until the bear wants to stop."

It is interesting to compare Brennan's experience at Montefiore with the experiences of McCool and Baker at Mobil. Montefiore and Mobil were both large, highly functional, centralized, and financially troubled entities that had lost touch with their customers. Both launched new strategies to become more efficient, to be more customer-focused, and to grow through increased market share and new products and services. The leaders implemented a massive reorganization, replacing the functional organization with decentralized, customer-focused units. The challenge was to take the leaders of the new decentralized units, whose professional careers had been within a narrow, functional organization, and give them a general management perspective and new management tools.

The Balanced Scorecard provided a mechanism for the new unit heads to participate in the initial high-level discussion to make the division/nation-level strategy explicit and show their commitment to the strategy. Both entities subsequently used the Balanced Scorecard as a mechanism to communicate and implement the strategy within the decentralized units. Mobil and Montefiore deployed the strategy by having each decentralized unit build its own Balanced Scorecard based on the high-level objectives established on the division/nation-level scorecard.

SUMMARY

The fundamental principles to create a Strategy-Focused Organization are applicable across all sectors. In addition to the private sector applications described in Chapters 3 and 4, this chapter has shown how organizations in national and local governments and a variety of nonprofit and health care organizations have deployed the scorecard effectively and gained benefits from it. The principal difference in these sectors has been a more careful consideration of customers. Customers become elevated to the top of the Balanced Scorecard strategy maps as, ultimately, effective delivery of services to customers explains the existence of most government and nonprofit organizations. Also, the financial perspective may be portrayed at the top of strategy maps, concomitant with the customer perspective, to signal the importance of satisfying the donors and citizens who provide funding for the services that the organization delivers. Once these modifications have been made, managers in government and nonprofit organizations have used the scorecard to gain agreement on the strategy and then align the organization to deliver it effectively, much like their private sector counterparts.

NOTES

1. This framework was developed collaboratively with Professor Dutch Leonard of Harvard's Kennedy School of Government.
2. The Charlotte story is described in more detail in R. S. Kaplan, "City of Charlotte (A)," 9-199-036 (Boston: Harvard Business School, 1998).
3. Two obvious choices, education and social services, were under the jurisdiction of the county government, not the city. Hence they were not on the list.

4. Originally the city had twenty-one objectives. Over time, one internal objective was dropped and another was consolidated into the financial perspective.
5. Kaplan, "City of Charlotte (A)," 4.
6. *Balancing Measures: Best Practices in Performance Management* (Washington, DC: National Partnership for Reinventing Government, August 1999), 6 (publication available at http://www.npr.gov/library/papers/bkgrd/balmeasure.html).
7. Robert S. Kaplan and David P. Norton, *The Balanced Scorecard: Translating Strategy into Action* (Boston: Harvard Business School Press, 1996), 181–82.
8. We don't have space to document all the interesting scorecard applications occurring in government agencies around the world. One application in an enforcement agency has been implemented by the Swedish National Police Board.
9. The UWSENE operates in Rhode Island and adjacent communities in Connecticut and Massachusetts. The UWSENE story is described in more detail in R. Kaplan and E. Kaplan, "United Way of Southeastern New England," 9-197-036 (Boston: Harvard Business School, 1996).
10. Ibid., 4.
11. Ibid., 8.
12. Ibid., 7–8.
13. R. Kaplan and J. Elias, "New Profit, Inc.," 100-052 (Boston: Harvard Business School, 1999).
14. Ibid., 8.
15. Ibid., 8–9.
16. Details on one organization, Jumpstart, can be found in Kaplan and Elias, "New Profit, Inc."
17. Ibid., 10–11.
18. Ibid., 11.
19. Material taken from J. Meliones et al., "A Three-Year Experience Using a Balanced Scorecard to Practice Smarter" (Durham, NC: Duke Children's Hospital, 1999).

Aligning the Organization to Create Synergies

The Balanced Scorecard provides a powerful framework for business units to describe and implement their strategies. A Strategy-Focused Organization, however, requires more than having each business unit using its own Balanced Scorecard to manage a great strategy. Most organizations consist of many different business units as well as shared service (or support) units. For maximum effectiveness, the strategies and the scorecards of all such units should be aligned and linked with one another. The linkages across the scorecards establish the theory of managing shared service units and decentralized business units within a single corporate entity. We refer to these linkages as the "strategic architecture" of the organization. They describe how the organization creates synergies by integrating the activities of otherwise segregated and independent units.

CORPORATE-LEVEL STRATEGY

The strategic architecture starts with a clear definition of the corporate role. The corporation—or division, sector, or group—exists to create synergies among its component business and support units. If the corporation cannot create synergies across its component parts, then investors will wonder why the business units shouldn't be spun off, to operate independently without the cost and bureaucratic overhead of an unproductive corporate office.

Scholars have established a rich history explaining the existence and growth of complex business organizations. Alfred Chandler described how corporations in the United States, Germany, and Japan gained competitive advantage in the twentieth century by leveraging synergies across related business units.[1] These units exploited scale advantages in product development, manufacturing, and marketing and customer relationships to dominate smaller, more focused companies.

More recently, Goold, Alexander, and Campbell articulated a compelling theory of how multibusiness companies gain corporate advantage by influencing—called "parenting"—the businesses they own and control.[2] Successful companies create more value through their "parenting advantage" than do rivals owning the same set of businesses. The essence of the parenting advantage arises from a fit between the capabilities of the corporate parent and the critical success factors for the individual business units. The parenting advantage can come from different sources. Among these are managing and exploiting common capabilities, operations, customers, technology, core competencies, or external relationships (with governments, unions, lenders, or suppliers) among the business units. The parenting advantage could also arise from the ability of the corporate parent to implement effective management systems for certain types of companies (innovative startups that must excel at market identification and product development, or mature commodity-type companies that must be leaders in continual cost reduction). A third source arises from the parent's ability to allocate capital and people across the business units.

In a related stream of research, Collis and Montgomery describe a resource-based view for corporate-level strategy:[3]

> *An outstanding corporate strategy is not a random collection of individual building blocks but a carefully constructed system of interdependent parts. . . . [I]n a great corporate strategy, all of the elements [resources, businesses, and organization] are aligned with one another. That alignment is driven by the nature of the firm's resources – its special assets, skills and capabilities.[4]*

The parenting advantages described by Goold, Alexander, and Campbell and the resource alignment described by Collis and Montgomery can be implemented through Balanced Scorecard linkages. The corporate role or critical resources should be articulated in a corporate-level scorecard. The corporate role can be translated into a set of priorities and a scorecard that is communicated to the rest of the organization. For example, Figure II-1 illustrates the corporate scorecard for a fashion retailer. The company used the scorecard as a template to define the priorities shared by each business and support unit.

The financial component of the corporate strategy in Figure II-1 stresses aggressive growth targets for each strategic business unit that will dramatically raise shareholder value. In the customer perspective, the strategy clarifies marketing goals of *fashion leadership* and *brand dominance* that will project a consistent corporate image across its business units. The corporate strategy identifies opportunities to create economies of scale in corporate staff groups, such as *real estate* and *purchasing*, that will support the strategies and plans of each SBU. Finally, it defines the opportunity to share intellectual capital in the form of *key personnel* and *information systems*. In this company, each SBU subsequently developed its own strategy and its own scorecard, but these were guided by the corporate template. The synergies defined in the corporate scorecard created an organization in which the whole was greater than the sum of its parts.

While the need for a unifying linkage and alignment process may seem obvious and straightforward, many companies nevertheless fail to link their business and shared service units to divisional and corporate strategy. For example, an unsuccessful implementation of the Balanced Scorecard occurred in a large European bank that failed in this linkage process. This bank was an early Balanced Scorecard adopter, starting its process in 1994. We did not, however, feature this experience in Chapter 1 when describing companies' success stories with the Balanced Scorecard. By early 1998, the bank was experiencing declining profits. The bank's new strategy, around which its Balanced Scorecard had been built, was to offer innovative and sophisticated financial products and services to global customers (corporations) that could be accessed seamlessly from any location around the world. The strategy failed when the complex information technology required to implement this strategy was not deployed in a timely or effective fashion.

When questioned about the performance of the information services (IS) business unit, however, the CEO replied that this unit was performing very well according to its Balanced Scorecard. It turned out that when the directive from the top came to implement Balanced Scorecards in each busi-

Figure II-1 Link and Align the Organization around Its Strategy

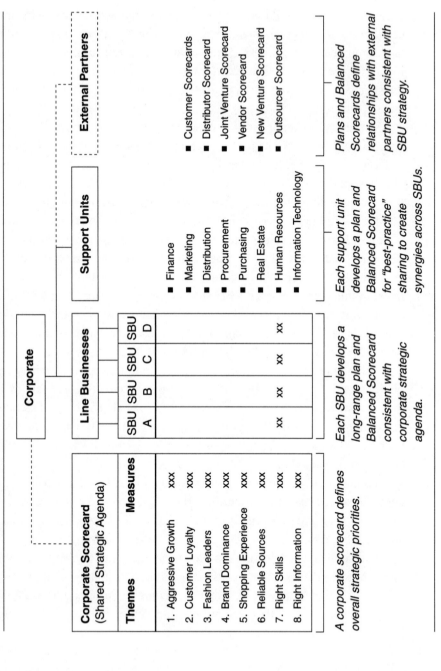

ness unit, the bank's IS unit went to what it perceived were the best, most admired IS units in the world. It benchmarked the performance of those IS units and adopted the metrics used by these "high-performing" information technology groups. According to these metrics, the bank's IS unit was now "world class," performing comparably to its top-tier benchmarked peer group. The IS unit, while performing well against externally determined metrics, had failed miserably to deliver the services that were vitally needed by a major business unit. Because of this lack of alignment, the business unit and the bank's strategy could not be implemented and eventually failed. The bank's experience is a classic lesson on the consequences from not aligning scorecards (and strategies) across the organization.

Synergies arise from excellent interactions among business units, and these potential interactions need to be explicitly recognized in the strategies—and the scorecards—of the individual units. We describe, in the next two chapters, how the Balanced Scorecard helps organizations to link effective corporate-level strategies to their business units and shared services.

NOTES

1. A. D. Chandler, *Scale and Scope: The Dynamics of Industrial Capitalism* (Cambridge, MA: Belknap Press, 1990); *Strategy and Structure: Chapters in the History of the Industrial Enterprise,* rpt. ed. (Cambridge, MA: MIT Press, 1982); *The Visible Hand: The Managerial Revolution in American Business* (Cambridge, MA.: Belknap Press, 1977).
2. M. Goold, A. Campbell, and M. Alexander, *Corporate-Level Strategy: Creating Value in the Multibusiness Company* (New York: John Wiley & Sons, 1994), and A. Campbell, M. Goold, and M. Alexander, "Corporate Strategy: The Quest for Parenting Advantage," *Harvard Business Review* (March–April 1995): 120–32.
3. D. Collis and C. Montgomery, "Competing on Resources: Strategy in the 1990s," *Harvard Business Review* (July–August 1995): 118–28, and "Creating Corporate Advantage," *Harvard Business Review* (May–June 1998): 70–83.
4. Collis and Montgomery, "Creating Corporate Advantage," 72.

Creating Business Unit Synergy

CORPORATIONS CONSIST OF A COLLECTION of divisions and business units that may compete in different industries, have different customers, and employ different strategies. Executives in the corporate office must determine how they add value to their collection of business units so that the whole is greater than the sum of its parts. The Balanced Scorecard provides a framework for clarifying the value created by the corporate headquarters, as the synergies generally can come from any of the four perspectives on the Balanced Scorecard. Figure 6-1 shows a spectrum of corporate synergies that we have observed in practice.

A conglomerate, such as FMC Corporation, creates few synergies across its diverse business units. The corporate role is primarily financial, creating synergy by operating an efficient internal capital market. FMC exploits the private information it has about the units' market opportunities, technologies, processes, and competencies to allocate capital to its most productive use. A corporate scorecard for FMC would stress cash flow, working capital efficiency, return on capital (or shareholder value metrics), and productivity of capital investments.

Organizations, such as the consumer banking groups of Citigroup, Inc., and Chase Manhattan Corporation, create synergies by providing customers with one-stop shopping for a broad set of financial products and

Figure 6-1 Spectrum of Corporate Synergies

Financial Perspective	Customer Perspective	Internal Process Perspective	Learning and Growth Perspective
Optimize Capital Allocation (Shareholder Value) **Balance Growth with Risk** (Risk-Adjusted ROI)	**Promote Cross-Selling** (Share of Account) **Create Customer Focus** (Customer Satisfaction and Retention)	**Shared Process Optimization** ■ Real Estate ■ Purchasing ■ Shelf Space **Economies of Scale** ■ Distribution ■ Manufacturing **Value Chain Integration** (Cost per Unit) (Share of Market)	**Best-Practice Sharing** **Core Competency Development**

services—credit cards, checking and savings accounts, mortgages, personal loans, brokerage, and investments. Each product or service is delivered by a different strategic business unit. Johnson & Johnson consists of more than 150 companies worldwide, all operating in the health and personal care field. Many of these operating companies share common customers—hospitals, health care delivery organizations, physicians, pharmacies, supermarkets, and general retailers—that deliver or sell health care products and services to consumers. For such broad suppliers of financial or health care products and services, each SBU benefits from the entire customer base of the organization. The corporate role should create synergies through the sharing of customers across SBUs, and its scorecard should emphasize themes such as share of customers' wallet, cross selling, and integrated products and services.

Many organizations share common *business processes* and require a corporate role to ensure their most effective use. Take the case of The Limited, an apparel retailer whose eight retail divisions include Victoria's Secret, Express, and Abercrombie & Fitch, each with its own targeted customer group and chain of retail stores. The company's real estate division, which acquires and manages retail properties, provides a single organization with deep expertise in its field that can be deployed to the benefit of each of the eight retail divisions. Also, The Limited has one division that manages the relationships with factories in low-labor-cost parts of the world that supply products for all eight retail divisions. It is both more effective and more efficient to concentrate the expertise in a single shared services division (a real estate division, a worldwide supply organization) than to have each of the eight operating companies develop its own capabilities in a critical area.

Many companies, particularly consumer goods companies, may have a single distribution division that supports multiple product and brand divisions. Customers—retailers and wholesalers—typically prefer to deal with a single organization for supply rather than have to negotiate directly with as many product divisions as the company has chosen for its internal organization. In this case, having the distribution function handled by a single shared service group enhances customer service and satisfaction.

Procurement is also often a shared business process. By aggregating the demands from diverse product and operating divisions, the company can enjoy the benefits of discounted prices and special supplier attention because of its purchasing volumes. A central procurement function also can invest in deeper and more specialized knowledge about the critical materials, components, and supplier performance than could separate purchasing units in each business unit.

Some company SBUs share common technologies and knowledge. Honda Motor Co., Inc., for example, uses its superb capabilities in engine design and manufacture to produce superior products in different market segments: motorcycles, automobiles, power lawnmowers, and power generators. NEC Corporation used capabilities in microelectronics and miniaturization to become a leader in televisions, computers, and telecommunications.[1]

The corporate scorecard should articulate the theory of the corporation, the rationale for having several SBUs operating within the corporate structure, rather than having each SBU operating as an independent entity, with its own governance structure and independent source of financing. A corporate scorecard can clarify two elements of a corporate-level strategy:

1. Corporate themes: values, beliefs, and ideas that reflect the corporate identity and must be shared by all SBUs (e.g., safety at Dupont or innovation at 3M Corporation)

2. Corporate role: actions mandated at the corporate level that create synergies at the SBU level (e.g., cross selling to customers across SBUs, sharing common technologies, or providing a central business process)

The following case studies illustrate some applications of these ideas.

FMC CORPORATION: MANAGING SHAREHOLDER VALUE

While we advocate that the Balanced Scorecard be driven from corporate strategy, often a formal corporate strategy does not exist. In a conglomerate (unrelated diversification) form of organization, the corporate office creates value by its ability to manage capital and people across its diverse business units, not by creating synergies and integration among them.

One of the first implementations of the Balanced Scorecard started at FMC Corporation in 1992. FMC was a collection of more than two dozen operating companies in diverse lines of business, including agricultural chemicals, industrial chemicals, food machinery, airport equipment, defense, gold, and lithium. Because the corporation generated its synergies through financial and people policies (not through customers or operating synergies), FMC did not build a corporate scorecard. Rather, the corporate office established a corporate theme that each operating company had to formulate a growth strategy that would then be expressed in its own Balanced Scorecard. The corporate executives would then monitor the performance of each company against its scorecard.

Some people wonder about the confusion from having different measures across divisions and operating companies. They search for a common set of measures that all divisions could use so that they can have a common reporting format. But we believe that FMC took exactly the right approach. With diverse operating units and diverse strategies, FMC would have been wrong to impose a standard reporting framework on its operating companies. The customized scorecards enabled senior FMC executives to focus their monitoring and reviews on the particular strategies being deployed by their companies, not on checking their companies' adherence to corporate-mandated indicators that may not have been central to their strategy. An FMC senior manager noted:

We have three businesses, three different processes, all of which could have elaborate systems for measuring quality, cost, and time but would feel the impact of improvements in radically different ways. With all the diversity in our business units, senior management really can't have a detailed understanding of the relative impact of time and quality improvements on each unit.[2]

The scorecard gave corporate executives a new and powerful parenting tool for managing the operating companies. Before, as long as the operating company presidents delivered excellent financial performance, no one questioned their strategy very closely. Now financial performance alone was not sufficient; the company presidents had to deliver against their Balanced Scorecard strategic objectives and measures.

FMC executives also felt that they now had ownership of the operating companies' strategies. Company presidents could not switch strategies without extensive dialogues with the corporate executive team. And when new company presidents were appointed, they were expected to continue the strategy already authorized. The company presidents could adapt the existing strategy, but then they had to propose a modified Balanced Scorecard measurement and accountability system for the new strategy and convince the corporate team of the desirability of switching to the new strategy.

FMC has continued to use the Balanced Scorecard with its operating companies. The general managers of about one-third of the companies felt it was not the right tool for them, and they were allowed to drop the scorecard for performance reporting to corporate. The remaining two-thirds of the companies have continued to use it aggressively to link their strategy to operations.

In 1998, FMC conducted a benchmarking study of the characteristics of best-performing NYSE corporations. The results from this study led (in mid-1999) to FMC's first "corporate-level" scorecard. The corporate scorecard (see Figure 6-2) contained measures in the financial, internal, and learning and growth perspectives. Apparently the relevant customer measures varied sufficiently across FMC's diverse operating units so that corporate-level reporting on customers could not be standardized. The corporate scorecard did not provide details on corporate strategy. It focused on the corporate responsibility to shareholders (creating shareholder value through the wise use of capital and the management of operating results) and on two simple process themes—safety and human resources development—to be implemented by all operating companies. The corporate

Figure 6-2 FMC's Corporate Scorecard for 1999

Financial **Perspective**	■ Return on Investment ■ Working Capital Efficiency ■ Cash Flow from Operations ■ EPS Growth and Predictability ■ # of Analysts Following Company ■ # of Acquisitions and Divestitures ■ Investment Level
Internal **Perspective**	■ Worker Safety ■ Process Safety
Learning and Growth **Perspective**	■ Employee Turnover ■ College Recruiting Success ■ Performance Appraisals Completed

scorecard communicated the high-level measures that FMC would use to assess its performance and, therefore, that the operating companies should be cognizant of when managing their own operations.

In summary, at FMC, a diversified holding company, the Balanced Scorecard served as a linkage mechanism between corporate and the operating companies to ensure better communication and accountability, and ultimately better judgments, about the strategies and performance of individual operating companies.

MOBIL NORTH AMERICA MARKETING AND REFINING: MANAGING CUSTOMERS ACROSS REGIONS

At Mobil, the first Balanced Scorecard was developed in the North America Marketing and Refining (NAM&R) Division. As we presented in Chapter 2, this Balanced Scorecard described a strategy to succeed with three targeted customer segments—Road Warriors, True Blues, and Generation F3—and to create win-win relationships with its dealers. The strategy required Mobil's dealer-operated stations to deliver a "fast, friendly serve" buying experience to attract consumers in the three targeted segments, even when gasoline was sold at a per-gallon price $0.06 to $0.08 higher than that offered at nearby, discounted gasoline stations. Mobil stations would need to be large, with sufficient space to contain a great convenience store as well as many gasoline pumps so that consumers would not have to wait in line to obtain gasoline. Each pump would have a credit card reader so that consumers in a hurry would not have to wait in line to pay.

Mobil NAM&R did not launch its Balanced Scorecard project by asking its eighteen geographical business units—such as New England, the Midwest, Florida, Texas, and California—that were actually closest to the customer to construct scorecards for their regions. Consider the problems that might have arisen if each regional business unit developed a strategy based on its local characteristics. The New England region, containing its legendary thrifty people, might want to focus on the Price Shopper segment. Texas, with its vast expanse, could opt for the Road Warriors. And California, with its youth-oriented culture in Hollywood and the Silicon Valley, could emphasize Generation F3. Such an outcome, however, would be chaotic. Mobil would mean something different in each local market. Consumers accustomed to seeing low prices in New England might be shocked to encounter premium prices in another market. And loyal customers from the Midwest, expecting Mobil stations with a dozen gasoline pumps and an extensive convenience store, would be disappointed when buying gasoline in New England, with long lines for a single set of pumps and no convenience store. Mobil would also encounter difficulties with a national dealer organization as it attempted to explain the different value propositions desired in different states. Having a common strategy for the entire country enabled a consistent message to be delivered to consumers and dealers throughout the United States. The Balanced Scorecard at the division level articulated the common strategy that each Mobil station, each buying experience, would deliver.

In addition to the common message for the customer perspective, Mobil NAM&R wanted common themes in each region for the internal business process perspective. In its primary operations—refining, storage, and distribution—Mobil wanted each region to emphasize the following:

- Low cost
- On specification, on time
- Environmentally friendly, healthy, and safe operations
- Effective asset utilization

While the strategy was articulated at the national level, NAM&R allowed each regional business unit to formulate its own Balanced Scorecard, as long as it delivered the high-level divisional themes. Each of NAM&R's geographical business units was asked to develop its own Balanced Score-card.[3] These scorecards were to be customized to local circumstances—competitors, market opportunities, and critical processes—based on the high-level divisional scorecard. Ed Lewis, the project leader at NAM&R, described the philosophy: "We used the [NAM&R] scorecard as a guiding light, but that's all it was, a light. When [a business unit] developed a score-card, it was their scorecard and they would live by it."[4]

In general, it is not critical or even desirable for all measures on the lower-level scorecards to add up to measures on the high-level scorecard. We have found it preferable for the lower-level unit to have the discretion to customize the measures to their own circumstance, rather than receive a drill-down component from a higher-level scorecard. The local units should feel empowered to choose appropriate measures that can influence higher-level objectives, not have to use measures that can add up to a divi-sion or corporate-level measure. As described in Chapter 2, Mobil's New England region developed its own strategies and measures to build win-win dealer relationships, and its dealer measures differed from those used in other business units.

BROWN & ROOT ENERGY SERVICES: INTEGRATING THE VALUE CHAIN

Many organizations have business units that operate at different points along their customers' value chain. The interfaces between the units that make up the value chain are generally filled with inefficiencies. Each busi-ness unit builds its own buffers, has its own systems and standards, and may follow different strategies (operational excellence, product leadership, or customer intimacy). A company can create significant strategic advan-tage by better integrating its business units along the value chain. Such in-tegration, however, typically cannot happen without active corporate intervention.

The Brown & Root Energy Services Division of the Halliburton Com-pany used the Balanced Scorecard to implement a value-chain integra-tion strategy across its six previously independent companies. These companies each supplied a different service for marine construction: en-gineering, purchasing, fabrication, installation, operations, and logistics and service (see Figure 6-3). Rockwater, a company we discussed briefly in Chapter 1, was the subsea-installation company in this division. Cus-

Figure 6-3 Brown & Root Energy Services

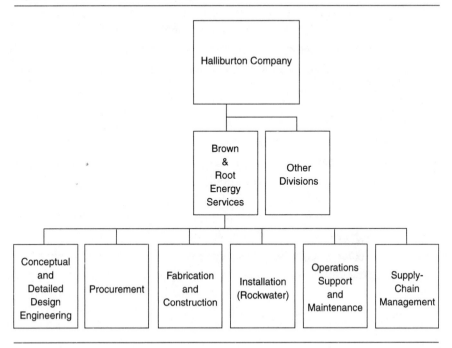

tomers, typically large oil and gas companies, contracted individually with each operating company to perform a particular function. While most of the operating companies had many customers in common, neither the customer nor the Brown & Root companies had attempted to gain benefits from such relationships.

When Norm Chambers, Rockwater's president, was promoted to become head of the Energy Services Division, he noted the inefficiencies, duplications, and confusion that existed at the interfaces of the Brown & Root companies. Each company was paid for the inputs it provided to customers: a ton of fabricated steel pipe, a man-hour of engineering. Such work was subject to fairly intense price competition.

Chambers and his senior management team believed that by combining efforts, the Brown & Root Energy Services Division could provide a unified and integrated—even turnkey—service. Chambers wanted Brown & Root to supply solutions and be paid for the outputs it produced, not the inputs it supplied. In its most complete form, Brown & Root could design the structure (such as a drilling rig), produce the critical parts for the structure, install the parts, operate the structure, and service the structure; it would offer, in effect, a cradle-to-grave service for the customer. If all of the business were of this turnkey type, then the rationale for having six independent companies would not be compelling. But much business, at least in the short run, would still be individual operating company bidding to perform a specific piece of work.

Chambers wanted the six companies to learn to work together so that they could offer a better integrated service for key customers, who could then be persuaded to outsource major parts of their noncore business. In effect, the new strategy would shift Energy Services from being a low-cost supplier to being the supplier that could best lower its customers' costs. With front-end investments of $1 billion to $2 billion required to bring a new undersea field into production, savings to the customer from a lower-cost integrated strategy could be substantial.

Brown & Root Energy Services expressed its strategic intent for more integrated strategies at the operating-company level by including, in the division-level scorecard, a strategic theme for integrated service delivery (see Figure 6-4). The financial perspective for this theme identified a new

Figure 6-4   Brown & Root Energy Services' Balanced Scorecard

Perspective	Objective	Measure
Financial	■ Increase Revenue from Integrated (Cross-Business) Services	■ % of Revenues from Integrated Projects
Customer	■ Build Strong Relationship ■ Lower Total Lifecycle Costs	■ Customer Satisfaction ■ Integrated Lifecycle Cost
Internal	■ Create New Market Opportunities	■ # of Contracts that Integrate Two or More Operating Companies
	■ Create New Service Opportunities	■ # of Integrated Services that Have Been Created
	■ Create Integrated Management Capabilities	■ Milestones in Achieving Specific Management Systems for Integrated Capability
	■ Become Low-Cost Producer	■ Product Cost vs. Benchmarked Target
Learning and Growth	■ Develop Incentives for Customer Teaming ■ Develop Culture of Systems Integrator	■ % of Projects with Customer Gain Sharing ■ Employee Survey on Awareness and Acceptance of New Cultural Values

objective: *increase revenue from services that involved multiple operating companies*. This objective communicated a goal of obtaining new business by providing integrated and turnkey services to customers.

The two objectives in the customer perspective were:

1. Build strong relationships with targeted companies that would be willing to allow Brown & Root to take on a broader scope of work.

2. Lower the lifecycle costs for customers who contracted with Brown & Root to offer integrated services across the value chain.

The second objective was measured by the lifecycle per barrel cost as a percentage of what independent companies, operating without collaboration, could achieve. This outcome measure reflected by how much the total cost curve could be lowered through its integrated operations. Brown & Root wanted to shift its mix of business away from being paid by the inputs it provided to customers (engineering and fabrication man hours, tons of steel fabricated) and toward producing outputs—lower costs—for its customer by becoming more focused on providing complete solutions. Internal and learning and growth objectives and measures were then defined that would enable the financial and customer objectives to be achieved. The cultural changes in the learning and growth perspective should not be underestimated. The engineers and the fabricators (construction people) had different backgrounds, spoke in different languages, and generally had very little communication between them. For Brown & Root to offer integrated solutions, cultural, national, and professional barriers would have to be broken down.

Each of Brown & Root's operating companies, when building their Balanced Scorecards, could now include objectives that reflected how they were contributing to the division-level theme for increases in integrated operations. The individual company scorecards signaled to organizational employees the importance of gaining new capabilities for integrated service delivery and measured the progress in winning the business and delivering cost-effective services in conjunction with the other Brown & Root companies.

In its first year of operating with the new, integrated service strategy, Brown & Root increased its revenues by 33 percent, and the total percentage of these revenues from integrated contracts rose from 11 percent to 30 percent. As one example of an early success from the new strategy, British Petroleum (BP) chose Brown & Root to manage an integrated team of seven different companies (four Brown & Root companies, three independent companies) to bring the new Andrew development field in the North Sea on-stream. Using the Balanced Scorecard as an integrating framework to align the objectives of all the alliance companies, Brown & Root succeeded in completing the new field development six months in advance of the twenty-five-month original schedule and $150 million under budget. As one example of the savings, the Brown & Root integrated team developed a creative approach for hookup of a new well in the Andrew field, a process that normally took about 90 days at a cost of $250,000 per day. With the new approach, the process was completed in 1.5 days. The total savings on the project were shared between BP and the alliance companies, with several of the companies receiving performance awards totaling 20 percent of the previous year's annual income.

CITY OF CHARLOTTE:
ALIGNING FUNCTIONAL DEPARTMENTS

Public sector organizations at the city, state, and federal level can also achieve integration and synergy across their diverse operating units. Once Charlotte, North Carolina, had developed its city-level scorecard (see discussion in Chapter 5), the city manager asked all operating units—such as police, fire, solid waste services, planning, community development, and transportation—to develop their own Balanced Scorecards. As at Mobil NAM&R, the operating unit scorecards reflected both the unit's operating performance and objectives and measures that linked to one or more of the city's five strategic themes. The process of building operating unit scorecards enabled the individual departments' objectives and strategy to contribute to the city's five strategic themes. As Deputy City Manager Del Borgsdorf observed:

> *Most cities are really just federations of operating units. The Balanced Scorecard became the vehicle to integrate across departments. It enabled us to ask, "What are you doing that either contributes to or subtracts from the 'strengthen neighborhoods' objective?" The scorecard enabled us to shift the city council agenda from departments and tactics to the five strategic themes.*[5]

The Charlotte Department of Transportation (CDOT) identified objectives in the four perspectives of the city's balanced scorecard that were most relevant for its operations (see Figure 6-5). In the customer perspec-

Figure 6-5 City of Charlotte's Scorecard

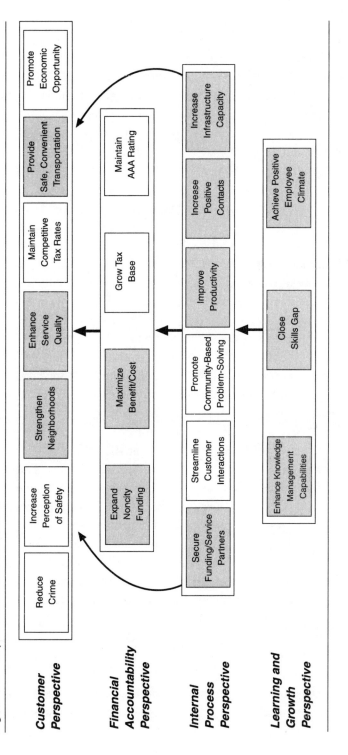

Corporate objectives affected by the Department of Transportation. This was based on the original Charlotte Scorecard.

tive, this naturally included "availability of safe, convenient transportation." The team also felt that "improve service quality" represented an important objective for their department. The team then expanded the city's transportation and service quality objectives to a departmental Balanced Scorecard. From this template, the team constructed lead and lag measures for the objectives in each perspective of the proposed CDOT Balanced Scorecard (see Figure 6-6). With this process, the CDOT developed a balanced set of lead and lag performance measures that were linked to higher-level city objectives and were consistent with the department's mission and strategy.[6]

The Police Department also developed its departmental-level Balanced Scorecard (see Figure 6-7).[7] The deputy chief for administrative services commented on the benefits from having a departmental Balanced Scorecard: "Before, each district had a long list of objectives and measures. People were just going through the motions to produce reports. The balanced scorecard is simpler and more meaningful. Our business plan connects to the scorecard measures. And the police officer in the street . . . will know more about the departmental objectives."[8]

The emphasis on some measures changed dramatically. The Police Department had historically been measured by the length of time taken to respond to emergency (911) calls. Surprisingly, their analysis revealed that rapid response time was relevant for less than 1 percent of the calls they received. Even when a crime had been committed, the criminal had usually left the premises, and victims were typically satisfied if the police arrived, as promised, within an hour, rather than within two minutes. The police also observed that there was no correlation between response time to a call and the crime rate. The Police Department, consistent with the total quality movement in the private sector, shifted its resource to preventing crimes rather than responding to defects (committed crimes) after they had occurred. The police chief commented that the department had been trying for several years to deemphasize response times as a performance measure but had been concerned about getting second-guessed by City Council. The Balanced Scorecard gave police the freedom to move away from the traditional response time measure and challenged them to find more meaningful measures, focused on community policing and long-term problem-solving.

The Police Department, however, felt that the crime rate would not be a reliable indicator by itself. With community policing, neighborhood police

Figure 6-6 City of Charlotte Department of Transportation's Balanced Scorecard

Perspective	Objective	Lead Measure	Lag Measure
Customer	C-1 Maintain the Transportation System	C-1 **Repair Response:** repair response action C-1 **Travel Speed:** average travel speed by facility and selected location	C-1 **High-Quality Streets:** condition of lane miles ≥90 rating
	C-2 Operate the Transportation System	C-2 **On-Time Buses:** public transit on time	C-2 **Safety:** citywide accident rate; # of high-accident locations
	C-3 Develop the Transportation System C-4 Determine the Optimal System Design	C-3 **Programs Introduced:** newly introduced programs, pilots, or program specifications	C-3 **Basic Mobility:** availability of transit C-4 **Plan Progress:** % complete on 2015 Transportation Plan
	C-5 Improve Service Quality	C-5 **Responsiveness:** % of citizen complaints and requests resolved at the CDOT level	C-5 **Commute Time:** average commute time on selected roads
	C-6 Strengthen Neighborhoods	C-6 **Issue Response:** defined situations where CDOT identifies, responds to neighborhood traffic and mobility issues	C-6 **Neighborhood-Oriented Programs:** programs implemented as a result of community-based problem-solving
Financial	F-1 Expand Noncity Funding		F-1 **Funding Leverage:** dollar value from noncity sources
	F-2 Maximize Benefit/Cost	F-2 **Costs:** costs compared with other municipalities and private sector competition	F-2 **New Funding Sources:** dollar value from sources not previously available
Internal Process	I-1 Gain Infrastructure Capacity	I-1 **Capital Investment:** $ allocated to capital projects in targeted areas	I-1 **Capacity Ratios:** incremental capacity build vs. required by 2015 Plan
	I-2 Secure Funding/Service Partners	I-2 **Leverage Funding/Service Partners:** new funding/resource partners identified	I-2 **# of Partners:** number of partners
	I-3 Improve Productivity	I-3 **Cost per Unit:** cost per unit I-3 **Competitive Sourcing:** % of budget bid I-3 **Problem Identification:** source and action	I-3 **Street Maintenance Cost:** cost/lane mile I-3 **Transit Passenger Cost:** cost/passenger
	I-4 Increase Positive Contacts with Community	I-4 **Customer Communications:** #, type, frequency	I-4 **Customer Surveys:** survey results concerning service quality
Learning and Growth	L-1 Enhance Automated Information Systems	L-1 **IT Infrastructure:** complete relational database across CDOT	L-1 **Information Access:** strategic information available vs. user requirements
	L-2 Enhance "Field" Technology		L-2 **Information Tools:** strategic tools available vs. user requirements
	L-3 Close the Skills Gap	L-3 **Skills Identified:** key skills identified in strategic functions	L-3 **Skills Transfer:** skill evidence in job
	L-4 Empower Employees	L-4 **Employee Climate Survey:** results of employee survey	L-4 **Employee Goal Alignment:** training/career development aligned with mission

Figure 6-7   Charlotte Police Department's Balanced Scorecard Objectives

Customer Perspective	▪ Decrease Crime Rate ▪ Improve Perception of Community Safety ▪ Respond Promptly to Citizen Phone Calls ▪ Improve Transportation Safety of City Streets
Financial Accountability Perspective	▪ Generate Funds from Noncity Sources
Internal Process Perspective	▪ Enhance Community-Based Problem-Solving ▪ Develop Partnerships with Public and Private Organizations ▪ Reengineer Police Patrol Services ▪ Improve Service in Animal Control Bureau ▪ Improve Police Officer Recruiting ▪ Develop Manpower Model for Community-Oriented Policing ▪ Strengthen Audit Process of Complaints about Police Misconduct
Learning and Growth Perspective	▪ Deploy Technology for Timely Information and Communication ▪ Increase Officer Skills for Community Problem-Oriented Policing ▪ Create Environment for Motivated and Empowered Employees to Be Responsive to Community Safety Objectives

would observe and report more crimes. Also, citizens would develop increased confidence that local police were responsive and skillful, leading to an increase in the number of crimes they reported to the police. Thus the number of crimes reported could increase even while the actual incidence of crimes was decreasing. Alternatively, the crime rate could be reduced by overzealous enforcement, leading some citizens to feel less safe because of aggressive police action.

The Police Department worked to develop a survey that would produce an index of the community's perception of safety. The police chief thought that this measurement was so critical to his organization's performance that he subsequently asked the Gallup Organization to refine and administer the survey to individuals in the city's neighborhoods. Using an experienced, trusted, and independent organization like Gallup would give the safety perception measurement added credibility. The 1999 Gallup survey indicated that 85 percent of Charlotte's citizens felt that the police officers in their community were service oriented; 84 percent indicated that they trusted the police officers in their community.

Another objective on the city's Balanced Scorecard was to strengthen neighborhoods. The police chief noted that an unusually large number of alcoholic beverage outlets in a neighborhood could not only contribute to a high local crime rate but also inhibit other types of businesses from operating in the community. He helped to form an interdepartmental team—consisting of a police officer and people from the zoning office and the Neighborhood Development Department—that could provide the documentation needed to revoke the liquor license of an alcoholic beverage outlet that had been the subject of numerous nuisance complaints. This integration across various city departments would have been difficult to accomplish without the shared understanding of the city objectives across departments.

For the learning and growth perspective, the department set an objective for all police officers to have access to a laptop computer. This would enable them to query the information base from their car as they were traveling to their destination or before questioning the driver of a car stopped for a traffic violation. In summarizing his experience to date with the scorecard, the chief noted, "When we first started with the training for the Balanced Scorecard, I thought 'Oh no, not another textbook program!' Now it's a relief to have the scorecard. Knowing exactly what outcomes the city is trying to achieve, we can be much more confident about how to set priorities, reallocate resources, and change the way we operate."

CITY OF CHARLOTTE: MANAGING STRATEGIC THEMES ACROSS ORGANIZATIONAL UNITS

The discussion so far in this chapter describes aligning high-level scorecards down to decentralized organizational units. Some organizations have used the scorecard not just for actual organizational units but for strategic themes that cut across multiple units.

Continuing the City of Charlotte story, City Manager Pam Syfert was not comfortable just having all of her departments (such as transportation and police) aligned to the city's scorecard, as described earlier. She wanted to highlight performance along the city's five strategic themes. Syfert established cabinets for each of the city's five strategic themes. Each cabinet met monthly to discuss progress in improving performance for the theme's strategic objectives. A cabinet consisted of the department heads whose departments could affect or influence the strategic theme. The cabinet provided a mechanism to assemble key operating people with a common interest in a strategic theme.

For example, the chief of police was an obvious member for, and in fact chaired, the Community Safety Cabinet. Initially, however, he had avoided membership in the four other cabinets, not wishing to have yet another set of meetings to attend. The chief soon noticed, however, that more people were being injured and killed in traffic accidents than in homicides and aggravated assaults. Also, many of the calls to the department were complaints about unsafe drivers. In response, the police chief decided to join the Transportation Cabinet. Chief Nowicki, with other Transportation Cabinet members, formed a Traffic Safety Advisory Committee, a collaborative effort among various city departments, such as police and transportation, as well as corporate communication and community organizations. The committee would conduct an extensive public information campaign to improve traffic safety, and to measure its impact.

Chief Nowicki described why he subsequently decided to join the Economic Development Cabinet as well.

> *Shortly after I arrived in Charlotte, an important retail store, in a brand new building, left a shopping mall. Did it leave because of a high local crime rate? I didn't know, but I should have known. Becoming more involved in the Economic Development Cabinet presented an opportunity to be more involved in that arena. Public safety is important for attracting businesses to locate and remain in our city, and for them to recruit our citizens to work in their urban locations.*
>
> *Likewise, it is helpful to have executives from other departments participate in the Community Safety Cabinet meetings. The Police Department doesn't have all the tools to solve all the city's safety problems. The Fire Chief and the heads of the Neighborhood Development and Solid Waste Services Departments now share responsibility for community safety. These other departments and agencies can mobilize additional resources to contribute to crime reduction activities.*[9]

Each cabinet developed its own Balanced Scorecard for its strategic theme (see scorecard for the city-within-a-city theme in Figure 6-8). No manager "owned" this scorecard or was evaluated against it. Rather, the cabinet Balanced Scorecard provided the framework that brought department heads together once a month to assess progress made to date, along with plans for new initiatives in the future to strengthen neighborhoods.

Figure 6-8 City of Charlotte: Defining the Balanced Scorecard for Strategic Themes

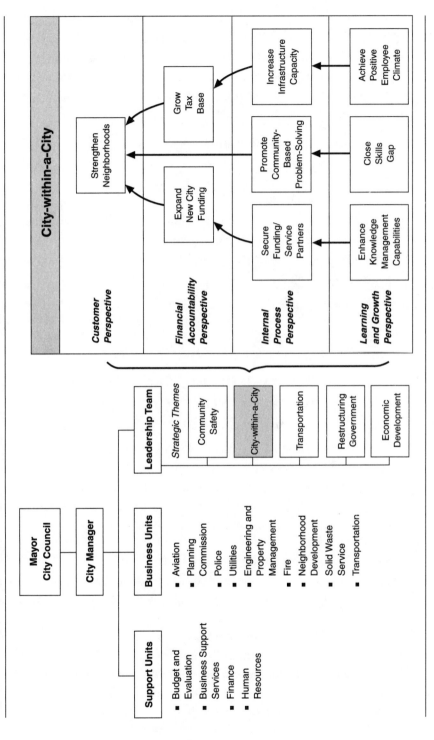

The cabinets used their scorecards for framing the discussion of the impact of major city projects—such as a new convention center, new highway construction, or airport improvements—on their cabinet's strategic theme.

Early successes from the partnerships created through the common goals, involvement, and integrated processes of the cabinets' virtual organizations included the following:

- A new transit–land use plan that combined strategic planning with appropriate changes in zoning regulations

- New "brownfields," inner-city developments accomplished with much lower regulatory and compliance costs. The brownfields were facilitated by active cooperation of the Planning, Engineering, and Transportation departments, working closely with private sector investors. A specific example was the transformation of an abandoned warehouse into a new design center.

- Community problem-oriented policing, involving, of course, the Police Department, but also the Neighborhood Development and Housing departments

STATE OF WASHINGTON: MANAGING STRATEGIC THEMES

As this book goes to press, the State of Washington is developing Balanced Scorecards for all cabinet agencies, and for the state's most pressing initiative: salmon recovery. The federal government has mandated, through enforcement of the Endangered Species Act, that the state make dramatic improvements in the quantity of salmon in the ocean and rivers around the state. But no single agency has complete control over all aspects of the environment that affect conditions that would lead to protection of salmon. Several relevant agencies are not even under the direct control of the governor, and some of the intervention has to be done in other governmental units such as neighboring states (Oregon), countries (Canada), and local counties and municipalities (King County, where Seattle is located). Left on their own, state agencies could set measurable objectives for outputs under their control that influence salmon production. Yet the decentralized efforts would likely fail because of lack of coherence across different organizational units.

The solution being implemented is to build a Balanced Scorecard for the strategic theme "preserve and enhance salmon," even though no czar of salmon exists. By getting each agency to agree, via a Balanced Scorecard about the general model for increasing the supply of salmon, the individual agencies could see how they could contribute to the high-level strategic theme. Their scorecards would include not only actions under their direct control, but also, and perhaps even more important, what linkages they would have to make with other government organizations, private citizens, and other entities for the entire effort to be a success.

The City of Charlotte and State of Washington illustrate how scorecards can be created for strategies even though a single organizational unit does not exist to implement the strategy. We encountered this situation in the private sector as well with an insurance company that was organized functionally, with central departments for underwriting, marketing, sales, and operations. Each department handled the full line of insurance products. The strategy for the company, however, involved multiple customer segments, each with its own marketing, distribution, and servicing requirements. The company struggled with developing a scorecard because of the diverse customer base and the different strategies required for each segment. The process became much simpler when they first developed separate scorecards for each customer segment. The scorecards described the strategy for a virtual organization—in this case a customer-focused business segment—that did not really exist in the company. But once the strategies could be expressed in a separate scorecard for each customer segment, each functional department developed scorecards that described how their internal processes would deliver the value proposition to the targeted customers in each segment. So the scorecard for the virtual customer-based strategic units provided the insight and direction to guide the operating strategies for the functional units.

SUMMARY

The case studies in this chapter have illustrated a broad spectrum of approaches used by organizations to achieve synergy across their units. For FMC and Mobil, the initial scorecards were developed below the corporate level. Mobil's NAM&R Division developed an explicit strategy—a sales growth in premium products that is faster than industry average, targeted consumer segments, win-win dealer relationships, and so forth—that it wanted each of its geographical and product business units to implement when developing their strategy and scorecards. Therefore the initial scorecard was developed at the NAM&R level and subsequently rolled out to its business units. Each business unit implemented the strategy in ways that were appropriate for its particular market and competitive situation.

In the case of Brown & Root Energy Services Division, the leadership team had an explicit strategy. They wanted the individual operating companies to work closely together to create value-added solutions that would reduce total lifecycle cost for shared customers that could not be achieved by allowing the business units to operate independently. The Energy Services scorecard explicitly identified the role for integration and used the objectives and measures in the Brown & Root scorecard to communicate the integration strategy across the business units. In the City of Charlotte, each functional department developed a scorecard that enabled it to integrate the city's five strategic themes into its daily responsibilities.

In general, there are many opportunities for coordination or integration. Many companies—for instance, Brown & Root Energy Services and the City of Charlotte—share common customers (or citizens) across diverse business units. For example, shared customers occur in financial institutions, consumer products companies, and pharmaceutical and medical device companies. In these cases, the customer perspective of the corporate/divisional scorecard must clearly identify the targeted customer and market segments. And it must articulate the value proposition that it wishes the business units, individually and collectively, to deliver to the customer. This will enable the business units to deliver more complete solutions to the customer with common corporate themes. The customer will understand that it is dealing with one integrated company, not an uncoordinated collection of diverse businesses.

Other companies achieve integration through shared internal processes. This occurs when economies of scale and the advantages of specialization and differentiation lead to the centralized provision of important business functions. For example, a company may have a single R&D division that supplies new product and process technologies to its individual operating groups. Another might have a manufacturing division that supports several business groups (usually organized by customer groups and marketing channels). Other examples of centrally provided goods and services include purchasing, real estate, distribution, and maintenance. We will discuss these situations in the next chapter.

The City of Charlotte and State of Washington cases illustrated how scorecards can define strategies even for virtual organizations. The scorecard provides the discipline to describe important strategic themes (in effect, a virtual organization). The scorecard contains both the outcomes desired (How would we measure success for the strategic theme?) and the performance drivers (especially in the internal processes and learning and growth) required for the outcomes of the strategic theme to be achieved. Individual organizational units then define their own strategies and scorecards that include their respective contributions to the objectives articulated in the strategic theme's scorecard.

NOTES

1. Examples taken from C. K. Prahalad and G. Hamel, "The Core Competence of the Corporation," *Harvard Business Review* (May–June 1990): 79–91.
2. R. Kaplan and D. Norton, "Implementing the Balanced Scorecard at FMC Corporation: An Interview with Larry D. Brady," *Harvard Business Review* (September–October 1993): 145.
3. The experience of building two business unit Balanced Scorecards is described in R. S. Kaplan, "Mobil USM&R (B): New England Sales and Distribution," 9-197-026 (Boston: Harvard Business School, 1996), and "Mobil USM&R (C): Lubricants Business Unit," 9-197-027 (Boston: Harvard Business School, 1996).
4. R. S. Kaplan, "Mobil USM&R (A): Linking the Balanced Scorecard," 9-197-025 (Boston: Harvard Business School, 1996), 6.
5. R. S. Kaplan, "City of Charlotte (A)," 9-199-036 (Boston: Harvard Business School, 1998), 6.
6. R. S. Kaplan, "City of Charlotte (B)," 9-199-043 (Boston: Harvard Business School, 1999).
7. The Police Department scorecard is also described in Kaplan, "City of Charlotte (B)."
8. Ibid., 4.
9. Ibid., 6.

Creating Synergies through Shared Services

CHAPTER 6 REPORTED HOW COMPANIES and public sector organizations have used the Balanced Scorecard to align and integrate their decentralized business units. Beyond aligning the business units that sell products and services to external customers, organizations can create synergies by aligning their internal units that provide shared services (once known as "corporate staff"). Shared service units are created at a corporate or division level because of economies of scale and the advantages of specialization and differentiation that these units can create. For example, a corporate role to "create economies of scale in the use of information technology," may require a central IT group to create these economies. If a corporate role is to "create a common brand and a common shopping experience" for the customer, a central marketing group can facilitate these objectives. Companies that want to leverage innovation may establish a single R&D division to supply new product and process technologies to its individual operating groups. Other examples of centralized provided goods and services include purchasing, manufacturing, real estate, distribution, and maintenance.

The challenge, of course, is for the centrally supplied service to be responsive to the strategies and needs of the business units it purports to serve. In practice, the shared service group, while established to provide benefits from economies of scale and specialization, frequently ends up becoming bureaucratic, unresponsive, and inflexible and doesn't deliver the desired economic benefits to operating divisions. We described earlier the failure in a European bank when the strategy of its IT group was not linked to the strategy of an important business unit. Creating a Balanced Scorecard for shared service units should align the strategies of these units so that they add value and are responsive to the strategies and needs of the business units they serve.

Most staff groups and support functions can be subjected to the "yellow pages" test.[1] Corporate managers can look in the Yellow Pages of the phone book and find independent companies that supply virtually all of the services currently provided by internal shared service departments. For an internal support group to be maintained within an organization, it should either supply the service internally at a lower price than what could be acquired from an external supplier, or it should offer a differentiated value proposition that is superior to that from an external vendor. Most support functions, however, do not have an explicit strategy—operational excellence, product leadership, customer intimacy—that demonstrates how they create competitive advantage for their parent corporation.

When shared service units cannot outperform external competitors, companies should outsource these functions. When outsourcing, companies can contract with their suppliers using a Balanced Scorecard rather than with just financial measures. This enables them to get the value and service levels they desire, not just a low price.

The Balanced Scorecard has been used in numerous ways to help link and align shared service units with business units and with the corporate strategy. In an ideal world, there would exist a top-down strategic architecture that defines the corporate role and how shared service units contribute to the corporate strategy. Often, however, such a strategic architecture will not exist. In the absence of an overall corporate scorecard program, shared service units will use the Balanced Scorecard in a somewhat different manner. In this chapter, we present the two models for developing shared service scorecards:

1. The Strategic Partner Model: The business units have developed Balanced Scorecards, reflecting their strategies and corporate priorities. The shared service unit is a partner in this process.

2. The Business-in-a-Business Model: The business units do not have

Balanced Scorecards. The shared service unit must view itself as a business and the business units as its customers. The shared service scorecard defines the relationships.

THE STRATEGIC PARTNER MODEL

Successful Balanced Scorecard companies typically first develop scorecards for SBUs that sell products and services directly to external customers. Subsequently, they develop scorecards for their shared service units (SSUs). This sequence is preferable because it allows the strategy for the business units that create value external to the company to be clearly articulated and understood. Once the SBU scorecards have been developed, the SSUs can develop strategies and scorecards for their customers—the market-facing business units. The SSU strategy can thereby deliver the value proposition that provides the greatest benefit to the SBUs.

Creating the linkage from SBUs to SSUs requires four components (see Figure 7-1):

1. Service agreement: A formal agreement between the SBUs and the SSU defines expectations about services and costs.

Figure 7-1 Creating Support Unit Linkage

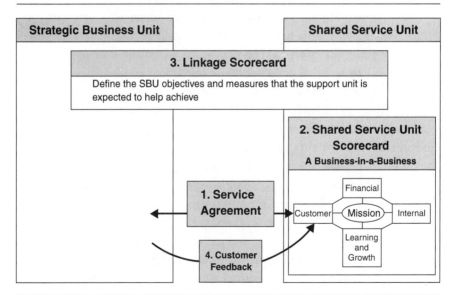

2. The shared service unit scorecard: The SSU develops a scorecard that reflects its strategy to support the service agreement with the SBUs.

3. The linkage scorecard: The SSU accepts accountability for improving selected measures on SBU scorecards.

4. Customer feedback: The SSU receives periodic feedback from the SBU about actual performance.

Various elements of this approach are illustrated by the following case studies.

Mobil North America Marketing and Refining

In Chapter 2, we described how Mobil North America Marketing and Refining (NAM&R) had its fourteen shared service units develop Balanced Scorecards after the division and eighteen business units had defined their strategies and scorecards. These scorecards were based on a service agreement between each shared service unit and a buyer's committee representing the business units. In developing scorecards for its shared service units, Mobil used a two-tier approach. We illustrate the approach with the process used by Mobil's Channel Management Group, the SSU that developed marketing and training programs used with dealers.

The Channel Management Group provided consulting services, programs, and support tools to help the dealers manage their businesses, consistent with Mobil's strategy. The two-tiered scorecard used by the group is shown in Figure 7-2. The lower tier of the scorecard identifies the strategies and measures for the group. The financial objective focused on operating efficiencies. A budget for the work of each shared service unit had been negotiated as part of the service agreement and the financial objectives related to becoming more efficient to meet the budgeted targets. For the customer perspective, the service unit designed and administered a survey to its customers—the geographic business units—to measure their satisfaction with the delivered services. The survey assessed whether the service unit was delivering the level and quality of services specified in the service agreement. The shared service unit then developed objectives, measures, targets, and initiatives for its internal process and learning and growth perspectives. These objectives were established for the service unit to achieve the customers' expectations within the cost constraints of the

Figure 7-2 Mobil Channel Management Group's Two-Tier Scorecard

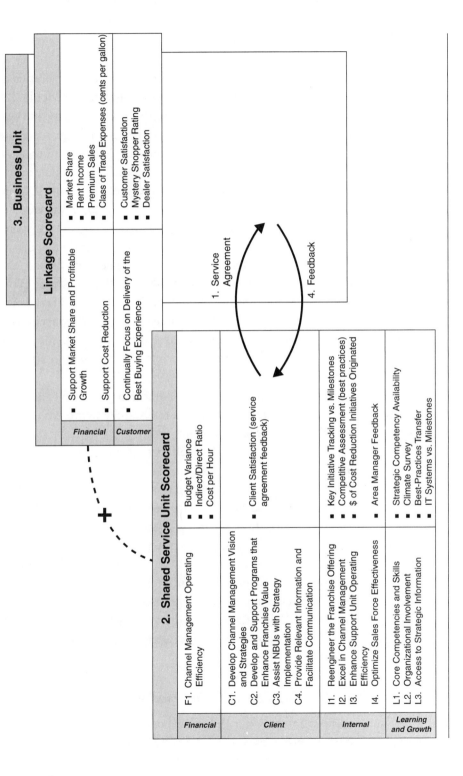

budget.[2] This part of the scorecard development was relatively standard for a shared service unit.

The novel aspect of the service unit's scorecard was the incorporation of a top-tier component, or "linkage scorecard," as it was called at Mobil. The linkage scorecard consisted of several measures from the financial and customer perspectives of the business unit scorecard. The linkage scorecard gave employees in the SSUs some responsibility for the needs of external customers and shareholders. An SSU chose measures for its linkage scorecard by identifying those financial and customer outcomes on the divisional scorecard that it had the greatest opportunity to influence. For example, the Channel Management Group included, in its linkage scorecard, a financial measure of premium gasoline sales volume, along with customer measures of the mystery shopper rating, dealer satisfaction, and consumer satisfaction. These measures expanded the thinking of employees in the SSUs beyond just serving internal business groups. They had to consider how to make a difference to the division's overall financial outcomes and to the division's external customers. The external focus helped to transform the service units from captive internal suppliers to strategic partners with the business units and division.

The Mobil "strategic partners" made one other change on their Balanced Scorecards—a seemingly minor one but actually quite symbolic of their value to the organization. The units were uncomfortable with using the word *customer* for their SSU scorecard. They felt that referring to their business units as *customers* put them in a subservient relationship to them; symbolizing that they had to supply whatever the business units asked for. The service units believed that a principal rationale for having SSUs in the division, rather than as a separate function within each geographic business unit, was that their scale of operations enabled them to create superior expertise and professionalism. They preferred to think of the business units as their clients, coming to them for advice, expertise, and differentiated service capabilities. So they renamed their "customer perspective" their "client perspective."

Each of Mobil NAM&R's fourteen business units updated their scorecards each year after renegotiating the service agreement with its buyer's committee.

Shell Services International

The Shell Services International (SSI) division of the Royal Dutch/Shell Group of Companies provides services to Shell operating companies and external customers around the world.[3] In 1999, SSI had more than 5,000 employees, and annual revenues exceeding $1 billion. Shell established the division in 1995 as part of an initiative to improve focus on core capabilities. Routine noncore activities—such as landscaping, mail, courier services, telecommunications, and office supplies—had already been outsourced to low-cost, focused external vendors. SSI managed the interface between these external vendors and the business units. Its main role, however, was to supply nonroutine services that were outside the core value-adding activities of the business units. The services were in four broad areas:

1. Consultancy and business solutions
2. Information technology and systems
3. Business services (accounting, finance, real estate, procurement, etc.)
4. Human resources services

By mid-1999, SSI was delivering 6,000 different products or services to more than 3,000 individual customers, most within Shell but to some external customers as well. The units of SSI each had a Balanced Scorecard to define their strategic priorities (see Figure 7-3).

The linkage between any service provider in SSI and a customer was accomplished with a Service Level Agreement (SLA). Shared services had existed in Shell since 1985, and their operating costs had already been cut by 50 percent. The goal of SSI had to be broader than low-cost delivery. The SLA established a clear understanding between the internal customer and the service provider. With so many products and customers, SSI could not just offer a single level of service; some business units wanted "gold-plated" services, whereas others wanted the "nickel-plated" variety. Each customer evaluated the cost/value tradeoffs in the service and selected the service requirement to fit its business needs. The service provider, in turn, committed to enhancing its capacity to supply and deliver the desired services at agreed levels of cost and functionality. The providers would also strive to continuously improve their cost and service quality.

Measurements played a key role in implementing the SLA system. SSI developed unit-level costs for all of its products and services. These unit costs could be cost per transaction for repetitive activities, or a cost per hour for engineering and consultative activities. In addition to cost, however, the SLA included a Balanced Scorecard of performance measures relating to the following:

Figure 7-3   Shell Services International's Balanced Scorecard

Financial		
	1996 Est.	1997 Plan
Revenue ($mm)	22.7	23.4
Revenue Growth (%)	n.a.	3.1
Pretax Income ($mm)	2.4	4.1
Cash Margin (%)	10.6	17.6
Pretax Income (stretch)	same	4.5
Net Income after Tax ($mm)	1.2	2.3

Customer

Positive Customer Feedback

	1995	1996	1997	1998	1999
Target	68%	75%	80%	85%	90%
Stretch	90%				

Market Share
- Share of Internal Customer—
  Current 70%—Target 80%
- External—xx%

Value Creation

Employee

Positive Employee Feedback
- Employee Satisfaction/Commitment
  – Attrition—4%
  – Employee Attendance Recognition
    Awards—40%
  – Employee Satisfaction—70%
- Leadership Performance
- Corporate Values
- EHS Leadership
  – Zero recordables
  – Zero reportables
  – Zero lost time

External

Performance vs. Competitors
- Revenue Growth
- ROA
- Cash Margin
Social Measure with Business Focus

1. Customer satisfaction (monthly survey)
2. Quality of support (measures on speed of response and on-time service delivery)
3. Technical end-to-end measurements (the measures are customized to specific service application)
4. Business alignment (ease of doing business with)

A sample of the SLA scorecard feedback is shown in Figure 7-4.

With its accompanying measures, the SLA committed the SSI unit to deliver the agreed-upon level of service at the least cost to the customer. The SSI unit could use the metrics in the SLA to construct its own Balanced Scorecard for measuring and motivating its performance. As a senior SSI manager reported, "The service-level agreements changed the mindset in discussions between customers and service providers from cost, cost, and

Figure 7-4   A Web-Based Service Level Agreement Scorecard

XYZ Company Scorecard

Customer Satisfaction		**Quality of Support**	
Satisfaction Survey—Help Desk and Delayed Resolution User Survey	**Very Good**	Time to Resolve a Problem	**Very Good**
		Service Request Response Time	**n.a.**
Satisfaction Survey—Business Management Survey	**Excellent**	% of Repeating Problems	**n.a.**
		Help Desk Answer Time	**n.a.**

Technical End-to-End Measurements		**Business Alignment**	
Availability	**Excellent**	Improvement of Speed and Efficiency of Implementation of New Ways of Working	**Very Good**
Reliability	**Excellent**		
Response Time	**Satisfactory**		

cost to how to develop and improve internal capabilities to help customers in their value creation activities."

U.S. Department of Energy

The Department of Energy Procurement (DOEP) Balanced Scorecard effort started with a new vision for the function: "To deliver on a timely basis the best value product or service to our customers while maintaining the public's trust and fulfilling public policy objectives."

Even this simple statement—stressing timely delivery—was a major departure. In the past, when purchasing only had to follow rules, it didn't have to worry about *when* the procurement function had been accomplished. Stephen Mournighan, director of management systems, described the cultural change required:

Prior to 1993, the only two performance measures for procurement were "Did you spend the money authorized?" and "Did you follow the rules?" The new vision required us to change the culture so that we could establish and maintain a customer focus, a sense of urgency, continuous and breakthrough process improvement, and an emphasis on results.

The Balanced Scorecard played a critical role in facilitating the major cultural change that would make the procurement function far more responsive to customers—to shift the focus from compliance to customer-based results.

Like other government and nonprofit organizations, the DOEP placed the *customer perspective* at the top of its Balanced Scorecard hierarchy (see Figure 7-5). Customer satisfaction was measured by a newly designed survey that asked customers to rate *timeliness*—of procurement processing, planning activities, and ongoing communication—and *quality* of the goods and services delivered. DOEP management used the results of this

Figure 7-5   Department of Energy Procurement's Balanced Scorecard

measure for internal benchmarking across all their field offices. They matched a high-performing office with one that scored low, so that learning and best-practice sharing could occur. This facilitated an environment of continual learning. The second customer objective—*creating effective service partnerships*—also was measured by survey questions relating to the procurement office's responsiveness to and cooperation with the customer.

The *internal perspective* communicated a major change in the way that purchasing was conducted. Previously, the rules-driven function required that even minor purchases have several forms and up to five signatures before an authorization to buy could be issued. For the objective *most effective use of contracting approaches*, the department authorized office managers to use a Visa credit card for purchases under $25,000. The measures for this objective were percentage of purchase card transactions under $25,000, as well as the percentage of these transactions made by a line manager, not a procurement manager. Within a couple of years, 85 percent of allowable purchases were made with the credit card, and an office manager, not a purchasing manager, made 84 percent of these. This improvement eliminated a huge amount of paperwork and delay in the system. Another measure for this objective was percentage of purchase and delivery orders made electronically.

For the *streamlined process* internal process objective, the DOEP measured the lead time from receipt of a request for a major contract to actual award. In 1987, the average lead time had been 287 days. In 1998, the DOEP reduced the lead time by about 50 percent, to 147 days. For standard contracts, the new processes reduced lead time to 15 days. These dramatic improvements required an enormous cultural shift in the procurement function. All employees were now focused on finding innovative ways to be more responsive for their customers.

In the *learning and growth perspective*, the DOEP initiated surveys to assess *employee satisfaction* with the new environment. The DOEP's new strategy asked people to operate with new rules and new measures. The surveys provided feedback about whether employees felt they were getting adequate training for the new mission and had new contracting and purchasing tools that enabled them to meet the stretch performance targets and access to appropriate data and information.

The primary *financial measure* was the *cost-to-spend ratio*, the cost of acquiring $1 of services. The procurement function had never before measured how much its activities cost. The DOEP benchmarked leading companies in the aerospace industry and found that the best procurement groups had costs of 2 percent to 3 percent of purchases. In the first year of operating with the Balanced Scorecard measurement system, the DOEP beat this target by achieving a cost-to-spend ratio of 1.8 percent. This financial improvement came through a large reduction in the number of people in the procurement function—possibly because of the operating efficiencies discussed earlier—and with significant improvements in customer service. This experience reinforced the message of the benefits from the Balanced Scorecard management system: Organizations can cut costs, become more productive, and deliver superior customer service at the same time.

With the success of the program internally, the DOEP extended its approach to private sector contractors that operated various DOE facilities—the University of California; AlliedSignal, Inc.; Lockheed Martin Corporation; Fluor Daniels, Inc.. It asked the major contractors to develop Balanced Scorecards for their procurement function, both to assess their own performance and to communicate with the DOEP on their progress.

As with the private sector examples, the Balanced Scorecard helped government service units become more productive, more responsive to customer needs, and a more effective partner in helping the line organization achieve its strategic objectives. The benefits were achieved without any linkages to compensation, which were not possible under federal government rules. The employees in the government agency liked the new strategy. Their jobs were now more interesting, they had more responsibility, and they had more challenges and opportunities for their initiative. The new approach created strong intrinsic motivation, and the reinforcement from financial incentives (extrinsic motivation) was not necessary to change behavior.

University of California, San Diego

Balanced Scorecards for SSUs are also occurring in higher education. The business support division of the University of California, San Diego (UCSD), won a 1999 Rochester Institute of Technology/*USA Today* Quality Cup for Education for its application of the Balanced Scorecard. Under the leadership of Vice Chancellor Steven Relyea, each of the 27 support units built Balanced Scorecards reflecting customer service and efficiency objectives.[4] Each business unit set targets for improvement and established an action plan aimed at attaining the targets.

For the customer perspective, an outside research organization visited the campus each year to conduct a survey among students, faculty, and administrators to assess the quality of campus services delivered by the business support units. Since the Balanced Scorecard was implemented at UCSD, customer satisfaction ratings have increased dramatically. Among the customer and financial improvements noted were the following:

- The payroll department reduced error rates by 80 percent.

  Travel reimbursement time was reduced from six weeks to three days.

- The custodial department reduced custodial cleaning expenses from $0.94 to $0.84 per square foot. With more than 5.6 million square feet of facilities, the annual savings from this improvement alone exceed $560,000.

- The human resources group cut the cost per new hire from $388 to about $200, while other California universities were seeing costs increase to nearly $900.

- Student housing costs were reduced $900,000 within two years and exceeded the five-year goal of $1 million savings during the third year of implementation.

The scorecard and customer feedback helped the units to focus on improving critical processes. In the human resources department, hiring costs were slashed through use of new electronic and Web-based technology and cross-functional team efforts. The dramatic improvements in custodial expenses were achieved by delegating responsibility to the people doing the work. Assistant Vice Chancellor Jack Hug said, "The people themselves have taken charge—recognizing what they are doing and how it impacts the bottom line. Our people are challenged to cover more space and cover it better." Relyea believes that "the constituents of higher education will, and should, demand this type of accountability out of institutions in the future."

THE BUSINESS-IN-A-BUSINESS MODEL

Many functional organizations such as information technology, human resources, finance, marketing, and R&D have developed Balanced Scorecard programs to manage their organizations without a broader corporate program. The scorecard enabled executives of these functional units to build a professional management approach that can motivate their organizations to be customer-focused and competitive. The "functional excellence" that this promoted for the organization offset some of the lost benefits and potential suboptimization created when a Balanced Scorecard is being built for a functional unit without explicit linkages to SBUs and corporate scorecards.

The functional scorecard should view itself as a "business-in-a-business"—in effect to compete on the Yellow Pages test. Figure 7-6 illustrates this perspective, using IT as an example. The IT organization views the SBUs as customers. It develops a professional interface with the SBU similar to approaches that external vendors would take. The IT unit is the "house brand." It has certain advantages through internal knowledge and relationships, but it still must develop a market-based relationship. In turn, the SBU bears responsibility for integrating IT into its business strategy.

Information Technology at Financial Services Company (FINCO)

FINCO IT was the centralized IT organization of a global, multidivisional, financial services organization. The corporation centralized the IT group in the 1980s to obtain scale economies with hardware and people, to develop a common communications infrastructure, and to enhance product-line integration to common customers.

Figure 7-6 The Support Function as a Business-in-a-Business

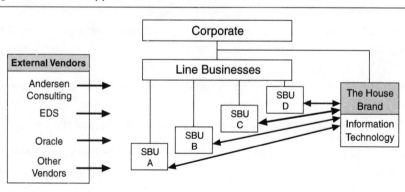

FINCO IT used the Balanced Scorecard framework to translate its vision into a more detailed strategic agenda (see Figure 7-7). With this agenda as the starting point, the management team met in a two-day workshop to develop the strategy map shown in Figure 7-8. The strategy map was designed from the IT group perspective. It would later serve as a template to be cascaded to the different departments within IT. The *financial* objectives attempted to balance efficiency and effectiveness. The cost productivity objective required each department to benchmark its unit costs against various external reference points (such as external vendors) to ensure that FINCO IT was competitive on cost. Strategic spending was linked to high-level measures of business return; it was separated from spending on operations and maintenance activities.

The *client* value proposition was divided into two components. The basic objectives defined the outcomes that internal clients expected— reliability and quality at a reasonable cost. The differentiators reflected a customer intimacy strategy to partner with the internal clients by providing knowledgeable people who could create innovative business solutions. The overarching goal was to create a long-term partnership between the IT and internal clients. Clients would provide survey feedback to measure progress toward these goals.

The *internal process* themes reflected the organization value chain:

- Understand customer needs
- Create and develop innovative solutions
- Provide infrastructure
- Manage technical and operating risk
- Service the client

The *learning and growth* strategy focused on key staff development, empowerment of employees, teamwork at the executive level, and an aligned goal system.

Clearly, FINCO's development of a scorecard for its IT group used the same underlying structure as we used elsewhere. The financial level of the scorecard is the only component that is not fully analogous to a true business, because the financial objectives of the functional unit do not stand alone. In many respects, the financial layer of the strategy is similar to that of a nonprofit or government organization (see Chapter 5). The organization must be efficient in its use of resources, but its higher-order goal is to create benefits for customers.

Figure 7-7 FINCO IT's Vision and Strategic Agenda

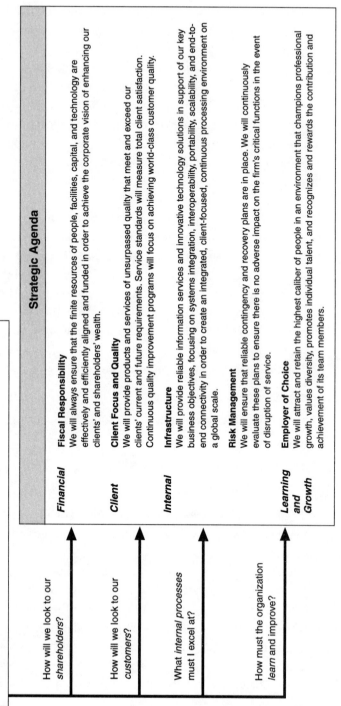

Vision

Our vision is to be the #1 client-driven team, providing unsurpassed quality, information services, and innovative technology throughout the world in order to enhance our clients' and our shareholders' wealth.

Strategic Agenda

Financial

Fiscal Responsibility
We will always ensure that the finite resources of people, facilities, capital, and technology are effectively and efficiently aligned and funded in order to achieve the corporate vision of enhancing our clients' and shareholders' wealth.

Client

Client Focus and Quality
We will provide products and services of unsurpassed quality that meet and exceed our clients' current and future requirements. Service standards will measure total client satisfaction. Continuous quality improvement programs will focus on achieving world-class customer quality.

Internal

Infrastructure
We will provide reliable information services and innovative technology solutions in support of our key business objectives, focusing on systems integration, interoperability, portability, scalability, and end-to-end connectivity in order to create an integrated, client-focused, continuous processing environment on a global scale.

Risk Management
We will ensure that reliable contingency and recovery plans are in place. We will continuously evaluate these plans to ensure there is no adverse impact on the firm's critical functions in the event of disruption of service.

Learning and Growth

Employer of Choice
We will attract and retain the highest caliber of people in an environment that champions professional growth, values diversity, promotes individual talent, and recognizes and rewards the contribution and achievement of its team members.

How will we look to our shareholders?

How will we look to our customers?

What internal processes must I excel at?

How must the organization learn and improve?

Figure 7-8 FINCO IT's Strategy Map

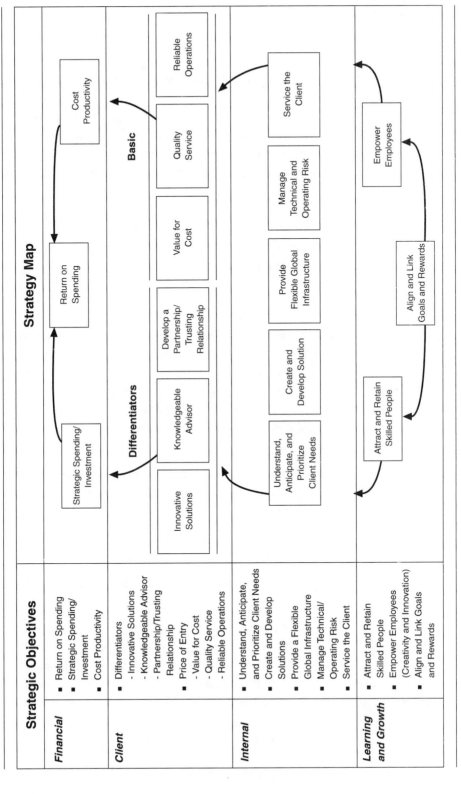

INTEGRATING EXTERNAL PARTNERS

Linkages between organizational units also arise when integration occurs across corporate boundaries—for suppliers, customers, outsourced services, and joint ventures. Companies such as J. P. Morgan Information Services and Caltex Petroleum Corporation—a joint venture between Texaco, Inc., and Chevron Corporation—have implemented Balanced Scorecards to define the performance model for the relationship. This enabled them to define how outsourced services and joint ventures could create new value, not just lower costs. No new principles were involved to develop scorecards for these external relationships. The external linkages had the same structure and served the same purposes as the linkages within the organization already described in this chapter.

SUMMARY

Balanced Scorecards for internal SSUs identify and articulate the opportunities for integration and synergy. They communicate how these organizations create value for the corporation and its divisions and business units. Scorecards should be constructed after a formal service agreement has been negotiated between the service unit and line operating business units. The service agreement and the SSU Balanced Scorecard should accomplish the following:

- Align the efforts of the unit to the priorities of its customers (primarily internal customers, although some service units may have the right to sell services to external customers as well)
- Provide a basis of accountability between the unit and its customers
- Track the progress in the performance of the unit
- Build a culture of customer-based performance and continuous improvement within the unit

The scorecard provides the measurements and the management system for aligning SSUs to the organization's strategic objectives.

While, ideally, strategy and scorecards should start at the top and then ripple down to local operating units and SSUs, often the motivation and commitment for the Balanced Scorecard management system can arise within a support unit. In this case, the unit can adopt a business-in-a-business model and develop a scorecard that reflects its estimated strategic role within the larger organization. Scorecards for external partners, such as joint ventures and outsourcing vendors, can be developed to define how value will be created with the external partnership.

NOTES

1. We first learned of this valuable test from Skip Stitt, who applied it in the City of Indianapolis's new approach for putting city services up for competitive bids with the private sector. Mayor Stephen Goldsmith realized that private sector counterparts existed for most city-supplied services (other than public safety services). See R. S. Kaplan, "Indianapolis: Activity-Based Costing of City Services (A)," 9-196-115 (Boston: Harvard Business School, 1996) and R. S. Kaplan, "Indianapolis: Activity-Based Costing of City Services (B)," 9-196-117 (Boston: Harvard Business School, 1996).
2. For details of this process for the Gasoline Marketing SSU, see R. S. Kaplan, "Mobil USM&R (D)," 9-197-028 (Boston: Harvard Business School, 1996).
3. Experience drawn from Dennis R. Wymore, "Beyond Cost Reduction: Using the Scorecard to Transform Shared Services into a Competitive Partner" (paper presented at the Balanced Scorecard Collaborative Best Practice Conference, Linking Scorecards to Create Organizational Alignment, Cambridge, MA, 12–13 April 1999).
4. Information on their application can be found on http://www.vcba.ucsd.edu/performance/cssemp.htm. See also "Balanced Scorecard Analyzes Performance in Businesslike Way," *HR on Campus* (LRP Publications, October 1999), and "Measuring Efficiency Responds to Customers, Impacts Employees," *HR on Campus* (LRP Publications, November 1999).

MAKING STRATEGY EVERYONE'S EVERYDAY JOB

YOU'VE FORMULATED THE STRATEGY, and you've built the scorecards—corporate, division, business units, shared services, and strategic partners. How do you now make the strategy happen? How do you get all employees to make strategy part of their daily job?

In the past, aligning all employees to the strategy was not critical. A century ago, at the height of the scientific management revolution, companies deconstructed complex manufacturing jobs into sequences of much simpler tasks. Industrial engineers and managers determined efficient work methods for each task and established standards for performance. Companies could then hire uneducated, unskilled employees and train them narrowly and deeply to do a single, relatively simple task. And the employee did this same job over and over, developing mastery and skill for the single task. As Frederick Taylor, the leader of the scientific management movement declared, "Simple jobs for simple people." In this environment, employees did not have to understand or implement the strategy. They just had to perform well the narrow task that engineers and management had assigned and trained them to do.

Today, this mode of work is virtually obsolete. For organizations to achieve their objectives—whether they are manufacturing or service, private or public, for-profit or not-for-profit—all organizational participants need to be aligned to the strategy. Much of the work done today is knowledge-based, not physical work. Automation and productivity have reduced the percentage of people in the organization who do traditional work functions. One report estimates that 50 percent of the work done in industrialized countries today is knowledge work.[1] Employees perform discretionary tasks in engineering, product development, marketing, customer relations, management, and administration. The challenge for organizations today is how to enlist the hearts and minds of all their employees.[2] Even employees still involved in direct production and service delivery must strive for continuous improvements in quality, cost reduction, and process times to meet customers' expectations and keep up with the competition. Employees have to understand who the customers are so that they can find innovative, new ways to create value for them. Doing the job as it was done last period is not likely to be adequate.

Dave Ulrich of the University of Michigan Business School has identified several critical trends that require intense alignment of employees to organizational objectives:

- Many companies now measure employee satisfaction on a regular basis.[3] But satisfaction is not the same as commitment. Employees may feel well compensated and well treated, but that does not imply that they understand the organization's goals and are committed to helping the organization achieve them.

- Companies may claim that their employees are their most valuable asset, but if you look at the frequency at which they check and validate their physical inventories versus the frequency with which they check employee attitudes and skills, their actions indicate that they value inventory much higher than they value employee capabilities.

- Not all employees are equally important. Ulrich asks companies to think about three groups of employees: those at the home office and headquarters; those in middle management; and frontline employees. Which group most directly affects customer experiences and relationships? Which group gets the most creative compensation schemes and has the most education and training programs? Usually the answers to the two questions are quite different groups.

- Some companies are learning how to involve their customers more directly in the hiring, training, and rewarding of key employees.

The companies consult with key customers when selecting employees, developing training programs for them, and even empowering the customers to give bonus slips when employees deliver exceptional service.

Strategy-Focused Organizations understand well the importance of engaging and aligning all of their employees to the strategy. Ultimately, the employees are the ones who will be implementing the strategy. And unlike in the scientific management era, companies look to their frontline employees for new ideas, as well as for information on market opportunities, competitive threats, and technological possibilities. The Balanced Scorecard provides organizations with a powerful tool for communication and alignment. It focuses the energies and talents of employees on the organization's strategic objectives.

Stragegy-Focused Organizations use the Balanced Scorecard in three distinct processes to align their employees to the strategy:

1. Communication and education: Employees must learn about and understand the strategy if they are to help implement it. Creating employee knowledge and understanding is the objective of an effective communications process.

2. Developing personal and team objectives: Employees must understand how they can influence the successful implementation of the strategy. Managers must help employees set individual and team goals that are consistent with strategic success. Personal development plans can be customized to achieving these goals.

3. Incentive and reward systems: the "balanced paycheck." Employees should feel that when the organization has been successful, they share in the rewards; conversely, when the organization has been unsuccessful, they should feel some of the pain. Incentive and reward systems provide the linkage between organizational performance and individual rewards.

In the next three chapters, we discuss each of these three vital processes that align individual employees to the organization's strategy.

NOTES

1. Thomas A. Stewart, *Intellectual Capital: The New Wealth of Organizations* (London: Nicholas Brealey, 1998).

2. See J. R. Katzenbach and J. A. Santamaria, "Firing Up the Front Line," *Harvard Business Review* (May–June 1999): 107–17.

3. In fact, such a measurement may prompt many organizations to claim that they already have a Balanced Scorecard, as they also measure customer satisfaction and quality in addition to employee satisfaction.

Creating Strategic Awareness

IMAGINE THAT YOU ARE THE MARKETING DIRECTOR of a large consumer goods company and are about to introduce a major new product. How would you let your customers know that something new is coming? Would you simply put the new product on the shelf, hoping that they notice it and understand what's different about it? Probably not! Product companies use well-defined processes when launching new products. They start with a major promotional campaign that informs customers about the new product (creating product awareness). They then track sales to see how many customers have tried the product (product market share). And they monitor to see if customers continue to purchase the product (product loyalty) and recommend the product to others (product missionary). Campaigns for new product introductions continually educate the market until behavior patterns have been modified and new buying patterns have been established.

Now imagine that you are the general manager of a large company about to launch your organization on a major new strategy. How do you let your employees know about the major new directions? If you're like most organizations, you don't. Our research indicates that less than 5 percent of the typical workforce understands their organization's strategy. But, logically, the changes in behavior required for a workforce to execute a new strategy are far greater than the changes required to get consumers to try a new product.

Executives should use communication processes at the launch of their new strategy similar to those employed for new product introductions. The processes start with education (creating strategy awareness) and are followed by testing that employees understood the message (strategy mind share), checking that employees believe the strategy is being followed (strategy loyalty), and, finally, determining how many are teaching others about it (becoming a strategy missionary). Each of these states of mind and commitment could be measured, just as companies do with their customers. And companies should authorize spending budgets to communicate and educate their employees, just as they commit to advertising and promotion expenditures to communicate to consumers about new product introductions.

As radical as these ideas may sound, they are becoming the norm for Strategy-Focused Organizations. CEOs of these organizations recognize that when a new strategy is being launched, all employees must understand the strategy so that they can find new and better ways to conduct their day-to-day business. For example, Gerry Isom, the CEO of CIGNA Property & Casualty, stated, "One of the most difficult things is to take a well-articulated executive plan and have the people sitting at their desks in Des Moines understand how they contribute to that plan. We need to educate all of our people to understand what they can do when they come to work every day to influence this company."

This is not top-down direction. This is top-down communication, leaving to individuals at their local work sites the task of finding innovative ways of helping the organization achieve its strategic objectives.

A study contrasting high- and low-performing organizations yielded the following data:[1]

	Well-Performing Organizations	Poorly Performing Organizations
Employees have a good understanding of overall organizational goals	67%	33%
Senior managers are highly effective communicators	26%	0%

Clearly, communication is a major lever for organizational success. Yet poor communication is prevalent. If employees don't understand the vision, they are even less likely to understand the strategy intended to realize that vision. Without understanding vision and strategy, employees cannot adapt their work to contribute to effective strategy implementation.

The leadership team should use every possible channel to communicate the strategy and to reinforce it at every opportunity. Gerry Isom of CIGNA used a graphic metaphor to emphasize the importance he placed on continual communication: "When you are introducing something like a Balanced Scorecard into a company that has never had it before, it's a real paradigm shift. It's a major cultural adjustment. It's like driving a nail into granite; you have to keep hitting the nail."

Companies must view the communication of the scorecard to employees as a strategic campaign, as critical as any communications program done for its external constituents of customers, investors, and suppliers. The creative and professional skills of its internal or external communications group should be mobilized for the campaign.

The communications program should have the following objectives:

1. Develop an understanding of the strategy throughout the organization

2. Develop buy-in to support the organization's strategy

3. Educate the organization about the Balanced Scorecard measurement and management system for implementing the strategy

4. Provide feedback, via the Balanced Scorecard, about the strategy

Ed Robertson, manager of employee communications at Federal Express Corporation, emphasized that the performance of the communications process must be evaluated by results, not activities. Counting the "number of messages sent" and "number of viewers" measures the *activities* of a communication process but not its *output*. George Bernard Shaw said: "The greatest problem with communication is the illusion that it has been accomplished." Just because a message has been sent, it doesn't mean that it has been received. The output measure for the communications process should be shared understanding among employees.

Several companies, to verify that the message was indeed "out," asked, as part of their annual employee survey, whether the employee knew about and understood the strategy. A Hay Group study of fifteen sophisticated Balanced Scorecard adopters found that eleven of them had formal systems to measure employee awareness. At Mobil North America Marketing and Refining (NAM&R), as reported at the end of Chapter 2, the initial awareness level (prior to introduction of the Balanced Scorecard) was less than 20 percent. Five years later, the awareness level exceeded 80 percent. The company felt that this deep penetration of the message was a great organizational asset.

COMMUNICATIONS MEDIA

Many media are available to communicate the strategy and the Balanced Scorecard to the troops. Some of the components that we have seen include:

- Quarterly town meetings. Initially, the executives use their town meetings to introduce the Balanced Scorecard concept. As the concept becomes established, they use quarterly meetings to brief the organization on recent performance and engage in Q&A discussions about the future.

- Brochure: A one-page document describes strategic objectives and how these will be measured.

- Monthly newsletters. The newsletters initially define and describe the scorecard. Subsequently they provide periodic reports on the measures and stories about employee initiatives leading to improved performance.

- Education programs. By incorporating the scorecard in all education and training programs, the message of the scorecard as a new way of doing business is reinforced.

- Company Intranet. The scorecard is posted on the Intranet, with voice and video segments of executives describing the overall strategy and explanations for individual objectives, measures, targets, and initiatives.

Few companies use only a single medium. Most use a comprehensive mix of media in a program of continual communications. Figure 8-1 shows a spectrum of communication channels used at New York University Medical Center to roll out a new strategy. "Rich channels," such as small group meetings, enable the communicator to focus the message in a personal

Figure 8-1   Using Multiple Media to Communicate the New Strategies

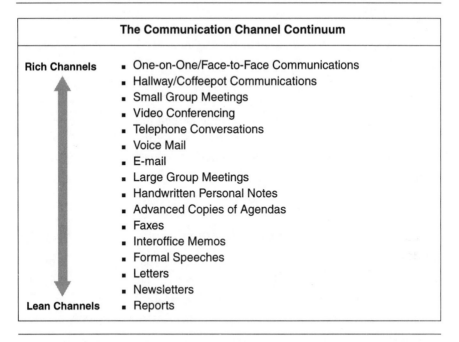

The Communication Channel Continuum

Rich Channels
- One-on-One/Face-to-Face Communications
- Hallway/Coffeepot Communications
- Small Group Meetings
- Video Conferencing
- Telephone Conversations
- Voice Mail
- E-mail
- Large Group Meetings
- Handwritten Personal Notes
- Advanced Copies of Agendas
- Faxes
- Interoffice Memos
- Formal Speeches
- Letters
- Newsletters

Lean Channels
- Reports

Source: Joseph N. Miniace and Elizabeth Falter, "Communication: A Key Factor in Strategy Implementation," *Planning Review* (January–February 1996): 29. Reprinted by permission of the authors.

manner and to respond to questions and feedback from the audience. Rich channels are highly effective but are the most expensive and limited in their reach. "Lean channels," such as newsletters, lack the personalization of rich channels but are much more economical and provide broader reach.[2]

Successful Balanced Scorecard implementers have used virtually every one of the channels listed in Figure 8-1 at one time or another, including a mixture of rich and lean channels. Eventually, when the scorecard becomes imbedded in ongoing management processes, the formal communications program ceases. It is no longer needed when scorecard use has become pervasive and routine.

Nova Scotia Power

Paul Niven, Business Performance Analyst at Nova Scotia Power, Inc., was assigned full time to oversee the deployment of the Balanced Scorecard. He distributed copies of the corporate scorecard to every manager with full accompanying notes. He used the company newsletter and Intranet to provide periodic updates, and he encouraged each business group to extensively communicate with its own people through presentations and newsletters. CFO Jay Forbes recalled, "Niven and I went to countless meetings and forums, any agenda we could wiggle our way onto, to try and help people understand the scorecard. We plastered the scorecard everywhere we could. Communication was my number one priority and my number one time allocation." Forbes noted the challenge of sustaining the effort: "To avoid the 'flavor of the week' problem, you have to embed the BSC into everything else you do. People need to live with it and enjoy the benefits of doing so. The implementation program needs to have visible executive support, constant promotion, continuous modification/enhancement, and, most of all, a relentless organizational focus, or it will fail."

The Mobil Experience: Sustaining the Communications Program

Mobil NAM&R, as we described in Chapter 2, started its deployment of the Balanced Scorecard by having a member of the executive leadership team visit every site in North America to explain the new strategy. The company distributed a one-page brochure that described the new balanced measurement system.

Once the notion of strategy and measurement had been communicated and embedded in the organization, Mobil moved to a systematic, ongoing communications program that reinforced the message in many ways. Monthly, the division and each business and shared service unit prepared an updated, one-page Balanced Scorecard report. The scorecard was posted and distributed at bulletin boards at every site. The report (see Figure 8-2) showed, on a single page, the objectives and measures in the four perspectives, current and year-to-date performance, and comparison with last year and with the current year's targets.

In addition, each business unit had a newsletter, with each issue featuring some aspect of the scorecard. The company produced a Balanced Scorecard Digest that summarized performance. And the scorecard was a component in every education class and training program at the company.

Quarterly, the division's president appeared for a one-hour briefing at the cafeteria of the company headquarters in Fairfax, Virginia, to review the scorecard performance for the preceding quarter and respond to questions about future direction. At the first such meeting, in April 1995, only about thirty people showed up. In 1999, more than five hundred people were regularly attending the meeting, and the company had to seek special

Figure 8-2 Mobil NAM&R's Monthly Report

Perspective	Objective	Measure	Frequency	Baseline	1997 Actual Results		1997 Plan	1999 Target Amount
					Current Period	Year to Date Amount		
Financial	Return on Capital Employed	ROCE (%)	S					
	Cash Flow	Cash Flow Excluding Dividends ($mm)	M					
		Cash Flow Including Dividends ($mm)	M					
	Profitability	P&L (after taxes)	M					
		Net Margin (cents per gallon before taxes)	M					
		Net Margin, Ranking out of 6	Q					
		Total Operating Expenses (cents per gallon)	M					
	Lowest Cost	Volume Growth, Gasoline Retail Sales (%)	M					
	Meet Profitable Growth Targets	Volume Growth, Distillate Sales to Trade	M					
		Volume Growth, Lubes (%)	M					
Customer	Continually Delight the Targeted Consumer	Share of Segment (%)	Q					
		■ % of Road Warriors	Q					
		■ % of True Blues	Q					
		■ % of Generation F3's	Q					
		Mystery Shopper (%)	M					
	Improve the Profitability of Our Partners	Total Gross Profit, Split	Q					
Internal	Improve EHS Performance	Safety Incidents (days away from work)	Q					
		Environmental Incidents	Q					
	Product, Service, and Alternative Profit Center Development	Alternative Profit Center Gross Margin/Store/Month ($m)	M					
	Lower Costs of Manufacturing vs. Competition	Refinery ROCE (%)	Q					
	Improve Hardware Performance	Refinery Expense (cents/unit output)	M					
		Refinery Reliability Index (%)	M					
		Refinery Yield Index (%)	M					
	Improve EHS Performance	Refinery Safety Incidents	Q					
	Reducing Laid-Down Cost	Laid-Down Cost vs. Competition's Supply—Gas (cents per gallon)	Q					
		Laid-Down Cost vs. Competition's Supply—Distribution (cents per gallon)	Q					
	Inventory Management	Inventory Level (millions of barrels)	M					
		Product Availability Index (%)	M					
	Quality	Quality Index	Q					
Learning and Growth	Organization Involvement	Climate Survey Index	M					
	Core Competencies and Skills	Strategic Competency Availability (%)	A					
	Access to Strategic Information	Strategic Systems Availability	A					

fire department approval for handling the overflow audience. The meetings were shown by video to all other locations and were taped so that those employees who could not attend the live meeting or remote broadcasts could view the presentation at their convenience.

Each January, more than one hundred top leaders from the company attended an annual State of the Business meeting at which the Balanced Scorecard provided the agenda for reviewing performance of the year just concluded and presenting and discussing plans for the upcoming year. Selected exemplars from the business and shared service units made presentations on their innovative programs. The executive leadership team used the scorecard as the discussion document when it met to review performance with business unit and shared service heads. Thus through active, continuous communication and use, the scorecard had become embedded into the organizational culture.

Motorola: New Channels

Motorola, Inc.'s employee communications department (ECOM) also followed a highly proactive approach to align employees with the company's high-level goals.[3] ECOM recognized that it could not use the CEO to communicate messages about every new program and initiative to employees. The CEO must focus on a maximum of two or three key messages per year (a survey of employees in benchmarked companies revealed that employees felt that the "CEO says too little about too much and was not a factor in motivating and persuading"). So any message from the CEO had to be comprehensive and powerful, explicating the rationale for the strategic theme and indicating the goals desired and the current status toward those goals. Managers throughout the organization would then reinforce the message. A typical rollout would be:

Person	Communications Role
CEO	Rationale, goal, status
President	Visible reinforcement, specific plan
Business unit general manager	"What will we do differently?"
Manager	How the initiative relates to everyday work
Employee	Understand and apply

Motorola went beyond traditional communication channels in ways that reinforced its mission to be a world leader in communication, especially electronic communication. It conducted satellite conferences with all business units to explain new initiatives. The CEO sent a weekly letter to all 140,000 employees discussing progress on his initiatives. The company established an interactive CEO Web site that provided daily company news (stock price; the "Motorola Minute," describing major events; and new products, services, and alliances). The daily news and update drew traffic each day to the site. The site included short tests on employees' knowledge of current initiatives and results ("Test your Motorola IQ") and sixty-second employee surveys. The surveys helped ECOM close the loop by measuring the outcomes from the communications process. It contained up to six yes/no and multiple-choice questions relating to the CEO's strategic themes.

In addition to the daily-changing information, the CEO Web site led employees on a Quick Tour, which contained the CEO's viewpoint, opinions on key issues facing Motorola, rationale for recent senior management decisions, discussion of corporatewide initiatives, and progress and status reports, including links to the company's Performance Excellence Scorecard. To reinforce the message, the site showcased great examples where theory had been turned into reality, case studies of strategy in action, and recognition of people who had achieved by breaking out of traditional organizational and performance boundaries.

The CEO Web site, with its continually updated information and features, soon became the most frequently visited location among Motorola employees. ECOM had recognized that if the rhetoric of "strategy execution coming from the bottom" were to happen, it had to invent new channels and an interactive communications environment. It took as its mission "the effective use of communication that allows an organization to make strategy everyone's job."

Sears: Learning Maps

Companies like Motorola and Sears, Roebuck and Co. have also used visual representations of the strategy to help employees understand the changes that are occurring and how they can contribute to successful implementation of the change initiatives.[4] A learning map visual consists of images and pathways designed to create employee discussions about a strategic theme. One such learning map visual at Sears (see Figure 8-3)

Figure 8-3 Learning Map at Sears

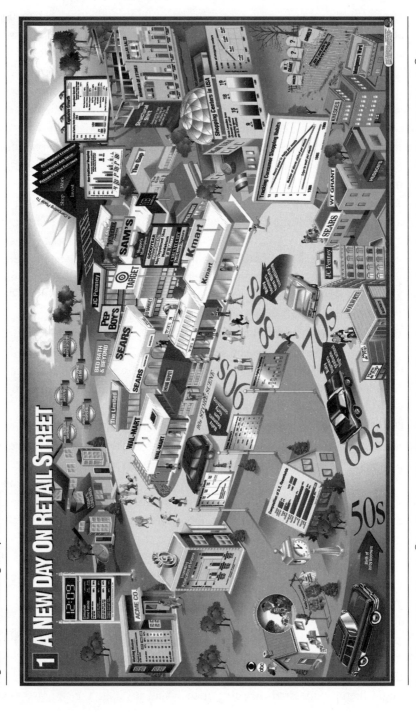

showed a winding street that started with pictures of the retail environment in the 1950s and wound through successive decades until the street showed the competitive environment of the mid-1990s: Wal-Mart Stores, Sears, J. C. Penney, The Limited, Toys 'R Us, Bed Bath & Beyond, The Home Depot, Target, and so on. The road ended by pointing to the somewhat unknown future. Every Sears employee—from top management, to stocking personnel, to salesclerks and checkout people—went through a facilitated learning map visual meeting with eight to ten colleagues. The maps and accompanying tables, charts, and graphs provided context for the employees to respond to questions about "What are the implications for our business and our team?"

After the small group meetings, the groups came together for a town hall meeting and action planning session at which the employees brainstormed about local actions that could be taken to help Sears succeed in its new and challenging competitive environment. The format was not senior management telling managers and employees what to do. Senior management had articulated broad strategic themes. Sears was to become[5]

1. A compelling place to shop
   - Great merchandise at great values
   - Excellent customer service from the best people
   - Fun place to shop
   - Customer loyalty

2. A compelling place to work
   - Environment for personal growth and development
   - Support for ideas and innovation
   - Empowered and involved teams and individuals

3. A compelling place to invest
   - Revenue growth
   - Superior operating income growth
   - Efficient asset management
   - Productivity gains

Within these three strategic themes, Sears wanted its employees to come up with the local actions that would help the company achieve its high-level objectives. Sears designed the learning map visual exercise and the follow-up town meetings to communicate the company's goals and vision more effectively, to provide the climate for managers to change their behavior toward employees, and to have both managers and employees understand the importance of making better customer-oriented decisions. The company wanted employees to become more responsive, take more initiative, and provide better service. Sears used the learning map visuals and town hall meetings to create small successes in employees' and managers' everyday life, not to aim for huge changes.

Strategy Trees

Many companies have constructed strategy trees to communicate how all the elements of their strategy are inter-related. A Texaco plant started by explicating how ROI could be affected by sales volume, which in turn would be driven by customer acquisition and retention. Then they showed a strategy tree (see Figure 8-4) for the value proposition expected to drive customer satisfaction: competitive price, product quality, service quality, and delivery. Employees could now see how local objectives such as maintenance costs, reliability, flexibility, and image contributed to overall organizational objectives. Employees learned about how the measures they could influence and control were linked to plantwide objectives.

At the Mobil Lubricants business unit of NAM&R, George Madden, the general manager, challenged his Balanced Scorecard project team to achieve two objectives:

1. Create an aligned and integrated organization in which every member has a clear understanding of the business's strategy: to function as one team

2. Drive the Balanced Scorecard down to every individual

The project started with a briefing to the team from the unit's top managers and function heads about the unit's strategy and organization. Once this was understood, the project team created a comprehensive cause-and-effect tree to help them accomplish their first objective. The actual diagram—consisting of several large brown papers that were taped together—filled a large wall. A simplified version is shown in Figure 8-5. The internal perspective on the actual tree contained more than one hundred internal processes.

After building the tree, the team rolled it up and took it to the field. During a period of twelve working days, the team held about forty meetings in

Figure 8-4   Texaco Refinery and Marketing's Customer Satisfaction Decomposition

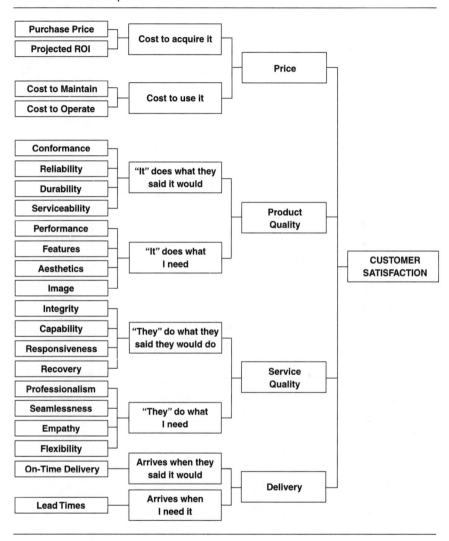

twenty different locations. Todd D'Attoma, the project team leader, described a typical meeting:

> *Most of the people had never heard of the Balanced Scorecard. We started off telling them what it was, our objectives in using the scorecard, and the role of the scorecard in the organization. Then we walked them through the tree, we talked about the alignment of ob-*

Figure 8-5 Mobil NAM&R Lubricants Division's Strategy Cause-and-Effect Tree

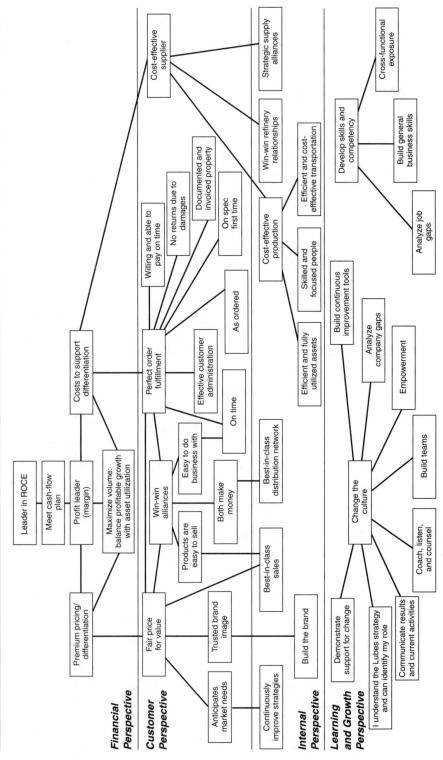

Source: Adapted from R.S. Kaplan, "Mobil USM&R (C): Lubricants Business Unit," 9-197-027 (Boston: Harvard Business School, 1996), 6. Reprinted by permission of Harvard Business School.

*jectives and strategies and about cross-functional relationships,
which the tree allows you to do. And then we asked them, "where do
you fit on the tree?" They were generally excited to find how their job
fit into our overall strategies and objectives. They went up to the tree,
pointed to their box, saw what they affected, and traced how their job
or position affected everything, eventually impacting ROCE. It was
powerful for individuals to see that.[6]*

With everyone now understanding the unit's strategy and where he or
she fit within that strategy, D'Attoma and his project team could move to
the second objective: to construct individual balanced scorecards (a
process that we describe in Chapter 9).

UNDERSTANDING THE MEASURES

Understanding the strategy, through extensive and innovative communication processes, is the initial building block for creating strategic awareness.
For any Balanced Scorecard project, managers should define clearly the
measures that will be used to guide and monitor the strategy on the scorecard, and how the measures will be calculated from underlying data. Employees must understand the measures clearly for their decisions and
actions to affect the strategy in the intended way.

As an example of the difficulty understanding measures that even
senior-level managers may have, we gave a list of thirty measures to one
ten-person executive team and asked them to identify the ones that they felt
should be on their Balanced Scorecard. Only one measure—ROCE—appeared on all ten lists. This concurrence on at least one measure was somewhat gratifying but not surprising, as the incentive compensation for every
executive in this capital-intense division was linked to ROCE. The lack of
consensus on the remaining measures indicated how much work would be
required to build the rest of the scorecard. Before proceeding with that task,
however, we gave the executives one more drill, asking them to write down
the formula used to compute ROCE in their organization. The ten executives produced ten different formulas! The lesson was clear. If the top ten
executives who managed the business didn't have a clear understanding of
their most common performance measure, imagine how poor the understanding was elsewhere in the organization.

We encourage organizations to be explicit about each measure used on
their Balanced Scorecards. Figure 8-6 shows a template that we have used
in several implementations. This template can be embedded in Balanced

Figure 8-6 Measurement Template

Strategic Objective: Measure: Measurement Intent:		Frequency of Update: Units of Measure:	
Measurement Definition/Formula:			
Notes/Assumptions:		Describes the plan to overcome any deficiencies in getting the required data	
Measurement Information Is:		**Data Elements and Sources:**	
Source for and Approach to Setting Targets:			
Target Setting Responsibility:	Accountability for Meeting Target:	Tracking/Reporting Responsibility:	Measure Availability: Target:

Target	1998 Actual	1999 Projected	2000	2001
	1Q 2Q 3Q 4Q Full Year			

Scorecard software systems so that users can easily access the measurement definitions.

The documentation of the measures should be complemented with ongoing education programs. Novacor, Inc., conducted an organizationwide education program to explain marketing and cost accounting concepts that appeared on the scorecard—for instance, segment share, customer profitability, and contribution margin (see Figure 8-7). Each employee attended a one-day training session to review the contents of the manual and to receive a better grounding on the economics of the business. In addition, the entire program was made available in an interactive forum on the company's local area network.

SUMMARY

Organizations follow comprehensive and creative programs to communicate their strategies and Balanced Scorecards. Companies use both tradi-

Figure 8-7 Educating about the Measures at Novacor

Internal Process Perspective

1. Focus on margin enhancement	Variable Margin = Selling Price – Variable Costs (e.g., feedstocks, energy, packaging, and delivery)

$$\frac{\$\$\$}{\$\$\$}$$

Raise selling prices and/or lower costs

1. Focus on Margin Enhancement

At the heart and soul of effectively managing our internal processes is the focus on margin enhancement. I referred to margin briefly in relation to customers. Before Business Transformation, we used to think we were doing a good job if we sold lots and lots of product. That's no longer a measurement of success. During Business Transformation, we shifted our thinking from just selling more and more product to determining which sales and customers are the most profitable.

When we go home at the end of the day, we should measure our achievement not on, say, the fact that we've sold five hopper cars full of polyethylene resin. Instead, we should consider it a successful day if we've generated a profitable margin on that sale—for example, a margin of $50,000 for Novacor.

Simply put, margin is the money we receive from our customers (sales revenue) minus costs to produce and deliver our product (revenue less variable cost × 100%).

The terms *variable margin* and *variable costs* are used when referring to margin to indicate the costs that change depending on production: feedstocks, packaging materials, etc. Fixed costs are those that don't change as the product volume changes, such as salaries and municipal property taxes. The Fixed Cost Productivity Measure, which we'll discuss later, deals with efficiencies related to fixed costs.

Variable margin reflects our pricing strategy as well as our ability to control costs. The goal is to improve margins through raising selling price and/or lowering costs. We can also increase our margins by selling value-added products, which we tailor to specific customer needs.

Feedstocks, such as the natural gas and crude oil we use to manufacture our products, offer a perfect example of where we have an opportunity to improve our efficiencies. Feedstocks are by far the largest single cost Novacor incurs in its operations. Every year, we pay in excess of $1.5 billion for raw materials. If we can drive our feedstock costs down, we will also make a definite positive impact on our margins.

tional channels (town meetings, brochures, newsletters, bulletin boards, and education and training programs) as well as effective new channels (Web sites, learning map visuals, and strategy cause-and-effect trees) to bring their strategy and the Balanced Scorecard to employees. They educate employees about the measures used on the strategy scorecard. The next steps reinforce the message: set individual goals consistent with the strategy (a topic presented in Chapter 9) and link incentive compensation to the achievement of individual, business unit, and company performance (the topic of Chapter 10).

NOTES

1. T. Stewart, "The Status of Communication Today," *Journal of Strategic Communication Management* (February–March 1999): 22–25.
2. J. Miniace and E. Falter, "Communication: A Key Factor in Strategy Implementation," *Planning Review* (January–February 1996): 26–30.
3. Material drawn from Steve Biederman, "Strategic Communication: A Two-Way Street at Motorola" (paper presented at the Balanced Scorecard Collaborative Best Practices Conference, Making Strategy Everyone's Job: Using the Balanced Scorecard to Align the Workforce, Cambridge, MA, 22–23 June 1999).
4. A. J. Rucci, S. P. Kirn, and R. T. Quinn, "The Employee-Customer-Profit Chain at Sears," *Harvard Business Review* (January–February 1998): 83–97.
5. Note that at this time Sears was using more of a constituent scorecard (see Chapter 3) than a strategy scorecard by featuring three stakeholders: customer, employees, and investors.
6. R. S. Kaplan, "Mobil USM&R (C): Lubricants Business Unit," 9-197-027 (Boston: Harvard Business School, 1996), 2.

Defining Personal and Team Objectives

FOR STRATEGY TO BECOME TRULY MEANINGFUL to employees, personal goals and objectives must be aligned with the organizational objectives. Setting objectives for individuals, of course, is not new. Management by objectives (MBO) has been around for decades.[1] But MBO is distinctly different from the strategic alignment achievable with the Balanced Scorecard. First, the objectives in an MBO system are established within the structure of the individual's organizational unit, reinforcing narrow, functional thinking. Second, the objectives are established relative to departmental goals, which, without a Balanced Scorecard strategic management system, are short-term, tactical, and financial. In effect, MBO reflects the traditional approach to job definition, whereby people are asked to do their existing jobs better.

The Balanced Scorecard, in contrast, provides individuals with a broad understanding of company and business unit strategy. It explicates where they fit in their organizations' strategy maps and how they can contribute to strategic objectives. Individual objectives established within the framework of the Balanced Scorecard should be cross-functional, longer-term, and strategic.

The City of Charlotte, described in Chapter 5, had a long history of performance measurement, having instituted an MBO program in 1972. Over the years, however, the MBO process had become burdensome and bureaucratic. City staff measured everything—workload, response time, cost per unit, and number of inspections. The MBO system led to an information overload, with 800 to 900 measures reported each year and lengthy reports that few people read. Pam Syfert, Charlotte city manager, described the city's dissatisfaction with its MBO process:

The city's management by objectives process served the organization well over the years and helped staff to track performance against targets. However, it did not reflect the '90s emphasis on strategic goals, mission-driven government, and rapid change. Our measurement system focused our attention backward, not forward. It was an audit tool, not a planning tool, and therefore did not relate to the city's vision, mission, or goals.[2]

Our research has shown that Charlotte's experience was not an aberration. Human resources systems, designed to provide clear objectives for employees, do not typically align to strategy:

- Only 51 percent of senior managers in the United States (and even fewer, 31 percent, in the United Kingdom) had their personal goals linked to strategy.
- Only 21 percent of U.S. middle managers (and 10 percent in the United Kingdom) had their personal goals linked to strategy.
- Only 7 percent of U.S. line employees (and 3 percent in the United Kingdom) had their personal goals linked to strategy.

Strategy-Focused Organizations, in contrast, can choose from a diverse set of methods to bridge from the strategic objectives that appear on a company or business unit scorecard across to personal and team objectives:

1. The "Super Bowl" approach
2. Alignment with strategic initiatives
3. Integration with existing planning and quality processes
4. Integration with human resource processes
5. Personal Balanced Scorecards

We illustrate each in turn.

THE "SUPER BOWL" APPROACH

At one Mobil business unit, New England Sales and Distribution (NES&D), the senior executive team introduced the Balanced Scorecard philosophy with a playful approach.[3] Unit CEO Tony Turchi felt that the scorecard was too complicated to communicate to his 300 employees in the field: "In 1995, we were doing Balanced Scorecard 101. We had to learn to walk before we could run. We needed to make it simple and understandable to all our people. We also wanted to create some fun and excitement."

In late January, the weekend after the Super Bowl, the NES&D leadership team organized a major meeting at a resort in New Hampshire. They decorated a meeting hall like a football field, gave everyone football sweatshirts, and showed videotapes of the great NFL professional teams like the Green Bay Packers and Pittsburgh Steelers. They had an announcer from NFL films describe how these winning teams had all the elements—offense, defense, coaches, the support groups—working together. The leadership team then announced that the New England region would have its own Super Bowl for 1995, with scoring based on five critical measures drawn from the financial, customer, and internal process measures on the NES&D scorecard:

- Gasoline volume
- Return on capital employed
- Customer complaints
- Mystery shopper rating
- Commitment to dealers

NES&D would win the Super Bowl if it could hit stretch targets on all five measures; the internal targets exceeded the performance levels committed by the leadership team to Mobil's headquarters. If NES&D reached all five targets, everyone would get a cash bonus of $250 and a great weekend next winter at a resort hotel in Vermont. If it failed in any one, there would be no reward.

The leadership team then rolled the Super Bowl program out to all people in the field.

We talked to the drivers, the union people and took them through the strategy, the Super Bowl concept, and asked for their support to help us achieve our goals, how they could impact the measures. The truck drivers didn't believe us. They said, "The marketing guys get all the good rewards and go out and have a good time; they never include the terminal guys." We had to convince them that we were serious. They were going to get the same reward as the marketing people.

After explaining the five measures and how the employees could affect them, the leadership team asked the employees to use the measures to set priorities for their work, and to stop doing work that didn't directly relate to improving the measures. As described in Chapter 2, truck drivers, on their own, started calling in from the field about stations that were dirty, poorly lit, and unfriendly to customers. The NES&D project team maintained communication through the year in meetings, e-mail, voice mail, and newsletters. The information included up-to-date reports on the five Super Bowl measures. At every meeting that Turchi and his senior leadership staff had with people in the field, performance was discussed against the Super Bowl targets.

By the end of the year, NES&D had greatly exceeded the stretch targets on four of the five Super Bowl measures. People acknowledged that the Super Bowl targets and the associated individual goals and objectives had driven this outstanding performance. But Turchi faced a dilemma:

Some said that the rules we established at the beginning required us to hit all five, or get nothing. But others argued that we exceeded four of the five, and came close on the fifth. We were about to enter 1996 with another set of very stretched targets, and I wanted people to be motivated to achieve them.

The NES&D leadership team eventually decided to award everyone the $250 bonus but not the free weekend in Vermont.[4] Turchi commented on the impact of the Super Bowl for his employees:

You can see the difference in our people. Pre-BSC, the scorecard for an area manager was pretty simple: sales, sales, and sales. For the manager of a terminal, it was cost, cost, cost, and perhaps a little safety. Now we are trying to have the people in both positions be mini-general managers, to have them think broadly about our entire business.

The Super Bowl approach provided a simple, clear, and focused set of measures and associated targets for all employees. It reinforced the new strategy and required little to no education about the Balanced Scorecard concept to make the measures and targets meaningful and actionable to frontline employees.

With the Super Bowl approach, however, the senior management group chooses the targeted measures. It is top-down, assuming that the executive team has superior information about the most critical elements of the unit's strategy. The leadership team had better get the critical measures correct, as they will likely get what they measure. The Super Bowl approach does not exploit any local information from middle managers and frontline employees for selecting measures and targets. For NES&D, a relatively homogeneous sales unit, the Super Bowl approach was likely fine, especially during the first year, to align all employees to the business unit's simple, common objectives through the five selected measures.

ALIGNMENT WITH STRATEGIC INITIATIVES

Government organizations tend to build their resource allocation and control processes around programs, as they are typically funded through authorized programs. Also, programs provide the linkage from employees' activities to the agency's mission. As a good example, the City of Charlotte's Department of Transportation (CDOT) drilled its scorecard down to employees by linking the department's scorecard measures to the department's high-priority programs.[5] In the past, the CDOT found it difficult to get employees and local supervisors to take time from their everyday jobs to focus on new initiatives. Terry Lathrop, CDOT deputy director, identified the Balanced Scorecard measures that would be affected by a successful implementation of each new program (see Figure 9-1). This process helped to influence the department's planning process:

Before, we couldn't get our people to focus on high-priority areas. People just wanted to talk about and plan for . . . what they did every day. This new planning process, based on the Balanced Scorecard, enabled department managers to pay serious attention to high-impact programs that had to be accomplished during the next 12 months.[6]

Second, Lathrop made sure that a work team then took ownership for each priority program, including measures of accountability and performance. The CDOT team developed a reporting framework for the high-

Summary of Division High-Impact Programs to Meet CDOT Objectives

Objectives	SMD 1	2	3	4	5	TOD 1	2	3	TPD 1	2	3	4	5	6	7	8	TSD 1	2	3	TED 1	2	3	PSD 1	2	3	4	STS 1	2	3	4	CTS 1	2	3	4	MKT 1	2	3	4	5	6	ADM 1	2	3	4	5	6	CDOT Measures
C-1 Maintain Transportation System	X																																															a. High-Quality Streets
		X	X	X		X	X	X									X	X	X																													b. Repair Response
																	X	X	X																												c. Travel Speed
C-2 Operate Transportation System																	X						X																									a. Commute Time
																	X	X					X																									b. Safety
																															X																	c. On-Time Buses
C-3 Develop Transportation System																											X																					a. Basic Mobility
									X	X							X						X	X																								b. Programs Introduced
C-4 Determine Optimal System	X	X									X	X	X	X	X	X	X			X	X		X																									a. Plan Progress
C-5 Improve Service Quality	X	X	X								X	X	X			X	X	X							X																							a. Responsiveness
F-1 Expand Noncity Funding											X									X			X													X												a. Funding Leverage
											X																										X											b. New Funding Sources
F-2 Maximize Benefit/Cost											X	X	X				X	X	X	X	X	X									X	X	X			X	X	X										a. Costs
I-1 Increase Infrastructure Capacity												X					X						X																									a. Capacity Ratios
																											X																					b. Capital Investment
I-2 Secure Resource Partners																					X									X				X													a. # of Partners
																																					X											b. Leverage Prospects
I-3 Improve Productivity									X	X											X			X			X	X	X	X	X	X	X	X						X	X							a. Cost per Unit
																											X	X	X	X	X	X	X	X														b. Street Maintenance Cost
																											X	X	X	X																		c. Transit Passenger Cost
																				X																												d. Competitive Sourcing
																									X																							e. Problem Identification
I-4 Increase Positive Contacts			X	X						X																						X			X													a. Customer Surveys
																						X										X				X												b. Customer Communication
L-1 Enhance Automated Systems	X																X						X																	X	X					X	X	a. Information Access
																																																b. IT Infrastructure
L-2 Enhance "Field" Technology	X																X														X															X		a. Information Tools
L-3 Close the Skills Gap	X		X	X		X	X																											X					X	X	X	X				X		a. Skills Identified
	X		X	X		X	X																																X	X	X	X				X		b. Skills Transfer
L-4 Empower Employees				X			X																															X										a. Employee Survey
			X				X																															X										b. Employee Goal Alignment

impact programs. Each of the forty-one programs had a one-page report that included the following:

- The Balanced Scorecard objectives and measures affected by the program
- The action steps required to implement the program
- The desired outcomes from the program
- The responsible managers
- The critical factors
- The program-specific performance measures

The report became the responsibility for each eight-person work crew. It provided the workers in each crew with a clear understanding of how their work contributed to citywide objectives, and how the work would be evaluated and judged. It gave ownership to the program and to the measures. It enabled the department to pass the workers' WIIFM ("What's in it for me?") criterion. The workers now had a context for their performance measures.

This method clearly delineated the responsibilities of frontline work teams. It also provided a validity check that each program and initiative, if successfully implemented, would have a significant impact on one or more Balanced Scorecard strategic measures. And it enhanced the motivation of the frontline teams by mapping their day-to-day activities up to high-level business unit and corporate objectives. One potential disadvantage is that the program was so structured that individuals were not left with much of a role for innovation and cross-functional initiatives. They may not find ways to have an impact on objectives and measures outside the specific jobs and tasks assigned to them.

INTEGRATION WITH EXISTING PLANNING AND QUALITY PROCESSES

United Parcel Service, with 344,000 employees, is the world's largest express carrier and package delivery company. Measurement has long been part of the UPS culture; the company strongly believes in the Vince Lombardi axiom "If you're not keeping score, you're only practicing."[7]

In December 1994, CEO Oz Nelson issued a directive to develop an improved measurement framework for a new UPS culture: to become a process-oriented organization. During 1995, the corporate quality group facilitated a process to establish that framework, which included the following:

- Senior management educated on TQM principles
- Point of arrival (POA) goals established at the corporate level
- Balanced Scorecard business plan for each region and district to achieve POA targets
- Deployment through a quality improvement process (QIP) at each business unit and quality performance reviews (QPRs) for every individual

Prior to the development of the Balanced Scorecard, employees did not understand how their local measurements and actions contributed to higher-level organizational goals. The goal of the new framework was to establish a clear line of sight from the frontline employees, who deliver to customers every day, up to the region, the district, and, finally, the corporation. Each employee had to understand how his or her job contributed to overall business goals.

The POA measures, selected by senior management, were indexes of

- Customer satisfaction
- Employee relations
- Competitive position
- Time in transit

The leadership team established stretch targets for these measures based on where UPS had to be to achieve its mission.

The Balanced Scorecards for the regions and districts contained measures in each of the four perspectives (see Figure 9-2).

Managers in each district conducted monthly business review meetings to develop and monitor strategic and cross-functional plans for improving the metrics on the Balanced Scorecard. The strategic plan included goals (targets) for the scorecard measures, root-cause analysis for problem areas, identification of the teams to attack the problems, and the time plan for implementation. Each operations supervisor developed action plans aligned to the strategic plan. The action plan components became elements in supervisors' QPRs.

Figure 9-2 UPS's Balanced Scorecard

Financial
■ Volume/Revenue/Cost Index
■ Profit Index

Customer
■ Claims Index
■ Concerns Index
■ Data Integrity

Internal
■ Quality Report Card
■ Operations Report Card

People
■ Injury Reduction
■ Employee Retention
■ Employee Relations Index

The QPR, derived from the district Balanced Scorecard, replaced the MBO local measures that had been used previously. In this way, district objectives were aligned with corporate objectives, and local success would contribute to achieving corporate goals. Scores on the performance reviews determined up to 50 percent of a manager's compensation; 80 percent of the rating came from the Balanced Scorecard results and 20 percent from an assessment of the manager's critical skills and competencies from supervisor, peer, and personal ratings.

UPS managers believe that the linked Balanced Scorecard measurements played a critical role in moving it from a functional to a process-oriented organization—a transition that most organizations fail to accomplish. The new system was implemented flexibly, so that perspectives could be emphasized differently, depending on the process and its level in the organization. The system built upon the existing emphasis on quality, so it was not viewed as a major change from the TQM culture that had been established in the prior several years. The new system was also widely accepted at UPS because it supplied employees with both intrinsic and extrinsic motivation. People wanted to know the big picture, the cause-and-effect relationships that linked their local job to corporate strategy and objectives. And because all employees could purchase the company's stock (even before it went public in November 1999), they had a natural interest in learning how they could influence the company's stock price.

INTEGRATION WITH THE HUMAN RESOURCES PROCESS

Winterthur International, a top-ten international property and casualty in-
surer, deployed its Balanced Scorecard through a performance management model developed by the human resources function. The company
had recently formulated a new differentiation strategy for industry leadership based on intellectual capital and competencies. Winterthur built a
performance model to link the strategy through eight themes:

1. Lower the cost base
2. Manage claims
3. Focus the sales force
4. Promote the value of the network
5. Be selective in underwriting
6. Institute team-based solution selling
7. Develop alternative risk transfer (ART) products
8. Manage portfolio and overall risk

These themes established the linkages from financial objectives to objectives in the customer, internal, and learning and growth perspectives.
Winterthur then developed lagging and leading measures for its Balanced
Scorecard. The company made the scorecard come alive by linking measures to specific employee development and change programs.

Winterthur's human resources group developed a new management
structure to attract, develop, and retain the highly motivated and strategy-
focused workforce required for the new business strategy (see Figure 9-3).
The HR management structure developed a set of specific job families. For
each family, the HR group defined accountabilities, skills and knowledge,
performance indicators (measures), and behavioral competencies. The
competencies and performance indicators defined the kinds of people the
company wanted and how they would make specific contributions to
the company's strategy. The new structure emphasized the outcomes from
the HR function, not the activities it performed.[8] The job family definitions
and measures identified training and development needs and served to
guide promotion and career-planning progression.

Many of the skills, knowledge, and competencies, of course, were difficult to measure, as they involved such subjective and difficult-to-observe

Figure 9-3 Winterthur International's Human Resources Management Process

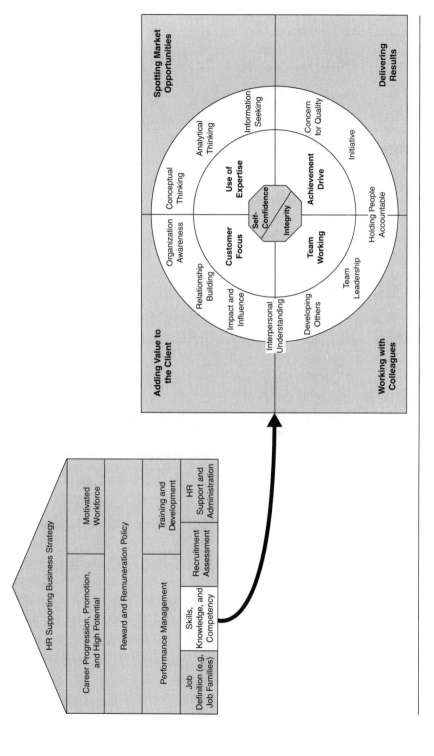

concepts as relationship-building, developing skills in others, conceptual thinking, and interpersonal understanding. The exercise, however, of deriving individual objectives from how people could contribute to achieving the strategy served to make Winterthur's strategic themes, objectives, and measures meaningful for all employees.

Nova Scotia Power, Inc., also used its human resources group to drive the scorecard down to individuals. The HR group analyzed what competencies the employees needed to have for the strategy to succeed. They asked every employee to perform a self-assessment about how they measured up against the competencies, with adequate validation (such as 360-degree feedback) to ensure that the assessments were realistic. Employees then defined personal development plans, which they validated with their managers, that would bridge the gap between the competencies and skills possessed today and those needed for the future.

PERSONAL BALANCED SCORECARDS

When individuals can construct their own Balanced Scorecards, then we have produced the clearest mechanism for aligning individual objectives to business unit and corporate objectives. In our previous book, we described how the exploration group of a large oil company created a small, fold-up personal scorecard (see Figure 9-4) for each person in the organization. The card contained three levels of information. The first level, preprinted on the left side of the card, described the corporate objectives and measures. The second level, printed in the middle, provided space for the business unit to translate the corporate goals into its specific goals. The third level enabled individuals and teams to define their personal performance objectives and the near-term steps of action they would take to achieve their objectives. Individuals also defined up to five personal performance measures for the personal objectives, as well as targets for these objectives that would be consistent with achieving the higher-level business unit and corporate objectives. The personal card kept the three levels of objectives, measures, and actions readily accessible on a daily basis for all employees. In contrast to the typical MBO approach, individuals did not develop their local objectives until they had a clear understanding of corporate and business unit objectives. They then articulated how their local, personal performance objectives would contribute to the accomplishment of business unit and corporate objectives.

Figure 9-4   Personal Balanced Scorecard

Corporate Objectives

- Double our corporate value in seven years
- Increase our earnings by an average of 20% per year
- Achieve an internal rate-of-return 2% above the cost of capital
- Increase both production and reserves by 20% in the next decade

	Corporate Targets			Scorecard Measures	Business Unit Targets			Team/Individual Objectives and Initiatives
	1997	1998	1999		1997	1998	1999	
Financial	160	180	250	Earnings (in millions of dollars)				1.
	200	210	225	Net cash flow				
	80	75	70	Overhead and operating expenses				
								2.
Operating	73	70	64	Production costs per barrel				
	93	90	82	Development costs per barrel				
	108	108	110	Total annual production				3.

Team/Individual Measures	**Targets**		
1.			
2.			4.
3.			
4.			
5.			5.
Name: Location: *1995 level = 100			

Source: Adapted from Robert S. Kaplan and David P. Norton, "Using the Balanced Scorecard as a Strategic Management System," *Harvard Business Review* (January–February 1996): 81. Reprinted by permission of *Harvard Business Review.*

Initially at Nova Scotia Power, personal scorecards were developed only for senior executives and sales account managers. Over time, the Balanced Scorecard has been adopted and cascaded throughout the business units. Managers from all other parts of the organization have begun to utilize personal Balanced Scorecards for themselves and their employees to promote individual alignment with department, business unit, and corporate objectives. The personal scorecards are now beginning to be used to integrate personal development goals and performance management to scorecard measures and results that are tied to compensation. In one group, Treasury

Operations, all thirty-five employees developed personal Balanced Scorecards in the first year of scorecard implementation and linked all their variable compensation to scorecard performance. Since that time, the number of employees in the Finance Group with personal Balanced Scorecards has increased each year. CFO Jay Forbes's goal for 2000 is for 80 percent (104 of 130) of his employees to have a personal Balanced Scorecard in place. Forbes observed:

We had situations that required a bit of imagination and creativity to define the right measure of success. For example, Investor Services finally took as a goal to eliminate phone calls from irate retail investors to the CEO or CFO. The groups learned that they had to measure and manage customer perceptions with the same vigor as salespeople.

Nova Scotia Power has had success in cascading the scorecard to the frontline employee in its Operating Business Unit as well. For example, in two of its generating stations, Balanced Scorecards were cascaded to the shop-floor (team) level, equating to twenty-six scorecards at two stations.

The standard for individual Balanced Scorecards, however, was established by Mobil NAM&R's Lubricants business unit. In Chapter 8, we described how the unit's project team used a cause-and-effect strategy tree (see Figure 8-5) to communicate strategy to the front lines. The team asked employees to develop individual Balanced Scorecards using the following rules:

- Scorecard should have a minimum of one objective and measure per perspective.
- Do not exceed fifteen measures.
- The individual's scorecard must support the supervisor/manager's scorecard.
- The scorecard must include a mix of lead and lag indicators.
- Every supervisor/manager must have an objective and measure related to coaching, counseling, or employee development.
- The scorecard must include an objective and measure that supports another part of the business.
- Any change must be agreed to by both supervisor and employee.

By having at least one objective and measure in each perspective, everyone would have a "Balanced Scorecard." For the financial perspective, each individual could identify a cost or revenue item that he or she could affect. For customers, employees had to recognize the internal or external person or group who benefited from their work. The internal process objectives reflected the activities performed by the individual that would improve financial and customer performance. And for the learning and growth objectives, the project team asked employees to develop personal development plans that would help them meet their objectives in the other three perspectives. The constraint of fifteen measures meant that the scorecards had to be simple. The team did not want this task to be complex and burdensome.

The linkage to supervisors and managers ensured that high-level objectives would cascade down through the organization (see Figure 9-5). It provided the linkage from business unit objectives to individual objectives. Individuals in the Lubricants unit reported that for the first time they understood what their supervisors and their supervisors'supervisors were trying to accomplish. This knowledge helped them do their jobs better.

One can see in Figure 9-5 how aggregate measures for the business unit general manager (George Madden at level 1) cascade down six levels to eventually reach a truck driver. Even in the seventh level, every measure in the truck driver's scorecard contributes in some way to the organizational strategy. Madden felt that the drill down to personal Balanced Scorecards enabled helped him to communicate a clear message about critical success factors: "I've been talking for four years about the need to fulfill the perfect order. But what did it mean? No one knew, outside of the order-fulfillment people. Now the vast majority of the people in this organization own a piece of that measure."

The mix of lead and lag indicators allowed employees to include measures that they could not directly control but whose performance was expected to improve as employees made improvements in the leading indicators (the performance drivers) on their scorecard. Thus employees learned the distinction between measures they could influence, through their actions, and measures they could directly control.

The measures on coaching and personal development were especially significant. Each individual developed an action plan for the learning and growth perspective: what will be done during the next period to maximize the likelihood of achieving scorecard targets and enhancing personal development. Thus, as at Winterthur, the Balanced Scorecard tied directly to personal development plans for achieving business unit strategic objectives.

Figure 9-5 Cascading to Teams and Individuals at Mobil NAM&R's Lubricants Division

Strategic Themes	Level 1 Division President	Level 2 VP—Order Fulfillment	Level 3 Manager of Plant Operation	Level 4 Facility Manager	Level 5 Delivery Supervisor	Level 6 Terminal Coordinator	Level 7 Motor Vehicle Driver
Financial Reward our shareholders by providing a long-term return which exceeds our peers.	ROCE (%) Cash Flow ($mm) **Integrated Cost ($mm)** Integrated Income ($mm)	**LOB Integrated Cost ($mm)** Net Integrated Income ($mm)	Inventory Value ($mm) **Transformation Cost ($mm)**	Inventory Carrying Cost **Line 44 Cents per Gallon** Formulation Giveaway ($m)	**Line 25 Cents per Gallon** Backhaul ($)	**Line 2 Cents per Gallon** Unavailable Hours Backhauls Savings	**Line 24 Cents per Gallon** ■ Idle Time ■ Out-of-Route Miles ■ Miles per Gallon
Customer Provide value-added business solutions to our customers and channel partners.	Market Share—Finished **Percent Perfect Orders** Develop/Implement Distributor Survey Customer Survey	**Percent Perfect Orders** Distributor Survey Develop/Implement Customer Survey	**Percent Perfect Orders**	**Percent Perfect Orders** Service Failures of Strategic Product Lines	**% On-Time Delivery** Develop Market Information Survey	**% On-Time Delivery** ■ Empty Drums Returned	**% On-Time Delivery** ■ Returns Drums ■ Customer Assessment
Internal Develop market-focused strategies and become operationally excellent.	**Safety Index** Environmental Index Continuous Improvement Cost Reduction ($mm) Develop/Implement Capital Plan	**Safety Index** Environmental Index Develop/Implement Standard Offering Asset Utilization Refinery Capacity (%) Network vs. Optimum (%) Inventory Accuracy	**Safety Index** Environmental Index Complexity Index Inventory Accuracy	**Days Away from Work** ■ Hits ■ Off-Spec Receipts ■ Transfers to Move 　Excess Base Stock	■ **Motor Vehicle Accidents** ■ **Days Away from Work**	Complete Environmental Self-Audit ■ **Safety Meetings Complete** ■ **% Attendance Safety Meeting**	Accurate Reporting Repts. 731, 601, 727 ■ **LOG Book Violations** Market Surveys
Learning and Growth Create a high-performance organization by equipping our people to succeed.	**Employee Development Plans Completed (%)** Develop/Implement/ Measure Progress of Change Program	**Employee Development Plans Completed (%)** Develop/Implement Marketing Comp. Plan, Product Management Plan, Distribution/Logistics Comp. Plan	**Employee Development Plans Completed (%)** Attendance	**Employee Development Plans Completed (%)** Develop Plan Climate Survey	**Employee Development Plans Completed (%)** Employees Trained ISO 9000 Certification	**Training on CCE**	**Develop Personal Improvement Plan**

SBU SCORECARD

Madden insisted on the criterion of choosing at least one measure outside the individual's normal job or work assignment. He wanted employees to think "out of the box." They had all seen the cause-and-effect strategy tree. Madden wanted them to think how they could help the business in a cross-functional or other innovative way.

As in the New England district, the truck drivers came through with the most innovative suggestion. The drivers noted that they drove 200,000 miles a year and basically lived in truck stops. While at truck stops—for fuel, food, or rest—they were around other truck drivers. The Lubricants truck drivers offered to work with the marketing research people in the commercial engine oil business to develop a survey that they would administer to learn about the other drivers' purchases and perceptions of engine oils. The truck drivers actually volunteered to conduct market surveys in truck stops that would provide feedback to people in the product development, marketing, and distribution side of the business.

If George Madden had ordered the truck drivers to conduct such surveys, the drivers would likely have imitated their French brethren and parked their trucks across highways, stopping traffic in all directions. But this suggestion did not come from the business head; it came from the frontline employees themselves. And the employees volunteered for the task, even though they likely would have refused the extra work if they had been ordered from above to perform it. This illustrates the power of intrinsic motivation. Madden trusted the workers and shared the business unit's strategy with them. The workers, seeing the whole picture for the first time, bought into the values of the organization, internalized them, and engaged in creative problem solution to propose an entirely new activity that would help the organization achieve its strategic objectives.

Our initial case study in this chapter described Mobil NES&D's use of the Super Bowl approach for its personal alignment process. It chose five measures from the scorecard and had every employee work to achieve stretch targets for the five measures. We argued earlier that the Super Bowl approach may have been fine for a relatively homogeneous and focused organization like a sales district.

Mobil Lubricants, in contrast, took the more complex and costly route by requiring that all 550 employees develop a personal Balanced Scorecard. The personal Balanced Scorecard approach required a strong project team to launch the concept and see that it was understood throughout the organization, plus the time of supervisors and employees to develop the cascaded scorecards and personal development plans. The Lubricants unit was a much more complex organization than a sales district. It had several different market segments, different distribution channels, and potentially different strategies. A single, high-level scorecard or a few Super Bowl measures may not have given sufficient guidance to people in the different segments, channels, and product lines. Therefore the cascading of score-cards down through the business allowed each Balanced Scorecard to be customized to the particular situation in which each team and individual found itself.

Arguably, the two business units—NES&D and Lubricants—each took the right approach for its business for linking scorecards to individual ob-jectives, even though the two approaches were diametrically different. This illustrates the importance of tying the Balanced Scorecard program to busi-ness strategy. One size cannot possibly fit all.

SUMMARY

Companies have many ways to link individuals' local behavior to higher-level business unit and corporate objectives. Homogeneous organizations whose outcomes are relatively easy to measure—such as a sales organiza-tion—can focus on relatively few measures, mostly outcomes in the finan-cial and customer perspectives. With only a few measures, executives ask individual employees and teams to improvise and innovate to find new ways of achieving the desired organizational outcomes.

More complex organizations will share the outcomes and strategy they are trying to achieve, and will allow each individual or team to define per-sonal objectives they can influence that will have an impact on the organi-zational objectives. The structure becomes even more formal when the personal objectives are developed either through personal Balanced Score-cards or integration with quality deployment and human resources devel-opment processes.

NOTES

1. Management by objectives was introduced by Peter Drucker in *The Practice of Management* (New York: HarperBusiness, 1954).
2. R. S. Kaplan, "City of Charlotte (A)," 9-199-036 (Boston: Harvard Business School, 1998), 2.

3. See R. S. Kaplan, "Mobil USM&R(B): New England Sales and Distribution Unit," 9-197-026 (Boston: Harvard Business School, 1996).

4. Some of the nonskiing employees thought this was a better outcome than receiving the free winter weekend at the resort.

5. R. S. Kaplan, "City of Charlotte (B)," 9-199-043 (Boston: Harvard Business School, 1999).

6. Ibid., 3.

7. Vince Lombardi was the legendary coach of the championship Green Bay Packer NFL teams of the 1960s.

8. The shift in emphasis for the HR function—from activity measures to outcome measures—matches the advocacy of leading HR scholars; see D. Ulrich, "A New Mandate for Human Resources," *Harvard Business Review* (January–February 1998): 124–34.

The Balanced Paycheck

THE FINAL LINKAGE FROM HIGH-LEVEL STRATEGY to day-to-day actions occurs when companies link individuals' incentive and reward programs to the Balanced Scorecard. As one plant manager noted after implementing a new reward program linked to its scorecard, "We have always had the measures. And we have always communicated them. Now our people are interested in them." A Mercer Consulting Group, Inc., study of compensation practices in 214 companies reported that 88 percent of responding companies considered the linkage of Balanced Scorecard measures to reward systems to be effective.[1] Likewise, a Hay Group study of fifteen sophisticated users of the Balanced Scorecard found that thirteen of them linked pay to the scorecard.[2] Fifty percent linked compensation to their first Balanced Scorecard. Those that did not link pay quickly to the scorecard had started with a pilot implementation and were still in the process of deploying the scorecard more widely in the organization. The companies had adopted the Balanced Scorecard to reinforce their transformation from a traditional functional organization to a new customer-focused one, as the following list shows.

Old Organization	New, Customer-Focused Organization
Functional	Process-oriented
Decision-making at top	Decentralized decision-making
Bureaucratic	Flexible
Measure tasks and activities	Measure outputs and outcomes
Little variable pay	Pay for results

The linkage to pay communicated the values of the new organizational form to employees.

No consistent program emerged across the thirteen firms in the Hay study. Twelve firms built the incentive pay into the annual cash bonus plan; six had long-term incentive pay linked to the scorecard, but only one of these used the scorecard linkage alone for the long-term program. About one-quarter to one-third of total direct compensation was influenced by the Balanced Scorecard approach. Eight companies had changed their pay system to increase the alignment of employees with the strategy.

All companies used *financial* metrics in the incentive scheme. Typically, companies used three financial measures and assigned 40 percent of the weight to the financial measures. The most common measures were net income, operating margin, and revenues, although ROCE, EVA, and revenue growth were also often used. The companies varied in the degree of stretch assigned to the financial targets: five companies used targets that were considered easily achievable, eight used stretch targets. Payouts typically started when performance reached 75 percent of the targets.

The *customer* measures, receiving about 15 percent to 20 percent of the weight, were, not surprisingly, "customized" to each company's local situation and strategy. Customer satisfaction, customer retention, and new customers were the most often used metrics. Respondents reported that their *internal business process* metrics—typically about two measures and accounting for about 25 of the weight—were more easily quantified than their customer perspective metrics. Often the internal process metrics—such as safety, efficiency, and new product development—were used as a multiplier, to leverage the total size of the award. As with the customer metrics, companies varied a great deal in which metrics they used. The *learning and growth* metrics, receiving about 15 percent to 20 percent of the weight, were, like the customer metrics, quite subjective and varied across the companies. Typical metrics were information technology deployment, employee satisfaction, individual development, and diversity.

The surveyed companies reported that having a multifunctional team design and communicate the incentive program made a big difference for employee understanding and acceptance. Companies did not want the new incentive program to be viewed as an initiative led by the human resources department. Active, continual, and effective communication of the program was also viewed as critical for success. The scorecard played a central role in overcoming the largest barrier to new incentive and reward programs: disagreement about the company's present state and performance. The scorecard made explicit the tradeoffs involved in implementing the new strategy. Finally, continual reinforcement and commitment from the CEO was critical for the success of the new incentive pay structure.

LINKING COMPENSATION TO BALANCED SCORECARDS

Incentive compensation is a powerful lever to gain people's attention to company and business unit objectives. When Brian Baker first linked incentive compensation to Mobil North America Marketing and Refining's Balanced Scorecard, his peers at the corporation chided him about how much time his people spent studying the scorecard results each month. He responded:

> *I think just the opposite. It's fabulous that people spend that time. For one hour each month, all employees are taking out the scorecard and looking at the most important things in their business and whether we were winning or losing against the targets. They're doing this to see how much money they were going to get. We would not have gotten that same focus on the scorecard, and the individual business objectives, if we hadn't made the link to pay.*

The linkage plays two important roles: It focuses employees' attention on the measures that are most critical for the strategy, and it provides extrinsic motivation by rewarding employees when they and the organization succeed in reaching their targets. But the particular details of how to link incentive pay to compensation differs for each of the companies we studied. No one approach has emerged as preferred or dominant.

Mobil North America Marketing and Refining

We described in Chapter 2 the three-tier compensation plan used by Mobil NAM&R. Here we expand on that description to describe how individual business units set targets for the plan.

Each business unit assigned its own percentage weights to the measures on the scorecard. These percentages determined the relative contribution of each scorecard measure to the bonus pool. The percentages, of course, had to sum to 100 across all the targeted measures. The business units chose to weight almost all of the measures on their scorecards. Only one business unit put more than a 50 percent weight on its financial measures.

The business units also established targets for each scorecard measure, along with a performance factor that represented the perceived degree of difficulty of target achievement (see Figure 10-1). The maximum index score of 1.25 occurred when the target would put the Mobil unit as best-in-class. An average target received a performance factor of 1.00, and a factor score as low as 0.70 would be applied when the target represented poor performance or was deemed very easy to achieve. While the individual business units proposed the performance factors for each measure, they had to explain and defend them in a meeting attended by several of their peers, the executive leadership team, and shared service unit heads. Col-

Figure 10-1 Mobil NAM&R's Metric Performance Factors

Performance Factor	Qualitative	
1.25	Best-in-Class	
1.20		**How to think about performance factors:**
1.15	Well above Average	
1.12		**1. Objective**
1.09		*External Benchmark*
1.06	Above Average	1.00 means target equals the
1.03		average of competition
1.00	Average	1.25 means target equals the
0.90		top of the competitive group
0.80	Below Average	
0.70		**2. Subjective**
0.60		*Internal Benchmark*
0.50	Needs Improvement	1.00 means the difficulty of
0.40		the target is average

lectively, this group had a great deal of knowledge about the degree of stretch in any proposed target.

The total performance amount is calculated by multiplying the performance factor by the actual value of the measure—much the way a diving competition is scored. In a diving competition, someone who attempts an easy dive may execute it flawlessly and be awarded the top score of 10 on merit. But because the degree of difficulty was low (say, 0.8), the total amount of points awarded to the dive (8) will be low. Another competitor may try an extremely difficult dive (triple reverse with two and a half spins, with a difficulty factor of 2.8), do it satisfactorily but not perfectly (be awarded a 7.1), and yet earn a much higher total score (19.9) for the dive.

Brian Baker was a strong advocate for the indexed targets:

Historically, people were rewarded for meeting targets and penalized when they missed a target. So sandbagging targets became an art form around here. I prefer the current system where I can give a better rating to a manager who stretches for a target and falls a little short than to someone who sandbags with an easy target and then beats it.[3]

Specific individuals, in shared service units, were designated to be the "metric owners." They collected and reported the data for their assigned metric. The use of metric owners gave specific responsibility to individuals for establishing reliable processes—ones with good internal controls and validity—for reporting on Balanced Scorecard measures, a critical feature when tying the scorecard to compensation. Sharing responsibility reduced what would otherwise have been a heavy burden on a single individual to do the data collection and reporting tasks, and it exploited the expertise of specific individuals and departments for data collection.

The metric owners participated in a leveling process, for all the business units, to ensure that the targets for individual units had comparable degrees of difficulty. And by having metric owners in staff rather than line departments, there was greater independence and objectivity for the data. This point was particularly important, as large amounts of compensation would be paid, or not paid, based on the performance reported by the metric owners against the targets.

Mobil's corporate portion of the award (the first 10 percent component) was recognized as a "below the operating profit" line in NAM&R's reporting statement to Mobil corporate. The bonus paid to employees based on the division and business unit's performance, therefore, was an expense charged against NAM&R's performance. Baker himself was only compensated on the corporate and divisional financial performance. So most of the bonus his division paid to employees detracted from his personal performance metric and compensation. Nevertheless, noted Baker, "Nothing would make me happier than to pay the maximum amount to all my employees. I really believe that if we are best-in-class on all scorecard measures, the return to the company on the bonus amount I pay our employees will be repaid many times."

The degree of alignment of individuals to the scorecard was highlighted by an incident that occurred in late 1998. Divisional headquarters received a phone call one morning from the wife of an employee who worked in the pipeline business unit. She asked whether anyone could tell her what the refinery environmental and safety indexes would be for the current month. After some investigation, someone reported back to her with the best estimates for those measures. But the headquarters people were perplexed by the phone call. Why would the wife of a pipeline employee be interested in measures about refinery operations?

Eventually, they learned that she was about to purchase a major new household appliance. She wanted to know how much she could afford to spend. She knew the formula for the bonus plan and that recent refinery performance had been falling short of target. She was curious whether a turnaround had occurred that would substantially increase the end-of-year bonus. Executives talk about the value of having all individuals aligned to the strategy. Imagine the alignment that occurs when not only the employees but also their spouses are actively discussing and trying to improve strategic performance.

Nova Scotia Power

Nova Scotia Power, Inc., linked 100 percent of its variable pay to the scorecard. Every vice president, in a meeting with the CEO, identified which Balanced Scorecard objectives and measures were most important for the upcoming year and agreed to an incentive plan based on these measures. Each business group set three targets for the next year: threshold, midpoint, and stretch. Threshold was the minimum performance for earning a bonus. Hitting the midpoint target earned a moderate bonus, and the maximum possible bonus was earned for meeting or exceeding the stretch target.

The company used a mixture of group and individual awards. Senior management had a personal Balanced Scorecard against which a personal bonus was awarded, based on performance against the three achievement levels. Employees further down the organization tended to receive group awards, although managers had the freedom to measure people on either individual or group results, depending on the nature of the work. Most employees at Nova Scotia Power had incentive compensation plans linked to the scorecard in some way.

CIGNA Property & Casualty

Gerry Isom of CIGNA Property & Casualty did not dictate a particular compensation plan. He subjectively assigned a bonus pool to each of the twenty-one business units and asked each unit to determine its own method for rewarding individuals. One unit developed an innovative Performance Share Plan (PSP) that other units all liked and subsequently adopted.[4]

With the PSP, all employees received a fixed number of "position shares" at the beginning of each year. The number of position shares awarded depended on the individual's job position. Throughout the year, supervisors awarded employees additional "performance shares" based on performance. All shares started out with a par value of $10 each, but at the time of pay-out, the unit recalculated the price of the shares based on its Balanced Scorecard performance. For example, one employee started the year with 50 position shares, having a par value of $10 each. During the year, she was awarded 100 performance shares, representing high individual performance. But because her business unit fell short of target for many Balanced Scorecard measures, the end-of-year price per share was $5. The employee received a bonus of $750, reflecting a strong individual performance but weak business unit performance.

Conversely, another employee at the same position level (receiving the 50 share initial endowment) performed weakly and received only 10 performance shares. But he was in a high-performance business unit whose end-of-year share price was calculated at $14. This employee received a bonus of $840 (see Figure 10-2).

The most relevant scorecard to the individual's work—corporate, division, or business unit—determined the price for each employee's shares. For example, the price for the shares earned by clerks working in the corporate claims processing unit was determined by the Balanced Scorecard

Figure 10-2 CIGNA Property & Casualty's Incentive Compensation System

Total Shares = Position Shares + Performance Shares

Unit Share Value Determined from Balanced Scorecard (Par Value = $10.00)

Strategic Objective	% Weight	Financial Measures	Nonfinancial Measures
(F1) Shareholder Expectations	20	Net Operating Income	
(F1) Operating Performance	15	Accident Year Combined	
(F3) Growth	20	Gross Written Premiums	
(E1) Producer Relationship	10		Producer Feedback (Councils, Surveys, etc.)
(I2) Underwriting Profitability	10		Underwriting Practice Reviews
(L2) Information Technology	5		Upgrade Computer Literacy
Other	20		

Example 1

$5.00/Unit Share x 50 Position Shares
+ 100 Performance Shares
= 150 Shares

Bonus = $750.00

Example 2

$14.00/Unit Share x 50 Position Shares
+ 10 Performance Shares
= 60 Shares

Bonus = $840.00

of the business unit they supported, such as the workers' compensation unit. Thus business unit heads received the attention and commitment not only of the people who worked directly in their department but also from people who provided service to the business unit from corporate support groups. Tom Valerio, chief transformation officer of CIGNA, noted, "It's not a question of centralizing or decentralizing corporate staffs. It's aligning them with the specific businesses."

The leadership team kept raising the performance targets, and employees continued to innovate to earn the maximum score on all fourteen measures of the PSP. And the company exhibited more balanced performance, with only 40 percent of the weight assigned to the financial measures, which in the insurance industry are highly lagging indicators of the critical underwriting and claims-processing processes. Isom believes that the PSP contributed significantly to CIGNA Property & Casualty's extraordinary turnaround: "Incentive compensation programs are all about reinforcing. If your people do a really good job on their BSC, I can't think of a better way to reinforce their accomplishments than linking them to an incentive program. For us, the linkage has been everything."

Winterthur International

Winterhur International placed a great deal of weight on the reward and remuneration component of its Balanced Scorecard management system. Annually, each individual received one of four ratings based on objectives and competencies, as shown in the following list.

Rating   Criteria for Rating

OS   Outstanding Performance

This level is achieved by few others and with no shortfalls. Objectives are exceeded; the individual may be performing regularly in situations of significantly increased responsibility, defining new standards of exceptional performance.

AT   At Stretched Target

Performance delivers against stretched targets and may exceed some targets, with no shortfalls. This is a fully effective performer who consistently meets job requirements across accountabilities as well as the stretched objectives in the performance plan.

GA   Performance Is Acceptable

Performance is generally acceptable and meets most objectives. Shortfalls are in noncritical areas. Some objectives are met, but definite improvements are needed.

NA   Performance Is Not Yet Acceptable

Performance is not in line with the requirement in the performance plan and job family. This person requires a closely monitored performance improvement plan.

Winterthur, like Mobil, established employees' base pay at 10 percent below the median. Not Acceptable (NA) performance received no bonus, so the individual received below-median pay for the year. Acceptable (GA) performance enabled the employee to receive a 10 percent bonus, bringing total pay up to the median for that job. Stretch target (AT) performance placed the employee at the seventy-fifth percentile of pay, and outstanding (OS) performance led to pay that met or exceeded the ninetieth percentile. The awards for outstanding performance (a 35 percent bonus for middle managers and supervisors; 80 percent to more than 100 percent for members of the executive board) greatly exceeded the bonuses typically paid to

European managers of any kind of enterprise, much less one in the insurance business. The executive board funding was based on the corporate Balanced Scorecard; the funding for managers and supervisors came from a budgeted pool to reward achievement of nonfinancial targets, including individuals' performance within the job family and performance model.

As the following list shows, the weighting for the bonus was a mixture of group, business unit, and individual performance.

Category	Group Level	Company Financial	Company Nonfinancial	Individual
Executive board	20%	30%	20%	30%
Managers/supervisors	0	33%	33%	33%

The group-level measures were mostly all financial and were specified by the Winterthur Group board. The company (Winterthur International) measured three or four financial and three or four nonfinancial measures. The individual measures represented up to four personal business objectives.

The particular measures used in the compensation plan evolved over time, although several measures remained the same from year to year. In any given year, they reflected the business priorities for that year. To be included, any metric had to be objectively measurable and sufficiently developed and comprehensive so that different levels of performance could be reasonably assessed across individuals. In this way, the performance awards were viewed as fair and transparent.

Texaco Refinery and Marketing, Inc.: Noncash Compensation

Texaco's U.S. refineries could not use a formal cash incentive program because of constraints in its union contract. Outside consultants helped the company institute a "Texaco Points" program. Texaco points had a $1 par value, but they could be redeemed only for merchandise, travel, and retail awards, not for cash.

Texaco points were awarded based on plantwide results, work-group team results, and individual performance. The awards were made frequently and based on monthly, quarterly, and annual performance. In addition, supervisors could make spontaneous awards to individuals based on exceptional performance.[5] The following list contains examples of the measures used in the recognition program.

Plantwide Team	Work-Group Team	Individual
Safety	Throughput	Perfect attendance
Utilization	No unscheduled downtime	No safety (OSHA) recordable incidents
Expenses (excluding utilities)	Expenses	
Energy expenses		

In implementing the new recognition plan, Texaco Refinery and Marketing, Inc. (TRMI) managers conducted extensive in-plant orientation meetings. They also mailed to employees' homes the brochures that described the awards that could be redeemed with Texaco points. In this way, the entire family learned about the program and participated in selecting the prizes that they would redeem with the employee's Texaco points.

In the first year (1995) with the new plan, two plants set new records for utilization ($11 million in increased value), expense reduction (a cost reduction of $0.13 per barrel—more than $18 million saved), and safety (the number of reported incidents hazardous to EHS was reduced by 36 percent). This performance was sustained and extended in subsequent years (see Figure 10-3). The TRMI experience illustrates how a noncash reward program linked to scorecard results could be implemented even in a heavily unionized environment and at a time when the parent corporation was encountering some financial shortfalls.

Figure 10-3 Texaco Refinery and Marketing's Business Results

Strategic Measure	Three-Year Average		Change
	1992–1994	1995–1997	
Utilization	79.9%	85.3%	+5.4%
Expense per Barrel	$3.53	$3.43	+$0.10
Energy Intensity Index	100.4	96.3	+4.1
Safety Index	5.6	3.1	+2.5

Other Organizations

Citicorp (now part of Citigroup, Inc.) was an early adopter of the Balanced Scorecard concept for its compensation plan. Like Mobil, it used a three-tier plan, but unlike Mobil, it assigned one of the tiers to individual performance. Citicorp's three tiers were corporate, business unit, and personal performance. The business unit performance scorecard encompassed six dimensions:[6]

1. Financial performance: primarily revenue and profit margin against targets

2. Customer/franchise performance: customer satisfaction and loyalty; use six sigma approach to eliminate incidence of problems; innovation in quality in new products and distribution

3. Strategy implementation: revenue in key segments; maintain revenue to expense ratio of 2:1

4. Risk and control: internal audit score. Bank branches had to score at least a 4, on a scale from 1 to 5, to be eligible for any bonus.

5. People: subjective rating, done by the executive overseeing the business unit, based on the proactive efforts of the manager to develop and communicate with subordinates, to develop training programs, and to serve as a role model for junior personnel. Employee satisfaction measures were an input to this rating.

6. Community standards: also a subjective rating assessing the manager's business ethics and involvement in community groups and trade associations

Each component of the business unit's scorecard was scored independently into three rating categories: below par, at par, or above par. Branch managers' bonuses were linked to the performance scorecard rating for their business unit. No bonus was awarded for an overall "below par" rating. A "par" rating generated a bonus of up to 15 percent to 20 percent of base salary, and an "above par" rating could generate a bonus of up to a 30 percent. If any of the six dimensions received a "below par" rating, the business unit could not receive an "above par" rating. This scheme provided strong incentives for managers not to underperform on any of the six performance dimensions.

UPS did not have a formal link between its Balanced Scorecard and individuals' compensation. But this formerly privately held company had recently granted the right for all employees to purchase UPS stock.[7] The Balanced Scorecard helped employees understand how their local actions contributed to the calculated company stock price. Thus, while not having the performance share linkage of the CIGNA Property & Casualty plan, the UPS plan did use a stock price calculated on Balanced Scorecard measures—for the company, financial measures plus the nonfinancial POA metrics—to motivate and reward employees' local actions.

Even government organizations have linked incentive pay to their scorecards. For the City of Charlotte, City Manager Pam Syfert initiated a gainsharing program in 1996 to motivate efficiency among city employees. A citizen's advisory group, consisting of human resources professionals from the city's major private sector employers, had requested this program. The program paid up to $600 per person, about two weeks' pay for lower-paid employees, based on two components. The first, worth $300 per employee, would be paid if the city achieved targeted budget savings of, say, $ 3 million. This savings could be accomplished by doing the required work with fewer than budgeted people and by savings from the privatization program. The second component was based on achieving selected local objectives from the unit's Balanced Scorecard. The city's HR department reviewed and approved each business unit's objectives and goals to validate that the targets were sufficiently challenging. As the city became more experienced with the incentive plan and the measurability of the key objectives, Syfert hoped to expand the amount of money that could be awarded under this incentive program.

Effective Compensation Design and Implementation

The only generalizable finding from all of the company experiences in linking compensation and reward to Balanced Scorecards is that they do it. We have yet to encounter an organization, well along with its Balanced Scorecard implementation, that either has not or does not intend to tie incentive compensation to achievement of targets for Balanced Scorecard measures. Some companies had yet to make the link to incentive compensation, but the reasons related to lack of readiness, not opposition to the concept.

Several design issues arise when tying compensation to the Balanced Scorecard:

- Speed of implementation
- Objective versus subjective measures

- Number of measures
- Team versus individual
- Frequency of updates

Speed of Implementation

It is reasonable for companies to be cautious in tying compensation to the scorecard. In fact, we have been somewhat surprised about how quickly most companies have moved to the linkage. This may say more about the dysfunctionality of the companies' previous incentive compensation system than about the desirability of rapid deployment of a Balanced Scorecard incentive system.

One reason for deferring the link to compensation for six to twelve months is that the initial scorecard represents only a tentative statement of the unit's strategy. The scorecard expresses hypotheses about the cause-and-effect relationships among the measures for creating superior, long-run financial performance. As they translate strategy into measures, executives formulate hypotheses about the linkages among the measures. They may not be completely confident that they have chosen the right measures. So they may be naturally reluctant to expose the initial measures to the efforts by highly motivated (and compensated) executives to achieve maximal scores on the selected measures.

For example, one of Mobil's initial revenue growth measures was a year-to-year increase in gasoline volume relative to the industry growth rate. With all the attention devoted to this measure, Mobil achieved its first-year target. Executives, however, didn't feel as successful as they thought they would with the achievement. Subsequent reflection and discussion revealed that their market segmentation strategy was intended to increase the percentage of sales in the premium grades, rather than in the more commoditylike regular product. So in the second year, the measure was modified to emphasize growth in sales of the higher-margin premium grades of gasoline, distillates, and lubricants.

A second reason for delay is that companies may not have good, reliable data for many of the measures at the early stages of their program. Companies' initial Balanced Scorecards often have several missing measurements, typically in the customer and learning and growth perspectives. Companies have to develop new processes that will generate the data for these new measures. Operating an "unbalanced" compensation scheme during the initial year, with the more objective and reliable data from the financial and internal business process perspectives, may send the wrong initial message to employees: "We can't measure what we want, so we have decided to want what we can measure."

A third reason for the delay is that unintended or unexpected consequences could result from how the targets for the measures are achieved. This concern arises when the initial Balanced Scorecard measures are not perfect surrogates for the strategic objectives, and when the actions that improve the short-term measured results may be inconsistent with achieving the long-term objectives. Executives may wish to see how managers achieve performance targets in scorecard measures to assess the likelihood of how easily the system can be distorted. CIGNA's Gerry Isom, who was among the fastest to tie incentive pay to his organization's new scorecards, made it known to everyone that he was prepared to override the reward tied to any measure if he felt that the underlying process had been manipulated or not managed well.

Objective versus Subjective Measures

Several executives stressed to us the importance of having compensation-based measures be more objective and outcome-based, rather than being measures of tasks and activities. For example, they don't want to reward the completion of initiatives and projects on time or to count the number of visits or phone calls made. They want compensation tied to the outcomes from these efforts: new customers signed up, number of new products and services sold to existing customers, and sales from new products. As another example of problems with subjective measures, many organizations tie commissions and compensation to a customer satisfaction measure. This often leads to dysfunctional behavior when salespeople and others with direct customer contact coach customers about how to respond to surveys or posttransaction third-party interviews. It is preferable to measure customers' actual behavior—repeat purchases, purchases of new products and services, and referrals to new customers—not their attitudes.

Number of Measures

Another design issue is how many measures should be in the compensation plan. Many executives want the compensation plan to be simple—say, no more than four to seven measures—feeling that employees cannot understand a system with upwards of two dozen measures. Often companies do use only a subset of their scorecard (the Super Bowl approach described in Chapter 9) for this reason, to increase focus and reduce confusion. But we are also impressed with Mobil's success in having employees understand and influence more than two dozen measures on both their business unit and divisional scorecards. A well-constructed strategy scorecard will not be as confusing as an ad hoc collection of two dozen metrics such as might arise from a stakeholder or KPI scorecard. The metrics derived from an integrated strategy map (see Chapter 3) should reflect a single strategy with only two or three strategic themes (e.g., revenue growth, cost reduction, and asset intensity). Employees can picture the cause-and-effect linkages that integrate the different performance driver and outcome measures.

Individual versus Team

Individual versus team metrics involve managing several tradeoffs and tensions. Mobil adopted a system that had no individual rewards, whereas several other companies (CIGNA, Winterthur, and Citicorp) used a mixture of organizational and individual rewards. Team-based rewards encourage cooperative behavior and group problem-solving. They encourage employees to identify issues and suggest solutions outside their normal, day-to-day responsibilities. On the other hand, team and organizational rewards can lead to what economists call the "free-rider problem," whereby individuals do not get the full benefit from their own initiatives and actions and can benefit from the good ideas and hard work of others. So they have some incentive to slack off and ride on the coattails (the source of the free-rider problem) of their coworkers.

The free-rider problem can often be mitigated in environments of high-visibility, where many people can observe and evaluate the effort and contributions of individuals. When sanctions other than pay can be deployed, the consequences of the free-rider problem can be minimized. In such circumstances, organizations get to enjoy the benefits from group problem-solving and having employees contribute suggestions to influence outcomes outside their day-to-day responsibilities and accountabilities, without paying a free-rider penalty.

On the other hand, such tasks as personal selling or breakthrough product innovation may require individual dedication and brilliance. In such settings, organizations may sensibly wish to provide explicit incentives that reward successful outcomes.

Some scholars advocate weakening the relationship between performance and individual pay. Jeffrey Pfeffer of Stanford Business School wants to deemphasize individual performance-related pay and shift more of the compensation, as Mobil has done, to organizational performance.[8] This shift acknowledges how organizational performance today increasingly depends on the consequences of collective behavior and performance. Several empirical studies indicate that the economists' free-rider problem could be less serious than purported, that individuals may be more influenced by peer pressures and social relationships than by individual merit pay. Pfeffer and others emphasize that many high-performing organizations motivate people by providing a fun place to work, excellent interactions with colleagues, clear statements of mission and purpose, and the freedom to act in ways that will make a difference.

Clearly, the Balanced Scorecard can be used to give a sense of overall purpose and mission, as many organizational behavior scholars advocate. And it can provide the measurement system for collective, organizational performance. Just how to choose the appropriate mix between group and individual rewards will be the subject of ongoing debate and mixed evidence. We don't know of good rules on how to manage these tensions and tradeoffs. We would expect some companies, such as CIGNA with its Performance Share Plan, to attempt to get the benefits from individual and collective actions by using a mixture of individual and group rewards. Others, such as Mobil, will choose to foster teamwork and collective responsibility by using only group rewards.

Frequency of Updates: Compensation in Rapidly Evolving Environments

An explicit, formula-based compensation plan tied to many nonfinancial measures from a Balanced Scorecard runs a risk of inflexibility. Consider companies operating in Internet time, where tactics and action plans may have to change rapidly owing to technological innovation, unexpected competitor initiatives, new competitors, and shifts in consumer preferences. While the basic strategy of these companies—attract new customers in targeted segments, deepen and broaden relationships with existing customers, reduce cost to serve—may not change, the value proposition, internal processes, critical skills, and information technology required to implement the strategy may have to undergo frequent updates. If a compensation system gets tied to nonfinancial metrics based on a now-obsolete set of processes, companies can find it difficult to execute frequent mid-course changes.

The issue of midyear changes in a Balanced Scorecard did not arise in our initial set of adopting companies—integrated petroleum companies, retail banks, construction companies, and insurance companies. The competitive environment for these companies was not subject to rapid change and obsolescence, so the strategy and the tactics for implementing the strategy varied slowly from year to year. Companies, however, that anticipate frequent within-year changes may wish not to link their incentive pay to a multitude of Balanced Scorecard measures in the four perspectives. Such a tight linkage will constrain rapid adaptation, because many people will have committed to actions based on the compensation plan derived from the previous strategy.

Companies in rapidly changing environments can base their incentive pay on customer outcomes and long-run financial performance, such as stock price or EVA over a three- to five-year period. In this way, their reward system is focused on long-term value creation, and they retain the option of modifying their Balanced Scorecard measures, particularly the performance drivers and leading indicators, without having to adjust their compensation plan. Used in this way, the Balanced Scorecard retains its powerful role for communication and alignment, as discussed in earlier chapters. And by not tying the scorecard too closely to compensation, the companies have the freedom to adapt the scorecard quickly to new circumstances.

SUMMARY

All of the companies we studied either made or were planning to make explicit linkages between the Balanced Scorecard and incentive pay. Often the incentive pay plans extended for the first time down to the front lines and back offices of the organization. The details of plans varied across companies. Some used team and organizational-unit rewards only; others used a mixture of individual and organizational rewards. Many organizations used several layers of incentives to reward performance at the corporate, division, business unit, and individual/team performance levels. Because of the attention given to incentive pay plans, managers must avoid the dangers of introducing plans too quickly, before good measures have been determined and good data for the measures are available. When all individuals understand how their pay is linked to achieving strategic objectives, however, strategy truly becomes everyone's everyday job.

NOTES

1. "Rewarding Employees: Balanced Scorecard Fax-Back Survey Result," William M. Mercer & Co., London, 20 May 1999.
2. Experience reported in M.A. Thompson, "Using Strategic Rewards as a Cornerstone of the Balanced Scorecard" (paper presented at the Balanced Scorecard Collaborative Best Practices Conference, Making Strategy Everyone's Job: Using the Balanced Scorecard to Align the Workforce, Cambridge, MA, 22–23 June 1999). Hay Group research conducted by Todd Manas and Michael Jensen.
3. R. S. Kaplan, "Mobil USM&R (A): Linking the Balanced Scorecard," 9-197-025 (Boston: Harvard Business School, 1996), 9.
4. The CIGNA plan was initially reported in B. Birchard, "Closing the Strategy Gap," *CFO Magazine* (October 1996).
5. TRMI tracked how many spontaneous awards each supervisor made. It discovered that it had to coach and counsel several supervisors who found it difficult to reinforce good behavior or to learn how to say "thank you" to their employees, which is not always a native skill for oil refinery supervisors.
6. See R. Simons and A. Davila, "Citbank: Performance Evaluation," 9-198-048 (Boston: Harvard Business School, 1997).
7. UPS became a public company in November 1999. At that point, the value of employees' stock holdings was determined by an active public market rather than an internal formula.
8. J. Pfeffer, "Six Dangerous Myths about Pay," *Harvard Business Review* (May–June 1998): 109–19.

MAKING STRATEGY A CONTINUAL PROCESS

IN CHAPTER 1, WE NOTED HOW MOST COMPANIES ENCOUNTER serious difficulties when implementing strategy. Our research indicates that the problem is more than a failure of CEO leadership. Systemic forces in organizations inhibit strategy implementation. As researchers have observed, managing strategy is fundamentally different from managing operations.[1]

We have found it useful to think of each of these processes—managing strategy and managing operations—as a self-contained control and learning loop. For managing operations, the budget serves as the planning and control system (see Figure IV-1). It defines the resources that will be allocated to business unit operations for the subsequent year, and the performance targets. During the year, managers review operating performance against the budget, identify variances, and take corrective action when necessary. In most organizations, the budget bears little relation to the organization's strategy, so management attention and actions are directed at short-term operational details, not implementation of the long-term strategy.

Yet organizations are becoming increasingly frustrated with the inflexibility of their budgeting process. Recent surveys have found that

- 20 percent of organizations take more than sixteen weeks to prepare a budget, with many budgets not even completed by the start of the fiscal year.[2]

Figure IV-1   The Problem: The Process for Managing Strategy Is Missing

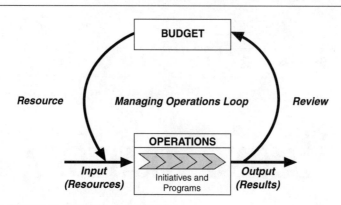

- 78 percent of companies do not change their budgets within the fiscal cycle.[3] The world may change, but not their budgets.

While the budget-based operations control process may have limitations in a dynamic, rapidly changing world, it at least exists. Most organizations don't have any process for managing strategy. Consider the following facts.

- 85 percent of management teams spend less than one hour per month discussing strategy[4]
- 60 percent of organizations don't link strategy and budgeting[5]
- 92 percent of organizations don't report on strategic lead indicators[6]

If this were a human system instead of a management system, we would be observing quite a sick patient. The brain is not functioning (no time is spent thinking about strategy), the body is not receiving any messages from the brain (there is no linkage from strategic intent to action), and the eyes are not observing (there is no feedback). With such a sick management system, is it any surprise that few companies can execute their strategies?

Strategy-Focused Organizations use a "double-loop" process that integrates the management of budgets and operations with the management of strategy. A reporting system, based on the Balanced Scorecard, allows progress against the strategy to be monitored and corrective actions to be taken as required. The scorecard serves as the linchpin of the *strategic learning* process, linking the operations control process with the learning and control process for managing strategy.

This new strategy-focused management system (see Figure IV-2) introduces three remedies to restore the management system to health:

1. Linking strategy and budgeting: Stretch targets and strategic initiatives on the Balanced Scorecard link the rhetoric of strategy with the rigor of budgets. Companies today, operating in continually changing environments, have begun to replace fixed budgets with rolling forecasts. These approaches are described in Chapter 11.

2. Closing the strategy loop: Strategic feedback systems linked to the Balanced Scorecard provide a new framework for reporting and a new kind of management meeting—one focused on strategy. Ac-

Figure IV-2   The Solution: Make Strategy a Continual Process

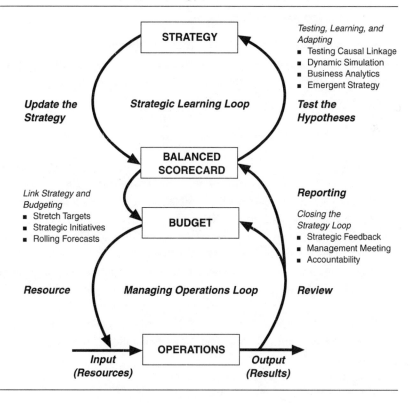

countability shifts from managing functional silos to managing integrated strategic themes. Chapter 12 describes this topic.

3. Testing, learning, and adapting: The Balanced Scorecard makes explicit the hypotheses of the strategy. Executive teams can be more analytical as they examine and test strategic hypotheses with the information from the Balanced Scorecard feedback system. Strategy evolves in real time as new ideas and directions emerge from the organization. These issues are also presented in Chapter 12.

With the strategy-focused management system, management teams

- monitor performance against the strategy
- work as teams to interpret the data
- develop new strategic insights
- formulate new strategic directions
- update the measures on scorecards
- change their budgets

Strategy-Focused Organizations must be able to adapt their strategies as the world changes or the strategy matures. The double-loop strategic management system provides the foundation for making strategy a continual process.

NOTES

1. For example, Robert N. Anthony identifies three layers to the management process: (1.) Strategic planning: the process of deciding on the organization's objectives, on changes in these objectives, on the resources used to attain these objectives, and the policies to govern their acquisition and use; (2.) Management control: the process by which managers ensure that resources are obtained and used efficiently and effectively in accomplishing the organization objectives; and (3.) Operational control: the process of ensuring that specific tasks are carried out efficiently and effectively. Robert N. Anthony, *Planning and Control Systems* (Boston: Division of Research, Graduate School of Business Administration, Harvard University, 1965).
2. "Many Companies Starting the New Millennium without a Budget," *PR Newswire,* 16 December 1999.
3. "Corporate Strategic Planning Suffers from Inefficiencies," Hackett Benchmarking PR Newswire, 25 October 1999.

4. David P. Norton, "Building a Management System to Implement Your Strategy," *Point of View*, Renaissance Solutions, Inc., Lincoln, MA, 1996.
5. Ibid.
6. "Corporate Strategic Planning."

Planning and Budgeting

INTEGRATING THE BALANCED SCORECARD with the organization's planning and budgeting processes is critical for creating a Strategy-Focused Organization. Most organizations use the budget as their primary management system for establishing targets, allocating resources, and reviewing performance. Yet more than half of surveyed companies indicated that their budgeting and performance review processes were done separately from the strategic planning process. With budgets serving as the primary means used to exercise control in organizations, management attention becomes riveted on achieving short-term financial targets.

The limitations of managing by the budget have become apparent. Jack Welch, CEO of General Electric Company, decried the role for budgets in corporations: "The budget is the bane of corporate America. It never should have existed. . . . Making a budget is an exercise in minimalization. You're always getting the lowest out of people, because everyone is negotiating to get the lowest number." Bob Lutz, former president of Chrysler Corporation, declared that "budgets are tools of repression, rather than innovation."

A 1998 reader survey in the journal *CFO* indicated that 90 percent of respondents thought their budgeting process was "cumbersome." Nor are problems with budgets a North American phenomenon. Bjartes Bogsnes, vice president of corporate control of Borealis, a Danish petrochemicals company, has expressed his concern with the centrality of budgets in organizations: "Traditional budgeting promotes centralization of decisions and responsibility, makes financial control an annual autumn event, absorbs significant resources across the organization and acts as a barrier to customer responsiveness."[1]

Yet before discarding the "bad old budget" entirely, we need to substitute new systems and processes to accomplish the critical objectives that budgets were intended to achieve. Managers use budgets to accomplish several vital organizational functions:

- Establish performance targets
- Allocate resources to enable performance targets to be achieved
- Assess performance relative to targets
- Update the targets based on new information and learning

If a traditional financial budget is not to be used for these purposes, what will take its place?

Our experience is that considerable confusion exists about the difference between managing strategy and managing tactics. Budgets were introduced at a time when the major issues were expanding production capacity and managing operations to control costs. The budget helped managers with these tactical processes. Strategic positioning and managing differentiated value propositions were not high priorities.

Today, with strategy being critical for organizational success, the Balanced Scorecard has emerged as a new system for managing strategy. But this new system must be linked to the old system—the budget—for managing tactics. This has yet to happen in most implementations, perhaps because the disciplines and cultures associated with strategic planning and budgeting for operations are so different.

The contrast between high-level strategic planning and detailed operational actions can be compared to a challenge also faced by airline pilots. While flying at 30,000 feet (strategic flying), pilots use only a few indicators to guide their course. The plane is often on autopilot and the cockpit atmosphere is generally relaxed. At some point, they must make the transition from high-level flight to an airport landing. As the plane approaches the airport, managing operational details and tactics becomes critical: the pilot constantly monitors traffic and weather conditions. Ground controllers give specific instructions that require precise execution. The pilot follows a "step-down" procedure to make the transition from strategic flying at 30,000 feet to the details and precision—budget control for operational flying—required for a landing.

Companies can follow an analogous step-down procedure to make the transition from high-level strategy to budgeting for local operations (see Figure 11-1):

1. Translate strategy into a Balanced Scorecard, defining the strategic objectives and measures.

2. Set stretch targets for specific future times for each measure. Identify planning gaps to motivate and stimulate creativity.

3. Identify strategic initiatives and resource requirements to close the planning gaps, thereby enabling the stretch targets to be achieved.

Figure 11-1 Linking Strategy to Budgets in a Step-Down Procedure

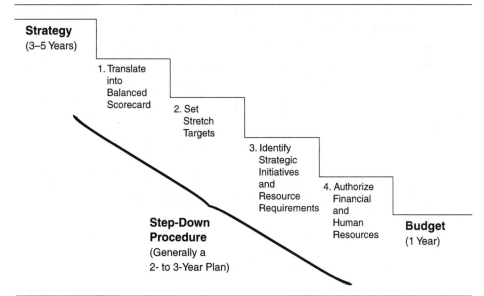

4. Authorize financial and human resources for the strategic initiatives. Embed these requirements into the annual budget. The annual budget comprises two components: a *strategy budget* to
manage discretionary programs and an *operating budget* to manage the efficiency of departments, functions, and line items.

Steps 2 and 3 form the core of the step-down procedure, frequently
being organized as a three-year plan. The plan allows the organization to
manage to longer-term strategic themes and provides a framework that allows rolling forecasts to be developed and incorporated into the annual
budget. In effect, the strategy budget launches the organization's trajectory,
in year one, toward achieving the stretch targets established in the three-
year plan.

The preceding four steps imbed the budget within a strategic planning
process, allocating resources and determining near-term performance targets. Most managers also think of the budget as a tool for reviewing and
evaluating performance. The two processes—planning and control—are
inextricably linked: how senior executives conduct performance reviews
strongly influences the target-setting process, the generation and selection
of initiatives, and the explanations for performance shortfalls.

We therefore have a "chicken and egg" problem. Do we start by developing effective processes for translating strategic plans into short-term operational targets? Or must we first modify the review processes for
assessing performance relative to the targets? We defer, for now, the detailed discussion of the management review process to focus on the target-
setting and resource allocation aspects of the budget. But we foreshadow
our preferences by indicating that the management meetings for comparing actual performance to budgeted targets will be conducted to stimulate
learning, problem-solving, and adaptation rather than to control and maintain performance on a trajectory established during the budget process.
Such interactive meetings stimulate managers to sign up for higher stretch
targets and be more candid and forthcoming when proposing strategic initiatives.

BRIDGING THE PLANNING-BUDGETING GAP

We illustrate two companies' experiences—ABB Switzerland and Mobil
NAM&R—to show how Strategy-Focused Organizations use the Balanced
Scorecard to integrate their planning and budgeting processes.

ABB Switzerland

ABB Switzerland provides an excellent example of how to use the Balanced Scorecard to bridge the gap between strategic planning and budgeting and reporting processes. The top half of Figure 11-2 illustrates the traditional front end of the planning process: reaffirm the mission and mar-

Figure 11-2 Integrating the Balanced Scorecard into ABB's Strategic Planning Process

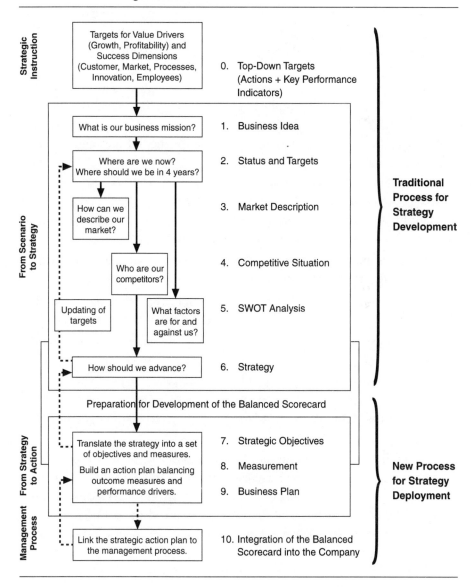

ket positioning of the business unit; develop stretch targets for financial performance four years into the future; scan the market space—customers, competitors, technology, government regulation, economic forecasts; perform a SWOT (strengths-weaknesses-opportunities-threat) analysis; and develop a strategy for the business unit.

While such a process for strategy development had existed at ABB for years, the company lacked a process for strategy deployment. The strategy had no direct linkages that would change the behavior and work of employees, strategy did not affect the budgeting process, and the reporting for periodic reviews did not adapt to the strategy. So the day-to-day work of employees, managers, and executives remained disconnected from strategy development.

Developing a Balanced Scorecard for the strategy, as shown in the bottom part of Figure 11-2, supplied the missing link. The actual development of the ABB scorecard followed the procedure recommended in Chapter 3. Managers developed strategy maps to describe the linkages among objectives and measures in the four scorecard perspectives. The deployment process consisted of developing strategic programs and actions that would enable the business unit to achieve the targets established in the strategic plan. Figure 11-3 illustrates how ABB then used the "step-down" procedure to integrate the scorecard into its management process.

1. Translate the strategy into objectives and measures on a Balanced Scorecard, as just described.

2. Develop a two-year business plan; establish stretch targets for each strategic objective, along with intermediate milestones.

3. Identify the strategic programs to implement the business plan. Each program had a person or department responsible for its implementation and a timetable. In addition, the programs themselves were represented on cause-and-effect diagrams that illustrated the linkages across the four Balanced Scorecard perspectives.

4. Drill each program, in turn, down into one or more action plans. These programs were included in the operating budget. ABB monitored the action plans on desktop software (in ABB's case, using Microsoft Project), and these became part of the periodic review processes of management, as shown in the feedback loop of Figure 11-3.

Figure 11-3 ABB Switzerland's Strategic Controlling Process

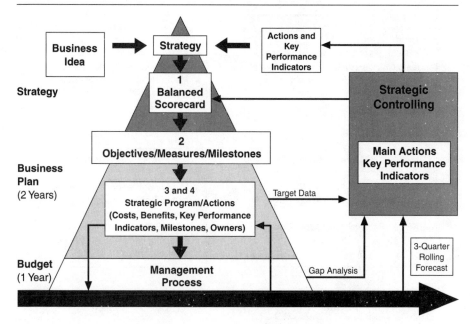

Mobil NAM&R

Mobil NAM&R integrated the Balanced Scorecard into its annual planning, budgeting, and reporting cycle (see Figure 11-4). The annual process started in the third quarter of the year when the metric owners—the people from NAM&R's strategic partners (the division's name for its internal SSUs) who were responsible for each measure on the NAM&R scorecard—reviewed midyear results and performed a strategic outlook review. They proposed changes in the objectives and measures for the upcoming year to the Executive Leadership Team, which then came to an agreement on the scorecard for the next year. The environment in the petroleum products refining and marketing industry had not changed greatly during the 1990s, and Mobil's strategy had been working well. So 95 percent of the objectives on the initial 1994 scorecard remained on the 1999 scorecard, and about 65 percent to 70 percent of the measures were also the same. One important change was the explicit incorporation of the market penetration of Mobil's Speedpass, a marketing innovation launched in 1996.

Figure 11-4   Mobil NAM&R's Planning and Targeting Process

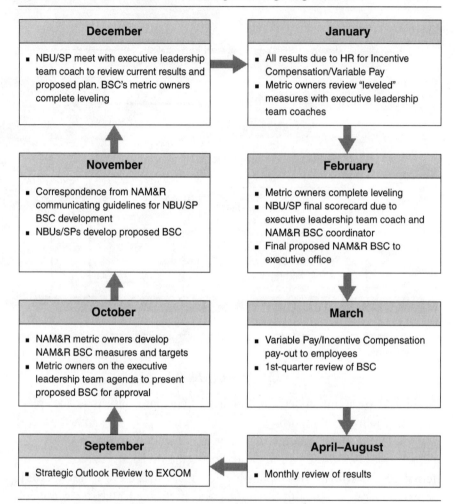

December	January
■ NBU/SP meet with executive leadership team coach to review current results and proposed plan. BSC's metric owners complete leveling	■ All results due to HR for Incentive Compensation/Variable Pay ■ Metric owners review "leveled" measures with executive leadership team coaches

November	February
■ Correspondence from NAM&R communicating guidelines for NBU/SP BSC development ■ NBUs/SPs develop proposed BSC	■ Metric owners complete leveling ■ NBU/SP final scorecard due to executive leadership team coach and NAM&R BSC coordinator ■ Final proposed NAM&R BSC to executive office

October	March
■ NAM&R metric owners develop NAM&R BSC measures and targets ■ Metric owners on the executive leadership team agenda to present proposed BSC for approval	■ Variable Pay/Incentive Compensation pay-out to employees ■ 1st-quarter review of BSC

September	April–August
■ Strategic Outlook Review to EXCOM	■ Monthly review of results

The updated NAM&R scorecard was then communicated down to each of the eighteen natural business units (NBUs) and fourteen strategic partners (SPs), who updated their scorecards based on the high-level scorecard. In November, the units developed their budgets, initiatives, and proposed targets for scorecard measures. In December, the leadership team of each NBU and SP presented their proposed plans at a meeting attended by the NAM&R metric owners, the Balanced Scorecard coordinator, and a senior member of the Executive Leadership Team. The meeting started by reviewing current-year Balanced Scorecard results to set the stage for next year's proposed scorecard. Then the group reviewed the measures and targets on the unit's proposed scorecard. With the advice and consent of the metric owners, the group ratified or adjusted the targets and performance factors for the unit. These meetings typically lasted for two hours and replaced a two-day meeting used in the previous budgeting process, in which all the focus was on financial numbers.

Because Mobil tied incentive compensation to achieving targets on the NAM&R and NBU/SP scorecards, the leveling process performed at this meeting played an important role. Prior to the meeting, the metric owners developed performance factor scores (discussed in Chapter 10) for each measure. A factor score of 1.25 represented performance at the top of competitors' performance; a score of 0.75 specified performance well below average for the industry. Achieving a target with a performance factor of 1.25 would generate a bonus of 20 percent of base compensation. A factor of 1.00 yielded a bonus of 7 percent, while achieving only at a 0.75 level generated a maximum bonus of 1 percent. Business unit heads proposed their own targets, which were assigned a performance factor based on where it landed in the range. They rarely proposed targets whose performance factor would be below 1.00.

Metric owners could follow up with a business unit or strategic partner to resolve difficulties on whether special circumstances for the unit would justify changes in the performance factors assigned to the unit's targets. With this process, a business unit in an area where Mobil NAM&R was weak or subject to strong, local competitive pressure could be rewarded for proposing and achieving a stretch target whose absolute value was considerably lower than that used by a business unit in a strong area for Mobil. The process helped to create a level playing field across all of NAM&R's operating units.

During January and February, the metric owners met with the Executive Leadership Team members to ratify the targets, performance factors, and linkages to incentive pay for the year. During the year, executives reviewed monthly performance, but without intense, lengthy meetings. By 1999, the planning and target-setting process had become well accepted by all units, the reporting of Balanced Scorecard measures against targets had become routine, and the process functioned without a great deal of active interaction. Unit heads knew what was expected from them and could function without extensive high-level intervention. Quarterly, Brian Baker reviewed the recent performance for all employees in a town meeting format that was videotaped and distributed to all locations. The highlight, of course, was a March meeting at which Baker announced the performance for the previous year and the amount of the annual bonus. Since the inception of the program, bonus pay-outs had ranged between 17 percent and 19 percent, and the meeting had become a celebration of Mobil's success.

INTRODUCING DYNAMIC BUDGETING

Mobil operated its planning and budgeting process on an annual cycle, with fixed targets for the upcoming year. Some companies, however, are trying to modify their process so that resource allocation decisions and even targets can be modified during the year to reflect changing situations. For example, a study of innovative practices identified several European companies—including Svenska Handelsbanken AB, Borealis, SKF, and IKEA Systems B.V.—that apparently operate without budgets. These companies use Balanced Scorecards for target-setting but update their forecasts and targets with a continuing series of strategic reviews designed to take advantage of emerging opportunities and to counter potential threats.[2]

We believe that to understand these new approaches, one should view budgets for financial numbers and resource allocation as arising from two different processes (see Figure 11-5). Only a small percentage of the spending and expenses in an annual (or quarterly) budget is discretionary. Most expenses are determined by the volume and mix of goods produced, services delivered, and customers served. The budget for such expenses reflects an expected level of spending based on forecasted revenue and the mix of products, services, and customers to generate the revenues. Activity-based budgeting provides a sound foundation for such operational budgeting.

The second process, which we refer to as the strategic budget, authorizes spending and initiatives that enable the organization to develop new products and services, new capabilities, new and enhanced customer relationships, and expanded capacity for future growth. The Balanced Scorecard helps organizations to determine the quantity and mix of spending in their strategic budget. Organizations need both budgeting processes so that they can manage both tactics and strategies. We describe each budgeting process in turn.

Figure 11-5 Operational and Strategic Budgets

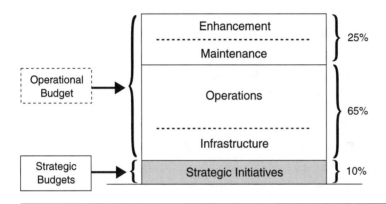

Operational Budgeting

The operational budget consists of a forecast of the revenues expected from sales of goods and services and the expenses expected to be incurred, under efficient operations, for the goods and services to be produced and delivered to customers. The operational budget specifies the ongoing expenses to maintain existing products and customers, as well as the expenses incurred to launch new products and attract new customers during the next period.

Many of the spending decisions in the operational budget can be determined by activity-based budgeting using the following sequence of steps:[3]

1. Estimate the production and sales volumes for the next period. Activity-based budgeting starts, as in a conventional budget process, with estimates of production, sales volumes, and mix of products and customers. The sales estimates must include not only the products that will be sold, but also the customers expected to buy them. And production and sales budgets need to be much more detailed than conventional ones. For example, the production budget must include information about the processes that will be used to achieve the total production volumes, such as the expected number of runs for each product, the frequency of materials orders and

receipts, and the method of shipment. For customers, estimates of the number of orders placed, average order size, and number and intensity of customer contacts are important inputs to forecast the demanded level of customer support activities.

2. Forecast the demand for activities. Activity-based budgeting continues by forecasting the demand for activities such as ordering, receiving, and handling materials, developing new products, selling to customers, and maintaining relationships with customers. Conventionally, companies construct detailed budgets only for activities such as materials purchasing, labor times, and machine times. Activity-based budgeting extends this analysis by estimating the demand for *all* activities required to make, market, sell, and deliver products.

3. Calculate the resource demands. Activity-based budgeting then estimates how many and what types of resources will be needed. It is at this step that the company uses information about next-period's activity and process efficiencies to forecast how many resources and of which type will be required to meet the demands for activities. If the company forecasts process improvements, the demands for resources will be modified downward to reflect the anticipated improvements in the forthcoming year.

4. Determine the actual resource supply. The activity-based budgeting process concludes by converting the demand for resources into an estimate of the total resources to be supplied. In general, each resource has a particular spending profile. (These range from very flexible—hourly labor, for example—to committed and fixed—plant floor space, for example.) For most companies, this final step will be a complex and iterative calculation. Establishing an activity's capacity will require looking at sales-order patterns; production, purchasing, and shipping schedules; resources that can perform multiple activities; and seasonal demands for activities. That's why activity-based budgeting is best performed in the information-rich environment of enterprise resource planning systems.

Conceptually, activity-based budgeting is simple to understand. In practice, however, it is not simple to implement. The organization has to specify far more detailed estimates than it would in conventional budgeting—details about the demand for activities from production and sales, about the underlying efficiency of organizational activities, and about the spending, supply pattern, and capacity of individual resources. When done successfully, however, the operational budget is truly bottoms-up; it is determined by the quantity of resources that must be supplied to match the future demands from production, marketing, and sales activities. It gives managers the opportunity to identify where excess resource capacity already exists in the organization, and to take steps to redeploy or dispose of the resources (equipment, facilities, people) that are no longer needed for activities in the forthcoming periods.

Take the example of the new planning, targeting, and budgeting process installed at Sprint Corporation during 1997–99.[4] The process started at the top, with senior executives setting targets for growth objectives. The planning group translated the growth objectives into an economic model that would deliver the growth targets. Based on the growth plan, the process forecasted the demands for the activity drivers, such as the number of calls and the number of switches, that the company would have to perform. The demand for activities could then be translated into the increased resource supply that had to be provided to meet the growth objectives.[5] Sprint's capital budget approval and review process would now be based on these driver-based economic plans. The finance group took the targeted revenue growth and forecasted changes in resource supply and incorporated them into financial plans for upcoming periods. In this way, the financial plan was linked tightly to the business forecasts. And rather than have a quantitative plan only for financial numbers, the finance group, as part of the same process, forecasted a set of key nonfinancial indicators, including the number of sales and installed accounts. As managers updated the business model for future periods (two to six quarters out), the system automatically updated the driver quantities, leading to dynamic forecasts for resource requirements and key, high-level indicators.

Nationwide Financial Services, Inc., followed a similar process, using its activity-based cost system to forecast activity and business process costs based on planned levels of activity volumes and anticipated business process efficiencies. The activities were taken from key scorecard measures, especially those in the internal and customer perspectives; for example, the number of accounts and transactions.

Thus operational budgets reflect expenses expected to be incurred to support recurring operations. Because of the large base of existing products, services, and customers that are expected to persist from period to period, most of an organization's spending on resources will be determined in its operational budget (as represented in Figure 11-5). This aspect of budgeting is informed by the Balanced Scorecard because of its connection to the business model for growth in existing businesses. But operational budgeting does not represent the most significant opportunity for the scorecard to redirect and align the organization to its growth strategy, particularly if the strategy represents a departure from the past.

Strategic Budgeting

The operational budget reflects incremental improvement to existing operations. The strategic budget authorizes the initiatives required to close the planning gap between desired breakthrough performance and that achievable by continuous improvement and business as usual. The strategic budget identifies what new operations are required; what new capabilities must be created; what new products and services must be launched; what new customers, markets, applications, and regions must be served; and what new alliances and joint ventures must be established.

For example, in Chapter 3 we showed the Balanced Scorecard strategy map, measures, and stretch targets for a major retailer's sourcing and distribution strategic theme. The retailer's leadership team identified and selected initiatives that would enable the stretch targets to be achieved. Each retail division, reflecting its specific situation, customer base, and employees, would do some of the initiatives independently. But some of the initiatives had to be done at the corporate level because they benefited all retail divisions. For example, an initiative to improve dramatically the capability of the company's network of manufacturing facilities in Asia was common across divisions. This initiative was critical to the objective of producing and distributing fashion merchandise of high quality with short lead times that would enable each division to respond rapidly to contemporary fashion trends.

The initiatives, once approved, received executive sponsorship, a project team, and a budget (see Figure 11-6). In this way, executives authorized adequate resources—both human and financial—for the strategic initiatives. Many organizations fail in strategy implementation because the necessary people, capital, and financial resources are not provided for in the budget, which, in these organizations, is done completely separately from the planning process. As a consequence, initiatives get implemented on the cheap,

Figure 11-6 Resource Allocation and Budgeting

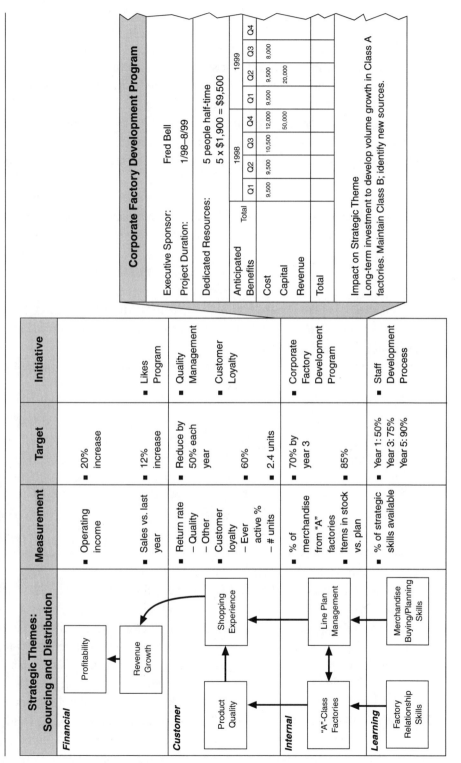

Corporate Factory Development Program

Executive Sponsor:	Fred Bell									
Project Duration:	1/98–8/99									
Dedicated Resources:	5 people half-time									
	5 x $1,900 = $9,500									

Anticipated Benefits	Total	1998				1999			
		Q1	Q2	Q3	Q4	Q1	Q2	Q3	Q4
Cost		9,500	9,500	10,500	12,000	9,500	9,500	8,000	
Capital					50,000		20,000		
Revenue									
Total									

Impact on Strategic Theme

Long-term investment to develop volume growth in Class A factories. Maintain Class B; identify new sources.

Strategic Themes: Sourcing and Distribution	Measurement	Target	Initiative
Financial	■ Operating income	■ 20% increase	
	■ Sales vs. last year	■ 12% increase	■ Likes Program
Customer	■ Return rate – Quality – Other	■ Reduce by 50% each year	■ Quality Management
	■ Customer loyalty – Ever active % – # units	■ 60% ■ 2.4 units	■ Customer Loyalty
Internal	■ % of merchandise from "A" factories	■ 70% by year 3	■ Corporate Factory Development Program
	■ Items in stock vs. plan	■ 85%	
Learning	■ % of strategic skills available	■ Year 1: 50% Year 3: 75% Year 5: 90%	■ Staff Development Process

trying to steal time from already busy people and with funding scraped to-gether from small improvements (or slack) in the operating budget. It is no wonder that so many strategies fail when required initiatives receive inad-equate staffing and financial support. Strategy-Focused Organizations *build human and financial resource commitments for strategic initiatives into organizational plans and budgets* and manage them separately from budgetary line-item expenses. This process makes achieving stretch targets far more likely.

A second important message from Figure 11-6 is that *initiatives must be viewed as means, not ends.* In constructing their Balanced Scorecards, or-ganizations often get this wrong. They use the following planning process:

Strategy → Initiatives → Measures (of initiative completion and cost)

Their strategic plan consists primarily of a list of initiatives that will be undertaken, and their internal business measures are milestones—time and cost metrics—about initiatives.

Such a planning process is backwards! Strategy is not about managing initiatives. The Balanced Scorecard strategic planning process is:

Strategy → Objectives → Measures → Targets (stretch) → Initiatives

The strategic planning process should use initiatives to help the organi-zation achieve its strategic objectives, not as ends in themselves. Public sector and nonprofit organizations are especially guilty of often confusing initiative completion as the target rather than improvements in mission ob-jectives and agency effectiveness.

Once all the initiatives have been defined, the organization can set perfor-mance targets for the Balanced Scorecard measures—including financial measures, as in a traditional budgeting process—for the upcoming year. For example, Figure 11-7 shows the complete picture of objectives, measures, initiatives, and short-term targets for a company's strategic initiative to "add and retain high-potential-value customers." The next-year's targets provide the basis for the periodic operating and strategic reviews in the subsequent year. They provide the baseline of expectations for near-term performance, based on initiatives being performed according to schedule and the com-pany's hypothesized linkages of cause-and-effect relationships being valid. The information in Figure 11-7 becomes the agenda for the strategic feed-back and learning process described in more detail in Chapter 12.

Figure 11-7 Objectives, Measures, Initiatives, and Short-Term Targets at National Bank Online Financial Services

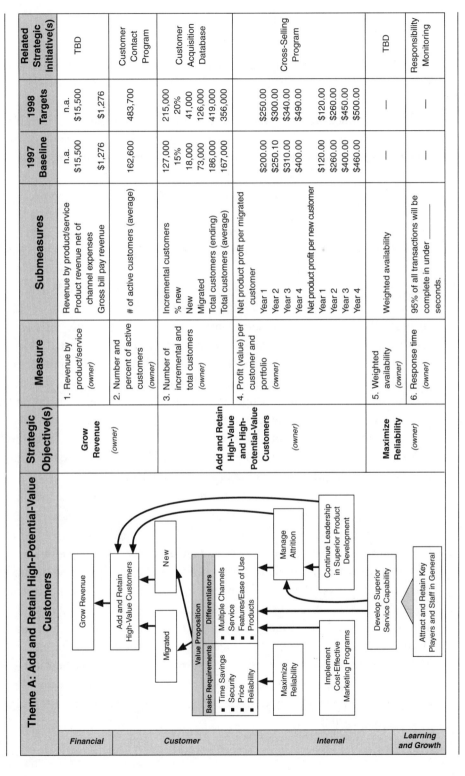

Theme A: Add and Retain High-Potential-Value Customers

Strategic Objective(s)	Measure	Submeasures	1997 Baseline	1998 Targets	Related Strategic Initiative(s)
Grow Revenue *(owner)*	1. Revenue by product/service *(owner)*	Revenue by product/service	n.a.	n.a.	TBD
		Product revenue net of channel expenses	$15,500	$15,500	
		Gross bill pay revenue	$1,276	$1,276	
	2. Number and percent of active customers *(owner)*	# of active customers (average)	162,600	483,700	Customer Contact Program
Add and Retain High-Value and High-Potential-Value Customers *(owner)*	3. Number of incremental and total customers *(owner)*	Incremental customers	127,000	215,000	Customer Acquisition Database
		% new	15%	20%	
		New	18,000	41,000	
		Migrated	73,000	126,000	
		Total customers (ending)	186,000	419,000	
		Total customers (average)	167,000	356,000	
	4. Profit (value) per customer and portfolio *(owner)*	Net product profit per migrated customer			Cross-Selling Program
		Year 1	$200.00	$250.00	
		Year 2	$250.10	$300.00	
		Year 3	$310.00	$340.00	
		Year 4	$400.00	$490.00	
		Net product profit per new customer			
		Year 1	$120.00	$120.00	
		Year 2	$260.00	$260.00	
		Year 3	$400.00	$450.00	
		Year 4	$460.00	$500.00	
Maximize Reliability *(owner)*	5. Weighted availability *(owner)*	Weighted availability	—	—	TBD
	6. Response time *(owner)*	95% of all transactions will be complete in under ____ seconds.	—	—	Responsibility Monitoring

Financial — Customer — Internal — Learning and Growth

Evaluating Initiatives

A critical component for linking strategy to short-term actions is selecting new initiatives. As described briefly in our first book, most companies do not suffer from having too few initiatives. For example, the executive teams at Chemical Retail Bank balked when they were asked to identify new strategic initiatives. They claimed that they had too many initiatives already under way and couldn't possibly handle any new ones, no matter how strategic the initiatives were. We asked them to identify all the initiatives, which they could not do right away, corroborating that they probably did have too many initiatives already. Two weeks later the project team produced a list of more than seventy named initiatives, each one with an executive sponsor, and some even with funding. We then made a second list, containing the twenty-three Balanced Scorecard measures, and asked the team to match each existing initiative with the one or more Balanced Scorecard measures that would improve significantly if the initiative was successfully completed. Not surprisingly, many of the existing initiatives failed to connect to any scorecard measure. These initiatives were all meritorious in some fashion (or else they would not have received initial approval), but none was truly strategic. These initiatives were canceled, consolidated, or reduced in scope, thereby freeing up both financial and human resources. So the executive team was absolutely correct in their initial response to us. They did indeed have too many initiatives. Without the lens of the Balanced Scorecard, they had no strategic tool for selecting, rejecting, or setting priorities among proposed initiatives.

Even more interesting, however, the exercise revealed that despite having more than three times as many initiatives as scorecard measures, almost one-third of the measures had no initiative designed to improve them. For example, no existing initiative would enhance employee capabilities or customer retention. Thus the company now saw the need to formulate entirely new initiatives that would generate improvements in these neglected measures. The exercise revealed a situation that we encounter in virtually all organizations. With strategy not linked to short-term planning and budgeting, companies have simultaneously too many and too few initiatives. The scorecard provides a framework and the discipline to screen initiatives, identify missing ones, and communicate to all employees—the ultimate source of new ideas, initiatives, and programs—where new initiatives could be most valuable.

National Bank Online Financial Services

One of the most elaborate linkages from the scorecard to initiatives occurred at National Bank Online Financial Services (OFS). In Chapter 4, we described one of the two principal motivations for OFS to develop a Balanced Scorecard—to communicate strategic objectives to senior bank executives and to the division's employees. The second, and equally strong, motivation was to help the senior management team cope with the flood of initiatives that continually came to them. OFS was resetting priorities among initiatives on a weekly basis, and with limited data on the strategic consequences from each initiative.

Once OFS built its Balanced Scorecard, it developed a new process to screen and rank initiatives. The process started by sorting initiatives into two categories: "strategic" and "business as usual." For an initiative to be classified as strategic, it had to rate high on three criteria:

1. Helps OFS achieve a strategic objective (defined by the three strategic themes outlined in the Balanced Scorecard)
2. Builds a competitive advantage
3. Builds a sustainable point of differentiation

For example, an initiative to offer a discount brokerage service would defend against customers defecting to major discount brokerage firms, some of which were encroaching upon the retail banking market. From an offensive perspective, National Bank believed that offering a discount brokerage service would give it a competitive advantage in attracting and retaining customers. The company felt that most customers placed a high value on the convenience of conducting its financial transactions in one place. The brokerage service would also differentiate the bank from its commercial banking competitors, as very few of them were then offering such a discount brokerage service. In addition, it would enable the bank to generate additional fee income from customers and encourage customers to keep more of their money in the bank, all of which would increase the bank's profits. Based on this rationale, the discount brokerage initiative rated "high" on each of the three criteria and was classified as a strategic initiative.

Conversely, another OFS initiative—to upgrade the look and feel of the National Bank Web site—would not significantly affect OFS's strategic objectives and was not likely to give the bank either a competitive advantage or a sustainable point of differentiation. Because this initiative did not rate "high" on any of the three criteria, it did not qualify as a strategic initiative.

OFS then applied a second screen to the initiatives to focus on those that drew upon resources from several functional units and required significant costs and time to implement. In effect, OFS used the two screens to separate its operational budgeting task from its strategic budgeting task. The process screened out projects that represented improvements of existing processes and business capabilities. The senior management team wanted to review only the strategic projects that could create new capabilities for supporting the organization's strategic objectives. The screening process maximized the organization's *return on management*, its most valuable resource.[6] Senior management wanted to use its scarce time to establish priorities among major cross-functional projects that required widespread support to succeed. After the two screens had filtered literally hundreds of initiatives to about a dozen, OFS developed an initiative ranking model in which the major weight was applied to the initiative's fit with the three strategic themes on the OFS Balanced Scorecard (see Figure 11-8).[7]

The new process was an immediate success in the organization. Before the scorecard project was launched, OFS had more than 600 initiatives under way. Soon after the new process for screening and ranking initiatives had been institutionalized, the total number of initiatives had been reduced to about 100. Managers did not use the ranking model mechanically. It was a guide that helped them focus on the most critical initiatives. As the CFO observed, "Scoring initiatives is very helpful in sorting out what we're *not* going to do. It doesn't do the greatest job of setting priorities among the things we are *going* to do, but it helped us reduce the number of initiatives we had to consider in more depth."

Management identified the following benefits from the Balanced Scorecard initiative ranking process:

- Enabled the unit to set priorities for initiatives that will contribute to strategic objectives while still being sensitive to shifts in the marketplace

- Adopted the right technologies to support the initiatives

- Allocated the right resources—both human and automated systems—for achieving targeted performance levels while lowering costs

Figure 11-8 Scoring Strategic Initiatives at National Bank's Online Financial Services

Criteria	Weight	Definition/Subcategories	●	◕	◑	◔	○
			Scores				
Strategic Importance	40%	■ Competitive edge ■ First to market ■ Value to customer ■ Gain market share ■ Window of opportunity ■ Match competition ■ Sustainable ■ Value to OFS	Very High *400 points*	High *320 points*	Moderate *240 points*	Low *160 points*	Very Low *80 points*
Initiative Cost	15%	■ Cost of implementing	Very Low <$300k *150 points*	Low *Use formula*	Moderate *Use formula*	High *Use formula*	Very High >$1m *30 points*
NPV	15%	■ Present value of net benefits (3-year)	Very High >$15m *150 points*	High $6–$15m *120 points*	Moderate $3–$6m *90 points*	Low $1–$3m *60 points*	Very Low NPV <$1m *30 points*
Elapsed Time	10%	■ Implementation time period (conception to deployment)	Very Short <4 months *100 points*	Short 4–8 months *80 points*	Moderate 8–12 months *60 points*	Long 12–16 months *40 points*	Very Long >16 months *20 points*
Interdependencies	10%	■ Degree to which the initiative is dependent on other initiatives	Stand-Alone *100 points*	Relatively Stand-Alone *80 points*	Moderately Interdependent *60 points*	Relatively Interdependent *40 points*	Very Interdependent *20 points*
Risk/Complexity to Implement	10%	■ Operational risk ■ Technology risk	Very Small Not New *100 points*	Not Significant Not New *80 points*	Moderate Not New *60 points*	Significant Beta *40 points*	Very Large Alpha *20 points*
Total	100%		Range for Initiative Total Scores: 200–1,000 Points				

Business Case — Implementation

In addition, all employees now understood both their unit's Balanced Scorecard as well as the criteria by which new initiatives would be judged. The strategic direction from the scorecard provided employees with more information to generate the innovative, entrepreneurial ideas that would help the organization achieve its ambitious strategic objectives. They could formulate and propose new initiatives that would likely have the greatest strategic impact on OFS. According to Douglas Newell, executive vice president, "The BSC contributed discipline and focus to our explosively growing Internet business. It permitted the orderly management of innovation as proposed initiatives were considered and prioritized from a strategic viewpoint."

SUMMARY

When using the Balanced Scorecard to integrate their planning and budgeting processes, companies can overcome important barriers to strategy implementation. The budget becomes transformed from a mechanical and tedious exercise, focused on short-term financial numbers, into a management tool that directs attention and resources to critical strategic initiatives. The *operational* budget, handled through an activity-based budgeting process, authorizes resource supply and spending based on anticipated demands for work and forecasted process efficiencies. This budget can be dynamic, allowing for changes in the environment, new opportunities, and competitor actions. The *strategic* budget focuses on decisions about new, discretionary funding and the assignment of critical human and capital resources to the new initiatives. The decisions are taken in rigorous reviews using the Balanced Scorecard as the lens by which proposed initiatives are proposed, ranked, and selected. The process also generates short-term performance targets across all Balanced Scorecard measures, financial and nonfinancial, for which managers and employees are held accountable and compensated in upcoming periods.

NOTES

1. J. Hope and R. Fraser, "Beyond Budgeting," BBRT, CAM-I Europe White Paper.
2. Ibid.
3. See Robert S. Kaplan and Robin Cooper, *Cost & Effect: Using Integrated Cost Systems to Drive Profitability and Performance* (Boston: Harvard Business School Press, 1997), 303–16; and "The Promise—and Peril—of Inte-

grated Cost Systems," *Harvard Business Review* (July–August 1998): 114–17.

4. Material taken from B. Conley, "Revamping Planning and Budgeting at Sprint" (paper presented at the Balanced Scorecard Collaborative Best Practice Conference, Redefining the Planning & Budgeting Process through the Balanced Scorecard, Cambridge, MA, 9–10 September 1999).

5. Sprint was fortunate in that demand for its services was growing rapidly, so its problem was how much new supply it had to add, rather than rationalizing and adjusting downward the supply of resources provided from previous periods.

6. R. Simons, "How High Is Your Return on Management?" *Harvard Business Review* (January–February 1998): 71–80.

7. In addition to strategic fit, the model reflected the cost, benefit, time, interdependencies, and risk of the initiative.

Feedback and Learning

ALIGNING STRATEGY TO TARGETS, initiatives, and budgets puts the organization in motion. Performance must then be monitored and guided to close the feedback loop. Beyond monitoring and fine-tuning, however, managers in Strategy-Focused Organizations must determine whether their strategy is still valid. In Chapter 1, we described how the Balanced Scorecard works like a laser to align and focus all organizational resources on implementing the strategy. Like a laser, such coherence can lead to nonlinear performance breakthroughs. But suppose the strategy articulated on the Balanced Scorecard is wrong. In this case, the Balanced Scorecard management system could cause an organization to fail that much faster, as all its energies focus on a losing strategy.

Companies that are stretching for high performance need management processes and systems to verify that their trajectory remains on course to a profitable future. They need feedback so that unprofitable strategies can be identified and corrected before much damage has been done.

THE NEW MANAGEMENT MEETING:
FROM TACTICS TO STRATEGY

The protocols for many management meetings are all too familiar. An executive describes the process previously used at AT&T Canada, Inc.: "Everybody told you what they did last month and what they were going to do next month. It was show-and-tell with no focus." Operational reviews and discussions of tactical issues dominate the typical meeting. Little time is left for strategic issues.

Strategy-Focused Organizations use a new kind of feedback process. Instead of reporting and control, the Balanced Scorecard focuses the agenda for the management meeting on strategic issues, teamwork, and learning. The meeting is used to manage and improve strategy, not tactics.

Managers need to perform several functions at their strategy meetings: controlling the strategy, testing the strategy, and adapting the strategy. Controlling the strategy, the bottom loop in Figure IV-1, is what most people think of as management control. The metaphor for such management control is a thermostat, responding to differences between actual and targeted temperature and adjusting the heating or air-conditioning unit to bring the outcome back to the desired state. In a management control meeting, managers receive a report on actual performance and variances that compare performance to the budget. People at the meeting attempt to determine a course of action that will get the organization back on track. Through this process, the assumptions about the measure, the target, and the strategy for achieving the target are maintained. The purpose is to detect when initiatives are not being deployed as planned, or to explain why results are falling short of targets.

Such management control meetings in the past focused only on financial measures. The Balanced Scorecard expands this process by having the meetings report and discuss all the measures relevant to the strategy plus the initiatives designed to improve measured performance. Using the scorecard, rather than the budget, as the agenda for the meeting maintains intense focus on the strategy and stimulates managers to devise actions to implement the strategy more effectively.

A good example of the new strategic control process occurred at AT&T Canada. CEO Bill Catucci inherited a process in which he met monthly with each head of the seven functional units to review the financial performance of the past month and the forecast for the next month. Once Catucci had the Balanced Scorecard in place, he canceled the seven individual meetings and replaced them with a new set of meetings for the entire executive team (see Figure 12-1). The meetings were organized around four strategic themes linked to the Balanced Scorecard:

1. New Business and Growth, chaired by the head of business development
2. Business Processes, chaired by the head of operations
3. Professional Development, chaired by the head of human resources
4. Strategic Management, chaired by the CEO

Catucci scheduled his Strategic Management meetings to last four hours, on a monthly basis, up to one year in advance. He made attendance com-

Figure 12-1 AT&T Canada Executive Team's Governance Model

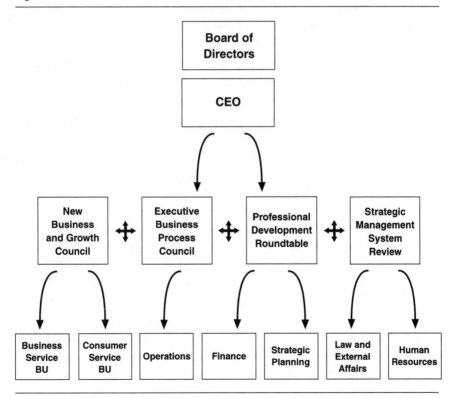

pulsory for himself and the eight business unit heads. Catucci emphasized that

> *how you conduct the meeting, how you react to the reported numbers, is tremendously important. In the past, the person reporting an unfavorable number was lonely and isolated. Now, I want people to admit to shortfalls and have everyone else respond, "How can we help?" Nothing that happens in this company is the sole responsibility of a single business unit head. If an indicator is in the Red [unfavorable] zone, we identify the people who can influence that indicator and ask them to come to the next meeting with an action plan. This is an entirely new management model for the company. We're sharing information and working together as a team to improve operations and fix problems.*
>
> *This monthly meeting soon became so interesting, people started to ask me if they could attend. I could have sold tickets to it.*

Catucci used the meetings focused on the Balanced Scorecard to introduce a new culture of teamwork and problem-solving around the strategy. Instead of reviewing and analyzing the past, the team was using data to influence the future in preferred directions. But even the team problem-solving described at AT&T Canada was single-loop control, working within the context of the existing strategy, not questioning or changing the strategy.

Managers also need to determine whether their strategies are valid: Will they deliver the intended performance breakthroughs? They need to engage in double-loop learning that enables the assumptions underlying their strategies to be examined.[1] Lee Wilson, chief of staff at Chemical Retail Bank, described the importance of questioning and updating the strategy at the management meetings:

> *When we started four years ago with the BSC, 80 percent of the time was spent on reviewing financial numbers and 20 percent on the strategy and its implementation. Now, it's just the reverse. We spend 80 percent of the time talking about our strategy and strategic initiatives, and only 20 percent on the financial results. Our industry is evolving and changing so rapidly, this focus on strategy is essential. If you stand still in financial services today, if you cast your strategy in stone, six months from now it will be out of date with what's happening in the world.*

For the City of Charlotte, City Manager Pam Syfert used the Balanced Scorecard to probe strategically in her periodic meetings with department heads. She asked each head several big questions:

1. How are you doing running your business?
2. How are you building the community and contributing to the focus areas?
3. How are you building your people?
4. How are you contributing to looking to the future?

The Balanced Scorecard was the common theme for the discussions on these questions.

People clearly noticed the difference in the meetings Syfert led:

[The previous] city manager would review progress on a major project, like the convention center, to see whether it was on time and on budget. Pam is more strategic. She asks: "Why did we build the convention center? What is its impact on neighborhoods, on economic development, . . . on employment, on transportation, . . . on the viability of downtown neighborhoods?"

This is a much broader discussion, requiring the active involvement of people from many departments. The questions are bigger and harder but they are also more fun and more motivating to work on.[2]

TESTING AND ADAPTING

In addition to using the meetings to engage senior managers in interactive discussions about the strategy, the strategy review meetings should explicitly allow for testing and adapting the strategy. We have seen three processes used to test and update the strategy:

1. Analytic methods: hypothesis testing and dynamic simulation
2. Examine impact of external discontinuities
3. Identify and support emergent strategies

We discuss each in turn.

Analytic Methods

Strategy, as we described in Chapter 3, consists of hypotheses. With the Balanced Scorecard, the hypotheses underlying the strategy are made explicit through the strategy map's cause-and-effect linkages across the four perspectives. But hypotheses are just assumptions about how the world works; they need to be continually tested for their validity and rejected when evidence accumulates that expected linkages are not occurring. So the first task in strategy adaptation is testing the underlying hypotheses.

Early in the implementation of its Balanced Scorecard, the Rockwater division of Brown & Root Energy Services examined the relationships among its measures and found correlations between employee morale and customer satisfaction, and between customer satisfaction and short collection cycles. Thus the managers could see how employee morale could lead to higher return on capital employed. Also, they saw higher employee morale leading to an increased number of employee suggestions implemented, which in turn led to reductions in waste and rework, lower operating expenses, and higher return on capital ROCE.[3]

Using data from its hundreds of retail stores, Sears performed extensive statistical analyses to determine patterns of causal linkages among scorecard measures.[4] The Sears analyst team described the motivation for their statistical analysis:

We wanted to go well beyond the usual balanced scorecard, commonly just a set of untested assumptions, and nail down the drivers of future financial performance with statistical rigor. We wanted to assemble the company's vast body of interview and research data . . . and construct a model to show pathways of actual causation all the way from employee attitudes to profits.[5]

The Sears strategy model was based on simple causal links between three key constituents (see Figure 12-2):

Investors	Customers	Employees
Compelling Place to Invest	Compelling Place to Shop	Compelling Place to Work

Managers believed that there could be up to a two-quarter lag from improvements in work measures to improvements in financial measures.

Figure 12-2   Testing the Hypotheses at Sears

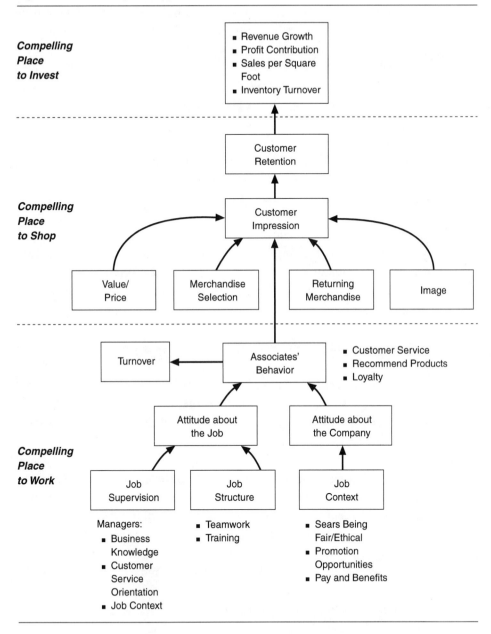

Using statistical factor analysis, Sears analysts mapped employee responses on up to 180 questions onto 22 underlying factors. For the shopping experience, the analysts mapped data from customer surveys into seven groupings. Four were related to perceptions of the buying experience—people, place, product, and value—and three to the outcome from the buying experience—satisfaction, the match between experience and expectations, and advocacy (Would customers recommend Sears to friends? Would they shop at Sears again?). The financial measures related to growth and to productivity. With the reduction in the dimensionality of the data, the analysts could then perform sophisticated causal modeling, factor analysis, and cluster analysis to identify systematic patterns in the data from 800 Sears stores.

The results proved fascinating and exciting. Sears saw how employee attitudes drove not just customer service but also employee turnover and the likelihood that employees would recommend Sears to family, friends, and customers. The statistical relationships revealed how improvements in training and employees' understanding of the business translated into higher revenues. For example, the model estimated that a 5-point improvement in employee attitudes led to a 1.3-point improvement in customer satisfaction, which in turn drove a 0.5% improvement in revenue growth. Thus a store with a 5-point improvement in employee attitude, in a district experiencing revenue growth of 4 percent, could actually be expected to have a revenue growth of 4.5 percent—nearly 15 percent higher than the average.

More detailed analysis showed how key drivers differed in their impact on different lines of business within the store. For example, analysts could compare the relative importance of employee measures versus product and place for their impact on customer satisfaction and loyalty. The impact of the factors varied across product lines such as women's intimate apparel versus large appliances. It also improved the explanatory power of the model, leading to insights about how to achieve double-digit sales productivity improvements in the apparel business. In this way, the statistical model of Sears's business strategy provided feedback on the business model and strategy. Initiatives and investments could now be targeted to the particular demands for each line of business and each type of store.

Statistical analysis requires considerable data such as can be captured in companies that—like Sears, Chemical Bank, or Mobil—have hundreds or thousands of relatively similar retail outlets. Each month, data on most scorecard measures become available for the sophisticated analysis. Time-series statistical analysis can also be performed but may require at least fifteen to twenty-four months of data before enough observations accumulate to estimate statistically reliable relationships, especially with lagged effects. When sufficient data are available for statistical analysis, managers have a powerful tool to not only confirm (or reject) the validity of their hypothesized relationships, but also to begin estimating quantitatively the magnitude and time-lags of linkages across measures.

Such statistical analysis enables managers to estimate historical relationships among Balanced Scorecard measures and to establish the validity of the causal linkages in the strategy map. The next step is to use the causal relationships to forecast the future trajectory of the strategy. Researchers at the MIT Sloan School of Management built a dynamic simulation model based on the scorecard used at Analog Devices, Inc.[6] The model helped to explain why Analog experienced difficulties initially translating dramatic improvements in its the scorecard's operational measures into improved financial performance.

Grupo Bal, a diversified Mexican business group (mining, insurance, retail stores, and financial services) with annual sales of $2.5 billion, built a dynamic simulation model to support its Balanced Scorecard initiative. Grupo Bal had introduced economic value added as a new financial metric in 1994, but the program was not successful because it did not link down to operational activities. Mr. Alberto Baillères, president and chairman of the board, decided to launch a major program of value creation in the group whose first phase was a pilot project in the insurance company to develop a Balanced Scorecard that would represent "a model of the strategy." The Balanced Scorecard provided the common language for communication about strategies for value creation. The simple Balanced Scorecard strategy maps, however, (see examples in Chapters 3 and 4) did not incorporate feedback loops and delays. So the development team went further to build a "model of the business" using a systems dynamics software language.[7]

The simulation model was more detailed than the Balanced Scorecard, requiring between 100 and 200 variables, as it had to include many operational variables, not just high-level strategic ones. The model also quantified the magnitudes and delays between changes in a driver variable and associated changes in outcome variables and explicitly incorporated feedback loops across measures and perspectives (see Figure 12-3). The model enabled managers to look several years into the future to see the impact of today's operations on tomorrow's results.

The first benefit from the dynamic simulation model came from the constructive dialogues that could now occur between corporate and business unit executives when evaluating the impact of different strategies on the dynamics of the business. It took the emotion out of the discussion by hav-

Figure 12-3 Grupo BAL's Dynamic Simulation Model

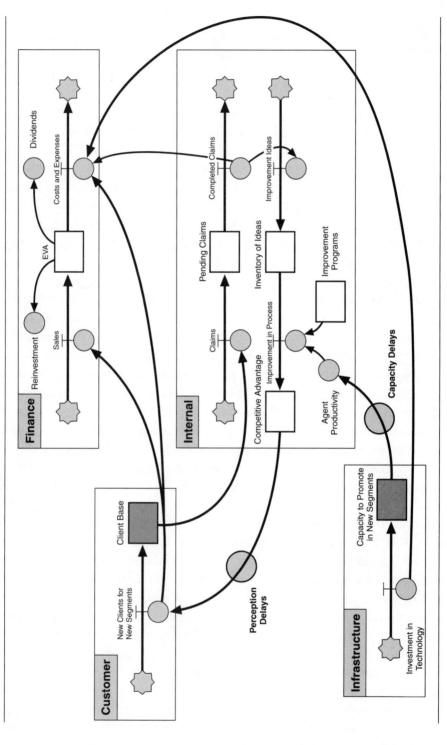

ing a formal analytic model as the language of the strategy and its evolution. Managers could understand better the trajectory of value creation from a given strategy, and they could fully evaluate strategic alternatives before committing resources for new investments and initiatives. The CEO saw where he could intervene to help the business unit create more future economic value. An unexpected benefit occurred when a new manager was brought into the business. By working through the simulation, the manager came up to speed in less than a day on the company's underlying business model.

Second, the model made explicit the key operational drivers of value creation. It identified the 20 percent of variables that drove 80 percent of the results. Managers came to understand the implications on feedback and delay among the key operational variables. The simulation model also facilitated an understanding of the interdependencies among strategic resources and the business unit's strategic objectives.

Third, the model transformed strategic planning from an annual event to an ongoing process. As new contingencies, opportunities, or threats emerged, their impact could be assessed by resetting variables within the simulation model. The process of building the model identified several variables that were key strategic drivers but that had not been measured before.

Sears's formal statistical model-building and hypothesis-testing and Grupo Bal's dynamic simulation model provided management teams with new insights about their strategy. Managers still faced the challenge of using these insights to enhance or adapt their strategy.

Examine the Impact of External Discontinuities

After managers formulate a strategy, the world can change in ways that undermine the assumptions that were used when the strategy map and Balanced Scorecard were created. Competitors may take unexpected actions, new competitors may emerge with attractive value propositions to targeted customers, a major and highly relevant technological innovation can arise, government regulatory or deregulatory actions can change the competitive playing field, and macroeconomic conditions—interest rates, exchange rates, energy prices, inflation, and recession—can shift. Companies whose growth strategies in 1997 included expansion into Southeast Asia markets would, by October 1997, have had an obsolete strategy owing to the financial meltdown that had just occurred in that part of the world. At least on a quarterly basis, management teams should be assessing the impact of external events to determine whether and how their strategies should be modified.

Some have expressed concern that the Balanced Scorecard may create an internal focus, leading managers to ignore competitors' performance and actions as well as events in the external environment that could affect the organization. Competitor forces and the external environment enter the formulation of the scorecard already in at least two ways. First, when the initial strategy is formulated, managers typically follow the standard strategic planning methodology of scanning the external environment to assess strengths, weaknesses, opportunities, and threats, and intensively studying competitors and customers. From this external assessment comes the judgments and tradeoffs that define the organization's strategy, which then gets translated into the scorecard. So the external environment and forces are present at the outset of any scorecard project.

Second, many scorecard measures are calibrated against the competition. The payoff in Mobil's corporate incentive plan was based on its financial performance as compared with its leading six competitors. The growth measures in the NAM&R Division's scorecard were benchmarked against industry averages. And the customer measure of market share was, by definition, calculated relative to the division's competitors. Important metrics in the value proposition—such as price, quality, lead times, and product attributes and functionality—can and should also be measured relative to those of competitors. Internal process measures can be benchmarked against best-in-class. Therefore the second influence of the external environment comes from establishing targets relative to competitor's performance.

Once strategies and targets have been established, however, the question remains about how the organization stays alert and vigilant to new threats and opportunities. If the organization has been successful in making strategy everyone's everyday job, it can mobilize the eyes and ears of its hundreds or thousands of employees. With everyone in the organization aware of the strategy, each person can be a scout, detecting when an external event has occurred that can affect the strategy. Software can play a powerful facilitating role. As we discuss later in this chapter, employees often access the Balanced Scorecard through the corporate Intranet. The Balanced Scorecard software should have a feature that enables individuals to send messages and engage in intranet discussions about any of the measures. If an employee learns of a new product introduction, a new hire, or a new initiative by a competitor, then, just like the Mobil truck driver phoning in feedback about bad retail stations to regional headquarters, the employee can post a message to inform others about the new development. In its monthly and quarterly meetings, management will have not only its own information to review and assess, but also the information that has been provided by the entire employee base.

There is no magical system that can capture all the relevant external information that might affect an organization's strategy. Organizations need to encourage all employees at all levels to participate in generating intelligence, both the positive and negative news, that has the potential for influencing the strategy. The scorecard provides the shared understanding that helps employees filter all of the information they receive each day to determine which events are the most significant for management to contemplate in future strategy meetings. Management meetings must be structured so that inputs on strategic opportunities and threats can come from the entire organization. In this way, strategy truly becomes a continual process.

Identify and Support Emergent Strategies

New strategies often emerge from within the organization. In an award-winning article, management scholar Henry Mintzberg has stressed the importance of such emergent strategies.[8] Many successful strategies arise from local initiatives and experimentation. Employees who already have a clear understanding of the existing strategy, because of the communication and alignment processes described in Part Three, may innovate and find new and unexpected ways to achieve high-level strategic objectives or identify variations in the strategy that open up new growth opportunities. Senior management should be encouraging employees to formulate emergent strategies and use their quarterly meetings to assess the viability of local initiatives. Recall Mobil NAM&R's Speedpass program, a powerful new way to provide customers with a "fast, friendly serve." Senior managers at Mobil rapidly incorporated this innovation, which had arisen from within the technology organization, into the strategy and the scorecard of the entire division.

National Bank Online Financial Services, as described in Chapter 11, used its Balanced Scorecard to screen initiatives that were continually proposed from within the organization. The scorecard helped managers select initiatives that had the best fit with the strategy. If followed too rigidly, however, this process could stifle emergent strategies from arising. In this case, though, the management team was alert to new possibilities. For example, the team was enthusiastic about one proposed initiative that scored low on the screening procedure. Rather than reject the proposal because it failed on the scoring criteria, the team reflected on what was attractive to them about the proposal. The team concluded that the proposal actually identified a new strategic opportunity that was not currently on their Balanced Scorecard. They not only accepted the initiative but changed a scorecard measure to reflect the insights from their discussion. In this way, the management meeting allowed the new initiative to modify the strategy and the scorecard. This is excellent "double-loop" learning—using the management meeting to reflect on the assumptions behind the strategy and being willing to modify the assumptions and the strategy based on an idea that had emerged from within the organization.

As with its facilitating role to encourage employees to report significant external events, Balanced Scorecard software on the corporate intranet facilitates the generation and communication of ideas within the organization. Companies can encourage employees to send e-mail and post proposals about new ways of achieving strategic objectives. Emergent strategies play an important role in allowing strategy to adapt even between formal strategy meetings.

UPDATING THE SCORECARD: CHEMICAL RETAIL BANK

As companies refine and adapt their strategy, the next level of value is created. Organizations find that up to 25 percent of the measures change every year, reflecting the learning that is taking place. The original strategies or the previous measures were not wrong. The evolution was caused by the organization reaching another level of sophistication around its strategy.

Lee Wilson uses the term *granularity* to describe this learning process. When Chemical Retail Bank introduced its first scorecard in 1994, service quality was a major priority, and the project team developed a sophisticated quality index incorporating about one hundred quality-related events. The quality index, however, included so many items that it lost meaning; it was just a number. People would sit around at the meetings having academic conversation about the measure, but nothing meaningful ever came from it. Finally, Mike Hegarty asked, "What's under that index?" At the next meeting, the composite was broken down. The number one problem identified by the index was "deposits not posted." Hegarty exploded: "Deposit not posted? We're a bank! The whole essence of a bank is trust. If someone gives us their money and we can't put it in their account, how are they going to trust us?"

Suddenly, the issue of service quality had come alive. The generality of a service-quality index had become tangible and focused on the critical few sources (granularity) of problems. The strategy had been translated to tactics; organization learning had taken place. A new measure on the scorecard reflected this learning.

The interplay of strategy, tactics, and learning is a subtle but fundamental process. Learning is not a "big bang." It takes place in hundreds of ways and in hundreds of places throughout the organization. The actual learning and the subject of the learning would be considered operational or tactical. It is the aggregate of the learning that is strategic. The Balanced Scorecard defines objectives, such as service quality, that are strategic. As the organization attempts to implement the strategic priority, it breaks the big picture into more granular pieces, learns where the leverage is greatest, and creates value. Ultimately, the learning that emerges becomes a strategic asset because it is embedded in linkages that drive high-level strategic objectives.

Again, the experiences at Chemical Retail Bank illustrate this. The initial Balanced Scorecard, introduced in the early 1990s, was designed to consolidate the merger of Chemical Bank and Manufacturers Hanover Trust. Customer retention was a major objective, especially while closing redundant branch offices that would deliver the cost benefits from the merger. An aggregate measure of customer retention appeared on the initial scorecard. As the program evolved, managers realized that not all customer turnover was undesirable. Some existing customers were not profitable or were not the targets of the new strategy. Thus the granularity of the customer retention increased to focus more specifically on retention of targeted, profitable customers. This narrow focus created tremendous learning because the executive team was now able to direct initiatives and evaluate their impact on targeted customers. Over a two-year period, Chemical retained 85 percent to 90 percent of its premerger assets despite closing hundreds of branches throughout the New York metropolitan area. And very few of the lost customers were in targeted segments.

In 1996, Chemical Bank, after its merger with Chase Manhattan Corporation, faced the same issue. This merger led to the closure of twice as many branches, yet the asset retention rate ranged between 95 percent to 100 percent of the balances. Chemical Bank's Chief of Staff Lee Wilson attributed this success to the learning that had taken place in the earlier merger: "We got tremendous value out of that process. It saved us several billion dollars of balances and added somewhere between 20 and 30 million dollars per year to earnings."

UPDATING THE SCORECARD: STORE 24

In Chapter 3 we described Store 24, a convenience-store chain attempting to introduce a new customer-intimacy strategy based on innovative in-store promotions that made shopping fun. Store 24's motto was "Ban Boredom." The strategy was introduced in 1998, along with the Balanced Scorecard shown in Figure 3-8. Two years later, CEO Bob Gordon scrapped the Ban Boredom campaign. Overall, financial performance was fine, with same-store sales growing at 4 percent to 6 percent, about the industry average. But customer feedback surveys showed low differentiation of Store 24 from its competitors. As Gordon noted: "Customers' recognition of the 'enjoyable experience' that we sought to create was particularly low. Customers told us that they valued fast service and good selection the most."

Gordon learned from the Balanced Scorecard measures that, despite acceptable financial performance, the innovative strategy to move from operational excellence to customer intimacy was not working.

It might have worked if we had done a better job of training our staff and had spent more on advertising to create customer awareness. But this is a difficult business in which to develop those kinds of employee skills. I guess we learned that this kind of differentiation strategy may not be realistic in the convenience-store industry.

Store 24 introduced a new customer strategy under the banner, "Cause You Just Can't Wait." This strategy focused on three features: fast and efficient (in and out), find what you want (selection), and good stuff (quality). The Balanced Scorecard was updated to reflect this shift. In the financial perspective, the measure "percent sales from new items" replaced "net sales from new concepts," to reflect the new emphasis on interesting selection. The customer feedback surveys dropped the customer-intimacy measurement of "enjoyable experience." In its place, a "competitive comparison" measure was added to determine whether Store 24 was succeeding in creating differentiation through its new strategy of speed, quality, and selection. This experience illustrates how the Balanced Scorecard provided a framework for Store 24's double-loop learning. The company introduced an innovative strategy, tested it in real time, learned what aspects of the strategy were not working, and adapted and modified the strategy based on what it had learned.

STRUCTURE AND FREQUENCY OF MEETINGS

How can you make meetings exciting and productive? Walt Disney Company CEO Michael Eisner described an important piece of his management philosophy: "Call meetings on subjects that really matter and show up."[9] This simple yet profound insight captures the essence of the approaches used by Strategy-Focused Organizations. The Balanced Scorecard defines the important topics, and the meeting is an open, team-based learning process led by the senior executive. Chemical Bank's Wilson described the power of the process this way: "One of the problems in large organizations is that you get to the top by being an expert. Everybody expects you to know everything. Sometimes there are magic moments in meetings when a leader actually learns in front of his subordinates. When this happens, the energy created is dynamite."[10]

We can paraphrase Hegarty's extension to Eisner's advice: "Call meetings on important topics, show up, be engaged, *and show that you are prepared to learn.*"

With the Balanced Scorecard, particularly when the information is accessible through a shared information system, the reporting and review of performance is continual, occurring between meetings. The actual meetings become more focused and shorter. Gerry Isom described the CIGNA Property & Casualty experience this way: "With the Balanced Scorecard, we were reviewing performance on a daily basis. We all knew what was going on. The quarterly reviews became shorter because of the simplicity and clarity of what we were trying to accomplish."

What does this new management meeting look like? In some organizations, the meetings are held less often; quarterly meetings become the norm, although reporting against the scorecard occurs monthly. Because strategic issues change less frequently, the quarterly meeting is adequate for reviewing strategy. The meetings are usually scheduled for half a day. This provides adequate time to review, say, twenty-five measures on three strategic themes. Each measure on the scorecard has an accountable executive. Each of these executives must attend if the meeting is to be productive. The attendees should not be based on the chain of command, but rather on who plays key roles in the strategy. Chemical Bank attendees, in addition to the president, included executive vice presidents, senior VPs, VPs, and assistant VPs. Knowledge replaced rank as a source of power.

An effective management process requires proper staff support. An administrator manages the agenda, handles meeting logistics, assists the reporting process, and coordinates action lists. Chemical Bank had a full-time assistant vice president and half the time of a VP from the Strategic Planning group managing this process. CIGNA Property & Casualty assigned one and a half people at the corporate level and one person in each SBU to coordinate the process. The agenda for these strategy reviews is generally organized around the measures on the scorecard. As experience is gained and reporting systems provide status information on a continuous basis, the agenda tends to become more issue oriented. Every effective meeting ends with an action list.

Often, data for several measures are not yet available after the initial design of the Balanced Scorecard. Some managers react to the missing measures by deferring the startup of management meetings until data on all of the measures are available. This is a bad decision. Our advice here, as suggested by the Nike commercial, is "Just do it." The primary benefit of a Balanced Scorecard is the *focus* that it produces. Focus doesn't always have to be measurable, especially in the early project stages. Every organization has "low hanging fruit" that can be easily harvested in the first pass if the pickers know what they are looking for. Thus simply convening the management meeting and using the topics of the Balanced Scorecard as the agenda create the first wave of benefits.

USING FEEDBACK SYSTEMS TO CHANGE CULTURE

The feedback and reporting system provides the structure around which management meetings work. Most of the discussion about reporting systems focuses on *technology:* availability of data, graphical interfaces, drill-down capability to detailed data and transactions, data mining, and e-mail links. Little time is spent discussing the *cultural* aspects of a feedback system. Yet the cultural context for reporting and feedback has far more potential for positive and negative impact than technology. Cultural assumptions, frequently overlooked and often embedded in the technology itself, can either create or inhibit the climate for change. Figure 12-4 shows the summary screen from the CIGNA Property & Casualty Balanced Scorecard reporting system. On the left-hand side of the screen, the strategic objectives from the corporate scorecard are listed. Each column represents an SBU (e.g., "D&O" is Directors and Officers Insurance). Each cell in the matrix shows a red-yellow-green indicator of performance. Executives drill down from any indicator to see more detailed screens showing measures, initiatives, and dialog boxes. The following seemingly simple questions, while technically elegant, have complex cultural implications:

- Who can access and use the system?
- How should performance be communicated?
- Does it create competition or cooperation?
- Is this an addition to our existing reporting system?

Who Can Access and Use the System?

Traditionally, reporting on strategic performance has been reserved for those at the top of the organization. Many of the benefits achieved at Chemical Retail Bank, for example, came from a reporting system designed only for the executive team. Increasingly, however, Strategy-Focused Organizations are concluding that more open reporting is better. Bill Catucci noted, "Because power is generally held at the top of corporations, information is also restricted to the top. Empowering employees means giving them information to make them powerful."

Several companies have begun distributing this power by making the performance data from Balanced Scorecards widely available. At CIGNA P&C, 70 percent of the workforce had access to the scorecards of all the company's SBUs. Lower-level staff saw the same information as division presidents. They could send e-mails to comment on performance. AT&T Canada had a similar program, giving all employees access to the performance data and allowing them to communicate with senior executives. Nationwide Mutual Insurance made its scorecard information available to its nearly 4,000 employees. Reuters America Inc. introduced a similar information-sharing scheme, although it indexed detailed quantity mea-

Figure 12-4 CIGNA Executive Team's Enterprise Management Software

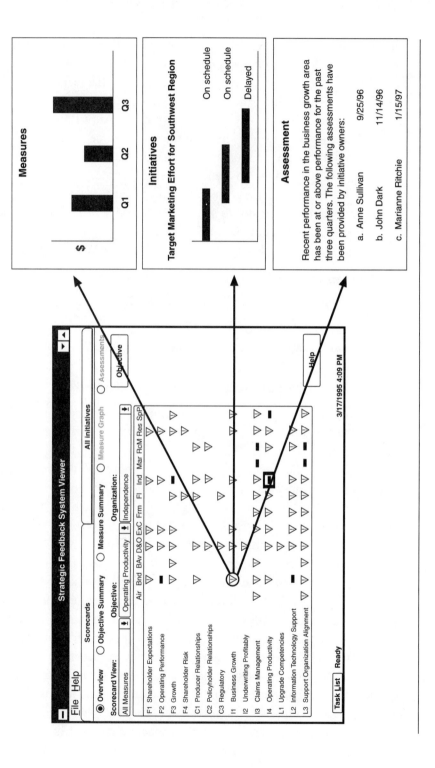

sures when they were considered too sensitive for wide-scale reporting.

Such extensive information sharing must overcome major cultural barriers. CIGNA's Gerry Isom noted:

> *If you can't accept that the CEO of the company will know what's happening in the unit as quickly as your immediate boss does, then you're probably not a candidate for the scorecard. But if you are open to communication about what's going on in your organization, you'll love a Balanced Scorecard.*

Open communication of performance information creates the opportunity for a new kind of infrastructure. It transcends functional and departmental barriers by allowing individuals to have a companywide view. More important, it helps individuals to build their own roadmaps to the knowledge and expertise they need to do their job. By showing who is responsible for what, and by showing performance in all parts of the organization, a "virtual organization" focused on strategic objectives emerges.

How Should Performance Be Communicated?

Traditional accounting control systems are dominated by a concern for precision. Auditing standards require that financial measures be absolute and objective. Strategic reporting is different. A strategic management system is a *communication* system, not a *control* system. We frequently find organizations replacing numeric reporting with performance coded into red-yellow-green indicators. Those with an accounting mindset sometimes have trouble with this. "Who determines red-yellow-green?" "What if they lie?" One cultural shift that takes place with open reporting systems is the integrity of the subjective information. In such an open environment, where everyone sees everyone else's performance, integrity becomes self-policing. When someone communicates a green status when others know differently, the feedback is rapid. "It's difficult to lie anymore," observed one participant.

A greater cultural challenge surrounds the public perceptions of status reporting. Individuals historically have been extremely reluctant to report performance landing in the "red" zone. "Better dead than red," they believe. As CIGNA's Gerry Isom noted, "It was a tremendous adjustment for people to report their problems because they knew that everyone in the company that had a computer would see their problems. It took a while for people to be totally objective about reporting performance."

The way the organization handles this issue tells a lot about the new culture that emerges. As described by AT&T Canada CEO Bill Catucci: "If you're not meeting your targets, and you get hammered, that sends a certain signal throughout the organization. If, instead, you discuss the problem and ask for the help of your colleagues, different signals are being sent."

Both Isom and Catucci had a common objective—to create teamwork based on sharing knowledge around shared goals. But they also realized that communication was as much a cultural phenomenon as a technical one. If they were to achieve their teamwork objectives, they had to set the tone for constructive, supportive dialogue, not criticism and micromanagement. For risk-taking and innovation to be encouraged, executives must create a climate that permits shortfalls and problems to be open for discussion and problem-solving. None of these organizations encouraged mediocrity, but they wanted people to report problems without fearing this would be a career-ending move. Public disclosure of a problem or shortfall launched a process to solve the problem.

In complex organizations, few strategic issues can be addressed alone. The red-yellow-green report on strategic indicators provides an early warning system to direct team problem-solving. People may initially be uncomfortable reporting on problems within their own area of responsibility. But, as described on a wall poster behind the desk of a military leader: The only thing worse than bad news is bad news late.

Does It Create Competition or Cooperation?

Humans are competitive beasts. Those who excel want to retain the advantages that they have. Open reporting systems make information available to all. The approaches used by the top-performing claims department at CIGNA Property & Casualty became visible to all other claims departments. The approaches used by leaders in plant safety at Mobil NAM&R were visible to all other plants. At one level, people take pride in being seen as the leader by their peers. At another level, people may wish to hold their approaches confidential so that their advantage can be retained. Companies need to break through such constraints. Large organizations can gain advantage from their scale by identifying and sharing their large information base of knowledge and experiences. For this to occur, however, they must promote a culture of information sharing. Open reporting around the Balanced Scorecard helps facilitate this cultural change. The scorecard identifies those with common objectives and roles. It points the way to a networked organization in which individuals can become linked together by their competencies instead of by their departmental or functional organization. The open reporting breaks down the barriers of selfishness. Incentive compensation systems based on team scorecard performance further reduce these barriers.

Is It an Addition to Our Existing Reporting System?

Does the Balanced Scorecard add more reporting? The answer is no, if the organization can reduce its reliance on traditional reports. J. P. Morgan & Co. Incorporated's IT Division formed an alliance with several vendors to manage its outsourced operations. Prior to establishing the alliance, J. P. Morgan had been measuring, in its global operations, more than 1,100 metrics. But only about 60 of these related to measures used in higher-level strategic reports. The scorecard with alliance partners enabled the company to focus on the data and information requirements for only 18 high-level measures. The focus on strategic reporting reduced the time required for measuring and reporting IT performance from 45 staff years to 12 staff years (a 75 percent improvement) and the goal was to make another 50 percent improvement in the near term. So the adoption of the Balanced Scorecard did not add another layer of reporting costs and complexity. It actually greatly simplified and lowered the cost of performance reporting.

Many organizations report similar experiences. Even though the Balanced Scorecard is a new reporting and information system, they now produce fewer reports and spend considerably less of their resources in collecting and reporting data. The City of Charlotte's traditional MBO system had been reporting nearly 1,000 measures. The scorecard measures were much fewer in number and much more meaningful to the frontline people and senior-level city administrators. Most organizations indicate that the scorecard enabled them to trash many of their reports that had accumulated over the years—reports to which no one was paying attention.

The elimination of traditional reports, however, can present another cultural barrier. At CIGNA P&C, once the Balanced Scorecard system had been installed, CEO Isom mandated that all previous reports be eliminated.

You would expect this decision to be greeted enthusiastically. To the contrary, it was resisted. "I had to literally tell people, 'I will not read your reports. I will read what you put in the computer each month within your Balanced Scorecard format. But I will not read written documents coming to me.'"

So the simple process of installing an information reporting system is fraught with cultural traps, but it is also loaded with cultural opportunities. Executives who avoid the traps and capitalize on the opportunities can establish a new performance-centered climate. An organization that shares information with employees generates new strategic opportunities from its front lines. It can respond quickly to competitive changes. An organization with integrity in its reporting will encourage risk-taking in a team environment. An organization with open communication will share and amplify strategic knowledge and competencies. And, finally, the organization will have developed a common language and agenda that promote teamwork for all.

THE ROLE OF TECHNOLOGY

When we began working with organizations on their Balanced Scorecard programs in the early 1990s, no off-the-shelf software products existed. Each organization had to develop its own method for acquiring and reporting scorecard information. CIGNA Property & Casualty started with a paper report. The first edition of this report had one page for each measure and one book for each of the twenty-one SBUs, leading to a monthly three-inch pile of paper on Gerry Isom's desk. He said, "Get this on a computer." Chemical's Retail Bank, a large but single SBU, maintained a paper-based system for more than a year. Each page of the report was supported by an information system of some type, but it required an assistant vice president to consolidate the information with a manual process. Mobil NAM&R required that each SBU develop a Microsoft Excel spreadsheet to report its Balanced Scorecard. Despite these technologically challenged solutions, each organization accomplished dramatic breakthroughs in performance with its Balanced Scorecard program. So sophisticated technology is not necessary for a successful implementation.

Once the new performance management system has been launched, information technology can unleash new dimensions of value that cannot be created in any other way. A simple low-tech system can support an executive team at the top of the organization. But to move the scorecard from the boardroom to the backroom, companies need more advanced information technology. CIGNA Property & Casualty moved quickly to developing a sophisticated computer system (Figure 12-4). While the initial goal of the new system was more efficient reporting to the executive teams (and reducing the height of paper on Gerry Isom's desk), the new system opened up the possibility of sharing the information with all employees. *Open reporting* would not have been possible without the system and its enabling network. *Cascading* the scorecard to function, department, team, and individuals is possible without technology, but an information system allows the scorecards and the organizations to be linked so that synergies can be achieved. We talked earlier of Chemical Bank's lessons about granularity and its impact on strategic learning. Technology enables Balanced Scorecard measures to be linked with more detailed data and transactions. The bank built a customer database that allowed it to measure customer satisfaction and retention by location and by customer segment. As reported earlier, the granular approach was instrumental for much of the bank's strategy. It could not have been accomplished without technology.

Many organizations are now capturing transaction data, operational data, and customer and supplier data in their enterprise resource planning (ERP) systems and making them available in their data warehouses. Companies with such ERP capabilities can link their Balanced Scorecards to their transactional databases, enabling automatic and continual updating of many scorecard measures. They can also link their Balanced Scorecard to their other analytic applications, such as activity-based costing, shareholder value, and customer relationship management. The scorecard strategy map becomes the top-level performance model, integrating across ABC/ABM, EVA, and CRM measurement systems.

SUMMARY

The Balanced Scorecard initially clarifies and communicates the organization's strategy. It starts to influence strategy by aligning business units, shared service units, and individuals to execute according to the formulated strategy, and by allocating resources—capital funds, discretionary spending, people, and technology—to new initiatives required to implement that strategy. Management needs opportunities, however, to measure progress on how well the strategy is being implemented and how well the strategy seems to be working.

Management meetings provide a forum for executives to work together in teams to identify problems, assess changes in the operating and strategic environment, and consider new opportunities that may have arisen since the strategy was formulated. The Balanced Scorecard becomes the agenda for such management meetings, enabling participants to work outside of their functional and departmental boundaries to solve problems affecting the entire organization. The meetings promote teamwork and organizational learning. Some have even reported that the meetings are fun to attend.

By giving employees continual access to the Balanced Scorecard, the organization greatly amplifies its problem-identification, problem-solving, opportunity-creating, and knowledge-sharing capabilities. It enlists the hearts and minds of all its employees, not just the chosen few at the top. Recent advances in information technology enable the performance data to be collected and shared at much lower cost and with greater linkages, visibility, and ease of understanding and use. Simple color-coding schemes, such as green-yellow-red, replace rows, columns, and pages of eight-digit numbers that only engineers and accountants could previously interpret. The feedback and review of strategic information helps to maintain enthusiasm about the strategic journey and to guide the organization to ever-higher levels of performance.

NOTES

1. The importance of distinguishing between single-loop and double-loop control is due to Chris Argyris; see Chris Argyris, *Reasoning, Learning, and Action* (San Francisco: Jossey-Bass, 1982), and "Teaching Smart People How to Learn," *Harvard Business Review* (May–June 1991): 99–109.

2. R. S. Kaplan, "City of Charlotte (A)," 9-199-036 (Boston: Harvard Business School, 1998), 9.

3. This example was described in Robert S. Kaplan and David P. Norton, *The Balanced Scorecard: Translating Strategy into Action* (Boston: Harvard Business School Press, 1996), 255–56.

4. A. J. Rucci, S. P. Kirn, and R. T. Quinn, "The Employee-Customer-Profit Chain at Sears," *Harvard Business Review* (January–February 1998): 82–97; see also S. P. Kirn, "Statistically Validating the Linkage between Employee Satisfaction, Customer Satisfaction, and Business Performance" (paper presented at the Second Annual Balanced Scorecard Summit, San Francisco, 12–15 October 1999).

5. Rucci, Kirn, and Quinn, "The Employee-Customer-Profit Chain at Sears," 89.

6. J. D. Sterman, N. Repenning, and F. Kofman, "Unanticipated Side Effects of Successful Quality Improvement Programs: Exploring a Paradox of Organizational Improvement," *Management Science* 4, no. 2 (1997): 503–21.

7. The simulation language, ithink, developed by High Performance Systems, Inc., is also the foundation for *Balancing the Corporate Scorecard,* a simulation produced by Harvard Business School Publishing.

8. H. Mintzberg, "Crafting Strategy," *Harvard Business Review* (July–August 1987): 66–75.

9. M. D. Eisner, *Letter From The Chairman,* The Walt Disney Annual Report, 1995.

10. L. Wilson, "The Management Meeting: Putting Strategy on the Table" (paper presented at the Balanced Scorecard Collaborative Best Practice Conference, Cambridge, MA, 15–16 December 1999).

Mobilizing Change through Executive Leadership

IMPLEMENTING NEW STRATEGIES REQUIRES LARGE-SCALE CHANGE. The term *transformation* has emerged to differentiate the scale of change required by business strategy from the continuous improvement that organizations routinely perform. The leaders of our Strategy-Focused Organizations clearly led transformations, not small-scale changes.

John Kotter carefully distinguishes between the words *management* and *leadership* when describing transformation: "Management is a set of processes that can keep a complicated system of people and technology running smoothly. . . . Leadership is a set of processes that creates organizations in the first place or adapts them to significantly changing circumstances. . . . Successful transformation is 70 to 90 percent leadership and only 10 to 30 percent management."[1]

The leadership process, as practiced by the executives in the successful organizations, can be seen throughout the previous sections of this book. In Part One, we saw how they created inspirational visions for new strategies. The Balanced Scorecard provided a framework to articulate and communicate the new vision and strategy. In Part Two, the leaders created new organization focus on the strategy. The Balanced Scorecard defined the linkages between business units, shared service groups, and external partners that were necessary to make the strategy work. In Part Three, the leaders decentralized power and responsibility to the lowest levels of the organization, using the power of the shared vision to align and reinforce local initiatives. In Part Four, the leaders used budget, feedback, and reporting systems to create a new culture and governance process. In Part Five, we focus on the way in which these leaders integrated these many activities to mobilize their organizations and to maintain momentum for strategic change.

Getting transformation started is often the biggest challenge. In Chapter 13, we study the different approaches used by the leaders. Several of the case studies were failing organizations; the leaders were able to use this "burning platform" to motivate change. In other cases, the companies were currently successful; the leaders created stretch targets to eliminate complacency and drive creative efforts. We also see that successful Balanced Scorecard programs don't always start in the CEO's office. Many effective programs started at lower levels, even in functional departments.

But getting started only planted the seeds for change. The change initiatives then had to be cultivated and sustained. Organizations used different approaches to build and sustain momentum. Each organization, however, used its measurement system, linked to the governance process, to sustain the change.

While the Balanced Scorecard has created benefits in many organizations, failures have also occurred. Several organizations failed to achieve benefits from their Balanced Scorecard programs. We can learn from failure. In Chapter 14, we will discuss the pitfalls that led to these missed opportunities. They serve as a counterpoint to the principles practiced by the leaders of our Strategy-Focused Organizations.

NOTE

1. John P. Kotter, *Leading Change* (Boston: Harvard Business School Press, 1996), 25–26.

Leadership and Mobilization

THE PROCESS TO INITIATE THE BALANCED SCORECARD management system starts with a leader creating the sense of urgency for change. The urgency can come from reversing recent underperformance, responding to a changing competitive environment, or stretching the organization to be much better than it currently is. Leaders who want to create dramatic change in their organization will find the Balanced Scorecard a highly effective management tool to motivate and accomplish the desired change.

Often the change is stimulated by poor organizational performance: Current performance is so dismal that new directions are clearly needed. At other times, the senior executive sees that future challenges will be very different from those of the past. The organization must adopt new ways of doing business even though no obvious crisis currently exists. Yet another trigger occurs when the senior executive wants to motivate employees to perform beyond current performance, which is adequate but not outstanding. In all of these cases, the executive recognizes the need to change, but then he or she must find ways to communicate the urgency to all managers and employees and provide a vision of what the change can accomplish.[1]

LEAPING OFF THE BURNING PLATFORM

Several of the CEOs of adopting organizations clearly sensed the need for urgent change because of current terrible performance. Bob McCool at Mobil NAM&R recalled that "expenses had doubled, capital had doubled, margins had flattened, and volumes were heading down. You didn't need an MBA to know we were in trouble."[2]

Gerry Isom of CIGNA was hired to turn around the Property & Casualty Division at a time when its combined ratio—the ratio of expense dollars going out to premium revenues coming in—exceeded 130, as compared with an industry average of 108.

Bill Catucci, the newly hired CEO of AT&T Canada, noted, "When I arrived in December 1995, the company was close to bankruptcy. The only core competence we had was losing money. We were good at that, losing C$1 million every day."

For Chemical Retail Bank, competition in its traditional retail deposit business had become very tough. Revenue growth had slowed because of lower interest rates on core deposits; deposits were leaving the bank for non-banking service providers, such as mutual funds and money market funds; core operating expenses for real estate and personnel in the expensive New York region were increasing; and heavy funding was required for expensive new electronic delivery systems. While the bank was still marginally profitable, President Michael Hegarty also saw the threat from electronic banking to Chemical's historic reliance on brick and mortar branches.

Each of these business leaders saw the need for dramatic change. Whatever their organizations had been doing in the past, it either was not working any more or would not work in the future.

CREATING A NEW FUTURE

Launching major organizational change need not be done just out of fear. Effective leaders can also motivate change by providing inspiration about the future. Pam Syfert, Charlotte's city manager, drove the development of Balanced Scorecards because she believed they would help the city's departments and employees deliver on the vision to become the number one city in the United States for people to live, work, and take their leisure activities. Similarly, in the State of Washington, Balanced Scorecard projects were launched at a meeting when Governor Gary Locke challenged his senior officials to think about what they wanted to be remembered for after their years of state service: "Do you want to be remembered for incremental improvement, and no major scandals on your watch, or do you want to look back and appreciate that something truly significant and revolutionary happened under your leadership that made the lives of citizens in the state demonstrably better?"

Douglas Newell, head of the fledgling Internet banking division of National Bank Online Financial Services, set a goal to become the number one Internet banking company in the world. The OFS division already enjoyed first-mover advantages and seemed to be doing well. But in the extremely dynamic Internet marketplace, Newell knew that continuous improvement was far from sufficient. He motivated the development of the Balanced Scorecard by setting stretch targets: triple the customer base in less than three years to become the first Internet bank with one million customers; increase the revenue per customer by more than 50 percent; and reduce the cost per customer served by more than 35 percent. At Reuters Americas, the president launched the Balanced Scorecard program by challenging the organization to double shareholder value within five years. The founder/CEO of a major apparel retailer challenged his senior executive team to develop plans that would raise sales from $8 billion to $20 billion during the next five years.

Stretch targets to inspire and drive change have been described in a best-selling book as "Big Hairy Audacious Goals" (BHAG). "A BHAG engages people—it reaches out and grabs them in the gut. It is tangible, energizing, and highly focused."[3]

Jack Welch, shortly after becoming CEO of the already successful and respected General Electric Company, energized the company by declaring a BHAG: Every division should become number one or number two in every market we serve and revolutionize this company to have the speed and agility of a small enterprise.

BHAGs must fall outside the comfort zone, must be almost unreasonable. They require a total organizational commitment to achieve them. Senior executives can energize even their currently successful companies for innovation and breakthrough performance by setting stretch targets or BHAGs that cannot be achieved by business-as-usual operations. The stretch targets break employees out of their complacency that current performance is both good and adequate.

Steve Kerr, the chief learning officer of General Electric, identified problems, however, if stretch targets are viewed as just a rhetorical or inspirational exercise: "Most organizations don't have a clue about how to manage stretch goals. It's popular today for companies to ask their people to double sales or increase speed to market threefold. But then they don't provide their people with the knowledge, tools, and means to meet such ambitious goals."[4]

In order to achieve the stretch target, managers and employees must find ways to both expand revenues and improve productivity. A well-constructed Balanced Scorecard provides the roadmap for such dramatic change. It decomposes high-level stretch targets into ambitious targets for the linked objectives and measures on the scorecard. The organization can then define the strategic initiatives designed to close the planning gap between the stretch targets and the organization's current performance. In this way, the organization provides the knowledge, tools, and means to achieve the stretch targets, overcoming the barriers that Steve Kerr identified. The Balanced Scorecard helps the organization mobilize for change by focusing and aligning all of its resources and activities on the strategy for breakthrough performance. Employees are more willing to sign up to the stretch targets because they can see the linkages, integration, and initiatives that make achievement possible.

GETTING STARTED

People often ask us where they should build their first Balanced Scorecard. There is no simple answer to this question. The answer depends on organizational structure, corporate strategy, and leadership.

FMC Corporation

FMC Corporation started by identifying six "volunteer" operating companies to develop prototype scorecards for their organizations. This enabled the scorecard concept and process to be validated at these six pilot sites. This acceptance provided the internal support for deploying scorecards to all of the corporation's other operating companies. The main role of the corporation in this process was a corporate requirement for each operating company to formulate a growth strategy that could be expressed in its Balanced Scorecard—a strategy that would subsequently serve as the accountability document between the operating company and corporate.

FMC followed a highly sensible approach. As a conglomerate, it did not have an overarching corporate strategy that could be captured in a corporate-level scorecard. Attempting to start by building a corporate-level strategic scorecard would have led to frustration and, likely, to failure. At FMC, strategy existed at the individual operating companies, and these were the appropriate levels at which to construct the initial Balanced Scorecards. Few if any synergies or opportunities for integration existed across the diverse operating units. Consequently, little was lost by having each operating company formulate its own growth strategy and scorecard to represent its new strategy.

Mobil

Mobil Corporation would seem to be just the opposite of FMC. It is a vertically integrated company with three large sectors: exploration and production (E&P), marketing and refining (M&R), and chemicals. Given the high degree of vertical integration, one would expect the initial Balanced Scorecard to be developed at the corporate-headquarters level of Mobil. In fact, however, the initial scorecard, as described in Chapter 2, was developed at an M&R division, not at the corporate level. We believe that this was fine, even better than attempting to build the initial scorecard at the corporate level.

Mobil, while vertically integrated, transferred mostly commodity products between its three sectors. These products could be bought and sold in highly competitive markets. The existence of active markets for crude oil provided a natural buffer between the operating strategies of the E&P and the M&R sectors. And similarly, the active markets for processed feedstocks enabled the M&R sector to operate largely independently from the chemicals sector. So the M&R sector could plausibly develop its own strategy without detailed consultations and integration with its upstream E&P divisions and its downstream chemicals divisions. Of course, if no unifying strategy existed across the three major sectors, observers could reasonably question whether Mobil was receiving significant benefits from its vertical integration. How did the corporation add value, beyond the independent performance of its E&P, M&R, and chemicals sectors? Eventually, as Mobil (now ExxonMobil) answers that question, it will define a corporate-level strategy that can then be translated into a corporate Balanced Scorecard.

Mobil's first Balanced Scorecard, however, was not even done at the sector level. It was done in a division representing a geographic region—the United States (subsequently extended to include Mexico as well). Mobil M&R included not only North America but also operations in South America, Europe, Asia, Australia, and Africa. The development of a Balanced Scorecard at an important but still local region, such as the United States, had the potential for suboptimizing the entire M&R sector.

As with the corporate level, however, the opportunities for integration and synergies across Mobil's worldwide M&R operations were not compelling. The U.S. market—both its consumers and its independent dealers—were almost completely separated from marketing operations in the rest of the world. Strategies for the U.S. market could be developed and implemented without affecting the strategies for consumers in other parts of the world—people who did not watch advertising messages delivered in the U.S. media or purchase gasoline and snacks at U.S. gasoline stations. Also, dealer organizations did not cross national boundaries, so that quite different dealer strategies could be required for each region. So for the M&R sector, natural geographic boundaries enabled each region to develop strategies, customized to local conditions, that did not have to be coordinated internationally. We believe, therefore, that no loss occurred by developing the first Balanced Scorecard at the NAM&R level, without having formulated a worldwide M&R strategy. Of course, as at the corporate level, if a global M&R strategy does not exist, it raises the question of the benefits from having a worldwide M&R organization. The answer for why it makes sense for Mobil to have a global M&R division—rather than selling off each geographical unit as a freestanding and independent company—will create a sector-level strategy that could then be translated into a global M&R scorecard.

As a company like Mobil works through the logic of where to construct Balanced Scorecards, it confronts the rationale for its existence. If clear corporate- or sector-level synergies cannot be identified, the corporation may not be adding value to its collection of divisions and business units. Some corporate-level benefits arise from consolidating financial and tax reporting and establishing banking relationships. But there are also the costs of operating the corporate headquarters and, more important, those from slowing down or inhibiting decision-making in the operating units where value is being created. Often corporations encounter difficulty in constructing corporate-level scorecards, because corporate-level strategies and opportunities for integration do not exist. These companies are receiving a diagnostic signal that the whole may be worth less than the sum of its parts.

Mobil's NAM&R divisional scorecard established the common themes and strategies that lower-level business units incorporated when they constructed their Balanced Scorecards. The high-level scorecard explicated the synergies, the rationale, for how value could be created by having business units, in their individual strategies, reinforce the common themes. Building the initial scorecard at too low a level loses the opportunity for value-creation from integrating and coordinating business unit strategies. But attempting to build the initial scorecard at too high a level (e.g., at Mobil Corporation) may be difficult and frustrating because a comprehensive integrated strategy may not exist at that level. In such a case, better results will occur when the initial scorecard is built at levels below that of the corporation or sector.

Shared Service Units

The initial Balanced Scorecard can even be launched at a shared services unit. An excellent example occurred at GTE Service Corporation, where the initial Balanced Scorecard was created for the human resources organization. At first, we were skeptical about launching the Balanced Scorecard from the HR group. It seemed unlikely that such a group would be able to understand the skills, knowledge, and competencies required from their hiring, training, retention, and promotion decisions without having explicit guidance from the strategies communicated in business unit, division, and corporate scorecards. But the HR scorecard at GTE was, in fact, constructed with just those strategies in mind. GTE had recently completed an extensive strategy exercise to reposition itself in the rapidly evolving telecommunications industry. The new strategy was communicated to everyone in the organization with extensive documentation (but no new measurement system). The strategy included "people imperatives," specific requirements for what the business strategy required of GTE employees. Recognizing the existing skill base in network management, customer support, international capabilities, and voice product expertise, the strategy required enhanced capabilities for leadership, union relationships, customer support, learning and innovation, and teaming. And it required entirely new skills in marketing and distribution, data management, partnering and managing alliances, and integration. With such an explicit strategy and demands for enhanced and new skills and capabilities, the HR group could embark on a project to produce a highly informative and credible Balanced Scorecard for the HR function.

Another unconventional evolution occurred at General Motors Corporation. GM was in the midst of a massive transformation program in its worldwide operations. As one manager noted, the company, in the past, made and designed products that consumers did not want, and did it inefficiently. Under CEO Jack Smith's leadership, GM was transforming itself from a product-oriented "make and sell" philosophy to a customer-driven "sense and respond" strategy. Such a transformation in an organization with nearly $200 billion in worldwide operations and sales involved massive changes in process, organization, and incentives.

While, in principle, a corporate-level Balanced Scorecard might have facilitated such a massive transformation, senior corporate executives would likely not have had much share of mind available to launch such a project in the midst of all the other transformations occurring simultaneously. Also, with such a complex, diverse, and dispersed organization, doing the first scorecard at corporate would have been an extraordinarily challenging task.

The Balanced Scorecard was introduced for GM in its European information technology organization, a shared service function. The IT group had a charter to "be the engine and turbocharger of change in systems and processes."

This charter gave the IT group access to the entire breadth of activities— marketing, design, concept engineering, manufacturing, vehicle sales, and after-market sales—in the organization. The IT project team built its initial Balanced Scorecard by aligning with the business units' strategies. This gave the team experience and credibility in how to measure a broad set of performance indicators related to a strategy. With this initial success, the team was then asked to transfer knowledge and facilitate the development of scorecards for all of GM Europe. This encompassed eight business units (Germany, Vauxhall, Belgium, Spain, Austria, Hungary, Poland, and National Sales Centers) and eleven functional units (e.g., engineering, manufacturing, sales/marketing, quality, financial, personnel, and purchasing). Based on the experience with building the initial IT scorecard, the IT group then helped the project teams in the various business and functional units choose measures and locate data for the measures—particularly the lead indicators. The IT team also taught the project teams about cause-and-effect linkages to ensure that the scorecards related to strategic objectives, not just to operational improvements.

By the end of 1998, Balanced Scorecards had been developed for most of GM Europe's business units and functional units, and the management system based on the scorecards was operating. At that point, the General Motors corporate office asked the Europe IT group to assist in developing and deploying scorecards worldwide. The project started with the IT group in North America (just as in Europe), and from that experience it was migrated upwards to GM's North American operations. As of mid-1999, plans have been formulated to roll the scorecard process out to GM Latin American and Asia/Pacific.

Thus a project that had started in a shared services department in a region far from the U.S. headquarters eventually led to a corporate, world-wide implementation. At least in this large, somewhat traditionally centralized and bureaucratic company, implementing the new idea in a local "skunk works" environment enabled it to develop and subsequently seed the rest of the organization in an incremental way, allowing experience, visibility, and credibility to develop from within the organization.

Arguably, the specific objectives and measures of the first IT scorecard might have been better if General Motors had previously established a comprehensive worldwide and European strategy. But waiting for such a revelation would have delayed the local project—perhaps for many years. The Europe IT group did not let "the best be the enemy of the good." They got the process under way in an area where it had local support. The project demonstrated feasibility and provided an experienced base of implementers who could subsequently be deployed to coach and facilitate the development of scorecards throughout the organization. At some point, after the GM Europe and GM corporate scorecards had been developed, the Europe IT group could update its own scorecard to reflect new strategic insights. Scorecard development is not a single event. It is a process that enables continual improvement and enhancement. Better to start and improve than to wait for perfect guidance. As Jim Noble, the global head of IT strategy, reflected on this evolution of the scorecard at GM, "If you succeed, you are at first base on a Dynamic Resource Management process."

The Danger of Starting Too High

We were reminded of the importance of the principle of building a score-card where a strategy exists when talking about a relatively unsuccessful Balanced Scorecard project with a senior executive of a large international corporation. The executive told us how the CEO and the board had added several nonfinancial measures to the compensation system for senior corporate executives. The performance of the nonfinancial measures had improved, but financial results had not improved. The company was paying out substantial salary bonuses without any improvement in financial performance.

The conversation proceeded, and we asked how the nonfinancial measures had been chosen. The response was that the new measures represented certain stakeholder interests, such as environmental and safety performance and hiring practices, for which the organization wanted to increase emphasis. But the measures had not been chosen as elements of an integrated, comprehensive strategy in which improvements in nonfinancial measures were hypothesized to lead to improved financial performance. In effect, the company had created a checklist of measures—a KPI score-card—but not a strategy scorecard.

We pressed on with the company executive, asking about the strategy at the corporate level, and learned that an integrated corporate strategy did not really exist. We recommended that the initial Balanced Scorecard would have been, as was the case at FMC and Mobil, better developed at the divisional level, below the corporate level, as divisional strategies did exist. In this organization, the initial Balanced Scorecard had been built at too high a level. A clear strategy did not exist at the corporate level, so the scorecard was constructed by adding an ad hoc collection of nonfinancial measures to the existing financial measures. We were not surprised to learn that improvement in the nonfinancial components of the scorecard did not lead to improvements in financial performance.

Contrast this experience with that of Mobil NAM&R, where safety and environmental measures were incorporated into the cause-and-effect relationships of the Balanced Scorecard. Brian Baker, NAM&R's executive vice president, noted that safety and environmental performance were usually leading indicators of future financial performance. He had observed that an increase in incidents that were harmful to safety and the environment indicated that operators were not paying attention. And if they were not paying attention when their own well-being was at stake, they certainly were not paying attention to how well company assets were being operated and maintained. So for Mobil, the nonfinancial indicators, chosen as part of an integrated strategy, were correlated with future improvements in financial performance.

USING MEASUREMENT TO LEAD THE CHANGE

Companies have been attempting to implement change for decades. Why do we advocate that change initiatives now be accompanied by a change in the measurement system to the Balanced Scorecard? Adapting the organization's measurement system to the change agenda is critical for success. When addressing an audience of financial managers and executives, we suggest to them that if they object to changes being advocated in their organizations, they should not stand up and express their concerns. They don't have to write memoranda or send e-mail with their objections. Just continue to measure performance and provide reports as they have been doing. Eventually, the change initiative will be choked off. In a famous article entitled "On the Folly of Rewarding A, While Hoping for B," Steve Kerr described how management espoused its desire for long-term growth but rewarded quarterly earnings performance.[5] Not surprising, managers delivered quarterly earnings performance but did not invest for long-term growth. Managers evaluated by short-term financial measures will manage to those measures, and likely shortchange new initiatives for growth, customer focus, innovation, and employee empowerment.

The CEOs who adopted the Balanced Scorecard for their new strategies understood the need for a new measurement framework. They saw it as a powerful tool for driving the new change initiatives. Bob McCool commented on why he changed Mobil NAM&R's measurements:

We were in a controller's mentality, reviewing the past not guiding the future. The functional metrics didn't communicate what we were about. I wanted metrics to be part of a communication process by which everyone in the organization could understand and implement our strategy. We needed better metrics so that our planning process could be linked to actions, to encourage people to do the things the organization was now committed to doing.

The executive leadership that creates the Balanced Scorecard becomes the guiding coalition for driving change in the organization. The process of building the scorecard builds both the team and its commitment to the strategy. And the scorecard provides the means for making the vision and the strategy operational. Words are not sufficient to communicate the change initiative. The same words mean different things to different people. It is only when word statements are translated into measures that everyone understands clearly what the vision and the strategy are about.

The CEOs of adopting organizations all had strategies that included a strong growth component. They did not want to increase profits just by cutting costs, downsizing, and eliminating unprofitable business units. While cost and productivity improvements were certainly part of their change agenda, they were only a part; they were mainly intended to deliver the strategy's short-term component. The implementing CEOs also wished to improve profitability through expanding revenues—a longer-term growth strategy. That these companies found the Balanced Scorecard useful for a growth strategy is not surprising. Organizations that have identified cost leadership as their strategy, or that wish to regain competitiveness by cost reduction and productivity enhancements, may not find the Balanced Scorecard that helpful. Financial measurements, especially when enhanced by activity-based costing, do a fine job in motivating cost reduction and productivity.[6] Financial measurements also provide good feedback as to whether costs have actually been reduced and productivity improved. By themselves, however, financial measurements may not be adequate for communicating how the top line—revenues—can be increased.

Anyone can build a business plan on a spreadsheet to meet specified growth objectives. If the current assumptions for growth do not meet corporate objectives, managers can easily increase assumed percentage growth rates in their spreadsheet programs. Eventually, the estimated growth rate will satisfy corporate planning objectives. This analytic part is easy. The hard part is identifying how the assumed growth rate will be achieved. Which new customers will the company acquire and retain? How much must be sold to each new customer? Which of the existing customers will purchase more products and services, and at higher margins? Which new regions, new applications, or new products must be launched for the growth assumptions to be realized? The Balanced Scorecard helped the adopting organizations specify in detail the critical elements for their growth strategies:[7]

- Targeted customers where profitable growth would occur
- Value propositions that would lead customers to do more business and at higher margins with the company

- Innovations in products, services, and processes
- Investments in people and systems to enhance processes and deliver differentiated value propositions for growth

Without such a clear specification, employees could not reinforce one another's efforts to implement the new growth and effectiveness strategy.

Financial measurements cannot even communicate and monitor a true operational excellence strategy, in which success with customers involves not only low costs and prices but also defect-free quality and short lead times from customer request to order fulfillment. Differentiating strategies that can lead to sustainable competitive advantage will require a much broader set of measurements than purely financial ones.

The CEO and senior leadership team also recognized that they could not implement the new strategy by themselves. They required the active contributions of everyone in the organization. For their new strategy to be successful, they had to move it from the boardroom to the back room, and to the front lines of daily operations and customer service as described in Part Three. The measurement system in the Balanced Scorecard provided a simple, clear message about the new strategy that all employees could understand and internalize in their everyday operations.

BUILDING EXECUTIVE TEAMS

The dynamics of the Executive Leadership Team frequently determines whether the Balanced Scorecard can be sustained so that the strategy can be successfully executed. Most executive teams consist of functional specialists, each with intense specialist knowledge. Such functional executives often have surprisingly little awareness of how other functions work. Strategy-Focused Organizations must transform their collections of functional specialists into cross-functional, problem-solving teams.

Some functions seem to be more segregated than others. From our experience, we have determined that many executive teams have low levels of shared understanding about marketing and human resources management. Yet these two areas are often critical for today's strategies. The executive team, as it goes through the process of building a scorecard, frequently realizes that it does not have the required understanding of market segments, customers, or employees. To remedy this lack, it adds marketing and human resources executives to the team, who now have a higher platform to educate others on their disciplines and contributions.

At Mobil, the finance and the operations disciplines had historically dominated the executive team. Brian Baker, the executive vice president of Mobil NAM&R, remarked, "We were a company with a lot of engineers—analytical people—and pretty introspective. We hadn't looked outside the business at the customer, and we hadn't understood the importance of the customer."

Mobil's executive team had no consensus on customer issues. As the senior managers tried to become consumer-driven and sell products other than petroleum to customers, they had to elevate the role for the marketing executive. Five years later, every executive understood the nuances of the market segments, how Mobil differentiated itself, and the drivers of consumer behavior. The cultural transformation occurred by putting the customer on the agenda and getting an intelligent spokesperson to help bring the rest of the team along.

The creation of the shared vision and strategy was an effective way to build an executive leadership *team* from the previous collection of individual business unit heads. The framework of the Balanced Scorecard provided a structured way for the team to work together to guide the development of a new vision and strategy. A tremendous amount of cross-fertilization took place as each element of the strategy was translated to the scorecard format. The strategic issues surrounding customer segments (marketing), yield optimization (manufacturing), cost of capital (finance), and supply-chain management (transportation, pipeline) now became the shared issues of the executive team. Historically, each of these issues had been considered the domain of a single functional executive.

The creation of an effective Leadership Team requires the breaking of many traditions. Management by silos is deeply entrenched. As noted earlier, AT&T Canada CEO Bill Catucci disbanded his monthly management meetings with individual department heads and replaced them with meetings about the most important business processes, including the management of strategy. According to Catucci, "At the Strategic Management meeting, the entire leadership team would get together and talk about the company in its totality—a holistic approach to the business. Instead of the chimneys, we would focus on what was happening throughout the company."

Catucci went a step further in signaling a new approach to teamwork and culture by appointing four women to strategic leadership roles on the formerly male-dominated executive team: "The mindset that there are certain people for certain jobs was another barrier to performance that had to be eliminated." The real message was that, in a performance culture, it's performance, not gender, that matters.

A functional or technical culture is frequently at odds with creating a Strategy-Focused Organization. The U.S. National Reconnaissance Office (NRO) existed for decades as a super-secret spy organization, with three completely isolated and segregated operating programs.[8] Each program came from a very different culture (Air Force, Central Intelligence Agency, and Navy) with little communication and, in fact, high competition among them. Senior executives were engineers with strong records of technical accomplishments. "Soft" managerial tasks, such as strategic planning and implementation, were considered less interesting than solving new technical problems.

In response to a changed external environment, NRO had been reorganized into directorates such as Imaging, Communications, and Space Launch. People from previously highly competitive programs were expected, in each directorate, to cooperate and agree on a unified approach to space reconnaissance. NRO, like many public sector (and private) organizations, initially established a staff level group, the Office of Plans and Analysis, to develop strategic plans. This staff-driven process faltered and plans were never implemented.

In 1996, a new NRO director led a strategy planning exercise, based on the Balanced Scorecard, to actively engage his senior executive team in formulating and modifying the organization's strategy. After a briefing on the Balanced Scorecard to the director and key senior staff, the executive team got engaged by changing the scorecard to their situation—they moved the customer perspective to the top of the diagram[9] and renamed the learning and growth perspective to employee satisfaction. Modifying the labels and rearranging the scorecard gave a sense of ownership to the executives. As the project facilitators noted, "By changing boxes, labels, and arrows, the executives had begun the process of understanding the cause and effect relationships unique to the NRO. . . . The Balanced Scorecard provided a common, structured environment and vocabulary for executives and employees to learn how to 'do strategy.'"[10] These discussions were the first in which the senior executive team discussed a comprehensive, shared NRO strategy, rather than a strategy for each executive's individual unit.

Once the ice had been broken for senior-level discussions of NRO strategy, the director established monthly strategy meetings in which executives provided continued updates and reports. At quarterly off-site meetings, the executive team considered the impact of new issues and requirements on the NRO strategy. As the details and assumptions in the strategic model became clearer, conflicts and contradictions arose that required the senior executives to expand the dialogue to include other members of their organizations. The process gave organizational members the opportunity to learn more about the strategy model, test their ideas, and explore how to talk among themselves about strategy. The director had used the Balanced Scorecard model to create an executive leadership team that could think beyond the mission and strategy of each individual directorate. They could now work together to formulate and implement new organizationwide strategies.

The City of Charlotte example described in Chapter 5 also showed how the leader, Pam Syfert, used the scorecard to break down functional barriers and create a culture of teamwork and cross-functional problem-solving. Execution of the five strategic themes, such as "city-within-a-city," required integrated teamwork from each city department. Syfert introduced a new structure, a cabinet, for each of the five strategic themes. Membership on the team came from many city departments and also included representatives from the private sector. The cabinets had their own scorecards and held monthly meetings to discuss how to integrate specialist department activities toward meeting the holistic citywide goals.

LEVERS OF CONTROL

One final set of concepts is important for leaders who want to embed the Balanced Scorecard in organizations. Robert Simons[11] has articulated a powerful framework for viewing the multiple control systems used by senior executives to implement organizational strategy (see Figure 13-1). The beliefs system in the upper left-hand quadrant of Figure 13-1 is the explicit set of documents, communicated to employees, that provides the basic values, purpose, and direction for the organization. Documents such as credos, mission statements, vision statements, and statements of purpose or values are examples of how the organization communicates its most fundamental values and goals to its employees.

In addition to communicating the grand purpose of the organization, managers also need to communicate what behavior and actions are unacceptable in pursuit of the mission. Companies need boundary systems that

Figure 13-1 Levers of Control

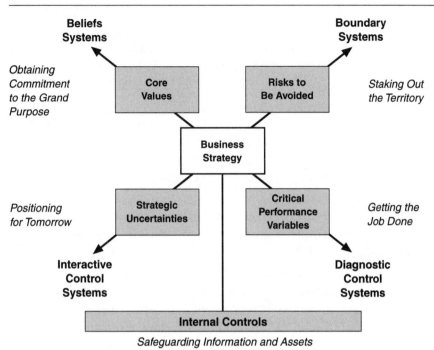

Source: Adapted from Robert Simons, *Levers of Control: How Managers Use Innovative Control Systems to Drive Strategic Renewal* (Boston: Harvard Business School Press, 1995), 159. Reprinted by permission of Harvard Business School Press.

describe the actions that must never be taken. Boundary systems include legal constraints and codes of conduct that clearly identify forbidden actions. They are intended to constrain the range of acceptable behavior.

Organizations also need strong internal control systems to safeguard critical assets, such as cash; equipment; information, such as databases; accounting; and customer records. Performance measurement systems in many organizations relate to such internal control tasks. These are important, but focusing only on internal control confuses adherence to rules and regulations with accomplishing mission and outcomes.

The diagnostic systems in Figure 13-1 are what many people think about when they describe performance measurement systems. Diagnostic systems provide signals about organizational health; they represent important dimensions of performance in the same way that body temperature and blood pressure (the body's vital signs) provide signals about the personal health of individuals. Organizations may have hundreds or thousands of variables that are vital for success, but none of these may be a driver of strategic success. Some of these variables may be called "critical success factors." They indicate that operations are "in control." Diagnostic variables should be measured, monitored, and controlled. But their reporting to higher management is on an exception basis only, when a value falls outside a normal control limit and corrective actions need to be taken.

The interactive system, which is the fifth major control system, focuses on the relatively few measures that drive breakthrough performance. Interactive systems are the formal information systems that senior managers use to engage in active dialogue with their subordinates about strategy and strategy implementation. Interactive control systems focus attention and force dialogue throughout the organization. Such systems serve as catalysts for the continual challenge and debate of underlying data, assumptions, and plans that will drive learning and improvement. The questions asked in a diagnostic system start with "how much" and "what." The questions with an interactive system are designed for interpreting, discussing, and learning; managers ask "why," "how will," "what if," and "suppose that."

Diagnostic systems, boundary systems, and internal control systems are all necessary, but they do not create a learning organization aligned to a focused strategy. Some Balanced Scorecard implementation failures occurred because organizations used their scorecard only diagnostically, and failed to get the learning and innovation benefits from an interactive system. The CEOs of successful Balanced Scorecard adopters, such as those described in Chapter 1, succeeded because they used the scorecard interactively, for communication and to drive learning and improvement. They set overall strategy and then encouraged people within their organization to identify the local actions and initiatives that would have the highest impact for accomplishing the scorecard objectives.

LEADERSHIP STYLE

Perhaps the most critical ingredient for scorecard success, however, is not the analytic, structural explanations already provided. It is the leadership style of the senior executive. The individuals who led the successfully adopting organizations felt that their most important challenge was communication. These leaders knew that they could not implement the strategy without gaining the hearts and minds of all of their middle managers, technologists, sales force, frontline employees, and back-office staff. The leaders did not know all of the steps required to implement the strategy. They did have a good vision about what success would look like and the outcomes they were trying to achieve. But they depended on their employees to find innovative ways to accomplish the mission.

At first we were surprised to learn that two of the most successful early adopters, Bob McCool at Mobil and Michael Hegarty at Chemical Retail Bank, were ex-Marine officers. Military officers are stereotyped as command and control managers. But the best military officers, particularly in the Marines, recognize that when the battle is taking place, the generals are far from the front lines. In the uncertain environments where Marine battles occur, whatever has been planned is almost surely not going to occur. Frontline officers may have been killed; equipment may have been dropped off at the wrong location or destroyed before it could be deployed; and the enemy may have appeared in unexpected places and in different strengths and resources. At that point, the mission depends on frontline troops reorganizing and adapting to the local situation. In the heat of battle, the intangible assets that the troops can draw upon are a clear knowledge of the mission and objectives they are expected to accomplish and an ability to improvise and work together to achieve the mission and objectives.

Senior Marine officers communicate, educate, and train their troops with the goal "that every private can become a general." Every member of the corps must be able and prepared to lead. Our casual observation was reinforced by a study conducted by McKinsey & Company and the Conference Board about the organizations that were the most successful in engaging the emotional energy of their frontline workers. The study examined many exemplary organizations in the private sector but finally concluded that the Marine Corps "outperformed all other organizations when it came to engaging the hearts and minds of the front line."[12] Given this culture, it is not at all surprising that Marine officers leading organizations in the private sector constantly look for ways to communicate mission and objectives and to inspire employees to find innovative ways to help the organization succeed.

In our initial interview with him, Bill Catucci of AT&T Canada described his management style of communication, team-building, and empowerment. It sounded very much like what we had heard from McCool and Hegarty. When we asked him whether he had been a military officer, he was initially surprised by our question but then replied that he had been an army officer, and concurred that his business leadership style had been influenced by his military officer's background.

The Balanced Scorecard strategic management system works best when used to *communicate* vision and strategy, not to *control* the actions of subordinates. This use is paradoxical to those who think that measurement is a control tool, not a communication tool. Excellent leaders recognize that the biggest challenge they face in implementing change and new strategies is getting alignment throughout the organization. Gerry Isom of CIGNA Property & Casualty expressed this well:

> *How do you get 6,000 people's minds aligned to the strategy? How do you get the functions people are performing aligned with the businesses they were supporting? The Balanced Scorecard became my key communicating vehicle for reporting, planning, and budgeting processes. It shifted us from a bureaucratic, autocratic, top-down company with people working within organizational silos to one that was streamlined and participatory, had top-down and bottom-up communication, and with people that worked across organizational boundaries.*

So when people ask us where they should start to build a Balanced Scorecard in their organization, we often give the "left-brain" analytic answer articulated at the beginning of this chapter: Choose a level in the company at which an integrated, holistic strategy exists that requires alignment and integration from organizational subunits and employees. But we always follow by providing the "right-brain" answer: Make sure that the head of that organizational unit has a management style that emphasizes vision, communication, participation, and employee initiative and innovation. Avoid organizational units in which the leader likes to be completely in control. Avoid leaders who use management control systems to ensure that all subunits and employees are following directions and adhering to plans determined at the top of the organization. And when the left-brain and the right-brain recommendations conflict, follow the right-brain rule. The choice of initial implementation should be determined more by leadership style than by the analytics of where strategy is ideally formulated. If this rule leads to the initial scorecard being built at a business or shared service unit rather than a division, that's all right. The Balanced Scorecard can subsequently be updated to reflect interactions and potential synergies initially unrecognized. It is much harder to modify and update the leadership and management style of a recalcitrant senior executive.

SUMMARY

The Balanced Scorecard is most effective when it is part of a major change process in the organization. Often the need for change is obvious: The unit is underperforming, or major shifts are occurring in the unit's competitive and technological environment. Even if the need for change is not obvious, leaders frequently motivate their organization to higher performance by setting ambitious targets. Whatever the initiating set of circumstances, adopting the new measurement and management system of the Balanced Scorecard helps organizational leaders to communicate the vision for change and empower business units and all employees to devise new ways of doing their day-to-day business to help the organization accomplish its strategic objectives.

Scorecard projects can be launched from different organizational units. Ideally, the project should be initiated at an organizational level where a comprehensive strategy exists or can be formulated. The scorecard provides the mechanism for translating that strategy into linked cause-and-effect objectives and measures for communication to organizational sub-units and individuals. But scorecards can also be started in shared service units. The most important criterion is that the initiating unit have a senior executive whose leadership and management style emphasizes communication, participation, and employee initiative and innovation.

Finally, the Balanced Scorecard should be viewed as the organization's interactive system, a system to provoke questions, discussions, debate, and dialogue. The scorecard is most powerful not to explain the past but to stimulate learning and to guide questions and discussion about how to proceed into the future.

Ultimately, however, the ability to create a Strategy-Focused Organization depends less on such structural and design issues and much more on the leadership of the organization's senior executive. The lead executive creates the climate for change, the vision for what the change can accomplish, and the governance process that promotes communication, interactive discussions, and learning about the strategy.

NOTES

1. John P. Kotter, in *Leading Change* (Boston: Harvard Business School Press, 1996), has similarly described the critical role of the senior executive for galvanizing organizational change.
2. R. S. Kaplan, "Mobil USM&R (A): Linking the Balanced Scorecard," 9-197-025 (Boston: Harvard Business School, 1996), 2.
3. James C. Collins and Jerry I. Porras, *Built to Last: Successful Habits of Visionary Companies* (New York: HarperBusiness, 1994), 94.
4. S. Sherman, "Stretch Goals: The Dark Side of Asking for Miracles," *Fortune,* 13 November 1995, 231.
5. S. Kerr, "On the Folly of Rewarding A, While Hoping for B," *Academy of Management Executive* (February 1995); originally published in 1975.
6. Robert S. Kaplan and Robin Cooper, *Cost & Effect: Using Integrated Cost Systems to Drive Profitability and Performance* (Boston: Harvard Business School Press, 1997).
7. Government agencies or nonprofit organizations, for which the growth option may not be a viable strategy, may interpret the "growth" theme as emphasizing effectiveness, not just efficiency.
8. The NRO experience is drawn from the more extensive description in J. A. Chesley and M. S. Wenger, "Transforming an Organization: Using Models to Foster a Strategic Conversation," *California Management Review* (Spring 1999): 54–73.
9. Recall from Chapter 5 that this re-arrangement to place the customer at the top was done, independently, by several other government and nonprofit organizations.
10. Chesley and Wenger, "Transforming an Organization," 65.
11. Robert Simons, *Levers of Control: How Managers Use Innovative Control Systems to Drive Strategic Renewal* (Boston: Harvard Business School Press, 1995), and "Control in an Age of Empowerment," *Harvard Business Review* (March–April 1995): 80–88.
12. J. R. Katzenbach and J. A. Santamaria, "Firing up the Front Line," *Harvard Business Review* (May–June 1999): 108.

CHAPTER FOURTEEN

Avoiding the Pitfalls

WE HAVE NOW DESCRIBED THE FIVE FUNDAMENTAL PRINCIPLES for organizations to become strategy-focused. Many organizations, since 1996, have been able to implement successful Balanced Scorecard programs. We have provided examples throughout the book of such organizations, and the evidence for success is larger than these individual stories. For example, the Metrus Group, Inc., surveyed 122 organizations to compare the performance of measurement-managed organizations with non–measurement-managed ones.[1] In a measurement-managed organization, "senior management was reported to be in agreement on measurable criteria for determining strategic success and in which management updated and reviewed semi-annual performance measures in . . . primary performance areas." The survey (see Figure 14-1) also showed that measurement-managed companies tend to have better teamwork at the top, better communication throughout the organization, and better self-management at the bottom. Better alignment translated into better results for the Balanced Measurement companies:

- 83 percent had financial performance in the top third of their industry

Figure 14-1   Impact of Measurement Systems on the Alignment and
Awareness of Organizations

	"Balanced Measurement Companies"	"Non–Balanced Measurement Companies"
■ Agreement among senior management on strategy	90%	47%
■ Good cooperation and teamwork among management	85%	38%
■ Open sharing and communication	71%	30%
■ Effective communication of strategy	60%	8%
■ High levels of self-monitoring by employees	42%	16%

Source: Data from J. H. Lingle and W. A. Shieman, "From Balanced Scorecards to Strategic Gauges: Is Measurement Worth It?" *Management Review* (March 1996): 56–62.

- ■ 74 percent were perceived as industry leaders by their peers
- ■ 97 percent were perceived as pioneers or leaders on changing the nature of their industries

A survey of 113 worldwide organizations conducted by the Conference Board for A. T. Kearney, Inc., showed that for companies linking their formal performance management systems to strategy,[2]

- ■ 52 percent had stock performance above their competitors
- ■ 30 percent had the same stock performance as competitors
- ■ 18 percent had performance below competitors

A survey conducted by the Institute of Management Accountants (IMA) concluded that Balanced Scorecard performance management systems were providing better results than traditional approaches (see Figure 14-2).

In the IMA study, Balanced Scorecard performance management systems were significantly more effective than non–Balanced Scorecard users, although neither approach was deemed more than "adequate" in the scales that were used. Perhaps more significant, when asked, "Is the Balanced

Figure 14-2   Effectiveness of the Performance Measurement (PM) System

Question	Overall	Non-BSC Adopters	BSC Adopters	BSC Users
Effectiveness of Current PM System	2.08	1.74	2.62	2.92
PM Supports Business Objectives	2.02	1.65	2.60	2.92

1 = Poor   2 = Less than adequate   3 = Adequate   4 = Good   5 = Very good   6 = Excellent

Scorecard worth implementing?" 60 percent of the respondents answered yes, 30 percent answered "not yet, but will be," and 7 percent answered "too early to tell."

But not all adopting organizations have succeeded with their Balanced Scorecard programs. Several, despite spending considerable effort, and in some cases considerable resources, could not implement the new measurement and management framework.[3] Many organizations report to us that the Balanced Scorecard is "harder than it looks."

In our first book, we provided a generic approach for building an initial Balanced Scorecard.[4] We are still using essentially this process today in contemporary implementations. With more experience during the past five years, and with templates relevant for particular strategies and particular industries, the initial process can now be shortened by 50 percent or more from the sixteen weeks typically required back in 1996.[5] But the basic process remains otherwise unchanged and hence does not require a new or modified treatment in this book. Even with our publication of this generic approach, some companies still experience difficulties in applying the concept. We have identified three classes of problems that inhibit the creation of Strategy-Focused Organizations: transitional issues, design issues, and process issues. We discuss each class in turn.

TRANSITIONAL ISSUES

Some disappointments arose after major organizational changes. As one example, several companies, well along in their Balanced Scorecard implementations, were acquired or merged. The senior management team in the new organization had no interest in the new approach and abandoned the project. Even successful companies, well along in their Balanced Scorecard management system, can experience this source of failure. For example, the ACE Group of Companies acquired CIGNA Property & Casualty, one of our leading exemplars, in December 1998. ACE did not retain the management system or management team that had led CIGNA P&C, in four years, from its position at the bottom of the fourth quartile to a top-quartile performer. Within six months, CEO Gerry Isom had left, along with Tom Valerio, the vice president of transformation who had championed the Balanced Scorecard management system. AT&T Canada merged with MetroNet Communications Corporation in January 1999. CEO Bill Catucci left at the conclusion of his three-year management contract. Soon thereafter, the project champion also left. One year later, the Balanced Scorecard is being revived, but only after several of its most important champions had left. The future of the Balanced Scorecard in the new ExxonMobil company was similarly uncertain as of February 2000.

Companies typically pay high premiums for their acquisitions. When they want to emphasize a cost-cutting strategy to justify the premium paid, the Balanced Scorecard may not be perceived as a valuable downsizing tool. And if the senior executives of the acquiring company are most adept at cost-cutting and driving productivity improvements, they may undervalue the growth-enhancing features of the scorecard. People who have become good surgeons—cutting waste and inefficiency wherever they can find—don't suddenly become creative architects, designing new organizational forms and developing innovative growth strategies.

One failure reported in the literature[6] actually was a story in which the scorecard won a local battle but got lost in a larger war. The first reports from the new Balanced Scorecard system made it clear that the current president's strategy wasn't working, so the company changed course. This was the local success as the scorecard provided feedback on a bad strategy. But the company's owners attributed the bad strategy to the president, who was summarily fired. The new president implemented a new strategy and, in the process, discarded the Balanced Scorecard, which he associated with the old, failing strategy.

These transitional issues arose in two of our first projects in the nonprofit sector as well. The Balanced Scorecards at both the United Way of Southeastern New England (UWSENE) and the United Way of America did not survive a change in leadership. The chief executive officer at the UWSENE retired from the organization shortly after the initial scorecard project had been completed. During the project, he had not actively involved his board in developing the scorecard, believing that the board should monitor the strategy but not participate in its formulation. In the search process for a new chief executive, the board did not place high weight on finding a leader who would be committed to the new strategic performance management system. It selected a retired bank executive who felt that his immediate priorities were to deal with operational issues left by his predecessor and to ensure that each position had a complete job description. The Balanced Scorecard was new to him, he had no commitment to it, and he never implemented it, much to the disappointment of several managers who had invested much time and energy in the new system. The board, given its lack of involvement with the Balanced Scorecard, did not press the issue.

At the United Way of America (UWA), the CEO resigned unexpectedly during the project. The new CEO, hired from outside the UWA, arrived with her own management style and highly formalized planning process that she wanted to implement. The Balanced Scorecard did not fit within her planning process and did not survive the transition.

Even these two projects, however, were not complete failures. The projects at both the UWA and the UWSENE had become highly visible throughout the national United Way organization and in many other nonprofit organizations. The internal project leaders at the UWA and the UWSENE became highly visible spokespersons and trainers for nonprofits around the United States that wanted to implement the concept. So the first two pilot projects in nonprofit organizations could be viewed as local failures, but perhaps national successes. The projects demonstrated the concept and created skilled and articulate implementers who subsequently served as national resources for many other agencies.

In Chapter 13, we discussed the type of leader for whom the Balanced Scorecard represents a fit with regard to leadership and management style. This style emphasizes vision, communication, participation, and employee initiative and innovation. When such a leader is replaced by a manager who likes to be completely in control—a leader whose management style includes formal, hierarchical planning systems; extensive job descriptions to ensure that individuals operate within their functional slots; and management control systems to monitor that all subunits and employees are complying with centrally determined plans—then the Balanced Scorecard is not likely to survive the transition.

As disappointing as these events are, they represent the minority of Balanced Scorecard implementation failures. Our experience is that disappointing results are more often self-inflicted, owing to factors internal to the business rather than attributable to external events.

DESIGN FAILURES

Some failures occur when companies actually build poor Balanced Scorecards. For example, companies may use too few measures (only one or two measures per perspective) and fail to obtain a balance between the outcomes they are trying to achieve and the performance drivers of those outcomes. Others include far too many measures and never identify the critical few. As another example, Art Schneiderman claims that some scorecards fail because they don't contain the correct "drivers" of the desired organizational outcomes, or don't link to specific improvement programs for the scorecard process measures.[7] While this is certainly possible, our experience is that companies who imbed the scorecard in active strategic learning and improvement processes (see the discussion in Chapters 12 and 13) learn over time about the appropriate and effective drivers of organizational performance. Companies whose scorecard projects fail because of poor design are typically not designing scorecards to tell the story of their strategy.

For example, companies that build KPI scorecards are not likely to realize performance breakthroughs. KPI scorecards can drive improved operational performance, but unless they are accompanied by an explicit strategy to capture the benefits, the organization will experience disappointing outcomes.[8]

A similar problem exists with stakeholder scorecards. Performance measurement systems that focus on keeping customers, employees, suppliers, and the community satisfied usually lack a strategy to create sustainable competitive advantage. Both KPI and stakeholder scorecards omit critical internal processes and the linkages for driving breakthroughs for customers and shareholders.

Failures also occur when business and shared service units are not aligned with an overall strategy. We described in the introduction to Part Two how a European bank's strategy failed, even while using the Balanced Scorecard, because it had failed to align the strategy and the scorecard of its IT division to the business units' strategy. If each business unit follows its own path in developing a Balanced Scorecard, organizations will not have a common strategic vocabulary; they will have instead "Scorecard

Babel." Many large enterprises lost interest in the scorecard concept because each unit did it differently, with no overall coordination or linkage for group and corporate-level synergies. Senior executives lacked a coherent framework for the diverse Balanced Scorecards used by their operating and service units. Without common high-level management processes, either in deployment or feedback and review, any local Balanced Scorecard success is likely to be temporary.

PROCESS FAILURES

The most common causes of implementation failures, however, are poor organizational processes, not poor scorecard design. We have seen at least seven different types of process failures in companies' scorecard projects:

1. Lack of senior management commitment
2. Too few individuals involved
3. Keeping the scorecard at the top
4. Too long a development process; the Balanced Scorecard as a one-time measurement project
5. Treating the Balanced Scorecard as a systems project
6. Hiring inexperienced consultants
7. Introducing the Balanced Scorecard only for compensation

1. Lack of Senior Management Commitment

Perhaps the biggest source of failure occurs when the project has been delegated to a middle-management team. A clear symptom of this occurs when the team refers to the project as a metrics or performance measurement project. Often the middle management team has been actively engaged in a TQM or continuous improvement project, and the Balanced Scorecard is viewed as the logical extension of the TQM measurement philosophy. The Balanced Scorecard is certainly compatible with TQM and continuous improvement initiatives (such as the Baldrige Award in the United States or the EFQM framework in Europe). But to position the Balanced Scorecard as a quality improvement project is to miss its enormous potential to focus and align the organization on strategy, not merely operational improvements. Quality programs help organizations do things right. Strategy is about doing the right things. Middle management teams can help organizations improve existing operations. But to transform and align organizational processes and systems to strategy requires leadership from the top.

Senior management commitment is required for several reasons. First, senior management must articulate the organization's strategy. Our research has revealed that few middle managers understand the organization's strategy. Therefore a middle management team is unlikely to capture the organization's strategy when building a Balanced Scorecard. Only the senior executive team has been empowered to make the difficult choices and tradeoffs required for an effective strategy. Senior management is unlikely to delegate to a middle management task force the right to select targeted customer and market segments, and to identify the value proposition that will attract, retain, and deepen relationships with targeted customers. Lacking either knowledge or decision rights about strategy (usually both), the middle management team cannot formulate a Balanced Scorecard linked to the business unit's strategy. Senior management is also required if consensus about the strategy is difficult to achieve; the business unit CEO must serve as the tie-breaker if the project reaches an impasse because of a lack of consensus about the strategic choices.

But even more important than the senior executive team's knowledge and authority, the process of building an effective scorecard requires an emotional commitment from them. We refer to this as the "bacon and eggs breakfast" requirement. The chicken is *involved* in creating this meal, but the pig makes a real *commitment* to it. The senior executive team needs to have real "skin in the game." They should be investing hours of their time. Some of this time is consumed in one-on-one interviews with the project team. More important is the time spent in actual meetings where the senior executives debate and argue among themselves about the objectives and measures on the organizational scorecard and the cause-and-effect linkages on the strategy map defining the strategic hypotheses. These meetings build an emotional commitment to the strategy, to the scorecard as a communications device, and to the management processes that build a Strategy-Focused Organization. Such senior management commitment seems both necessary and also sufficient for success.

2. Too Few Individuals Involved

In some companies, a senior executive, such as the chief financial officer or the chief planning officer who was an important member of the senior leadership team, built the scorecard by himself. Rather than lead a team process to develop the scorecard, the lone executive made two assumptions. First, he believed that the senior leadership team was already busy dealing with many initiatives, both collectively and within their own responsibilities, and had too many meetings already on their calendars. Adding another series of meetings to build a Balanced Scorecard with this team would be difficult. Second, with his analytic abilities and deep knowledge of the organization's strategy, he could build the scorecard by himself. And he did. Arguably, he built an excellent scorecard—one that captured the organizational strategy well and had an appropriate balance of outcomes and performance drivers in the four perspectives.

Subsequent interviews, however, revealed that nothing had changed in the organization. Sure, the senior leadership team had less financial data to review and more nonfinancial statistics. But the staff executive who built the scorecard had to admit that decisions were still being made the same way, and the leadership and management style of the organization still focused on influencing the variables that had always been used by senior management.

The commitment both to the strategy and its implementation requires that the senior leadership team be actively involved in formulating the scorecard objectives, measures, and targets. Otherwise, their attitudes and their behavior will not change. If people claim that they already attend too many meetings, the project leader should use meetings already scheduled—such as the so-called strategic reviews—to drive the scorecard development process. Organizations that currently have too many meetings are the ones for which a Balanced Scorecard management system is most needed.

Of course, trying to build a scorecard with too many people can also prove fatal. The intensive interactions suggest that group sizes be kept to a number at which active discussion from all participants can occur and achieving consensus is a realistic goal. Companies can involve a broader set of people in the scorecard creation process by cascading scorecards from the top level down to divisions, business units, and departments. Also, rather than have everyone work simultaneously on the scorecard at their level in the organization, smaller subgroups can be formed to focus on a single perspective or on one of the several strategic themes that define the overall strategy. The work of the subgroups becomes integrated in a broader, larger meeting.

3. Keeping the Scorecard at the Top

The opposite error of not involving the senior executive team is to involve only the senior executive team. For the scorecard to be effective, it must eventually be shared with everyone in the organization. The goal is to have everyone in the organization understand the strategy and contribute to implementing it (as described in Part Three).

When the scorecard is disseminated throughout the organization, it provides the basis for setting local initiatives and promoting knowledge and learning on key organizational processes. It facilitates the sharing of best practices, either through publicized stories in company newsletters or, more formally, through knowledge-sharing networks. Companies that do not deploy the scorecard throughout their organization lose the potential for employee innovation, creativity, and learning. They fail to make strategy everyone's everyday job.

4. Too Long a Development Process; Treating the Balanced Scorecard as Onetime Event

Some failures have occurred when a project team allows the "best to be the enemy of the good." The team, believing in the big-bang theory of organizational change, feels it has only one chance to launch the scorecard, so it wants to produce the perfect scorecard. The team believes that it must have valid data for every measure on the scorecard, so it spends months refining the measures, improving data collection processes, and establishing baselines for the scorecard measures. Eighteen months after the start of the Balanced Scorecard project, management has yet to use it in any meeting. When interviewed, executives at the company respond, "I think we tried the Balanced Scorecard last year, but it didn't last." The problem was not that it didn't last. It had never begun.

As we mentioned in Chapter 12, most successful implementations of the Balanced Scorecard start with missing measurements. Sometimes up to one-third of the measures are not available in the first few months. Yet management still uses the scorecard as the agenda for its review and resource allocation processes, thereby embedding it into the management system. The scorecard becomes a living document. Conversations take place around objectives and measures, even without specific data on the measures. And the measures themselves evolve with use and experience.

Learning by doing is a powerful paradigm. The scorecard is not a onetime event. It is a continuous management process. The objectives, the measures, and the data collection will be modified over time, based on organizational learning.

5. Treating the Balanced Scorecard as a Systems Project

Some of the most expensive failures have occurred when companies implemented their Balanced Scorecard as a systems project rather than as a management project. These failures typically occur when an outside consulting organization, particularly one specializing in installing large systems, convinces someone in the company to hire the consultants to install a Balanced Scorecard management system. The consultants spend the next twelve to eighteen months, and several million dollars, automating all existing data-collection systems and providing a standard reporting interface, and perhaps even data mining capabilities, so that managers can have an executive information system on their desktop. The executive information system enables managers to access any existing piece of data or sort through the extensive database in many different ways. Not surprisingly, hardly anybody uses the new system. Automating and facilitating access to the thousands and millions of data observations collected in a company is not what we had in mind when we developed the Balanced Scorecard.

Recall that organizations that already had extensive databases and systems still lacked up to one-third of the measures on their initial Balanced Scorecard. Automating and mining existing data would never identify the critical missing measurements. Recall as well the notion of balance. Giving managers access to more than 100,000 possible pieces of data is not a substitute for having an organized strategy map, with cause-and-effect linkages across the twenty to thirty measures that truly represent the most important strategic variables.

And, most important, consider the issues raised by the first two pitfalls. Organizations that delegate the scorecard to an outside systems consulting and implementation firm will rarely engage the senior management team in a strategic dialogue. It should not be surprising, therefore, that the senior managers don't use their new desktop information system and certainly never manage the company differently just because they now have direct access to the minutiae of all the data in their company.

The Balanced Scorecard must start with a comprehensive strategic review that engages the managers within the organization. It cannot be delegated to an IT group or a systems implementation firm. The scorecard should start with a management process, not a systems process.

Systems and technology are important, as we discussed in Chapters 11 and 12. By imbedding the scorecard into ongoing data collection, information reporting, and learning and review processes, the scorecard becomes a living part of the organization. But the systems and technology input comes after the initial management process that generates the objectives, measures, targets, initiatives, and linked scorecards throughout the organization. And more important, the front-end management process generates the commitment to manage the organization via the scorecard.

6. Hiring Inexperienced Consultants

Hiring consultants who treat the Balanced Scorecard as a systems project is related to another pitfall: hiring consultants for whom the project represents the first scorecard implementation they will have done. After our articles and book were published, many consulting organizations responded to companies' requests for assistance in implementing the scorecard. All too often, unfortunately, consultants just renamed whatever measurement or information systems approach they were accustomed to delivering as "the Balanced Scorecard." Using inexperienced consultants or consultants who deliver their favorite methodology under the rubric of the Balanced Scorecard is almost surely a recipe for failure.

This point was driven home forcefully to us when we learned of a large financial institution that had just spent several million dollars on a Balanced Scorecard project that was widely perceived as a major failure. We made an appointment to meet with the president of the division to learn what had occurred. Was it a problem with the scorecard concept and management system that we needed to address? Upon arrival at the meeting, the president told us immediately:

We screwed it up; the scorecard is fine. I saw it work with great effect at my previous company. But the project wasn't positioned well in this organization, and the consultants we hired, while claiming great expertise on the subject, didn't have a clue about how to organize the project or implement the system.

7. Introducing the Balanced Scorecard Only for Compensation

We like the idea of tying compensation to the strategic measures on the scorecard, as we described in Chapter 10. Companies use the link to compensation as a powerful lever to gain the attention and commitment of individuals to the strategy. But some companies skip the strategy translation part of the scorecard process. They just introduce new, nonfinancial measures to their incentive compensation plan. This can happen when companies build a stakeholder scorecard by including indicators on environmental performance, employee diversity, and community ratings. Managers, of course, now focus more attention and energy on the new indicators. Performance on the nonfinancial measures improves. But overall financial and customer performance do not improve, leading to some tension and conflict in the organization. Managers wonder why the Balanced Scorecard did not work for them. The answer is quite obvious. Scorecards used to introduce nonfinancial indicators into a compensation plan do not capture how the nonfinancial measures lead to improved customer and financial performance. The link to compensation drives financial performance when based on a strategy scorecard, not a stakeholder or KPI scorecard.

SUMMARY

Many companies are already enjoying benefits from their Balanced Scorecard management systems. Implementation failures do occur, but most are self-inflicted. After a change in leadership or change in control, organizations may revert back to traditional management systems because the new leader has not experienced the benefits from operating a Strategy-Focused Organization. Other failures represent breakdowns in implementing the concept, such as inadequate sponsorship and commitment from the senior management team, designing scorecards not linked to a strategy, using inexperienced consultants, and deploying inadequate resources.

In this book, we have provided the principal steps that enable the Balanced Scorecard to create the Strategy-Focused Organization:

1. Translate the Strategy to Operational Terms
2. Align the Organization to the Strategy
3. Make Strategy Everyone's Everyday Job
4. Make Strategy a Continual Process
5. Mobilize Change through Executive Leadership

The journey is not easy or short. It requires commitment and perseverance. It requires teamwork and integration across traditional organizational boundaries and roles. The message must be reinforced often and in many ways. But organizations that sustain the effort and maintain adherence to the five principles will avoid the pitfalls and be on the road to breakthrough performance.

NOTES

1. J. H. Lingle and W. A. Schiemann, "From Balanced Scorecards to Strategic Gauges: Is Measurement Worth It?" *Management Review* (March 1996): 56–62. See also W. A. Schiemann and J. H. Lingle, *Bullseye: Hitting Your Strategic Targets through High-Impact Measurement* (New York: The Free Press, 1999).
2. "Making Strategy Pay," a report describing a 1999 research study performed for A. T. Kearney by The Conference Board (Chicago: A. T. Kearney, 1999).
3. B. Birchard, "Where Performance Measures Fail," p. 36 in "Closing the Strategy Gap," *CFO Magazine* (October 1996); J. Kersnar, "Hitting the Mark," *CFO Europe* (February 1999): 46–48; A. Schneiderman, "Why Balanced Scorecards Fail," *Journal of Strategic Performance Measurement* (January 1999): 6–11.
4. Robert S. Kaplan and David P. Norton, "Building a Balanced Scorecard: The Process," pp. 300–10 in *The Balanced Scorecard: Translating Strategy into Action* (Boston: Harvard Business School Press, 1996).
5. See, for example, the Balanced Scorecard Fast Track Development program offered by the Balanced Scorecard Collaborative (http://www.bscol.com).
6. See Birchard, "Where Performance Measures Fail."
7. See, for example, Schneiderman, "Why Balanced Scorecards Fail."
8. See, for example, the problems encountered after implementation of a corporate scorecard at Analog Devices in R. S. Kaplan, "Analog Devices: The Half-Life System," 9-190-061 (Boston: Harvard Business School, 1990). The subsequent decline in performance is described in the teaching note to the case (5-191-103) and in J. D. Sterman, N. Repenning, and F. Kofman, "Unanticipated Side Effects of Successful Quality Improvement Programs: Exploring a Paradox of Organizational Improvement," *Management Science* 4, no. 2 (1997): 503–21.

Frequently Asked Questions

As we give public talks and seminars, generally covering the substance of the material in this book, several questions recur about the Balanced Scorecard and how it gets implemented in organizations. We thought readers might find it useful to hear our responses to these frequently asked questions.

FAQ: Many of your examples come from large companies in mature industries: banking, insurance, oil and petroleum products, and large retailers. Can the Balanced Scorecard be applied to small businesses, new businesses, and rapidly changing businesses?

The answer is yes for all three questions. Our initial work was with large companies. Their platforms had the largest fires. Many of these companies were doing poorly and clearly most in need of a new strategy and business model. But their size and associated organizational inertia made the deployment of any new strategy more difficult. The scorecard accelerated their turn toward a new strategic direction. Since that time, we have seen many successful implementations in small divisions embedded in larger companies. We mentioned in Chapter 1 the success story of Southern Gardens Citrus with 200 employees. We have assisted Guideposts, a 500-employee, nonprofit Christian magazine and book publishing firm, as well as a small satellite systems design and fabrication company. Of course, several of the nonprofit organizations—New Profit, Inc., Duke Children's Hospital, and the May Institute—had employees ranging in number from about a dozen up to a couple of hundred. The key issue for any organization, regardless of size, is the alignment of individuals and processes to the strategy. Small companies as well as large benefit from having everyone understand the strategy and implementing it in his or her everyday job.

For new businesses, the example of National Bank Online Financial Services (see Chapter 4) provides a roadmap for applying the Balanced Scorecard to an Internet-based company. We are currently working with several e-commerce companies to develop Balanced Scorecards to guide their operations. The benefits arise from having the business founders completely aligned to the strategy. Also, they have a great tool for communicating and educating new hires about the underlying business model, and how they can contribute to rapid growth.

As for companies in rapidly changing environments, Cisco Systems uses a Balanced Scorecard–like measurement system for its operations. Microsoft Corporation in Latin America uses the scorecard to align all country managers to evolving strategies for new product introductions, new services, and new relationships with distributors and end-use customers.[1] The Balanced Scorecard for such companies becomes a powerful tool for rapid midcourse changes, as discussed in Chapter 12 in the context of emergent strategies. The entire scorecard does not have to be redone each time a new opportunity is seized or a new threat countered. Rather, the objectives and measures, particularly in the financial and customer perspectives, will be largely unaffected. What changes are the new initiatives launched, existing initiatives curtailed, and perhaps one or two new internal processes becoming critical. The scorecard becomes the language by which the executive team communicates the changes in tactics and direction, enabling changes and new initiatives to be executed that much faster. And the direction is not always top-down, as discussed in Chapter 12. Understanding the current status and direction of the company, employees can identify valuable new opportunities and communicate them to others using the shared language of the scorecard.

FAQ: Are there any new issues, such as differences in culture, when the Balanced Scorecard is applied in different parts of the world?

Our first book on the Balanced Scorecard has already been translated into nineteen languages, suggesting that the issues and principles for the scorecard apply well in cultures around the world. We have consulted and lectured to managers on every continent and have not encountered any cultural barriers to implementing the scorecard. Consulting companies in the major geographic markets have taken the Balanced Scorecard and customized it to the intellectual and business practice traditions in their markets. We haven't seen major changes from our basic framework as the scorecard has been customized to these local applications.

The scorecard does require some management maturity and sophistication. It requires a participative, not authoritative, style of management. Some companies may have to adapt to the new management style before getting full benefits from the scorecard.

FAQ: How can I get senior sponsorship for the Balanced Scorecard project?

We are reminded of the story about a customer inquiring into the price of a yacht: "If you have to ask, you can't afford it." If you have to persuade a reluctant senior executive to support the Balanced Scorecard, you probably aren't going to get the necessary commitment. As we discussed in Chapter 13, the Balanced Scorecard works best when senior executives are already looking for ways to communicate more effectively the strategy and objectives of their business units. Executives who value vision, communication, participation, and employee initiative and innovation should find, without any persuasion, the scorecard to be a natural and powerful management tool. If they need a little encouragement, the success stories described in Chapter 1 reveal the power of the scorecard for helping to create breakthrough performance.

Executives who manage with financial statements and who want subunits and employees to follow directions and adhere to centrally formulated plans will not find the Balanced Scorecard a very compatible management tool. We would not spend much energy trying to get such executives to "sponsor" a Balanced Scorecard project. They wouldn't follow the principles to become a Strategy-Focused Organization, even if they eventually provided the funds and other resources that permitted an initial scorecard to be developed. We would encourage advocates to look elsewhere in the organization rather than solicit sponsorship from such executives. Find a unit with an executive for whom the scorecard represents a more natural complement to his or her management style.

FAQ: Can the Balanced Scorecard be applied in a unionized work force?

The implementations in the petroleum industry (such as Mobil and Texaco) and automobile industry occurred in places where many front-line employees were unionized. Similarly, many applications in the government sector are with unionized employees. The scorecard communicates a more sustainable business model to employees. It challenges employees to search for new ways to do their job to create value for the organization. Resistance likely comes more from front-line supervisors and middle managers—people accustomed to giving orders and being "in control"—than from the front-line workers.

The only aspect of the Strategy-Focused Organization that unions have not embraced is the linkage to compensation. Texaco used the noncash awards described in Chapter 10 to avoid incentive pay for unionized workers. At Mobil, the union was happy to be included in the company's variable pay plan, but it objected to having its base wages set at 90 percent of the prevailing wage and having the remaining 10 percent at risk. Mobil executives did not want unionized workers to participate in the incentive plan without having some percentage (perhaps as low as 5 percent) of base pay at risk. The union did not agree to this, and hence it has been excluded from the variable pay plan that averaged between 17 percent and 19 percent of payouts from 1996 to 1999.

FAQ: Do I need to have a strategy before I build a Balanced Scorecard?

Strictly speaking, the Balanced Scorecard is a strategy implementation tool. For organizations that already have an explicit strategy, the Balanced Scorecard can help them implement their strategy faster and more effectively by following the principles described in this book.

Some management groups initially believed that all their members concurred with an existing strategy. While building the initial scorecard, however, they discovered that each member of the team had a quite different interpretation about the strategy. They disagreed about who were the targeted customers, what was the differentiated value proposition, and what role would innovation and shared services play in the strategy. The process of building the scorecard forced clarification and consensus about exactly what the strategy was and how it could be achieved.

Organizations without any explicit or shared strategy have used the process of building a scorecard as the mechanism to develop a strategy for the business unit. The scorecard stimulates an intense management dialogue to define the strategy. As described in Chapter 3, the Balanced Scorecard provides a common language and architecture for strategy that did not exist before. Strategy maps and templates provide a framework for strategic discussions.

So the answer to the question is that having an explicit strategy that everyone truly understands and agrees to will shorten the time required to build the initial Balanced Scorecard. But organizations don't have to defer the building of a scorecard until they have achieved consensus about a strategy. They can use the process of building the scorecard as a mechanism for a simultaneous process that creates the strategy.

FAQ: What about data security and privacy concerns? Can we share all Balanced Scorecard information with employees on our intranet?

Privacy and security concerns raise an interesting tension. On the one hand, Strategy-Focused Organizations want employees to have access to the strategy and deep awareness and understanding of the strategy. Communication and awareness stimulates intrinsic motivation as employees see how they can contribute to the organization's success. It unleashes their creative energies to find new ways to contribute.

On the other hand, such a clear articulation of strategy creates risk. In our first book we told what a division president said when he turned in his first Balanced Scorecard to the company's president:

In the past, if you had lost my strategic planning document on an airplane and a competitor found it, I would have been angry, but I would have gotten over it. In reality, it wouldn't have been that big a loss. Or if I had left my monthly operating review somewhere and a competitor obtained a copy, I would have been upset, but, again, it wouldn't have been that big a deal. This Balanced Scorecard, however, communicates my strategy so well that a competitor seeing this would be able to block the strategy and cause it to become ineffective.

We want scorecards to tell the story of the strategy. That is the ideal outcome from building strategy maps. But the risk from sharing such a strategy scorecard with hundreds and thousands of employees is obvious. People leave the company all the time. Companies cannot count on having 100 percent of its employees 100 percent aligned to the company's values, mission, and sustained success. As the wartime expression says, "Loose lips sink ships." To avoid disclosure of sensitive information, companies can index the numbers on the scorecard to avoid the risk of disclosure to competitors. In this way, most employees see directional information but not actual quantities.

Many companies believe, however, that their competitive success does not come from a superior strategy, which is kept secret by members of their senior executive team. They believe their competitive advantage comes from implementing their strategy faster and more effectively than their competitors. And they believe that the scorecard—communicated, understood, and acted upon by all employees—gives them the capability for such rapid and effective strategy implementation. Therefore the secret is not the strategy but the internal leadership and management processes leading to a Strategy-Focused Organization.

We are often asked why Mobil NAM&R was so generous with allowing its strategy to be disclosed and used as a case example. In the first place, Mobil NAM&R must implement its strategy through its retail dealers, who are businesspeople independent from Mobil. Any new strategy communicated to its dealers is soon known by all of Mobil's competitors. Conversely, Mobil knows the strategy of all of its competitors (most have strategies quite similar to Mobil's), and the competitors all know Mobil's strategy. The differentiation comes from how well the company implements the strategy, and that is where the scorecard gave Mobil some sustainable first-mover advantages. Second, by publicizing its strategy, Executive Vice President Brian Baker made all employees understand that success would not flow from a winning strategy dreamed up by geniuses at company headquarters that competitors could not attempt to imitate. It would come from how well employees implemented the strategy. And third, Baker believed that by putting Mobil NAM&R's initial strategic move into the public domain, managers and employees would have more incentive to find new ways of competing—perhaps developing emergent strategies, as discussed in Chapter 12—that would help Mobil to sustain and extend its first-mover advantages.

The disclosure issue surfaced as a major barrier in one company when the company lawyers reviewed the scorecard and discovered that it contained financial and other projections. They asked, "What if an employee copies and distributes this forward-looking information to analysts? We could be liable for violation of the Securities and Exchange Commission acts on corporate disclosure." Their objection stopped the deployment of the scorecard in its tracks for two months until a solution could be found. The scorecard was released after the company built two levels of access into its intranet. The executive leadership team could see the actual numbers on the vertical scale for the scorecard measures. All other employees could see the trends and the color coding of red-yellow-green of scorecard measures. They could not see the actual values of the displayed measures.

FAQ: Suppose some measures for the scorecard are missing. Should we delay introduction until we have data for all the measures before starting the Balanced Scorecard management system?

After the initial design of a Balanced Scorecard, many measures are often not yet available for reporting. Chemical Bank was missing about 33 percent of the measures, Mobil was missing 25 percent, and Reuters America was missing 40 percent. The first reaction is predictable: "If we can't measure what we want, let's want what we can measure; let's use some measure for which we already have data!" This is a mistake. If the scorecard has been thoughtfully designed, the measures represent the most important information in the company. If measures don't exist currently, critical management processes are likely not being managed. The organization will be exploring new ground on which management processes and systems have yet to be developed. We advise organizations to be patient and institute new processes to get the new information. Upon learning of his information gap at Chemical Retail Bank, Chief of Staff Lee Wilson recalled, "We invested a tremendous amount of time, energy, and money in the systems and procedures to collect the new information. The process of looking at the new measures gave us the benefits from our strategy."

FAQ: How many measures should be on a Balanced Scorecard, and what should the mix be across the various perspectives?

From our own experience, we expect strategy scorecards to have twenty to twenty-five measures. Here is a typical allocation across the four perspectives:

Financial	five measures (22 percent)
Customer	five measures (22 percent)
Internal	eight to ten measures (34 percent)
Learning and growth	five measures (22 percent)

An independent 1998 study conducted by Best Practices, LLC, analyzed the scorecards of twenty-two organizations that had successfully implemented Balanced Scorecards and found just about the same distribution of measures.[2] The higher weighting for the internal perspective reflects the importance of emphasizing the drivers of financial and customer out-comes. Note also that nearly 80 percent of the measures on a Balanced Scorecard should be nonfinancial. Of the best-in-class companies, only Mobil departed from the preceding pattern; it had 50 percent of its twenty-four measures in the internal perspective, reflecting the emphasis on oper-ational excellence and environmental, health, and safety issues in its capital-intense business.

FAQ: How does the Balanced Scorecard differ from TQM?

The Balanced Scorecard is perfectly consistent with TQM principles. Initiatives to improve the quality, responsiveness, and efficiency of inter-nal processes can be reflected in the operations portion of the scorecard's internal perspective. Extending TQM principles out to the innovation process and to enhancing customer relationships will be reflected in the several other building blocks in the internal business process perspective. Thus companies already implementing the continuous improvement and measurement disciplines from TQM will find ample opportunity to sustain their programs within the more strategic framework of the Balanced Score-card.

Our experience with companies, however, indicates that the Balanced Scorecard does much more than merely recast TQM principles into a new framework. The scorecard enhances, in several ways, the effectiveness of TQM programs. First, the scorecard identifies those internal processes in which improvement will be most critical for strategic success. In many or-ganizations, local TQM programs succeeded, but their impact could not be detected in the financial or customer performance of the organization. The Balanced Scorecard identifies and sets priorities on which processes are most critical to the strategy; it also identifies whether the process im-provements should focus more on cost reduction, quality improvement, or cycle-time compression. Bill Allen, executive vice president of Commu-nity Services at United Way of Southeastern New England, commented, "The BSC provided a unity and focus to our TQM efforts. We had a lot of teams doing a lot of things, but the efforts were ad hoc. Our TQM experi-ence gave us a strong emphasis on teamwork and on good data gathering and measurement. The BSC brought this all together into a unified sys-tematic approach."[3]

The second enhancement from the Balanced Scorecard to TQM pro-grams occurs by forcing managers to explicate the linkage from improved operating processes to successful outcomes for customers and share-holders. While the linkage from quality to financial outcomes does often happen, it doesn't always happen. In the early 1990s, several companies that were recent winners of the Baldrige Award or apparent exemplars of TQM principles subsequently experienced financial difficulties.[4] In his final days as CEO of IBM Corporation, John Akers remarked remorse-fully about his visits to IBM manufacturing facilities. Employees proudly showed him charts of dramatic quality and cycle-time improvements but had few answers when he asked them why customer sales were contin-uing to decline.

Companies focusing only on quality and local process improvement often do not link operational improvements to expected outcomes in ei-ther the customer or the financial perspective. These companies are fol-lowing a *Field of Dreams* strategy for quality: "If we improve it, financial results will come." The scorecard requires that linkages be made explicit. One linkage is from quality improvements in the internal perspective to one or more outcome (not process) measures in the customer perspec-tive. A second is from quality improvements that enable companies to reduce costs—an outcome in the financial perspective. The scorecard framework enables managers to articulate how they will translate qual-ity improvements into higher revenues, fewer assets, fewer people, and lower spending.

FAQ: What about reengineering? How does that relate to the Balanced Scorecard?

Reengineering, the discontinuous improvement of existing processes, may be required when continuous process improvement (the TQM ap-proach) will not lead to achieving the desired performance.[5] But without the guidance from a strategy scorecard, reengineering, like TQM, can focus on processes that are not critical for strategic success so that im-provements in the reengineered processes don't have a major economic im-pact. Also, reengineering can become trivialized into cost-cutting and headcount-slashing programs. Without the strategic perspective of the non-financial outcome measures on a Balanced Scorecard, the default measure for reengineering programs ends up being cost savings. The Balanced Scorecard can enhance process-focused strategies by identifying several nonfinancial measures in the value proposition that can be the successful outcomes from reengineering efforts.[6]

FAQ: What is the relationship of the Balanced Scorecard to activity-based costing? Which should be done first?

At least one of us must admit to a fondness for both approaches and prefers not to have to choose between them. Activity-based costing gives managers a clear picture about the cost drivers in their organization and the opportunity for cost reduction through decisions about product and customer mix, customer relationships and terms, product designs, and activity and process improvements. No cost system, including ABC, however, can measure the *value* of what an organization does for its customers. The Balanced Scorecard is a complementary approach that specifically identifies targeted customers, what they value, and the processes, capabilities, and competencies that an organization must excel at to deliver unique value propositions to its targeted customers. Thus, the two systems work well together. ABC identifies an organization's *cost drivers* and the actions it can take to reduce costs, while still delivering the same value to customers. BSC identifies the *value drivers* of an organization's strategy and a new management system to align the organization to the strategy. The two systems intersect in several places. In the customer perspective, customer profitability can be measured only if a well-designed ABC system calculates the costs of serving individual customers. For the operational excellence theme in the internal perspective, an ABC system measures costs for critical activities and processes. And an ABC system can help in the strategy-formulation stage of building a Balanced Scorecard by identifying the costs of serving different customer segments, facilitating the choice of which segments should become the targets for a company's strategy.

Both approaches are valuable to organizations. Companies that need to gain clarity about their strategy and to align their organization to a new customer-focused strategy would likely find the Balanced Scorecard a higher immediate priority. Companies that need to focus immediately on escalating costs, proliferating products and customers, and cost competitiveness could start with an activity-based costing system. We believe, however, that organizations benefit by using both systems so that they can measure and manage their value drivers *and* their cost drivers.

FAQ: We are already implementing an EVA/value-based management approach. Why do we need a Balanced Scorecard beyond these enhanced financial measures?

Companies that have adopted shareholder value strategies, using EVA or other value-based management metrics, can certainly place such high-level financial metrics at the top of the scorecards.[7] The financial drivers of shareholder value such as revenue growth, operating margin, sales to assets, working capital ratios, and financial leverage are also represented within the financial perspective as value drivers. But value-based management implementations often stop with these financial drivers.

The scorecard framework enhances financial-based strategies by making explicit the specific customer outcomes and performance drivers that enable the financial targets to be achieved. Without the balance of the scorecard, value-based management strategies may pick the low-hanging fruit of cost reduction and increased asset intensity but miss the opportunity to create additional value by a longer-term revenue growth strategy through investments in customers, innovation, process enhancements, information technology, and employee capabilities.

FAQ (related question to the preceding): Why can't I achieve the same results by communicating and rewarding people on the financial targets we want to achieve?

Attempting to drive strategy by communicating and rewarding financial outcomes alone is a lot like teaching people to play tennis by explaining how to keep score. The class starts with "love" (the tennis term, not the intimate feeling or act); proceeds quickly through "15, 30, 40"; pauses for an advanced lesson on "deuce"; and then explains "game." For students who get this far, the class continues by explicating "sets" and "tie-breakers." The instructor then tells the students, "OK, now you know what outcome you must achieve. Go out and win!" The students soon find their opponents' shots whizzing past them, while most of their attempts at returns end up hitting the net or flying out of bounds. At the end of the exercise, the students know the score—6-0, 6-0—and understand that this may not have been the desired outcome, but they have no idea how to improve their performance in future periods.

Obviously, good tennis classes require that students understand not only how to keep score but also what performance drivers—backhands, forehands, overheads, volleys, lobs, chips, and serves—will generate the desired outcomes, along with the successful court management that ties the components together into a winning strategy. Similarly, beyond adopting a good set of financial metrics to keep score, managers must help employees understand the components—customer relationships, value proposition, innovation, process management, employee capabilities and motivation, and information technology—and the strategy that links these together for the desired financial outcome. This is how the Balanced Scorecard incorporates financial-based strategies into its framework and enhances pure shareholder-value strategies by explicating the logic of how shareholder value will be improved.

FAQ: Should the Balanced Scorecard be shared with financial analysts and shareholders?

Few companies have Balanced Scorecards at the corporate level and for all their business units. Financial measures have this wonderful property that you can sum them up across completely diverse business units to obtain overall corporate financial performance. Customer measures and value propositions are not additive, particularly when business units have different strategies. It's still unclear whether corporate-level Balanced Scorecards have much meaning, except when companies operate within a single industry segment. In addition, the confidentiality of strategic scorecard measures becomes even more sensitive if the data are included in public reports and statements.

Having said this, we must note that some divisional company executives—for instance, Brian Baker at Mobil and Michael Hegarty at Chemical Bank—did use the scorecard framework in their briefing sessions with analysts. They convinced analysts that their recent excellent performance was not due to luck or one-time events by communicating the underlying logic and structure of an integrated strategy. They explained targeted segments, value propositions, and the role for technology. The analysts left with renewed enthusiasm for the company's stock and future prospects. We believe that the scorecard, by structuring executives' communication about strategy, can enhance their credibility and, over time, encourage analysts and shareholders to focus on critical nonfinancial variables that are either the drivers or the outcomes from a successful strategy.

NOTES

1. A. Ballvé, A. Davila, and R. S. Kaplan, "Microsoft Latin America: Measuring the Future," 100-040 (Boston: Harvard Business School, 2000).

2. Best Practices Benchmarking Report, *Developing the Balanced Scorecard* (Chapel Hill, NC: Best Practices, LLC, 1999).

3. R. S. Kaplan and E. L. Kaplan, "United Way of Southeastern New England," 9-197-036 (Boston: Harvard Business School, 1996), 7.

4. R. E. Kordupleski, R. T. Rust, A. J. Zahorik "Why Improving Quality Doesn't Improve Quality (Or Whatever Happened to Marketing?)," *California Management Review* (April 1993).

5. J. Champy and M. Hammer, *Reengineering the Corporation: A Manifesto for Business Revolution* (New York: HarperBusiness, 1993).

6. Michael Hammer, *Beyond Reengineering: How the Process-Centered Organization Is Changing Our Work and Our Lives* (New York: Harper Collins, 1997).

7. R. Myers, "Metric Wars," *CFO Magazine* (October 1996); "Measure for Measure," *CFO Magazine* (November 1997); and "Valuing Companies: A Star to Sail By?" *The Economist,* 2 August 1997: 53–55.

Index

About the Authors

Robert S. Kaplan is the Marvin Bower Professor of Leadership Development at Harvard Business School. Formerly he was on the faculty of the Graduate School of Industrial Administration, Carnegie-Mellon University, where he also served as Dean from 1977 to 1983. He is the creator of the Harvard Business School video series *Measuring Corporate Performance* and the author or coauthor of more than 120 papers and ten books, including, with David Norton, *The Balanced Scorecard: Translating Strategy into Action*. Dr. Kaplan consults on the design of performance and cost management systems with leading companies worldwide. His research, teaching, consulting, and speaking focus on new performance management and measurement systems, primarily the Balanced Scorecard and Activity-Based Costing. He is the recipient of numerous honors, including the Outstanding Educator Award from the American Accounting Association and the Chartered Institute of Management Accountants (UK) Award for "Outstanding Contributions to the Accountancy Profession." Dr. Kaplan serves on the boards of the Technion (Israel Institute of Technology) and the Balanced Scorecard Collaborative. He can be reached at rkaplan@hbs.edu.

David P. Norton is President of Balanced Scorecard Collaborative, Inc., a professional services firm that facilitates the worldwide awareness, use, enhancement, and integrity of the Balanced Scorecard. Previously he was the President of Renaissance Solutions, Inc., a consulting firm he co-founded in 1992, and of Nolan, Norton & Company, where he spent seventeen years as President. Dr. Norton is a management consultant, researcher, and speaker in the field of strategic performance management. With Robert Kaplan, he is the cocreator of the Balanced Scorecard concept, coauthor of four *Harvard Business Review* articles, and coauthor of *The Balanced Scorecard: Translating Strategy into Action*. He is a Trustee of Worcester Polytechnic Institute and a former Director of ACME (The Association of Consulting Management Engineers). He can be reached at dnorton@bscol.com.